Profitability, Productivity, and Sustainability

This book presents an in-depth study of how the drive to optimize organizational performance can be significantly improved by investigating the causal relationships between profitability, productivity, and sustainability (PPS). This is presented through an assessment of a triple combined therapy that studies the interplay between Organizational DNA, Strategic Alignments for Value, and their implications for Sustainability. Through this approach, this volume seeks to answer critical mind-searching questions and provide useful guides as to how some firms are able to sustainably create higher value or wealth, especially through corporate entrepreneurship, or via the creation of new business models than others.

In tackling the three elements of profitability, productivity, and sustainability, this book also provides greater insight through an in-depth study of the pervasively unresolved and disturbing issues surrounding the prospects of increasing the chances of success for entrepreneurial start-off ventures, making it of value to researchers, academics, and students in the fields of organizational studies, strategy, and sustainability.

Dennis N. Onyama is the President and CEO of the International Research Institute for Innovative Studies, USA.

Routledge Studies in Management, Organizations and Society

This series presents innovative work grounded in new realities, addressing issues crucial to an understanding of the contemporary world. This is the world of organized societies, where boundaries between formal and informal, public and private, local and global organizations have been displaced or have vanished, along with other 19th-century dichotomies and oppositions. Management, apart from becoming a specialized profession for a growing number of people, is an everyday activity for most members of modern societies.

Similarly, at the level of inquiry, culture and technology, and literature and economics can no longer be conceived as isolated intellectual fields; conventional canons and established mainstreams are contested. *Routledge Studies in Management, Organizations, and Society* addresses these contemporary dynamics of transformation in a manner that transcends disciplinary boundaries, with books that will appeal to researchers, students, and practitioners alike.

Recent titles in this series include:

Analyzing Organization Cultures
Edited by Bruce Fortado

Public Sector Reform and Performance Management in Emerging Economies
Outcomes-Based Approaches in Practice
Edited by Zahirul Hoque

Founders and Organizational Development
The Etiology and Theory of Founder's Syndrome
Stephen R. Block and Katrina Miller-Stevens

Profitability, Productivity, and Sustainability
Organizational Behavior and Strategic Alignment
Dennis N. Onyama

Profitability, Productivity, and Sustainability

Organizational Behavior and Strategic Alignment

Dennis N. Onyama

Routledge
Taylor & Francis Group
NEW YORK AND LONDON

First published 2021
by Routledge
605 Third Avenue, New York, NY 10158

and by Routledge
2 Park Square, Milton Park, Abingdon, Oxon, OX14 4RN

Routledge is an imprint of the Taylor & Francis Group, an informa business

Library of Congress Cataloging-in-Publication Data
Names: Onyama, Dennis N., 1976- author.
Title: Profitability, productivity, and sustainability : organizational behavior and strategic alignment / Dennis N. Onyama.
Description: New York, NY : Routledge, 2021. | Series: Routledge studies in management, organizations and society | Includes bibliographical references and index.
Identifiers: LCCN 2020057606 (print) | LCCN 2020057607 (ebook) | ISBN 9780367608927 (hardback) | ISBN 9781003102410 (ebook)
Subjects: LCSH: Industrial productivity. | Organizational effectiveness. | Strategic planning.
Classification: LCC HC79.I52 O69 2021 (print) | LCC HC79.I52 (ebook) | DDC 658.4/012--dc23
LC record available at https://lccn.loc.gov/2020057606
LC ebook record available at https://lccn.loc.gov/2020057607

ISBN: 978-0-367-60892-7 (hbk)
ISBN: 978-0-367-60893-4 (pbk)
ISBN: 978-1-003-10241-0 (ebk)

Typeset in Sabon
by MPS Limited, Dehradun

Contents

Figures

Tables

1 Introduction

Introduction

This chapter identifies, introduces, and clarifies critical factors and processes that subtly impair a comprehensive understanding of the relationships between *profitability, productivity, and sustainability (PPS)* in their interplay with critical elements that underpin *organizational behavior* and *strategic alignment*. This is, indeed, a complex relationship that is least understood in the business world and beyond. That being said, while the focal points of many *"bestselling management books of all time"* emphasize one or two of the three things – namely, PPS – as constituting a driving force for optimizing organizational performance, this chapter presents these three elements not only as individual forces that drive organizational performance but also as triple combined forces that influence organizational performance concurrently.

The aforementioned polemic is exceedingly subtle as just a few company and industry leaders or pioneers get it right. Among them are those who constantly thrive to master the art of preparing their organizations as a learning hub for radical and disruptive change. However, a critical majority of those who get it right, get it most often by gambling their way through. But this latter approach would imply that such organizations have not grasped a foothold of the situation; as a result, the challenges of sustaining these gains gradually disappear over time. This is true because most of these companies find it extremely difficult to align sustainability with the changing landscape of productivity and profitability in the long run.

Essentially, this chapter also points to the argument that a successful relationship between PPS – as applicable within the framework of organizational behavior and strategic alignment – follows recurrent cycles.

From the foregoing, it reasons that each of these elements – *PPS* – does not work in isolation. At any point in time, an organization is confronted by one of these three problems – although at varying degrees of complexity when compared to other organizations in the same industry and sometimes across different industries. In more complicated scenarios, some entities are confronted with two of these problems at a time, and, in worse scenarios, other entities are afflicted by all three of the aforementioned problems at the same time. These problems are extremely time-sensitive and contagious. In the sense that, if a firm, for example, is confronted by, say, *profitability* problems and it does not resolve the issue within a *reasonable time,* it tends to produce a viral effect that naturally contaminates the elements of *productivity* and *sustainability.* This makes it imperatively critical for organizations to retain *strategic control* over these kinds of scenarios by taking into consideration both the combined and individual effects of each of these elements – *PPS* – on organizational performance, as well as the dynamics of the interactions between them. Let's throw some light on these three elements.

Productivity has been defined as the efficient use of resources, labor, capital, land, materials, energy, and information in the production of various goods and services. Higher productivity means accomplishing more with the same amount of resources or achieving higher output in terms of volume and quality from the same input.[1] In short, *productivity* is about *doing more with the same.*[2] The formula for measuring productivity is

$$\text{Productivity} = \frac{Units\ \ of\ \ Output}{Units\ \ of\ \ Inputs}.$$

In this regard, Chew (1988) argues that the central mission of a productivity index is to illuminate how a business can get more units of output per labor hour, per machine, or per pound of materials than its competitors.[3] This means that productivity is about *expanding* the *numerator* – that is, the *output* – in order to deliver greater top-line growth from the same workforce.[4] On the other hand, *efficiency* is about *doing the same with less.* Arguably so, because companies, most often, improve labor efficiency by finding ways to reduce the number of labor hours required to produce the same level of output. Consequently, *efficiency* is about *shrinking* the *denominator* – that is, *inputs* (reducing labor hours, producing high-quality low-cost materials, etc.) – in an effort to improve profitability.[5]

Profitability is the ability of a business to earn a profit. A profit is what is left of the revenue a business generates after it pays all expenses directly related to the generation of the revenue, such as producing a product and other expenses related to the conduct of the business activities.[6] Simply put, *profitability* is the ability of a company to use its resources to generate revenues in excess of its expenses.[7]

Sustainability is often defined as meeting the needs of the present without compromising the ability of future generations to meet their needs. The concept of sustainability is composed of three pillars – economic, environment, and society. It is also known informally as profits, planet, and people, respectively. According to Grant (2020), encouraging businesses to frame decisions in terms of environmental, social, and human impact for the long term, rather than for the short term, influences them to consider more factors than simply the immediate profit or loss involved.[8] To concur, Rosenberg (2015) argues that sustainability often requires short-term costs to secure a, sometimes uncertain, long-term benefit.

But in the context of this volume, the focus is on *organizational sustainability*. According to Action Inclusion (2020), unlike *environmental sustainability,* which is about the environment, *organizational sustainability* is about equipping organizations with the people and structures necessary for success in the global marketplace of the 21st century.[9] By implication, therefore, organizational sustainability means having the leadership, talent, global insights, and change strategies necessary to rise to the unique challenges facing organizations today.[10] Consequently, all businesses must have a strategy to deal with sustainability, and like any strategy, this involves making choices (Rosenberg, 2015).

Understanding the individual and tripled combined effects of PPS in a holistic way, in the lifecycle of a venture, is an art that requires careful and critical observation as well as successful strategy execution, among other things.

In relation to successful strategy execution, Neilson, Martin, and Powers (2008) identified four organizational *fundamental building blocks* that executives can use to influence successful execution of strategy. These are: *clarifying decision rights*, *designing information flows*, *aligning motivators*, and where applicable, *making structural changes that naturally or organically evolves from the combined effects of decision rights, information flows, and motivators.* In this regard, Neilson *et al.* (2008) define *execution* as the result of thousands of decisions made every day by employees acting according to the information they have and their self-interest.[11] Organizational fundamental building blocks are of two strands. The *first* strand is the *Organizational DNA (OrgDNA) formal building blocks* or *common bases.* We can simply refer to them as *decision rights, information flow, motivators,* and *structure.* The *second* strand is the *OrgDNA informal building blocks,* which are the synthesized templates of the OrgDNA formal building blocks. These synthesized templates include *norms, mindset, commitments,* and *networks*. Put together, both the formal building blocks and the informal building blocks make up what we can refer to as the *organization's genetic material.*

In addition, Neilson *et al.* (2008) found that the fundamentals of good execution start with clarifying *decision rights* and making sure *information flows* where it needs to go, and that once these two have been properly aligned, the correct *motivators* and *structure* become obvious. They found that when, on the contrary, an organization fails to execute its strategy, the first thing most managers think of as an effort to improve performance is to restructure.[12] As a result, such steps generally tend to reap some short-term efficiency quickly, but in so doing, address only symptoms of dysfunction and not its root causes. Several years later, such organizations usually end up in the same place they had started.[13] However, decision rights and information flow are not the only major influencing factors here. The informal organizational building blocks are also very powerful alignment factors to reckon with.

Finally, although this chapter also makes use of some primary data, the study leading to this book concentrated predominantly on secondary sources of information. For example, the literature review was conducted with the latest information from internet websites, journals, Google books, and government most-recent reports in the study area during the research period. It also describes, summarizes, and discusses information originally presented in other academic sources like publications, textbooks, journal articles, book reviews, commentaries, e-books, and so on.

1.1 Introduction to Leadership as the Framework of Value Creation

1.1.1 The Leadership Equation on Sustainable Value Creation

Be it start-up entrepreneurial ventures or the journey toward the creation of higher value undertaken by existing firms, they are two sides of the same coin in that they all want to create value. Eisenmann, Ries, and Dillard (2013) define start-ups as new organizations created by entrepreneurs to launch new products. As a result, a start-up's founders typically confront significant resource constraints and considerable uncertainty about the viability of their proposed business model.[14] The kinds of value that can create a competitive edge are the values that will be sustainable by consistently producing both accelerator and multiplier effects over time. This is what this book calls *strategic alignments* for value as opposed to traditional *value creation.*

Historically, traditional *value creation* via the process of *managerial thinking* has been known to maximize profits and reduce costs as much as possible in the short term, and it has also been the dominant business ideology. However, at best, it can only ensure moderate growth in the short term and low growth in the medium term. At the least, it might lead to declining growth rates and would tend to compromise the survival of the firm in the long term. Meanwhile, an overemphasis on long-term financial viability of the firm without due consideration on short-term profitability margins, as well as the firm's financial health in the medium term, runs a high risk of the firm collapsing quite early – probably so even in the short or medium term.

In a related development, Engel and Weber (2007) argue that while "*novel problem-solving modes*" can be constructed on the spot, this probably does not happen very often. Because most people, most of the time, would rather select between "*existing, tried-and-true problem-solving modes*" and available resources for the task in hand. In other words, they use this sequential logic in mind to employ the problem-solving mode that provides the best match.[15] As we would see ahead, this is typically the modus operandi of *recombinative innovation*. This mode of innovation is based on the systemic re-use or "recycling" of existing "components" or characteristics, which does not preclude the creation, and in some cases, of radically new "products" (requiring specific competencies, design work, and a certain degree of creativity).[16]

Relying on preconfigured problem-solving modes saves mental and external resources as the decision about how to decide reduces to a mere matching task, where the domain of the task at hand is matched against the domains in which existing problem-solving modes have performed well.[17] In concurrence, Barry and Halfmann (2016) define mindset as a manner of thinking or construing objects or actions.[18] In other words, *our mindset is an approach or manner of understanding information*. In addition, Barry and Halfmann (2016) found that William James, a leading early psychologist, was one of the first to suggest that goal-directed behavior, such as decisions,[19] is preceded by a cognitive representation (i.e., an approach or manner of understanding information).[20]

1.1.2 Leadership and the Attraction of a Growing Stream of Added Value

This book also argues that leadership has everything to do with the concept and final outcomes of value creation. So, it discusses the interplay between popular leadership styles or concepts such as visionary leadership, charismatic leadership, managerial leadership, servant leadership, strategic leadership, vertical leadership, transformational leadership, laissez-faire leadership, affiliate leadership, pacesetting leadership, democratic leadership, situational leadership, and sustainability leadership among others in the value creation pathway – with emphasis on the latter as a strategic choice. It equally acknowledges the existence of many other leadership styles that are not popular in the management literature. This book believes that this approach can provide greater impetus and insight to the modus operandi and the various outcomes of value creation. It also argues that the hidden patterns underpinning the interplay between the various leadership styles significantly dictate the modus operandi of productivity, profitability, and sustainability.

In a similar vein, Rowe (2001) argues that value-creation strategies in entrepreneurial and established organizations are a complex and challenging task in today's global and technologically advancing business environment,[21] more especially when it involves the process of *designing for a better quality of life*.[22] But, too often, it also requires complex decision making. In this regard, Barry and Halfmann (2016) found that most decisions we make are complex and involve time, risk, and several other factors (e.g., magnitude, importance, social, emotional, or learning aspects); and the more complex choices become, the more challenging it is to understand what factors determine choice patterns, and why.[23] Similarly, it argues that too often, people do not employ formal logic when thinking. This is true, more especially as the presentation of the results of thought does not necessarily reflect the deliberative processes that generated the results.[24]

In addition, Engel and Weber (2007) argue that such deliberation about the pros and cons of different modes may not be done consciously, and it may sometimes involve emotions,[25] and the mindset we adopt in a given context influences subsequent decision patterns.[26] Too often, this is typical of managerial leadership, whose organizational orientation is usually confined to the use of existing means to achieve predetermined goals. However, in the face of a radical change, or a disruptive change in the industry, this mode of problem-solving will clearly be counter-productive to the organization.

From the foregoing discussion, this book suggests a combination of strategy execution plans that integrate *strategic thinking* into *managerial thinking* and goes beyond that to include *strategic foresight* – so as to build a comprehensive strategic management program that is feasibly executable with viable business prospects.

1.2 The Human DNA and System Elements, Ergonomics, and OrgDNA

Based on the principle that each organization has exclusive genetic characteristics like any living organism, *management* – as a science – presents a new vision of organization based on the concept of OrgDNA. It also helps to explain its organizational performance.[27] That said, just as a double-stranded DNA molecule in humans is copied to produce two identical DNA molecules, referred to as its DNA synthesized templates, *organizations* too produce their own DNA synthesized templates from the DNA of their formal Organizational building blocks. However, it doesn't end there, as there is also the concept of ergonomics, which partly plays a similar role in organizations and product design, as well as the system elements within which these concepts interact with.

1.2.1 A Brief Description of the Structure of DNA in Humans

The cells of a human body are composed of protein, DNA, ribonucleic acid (RNA), sugar, and lipids. Being relevant to our topic, it is worthwhile to begin by giving a brief description of the structure of DNA so that you can better appreciate the entire subject matter.

DNA, which stands for d(eoxyribo)n(ucleic)a(cid), is defined as a nucleic acid that contains the genetic code. DNA is the polymer our genes are made of, and it carries the genetic information in cells and some viruses.[28]

The human DNA consists of two long chains of units called *nucleotides,* twisted into a double helix and joined by hydrogen bonds between the complementary bases: adenine (A) and thymine (T) or cytosine (C) and guanine (G).[29] *Nucleotide* is a molecule comprised of a nitrogen base, a 5-carbon sugar, and a phosphate group. It is the monomeric unit of DNA and RNA, depending on the type of sugar. Nucleotides link 5′end to the 3′end. For example, *deoxyribose* is the sugar in DNA, whereas *ribose* is the sugar in RNA, and contains adenine (A), uracil (U), cytosine (C) and thymine (T) ribo-nucleotides.[30]

DNA is the hereditary material in humans and almost all other organisms. Most DNA is located in the*cell nucleus* (where it is called *nuclear DNA*); however, a small amount of DNA can also be found in the *mitochondria* (where it is called *mitochondrial DNA* or *mtDNA*). Mitochondria are structures within cells that convert the energy from food into a form that cells can use.[31] The DNA double helix containing our genes is packaged with proteins and stored in the nucleus of the cell. The proteins protect our DNA and also coordinate the transcription of our genes. In addition, humans have two sets of 22 chromosomes (one set from mother and the other from father).[32] Of these chromosomes, one set is special as it determines our sex. Females have two copies of chromosome X. Males have one chromosome X and another chromosome, chromosome Y. Thus, men have 22 pairs of X:Y chromosomes; whereas, women have 22 pairs of X:X chromosomes.[33]

DNA Base Pairs

As we saw earlier, the double helix model of DNA consists of *two adjacent intertwined strands.* These strands are made up of nucleotides, which themselves consist of three component parts: a sugar group, a phosphate group, and a base. The sugar and phosphate groups combine to form the repeating "backbone" of the DNA strand.[34] In this arrangement, the sugar phosphate backbones face outward while the nitrogen bases face inward with base pair Guanine (G) to Cytosine (C), and Adenine (A) to Thymine (T).[35] The DNA strands are held together by hydrogen bonds between the two bases on adjacent strand.[36] Strong intermolecular forces called hydrogen bonds between the bases on adjacent strands are responsible for this. In human DNA, on average, there are 150 million base pairs in a single molecule.[37]

Human DNA consists of about three billion bases, and more than 99% of those bases are the same in all people. The order, or sequence, of these bases determines the information available for building and maintaining an organism, similar to the way in which letters of the alphabet appear in a certain order to form words and sentences.[38]

DNA Replication and Mutation

REPLICATION

An important property of DNA is that it can replicate or make copies of itself. In this regard, the cells in your body constantly divide, regenerate, and die; but for this process to occur, the DNA within the cell must be able to replicate itself. During cell division, the two strands of DNA split, and the two single strands can then be used as a template in order to construct a new version of the complimentary strand.[39] In other words, each strand of DNA in the double helix can serve as a pattern for duplicating the sequence of bases. This is critical when cells divide because each new cell needs to have an exact copy of the DNA present in the old cell.[40]

That being said, replication proceeds through A-T and G-C base pairing. When a cell replicates, it produces two identical copies of itself referred to as "daughter cells." Put in another way, replication is the process by which a double-stranded DNA molecule is copied to produce two identical DNA molecules. DNA replication is one of the most basic processes that occurs within a cell. Each time a cell divides, the two resulting daughter cells must contain exactly the same genetic information, or DNA, as the parent cell.[41] This process is carried out by a family of enzymes called DNA polymerases.[42] All the information needed to produce new organelles, proteins, sugars, membranes, and ribosomes is stored in the cell's genes made of DNA. The information stored in our genes actually guide the production of proteins with the help of its genetic code. Genetic codes consist of three letter codons.[43]

Process of Transcription When DNA is used to create proteins, an enzyme RNA polymerase *transcribes* DNA into messenger ribonucleic acid (mRNA). The mRNA, which is the working copy of the DNA gene, is translated via molecules called ribosomes to produce proteins from the *amino acids* coded for, by the mRNA. In this process, which is known as ***transcription,*** the mRNA splits apart the two strands that form the DNA double helix; it then *reads a DNA strand* and *copies the sequence* of its nucleotide[44] – a molecule comprised of a nitrogen base, a 5-carbon sugar, and a phosphate group.

RNA's structure is very similar to that of DNA but with a few key differences. Firstly, as mentioned earlier, it contains a different sugar group in the sugar-phosphate backbone of the molecule: *ribose* instead of *deoxyribose.* Secondly, RNA still uses the bases A, G, and C, but instead of the base T as in DNA, it uses base U. However, the structure of U is very similar to T, with the absence of a methyl (CH_3) group being the only difference.[45] In other words, RNA molecules use the nitrogen base U instead of T found in DNA.[46] Consequently, A–T and G–C base pair in DNA, while A–U and G–C base pair in RNA.

Process of Translation In multicellular organisms such as humans, the mRNA carries genetic code out of the cell nucleus to the cytoplasm. Here, protein synthesis takes place. "*Translation*" is the process of turning the mRNA's "code" into proteins. Molecules called ribosomes carry out this process by building up proteins from the amino acids coded for[47](*see* Fig. 1.1). Lately, a new method for estimating the biological sex of human remains based on reading protein sequences rather than DNA has been used to study an archeological site in Northern California.[48]

The genetic code is the set of 64 codons corresponding to the 20 natural amino acids (a monomer of proteins) + three Stop codons. The Stop codon is a codon that signals the termination of mRNA translation. The mRNA is the working copy of the DNA gene. Ribosomes *translate* mRNA to produce proteins. Stop codons appear at the end of the reading frame of an mRNA and thus indicate that the protein being translated has reached completion. There are a total of 64 possible codons (43 combinations), and they are read from 5′ to 3.′[49]

Replication occurs so quickly because multiple polymerases can synthesize two new strands at the same time by using each unwound strand from the original DNA double helix as a template. One of these original strands is called the leading strand, whereas the other is called the lagging strand. The leading strand is synthesized continuously. In contrast, the lagging strand is synthesized in small, separate fragments that are eventually joined together to form a complete, newly copied strand.[50] However, the process of *replication* is not always flawless, as mutation of the DNA can occur.

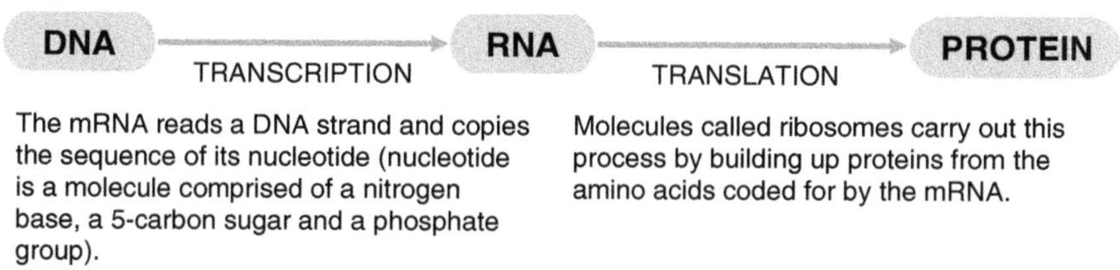

Figure 1.1 Chemical Structure of DNA – From DNA to Protein.
Source: Adapted from Compound Interest (2015c).

Mutation

Mutation is an error in DNA that can lead to a change in protein composition, structure, and function. Mutations can occur on several levels, including genetic, and can also take the form of *amino acid* replacements during protein synthesis.[51] With regards to *DNA,* errors can occur in copying DNA's sequence to mRNA, and these random errors are referred to as *mutations.* The errors can be in the form of a changed base, or even a deleted or added base. Some chemicals and radiation can induce these changes, but they can also happen in the absence of these external effects. With regards to *amino acids,* errors can lead to an *amino acids*[52] code being changed to that of another, or even rendered unreadable. That said, a number of diseases can result from *mutations* during DNA replication, including *cystic fibrosis* and *sickle-cell anaemia,* but it's worth noting that *mutations* can also have positive effects. The good news is that mutations that create "Stop codons" can entirely prevent the production of the mutated protein.[53]

Recently, new frontiers in medical science sometimes recommend the use of gene therapy in life-threatening cases. It is applicable in the form of either gene addition/transfer (the recommended approach) or gene editing that helps to correct the malfunctioning of the DNA as a way to treat hereditary disorders, infectious disorders, and cancer. So too, organizations in critical conditions may at some point in time need to correct the malfunctioning of some of its core hereditary components, ideally located in its organizational culture within the framework of its OrgDNA. Nafei (2014) maintains that identifying OrgDNA could provide great aids in improving these organizations.[54]

1.2.2 The Logic and Relevance of Human DNA and Its System Elements to OrgDNA and Ergonomics

Relevance of Human DNA and Its System Elements to OrgDNA

Fascinated by aging and mortality, West (2017) applied the rigor of a physicist to the biological question of why we live as long as we do and not longer. The result was astonishing, and it changed science. In this regard, West found that despite the riotous diversity in mammals, they are all, to a large degree, scaled versions of each other. For instance, he argues that if you know the *size* of a mammal, you can use scaling laws to learn everything from how much food it eats a day, what its heart-rate is, how long it will take to mature, its lifespan, and so on.

Furthermore, the efficiency of a mammal's circulatory systems scales precisely based on *weight.* For example, if you compare a mouse, a human, and an elephant on a logarithmic graph, you find with every doubling of *average weight,* a species gets 25% more efficient in its circulatory system and lives 25% longer. Fundamentally, he has proven that the issue has to do with the *fractal geometry* of the networks that supply energy and remove waste from the organism's body (West, 2017). A fractal has been defined as *a geometric pattern that repeats at every level of magnification.* Fractals help us study and understand important scientific concepts, for example, the way bacteria grow, patterns in freezing water (snowflakes), and brain waves. Their formulas have made possible many scientific breakthroughs. For instance, wireless cell phone antennas use a fractal pattern to pick up the signals better and, of course, pick up a wider range of signals.[55]

West's work has been game-changing for biologists, but then he made even bolder moves of exploring the applicability of his works. For instance, he found that *cities* too, are constellations of networks, and the laws of scalability relate with eerie precision (i.e., the quality or state of being very accurate). Recently, West has applied his revolutionary work to the *business world.* This investigation has led to powerful insight into why some companies thrive while others fail (West, 2017). That said, let's examine the relationships between DNA and OrgDNA bases pairs as shown on Fig. 1.2.

As shown in Fig. 1.2, the initiative to extend this phenomenon to OrgDNA is based on the principle that each organization has exclusive genetic characteristics like any living organism.[56] In this regard, Satell (2013) found that the need to find the structure of DNA was a very well-defined problem, but the answer eluded even *Linus Pauling,* the most talented chemist of the day. He also observed that usually these types of problems are solved through synthesizing across domains.[57] For instance, Watson and Crick solved the DNA problem by combining insights from chemistry, biology, and X-ray crystallography. In a similar vein, many companies are learning to embrace open innovation in order to pull in diverse resources.[58]

To throw more light on this, Satell (2010) found that in the early 1950s, the most coveted scientific prize was the discovery of the structure of DNA, where the greatest scientists of the day, including the already legendary *Linus Pauling,* raced to decipher one of nature's best-kept secrets.[59] However, Satell (2010) noted that the glory went to two young,

Human DNA Base Pairs			**Formal Organizational DNA Base Pairs**		
Guanine (G)	⟷	Cytosine (C)	Information flow (I)	⟷	Structure (S)
Adenine (G)	⟷	Thymine (T)	Decision rights (D)	⟷	Motivators (M)
			OrgDNA Base Pairs Synthesized Templates		
			Mindset (M)	⟷	Network (N)
			Norms (Nm)	⟷	Commitments (C)

Figure 1.2 Relationships between Human DNA and OrgDNA Base Pairs.
Source: Author created.

unknown scientists: *James Watson and Francis Crick.*[60] What they did was something no one else did; they put together the information needed to get the job done by spending most of their time talking about others' research rather than doing their own. That said, they put together biological expertise, X-ray defraction data, and chemical model building approaches needed to discover the DNA's structure. Whereas, all of the other people working on the problem, many perhaps more talented than Watson and Crick, were working feverishly on one aspect of the problem.[61]

According to Eisenmann *et al.* (2013), the approach to focus more on putting together all the needed information rather than uncovering new facts is known as *recombination.* New ideas often result from connecting seemingly unrelated concepts.[62] They argue that creative individuals are curious; they put themselves in situations of planned *serendipity*[63] where they will be exposed to diverse ideas in order to harness their associative thinking abilities. They may do this through the variety of contacts they keep in the real world or through the subject matter experts they follow online.[64] In many cases, having a fresh set of eyes to look at your problem can give you a fresh perspective. Thus, *the science of innovation has shown that breakthroughs happen when different ideas and perspectives clash and co-mingle.*[65]

In a similar vein, Satell (2010) found that increasingly, the ability to synthesize concepts across disciplines is much more valuable than domain knowledge, which is becoming a commodity. Thus, as information becomes more accessible, the trend is sure to continue. But argues that ironically, while empirical data is being devalued in the information age, what really matters is the ability to put the pieces of data together.[66] In concurrence, Nafei (2014) argues that as with many big problems, the answer to the fundamental genetic question is a matter of putting all the information together rather than uncovering new facts.[67] In the same vein, Soroush, Esfahani, and Poorfarahmand (2013) suggest that by combining the reality of biology and genetics with management science, effective steps could be made in improving and developing organizations.[68]

Relevance of Human DNA and Its System Elements to Ergonomics

Interestingly, the characteristics of the human DNA are not only mimicked by organizations within the framework of OrgDNA building blocks; humans and its system elements are also mimicked by *ergonomics.* In this regard, Acevedo (2020) defines *ergonomics* as the study of the interaction between humans and system elements with the goal of increasing efficiency and compatibility. Thus, through an understanding of the human form, muscle systems, and human limitations, ergonomic principles can be applied to products used in business and personal settings.[69] In a similar vein, Nibusinessinfo (2020) defines ergonomics as the science of designing spaces or equipment to fit the person using them. In other words, ergonomics is about ensuring a good fit between people and the things they interact with. This could include objects they use or the environment they live in. Therefore, it makes ergonomics an important part of *research* in the product development process.[70] Its purpose is to increase the safety, comfort, and performance of a product or an environment.[71] Put in another way, ergonomic products are any goods designed to increase ease of use and reduce injuries. Most of them are often associated with computer supplies, office equipment, production equipment, travel, and training videos.[72]

Ergonomics uses *anthropometrical data* to determine the optimum size, shape, and form of a product, and make it easier for people to use.[73] According to Marshall and Summerskill (2019), anthropometric data are data on human body size and shape and are the basis upon which all digital models are constructed.[74] According to Daanen and Reffeltrathe (2007), when anthropometric data are available, the data should be matched with the product under design or evaluation.[75] Skilling (2016) found that correctly selected anthropometric data assists in the design of work areas and workspaces to support neutral working postures and improve productivity, and this helps to reduce error and injury. But argues however that contrary to other products, vehicles presents some specific considerations.[76]

Consequently, ergonomics can help you identify which *user* characteristics you should take into account during your design process. This is important when you consider how much individuals vary in terms of body size, body shape strength, mobility, sensory sensitivity, mental ability, experience, training, culture, and emotions.[77] In addition, *anthropometric measurements* are series of quantitative measurements of the muscle, bone, and adipose tissue used to assess the composition of the body. Thus, the core elements of anthropometry are height, weight, body mass index, body circumferences (waist, hip, and limps), and skinfold thickness.[78]

Essentially, there are three categories of ergonomics: physical ergonomics, psychological ergonomics, and organizational ergonomics.

1.3 Leadership Roles in Today's Business Thinking and the Essence of Its OrgDNA

1.3.1 Attracting a Continually Growing Stream of Added Values: The Stakes

Clues to the Surrounding Environment

The essence of today's business is that of attracting or creating more value, and that such values need to be sustainable. In other words, the ultimate challenge is thinking about the best ways to attract a continually growing stream of added values, and in the case of the circular economy, with minimum resources.

In this direction, research findings of *Industry Canada (2012)* revealed that companies generally pursue a mix of two product innovation strategies. The *first* strategy is *new product innovation,* which is essentially: (1) to push the boundaries of existing markets; and (2) to discover and pursue new opportunities in the global economy. The *second* strategy involves *substantial investment in R&D and product design* to drive long-term profitability and future iterations of product development.[79] In this regard, Asongu (2011) argues that international business is very important for the mere fact that it comprises a large and growing portion of the world's total business – as virtually every company, be it large or small – is affected by global events and competition.[80] This is true, most especially, as almost every company sells its products or services to foreign countries, secures supplies from overseas, and/or competes against products and services that come from abroad. Of course, too often, they also compete for overseas labor.[81]

Little wonder, Sung and Wong (1998) argue that as a society progresses, three factors can be identified: *imitation, technology transfer, and innovation* – which are largely set in motion by global events and competition. That said, *technology transfer* can be due to technology spillover through firm-to-firm or person-to-person contacts (the contagion effect).[82] *Innovation* is the effort to develop a new technology to improve factor productivity, to invent a new product, or to improve the quality of some existing products. *Imitation* is an effort to learn and improve the technology developed by other firms. By implication, therefore, in the absence of technological progress, the growth of an economy, which may be positive in the short run, is not sustainable in the long run.[83] Consequently, intergenerational spillovers in terms of the accumulation of productive knowledge are increasingly becoming a strong force to reckon with.

The Leadership Equation in Value Creation

To pursue such product innovation strategies as discussed earlier, it becomes imperative to put in place the right combinations or mixes of value creation mindsets and skills required for the successful nurturing of the culture of value creation. But this process is not without its own complications. Different leadership strategies tend to tackle these issues with varying degrees and approaches, notably: their style, emphasis, and contents.

In this regard, Rowe (2001) maintains that organizations led by *visionaries* who are not properly supported by strong managerial leadership may destroy wealth even more quickly than organizations led by *managerial leaders.*[84] However, Nyangena, Akujah, and Okanga (2019) found that conventional leaders (managerial leaders inclusive) generally enact changes as short-term solutions to immediate problems and do not diligently seek answers to the issues and challenges concerning sustainability or sustainable development.[85] This introduces another vital element – that of *sustainable leadership*.

Davis (1994) and Hargreaves (2006) define sustainable leadership as *the ability for individuals and institutions to continue to adapt and meet new challenges and complexities in demanding and changing contexts*. In addition, sustainable leadership empowers others to improve human and resource capacity and provides opportunities for leaders and stakeholders to network, learn from, and support each other in achieving organizational goals for the future (Hargeaves, 2006; Fullan, 2005).[86] Finally on this queue, Philips (2003) opines that sustainable leaders tend to embrace new ways of seeing, thinking, and interacting that lead to innovative and sustainable solutions.[87]

With regards to the attributes of *servant leadership*; Smith, Montagno, and Kuzmenko (2004) found that the servant leader's primary motivation is not to *ensure organizational success,* but to *serve*. They do so with *greater emphasis* on *enhancing their follower's personal growth and development*. However, when an organization grows larger and more diversified, the effect of servant leadership tends to face increasingly difficult challenges to achieve its objectives – as the task to manage insightfully depends on the direct experience and personal knowledge that comes with intimacy.[88] This brings to the limelight, another key element – that of *transformational leadership*.

Empowered by a dynamic culture and motivated by a sense of mission to survive in a dynamic and ever-changing external environment, the *transformational leader's* motivation is to *lead*. They do so by focusing on *developing their follower's innovation and creativity*, which *emphasizes on organizational success*.[89]

It is necessary to improve on the personal wellbeing of the individual, especially in the phase of immediate and short-term challenges, as in *servant leadership*. But more importantly, leaders should be able to transform the creative and innovative capacity of their followers toward the long-term goals of the organization to ensure long-term prosperity and survivability. Undeniably, this task involves core elements of *transformational leadership*. Hence, transformational leadership could be said to be more effective in a *dynamic environment,* and servant leadership could be more effective in a *static environment*.[90] Consequently, we can draw inspiration from this fine distinction to arrive at the reasoning that *sustainable leaders are transformational leaders equipped with the added qualities of servant leadership*.

1.3.2 The Dilemma of Adding New Frontiers of Value Creation Outside the Existing Model

Business Model and Sustainability

Eisenmann *et al.* (2013) define a business model as an integrated array of distinctive choices; which specifies a new venture's unique customer value proposition, and how it will configure its activities to deliver that value and earn sustainable profits.[91] According to Neilson *et al.* (2008), you should first take steps to clarify decision rights and design information flow, align motivators, and then make the necessary changes to the structure to support the new design.[92] Blank (2013) argues that one of the main differences between existing companies and start-ups lies in the business model issue. For example, while existing firms execute a business model, start-ups look for one.[93] In a similar vein, Lemus-Aguilar *et al.* (2019) found that *sustainability* and *business models* are two of the most popular topics for managers, academics, and policymakers.[94]

With regards to *sustainability,* they noted, however, that although there is consensus regarding the importance of sustainability for firms, the scientific discourse on how to create or transform into a sustainable organization is blurred.[95]

In relation to *business model,* an entrepreneur may choose to pivot along one or more dimensions of a business model;[96] more especially as a *pivot* changes some business model elements while retaining others. In particular, core aspects of the start-up's original vision are typically retained, for example, a commitment to solving a broad problem, to serving a certain customer segment, or to employ a proprietary technology.[97] Consistent with this, Ries (2011) *defines a pivot as changing strategy while retaining one's original vision.*[98] In relation to this, Satell (2013) defines strategy as a coherent and substantiated logic for making choices.[99] Thus, pivoting is neither a goal nor something to be avoided. While pivoting can be costly and disruptive, failing to pivot when assumptions are known to be flawed can be fatal.[100] That said, pivoting choices can be grouped into four elements: (1) those that define the new venture's customer value proposition, (2) technology and operations plan, (3) go-to-market strategy, and (4) cash flow formula.[101]

With regards to *new venture's customer value proposition,* Eisenmann *et al.* (2013) found that it can take two forms. It can use *customer value proposition – feature set,* where a new venture may pivot to a new customer value proposition by expanding, contracting, or entirely changing its feature set. It can use *customer value proposition – customer set,* where a start-up may also pivot to a new customer value proposition by expanding, contracting, or entirely changing its customer set.[102] As regards *technology and operations management strategy,* an entrepreneur may choose to expand, contract, or shift the scope of activities that are performed internally, rather than externally by partners. With respect to the *go-to-market plan,* a start-up may change its main methods for acquiring customers. Finally, with the *cash flow formula,* a start-up may pivot by changing its monetization approach.[103]

From the aforementioned, undeniably, a *business model* need not only to be successful but equally needs to be *sustainable* in order to create or transform into a sustainable organization. Within this framework, Lemus-Aguilar *et al.* (2019) found that in addition to *sustainability* and *business models* being two of the most popular topics for managers, academics, and policymakers, they have been interpreted somewhat as rather dispersed concepts in most of the literature, notably; from the *business models* perspective and the *organizational theory* perspective.

Business Model and Organizational Theory

Pertaining to *business models,* Casadesus-Masanell and Ricart (2010) posited that it refers to "the logic of the firm, the way it operates and how it creates value for its stakeholders". This can be traced in the literature as far back as the writings of Peter Drucker (Drucker, 1955), where he referred to it as *"the theory of a business.*[104] However, Porter and Kramer (2011) observed that lately there has been a shift toward proposing *sustainable business models* in which the value created and delivered by a firm should not only be appealing to the customer but also fair for the society and friendly to the environment.[105] As a result, the business model literature has recently extended into sub-streams due to the increasing attention on sustainability and the popularity of topics such as circular economy, collaborative consumption, inclusive growth, targeting low-income consumers, and the sharing economy – a view shared by many leading scholars.[106]

Regarding *organizational theory,* Mohrman and Worley (2010) reasoned that it is the process of identifying the *organizational design* elements that must be articulated. These involve organizational design elements that aim to align the firm's strategy with its structures and processes to achieve effectiveness. In concurrence, Gebauer, Fischer, and Fleisch (2010) suggest a wide range of organizational design elements that need to be aligned, which include: coordination, corporate culture, power, human resources management, incentives, performance measurements, and so on.[107] Finally, it also emphasizes the importance of top management's understanding of how to design an organization in order to manage multiple stakeholders.[108]

BUSINESS MODEL AS A SUBJECT OF INNOVATION

Owing to the aforementioned complexities, Mitchell and Coles (2003) argue that in addition to adopting business models to facilitate technological innovation and the management of technology, firms can view the business model itself as a subject of *innovation.*[109] This also applies to entrepreneurial start-ups. With regards to the subject of innovation, Montague (2017) holds the view that innovation is by definition new and unfamiliar. And that people are not immediately drawn to the unfamiliar, and that's where product qualities like aesthetics come in. Aesthetics compels people to look, touch, and engage with something new, and it fosters the adoption of innovation by providing delight and sparking emotional connections.[110]

In a related development, Charles L. Owen (1991), a distinguished Professor Emeritus of Design, notes that in most product development processes, the process of collecting information consists of the examination of competitive products, market studies on existing products, and the elicitation of needs and/or ideas from potential users. As a result, the focus is almost always on existing products and their purchasers or users. He argues that two things are wrong with this approach: (1) usually there is no serious attempt to develop a new concept, and (2) the search for information usually reaches only the primary users of the product.

Owen (1991) argues that the *first* wrong thing is that there is usually *no serious attempt to develop a new concept.* Especially as the effort in this product development model almost always goes into the refinement of an existing concept. As an idea already exists, the challenge would be to focus on the current product to be improved, or that which can be obtained with little effort, especially when a product is fortuitously conceived (especially through a lucky chance) by someone with enough influence to have it considered.[111] Similarly, Mintzberg (1990) found that one common solution to approving projects has been to pick the person instead of the proposal. That is, the manager authorizes those projects presented by people whose judgment he or she trusts. But the manager cannot always use this simple dodge.[112] Owen maintains that market research is often suggested as a tool at this stage. But, unfortunately, it is not a good choice on the basis that market research can help evolve a concept but is inappropriate for inventing one.[113]

The *second* wrong thing is that *the search for information usually reaches only the primary users of the product* – that is, those at the top tier of the pyramid who operate it for its intended use. Those missing it are the many secondary users of the product – those at the middle and lower tiers of the pyramid. These are the very users who could reveal many of the needs that should be considered in its design; as they are usually those who form the bulk of those who distribute it, store it, sell it, maintain it, repair it, remodel it, recycle it, retire it, and so on.[114]

Obviously, it is at this juncture where the urgent need for the integration of design thinking comes in. In the argument of Hannon, Kuhlmann, and Thaidigsmann (2019), design *thinking* starts with observing customers in their everyday lives to learn about their material needs and about how well (or poorly) those needs are met by existing products. Product designers, marketing specialists, engineers, and others involved in making and selling products use the resulting insights on customer needs to rapidly prototype, test, and refine new concepts for products and services, without relying on old assumptions that might constrain their ideas. With respect to the circular economy, design thinking also means asking how to provide value to consumers using a minimum amount of material.[115]

It is obvious at this point that through the eyes of each of these "users," a product looks radically different. Each user sees it in terms of the *functions* he has to perform with it, and each can contribute to the development of a better concept.[116] This is especially true, for example, during the era that immediately preceded the conceptual design of the automotive engine; if one had to contact a marketing research company – about the need for a faster means of transportation, they would have probably suggested the financing of research on some kind of medication or drug that could be injected into the body of horses, so that they can run faster. Also, at the time the Wright brothers were discussing their airplane project, if they had contacted maybe a marketing department of a car manufacturing company, the latter would have probably hastily dismissed the idea as wasting resources that could have been used for another innovation project that was feasibly viable.

ORGANIZATIONAL THEORY: VISIONARY VS. MANAGERIAL LEADERSHIP

Tapping sense from the aforementioned, Rowe (2001) argues that visionary leaders have attitudes toward goals that are opposite to those of managerial leaders. Thus, as visionary leaders strive to develop choices and fresh approaches to long-standing problems, they tend to create excitement at work, especially from high-risk positions as they seek out risky ventures, when the rewards are high. In other words, visionary leaders are relatively more proactive, shaping ideas as opposed to reacting to them.[117] On the contrary, when an organization is in a transition phase, driven by a vision of what it should be, for example, to maintain and enhance long-term viability, it is very hard on those who are managerial leaders[118] to realize this target. This is not strange, as managerial leadership involves stability and order, and the preservation of the existing order. Managerial leaders are more comfortable handling day-to-day activities and are short-term oriented. Essentially, this involves issues of organizational change management.

From the foregoing, Prasad, Nair, and Raj (2014) contend that several organizational theorists have witnessed that organizational change management practices are failing today because organizations *are missing people as a human factor,* and only giving importance to them *in their strategies of change management in the organization.* They maintain that what best represents the ideals embodied in the human factor (HF) is servant-leadership.[119] This is true, but as we discussed earlier, there are many options to tap from in resolving the leadership equation.

Conclusion

To comprehensively identify, introduce, and clarify critical factors and processes that subtly impair the understanding of the relationships between PPS with regards to their interplay with critical factors that underpins organizational behavior and strategic alignment, is a difficult process as the relationships between PPS is a complex relationship that is least understood in the business world and beyond. This is because just a few industry leaders or pioneers get it right. Among them are those that constantly thrive to master the art of preparing their organizations as a learning hub for radical and disruptive change. However, a critical majority of those who got it right most often get it by gamble their way through. But this latter approach would imply that such organizations have not grasped a foothold of the situation; as a result, the challenges of sustaining these gains gradually disappear over time. This is true, as most of these companies find it extremely difficult to align sustainability with the changing landscape of productivity and profitability in the long run.

Essentially, this chapter also points to the argument that a successful relationship between PPS as applicable within the framework of organizational behavior and strategic alignment follows are recurrent cycles.

Consequently, retaining strategic control over the ***"PPS"*** is not a one-time or one-big-push, but a series of continuous alignment and realignment of the aforementioned three elements. Moreover, the core tenet of an entity's organizational behavior is not easily discernible at first sight. Even if it does, it is still subject to severe competitive forces both internally and externally that might cause its OrgDNA replication process to mutate or become obsolete in the course of improving organizational performance. By some measures, this largely explains why in spite of the presence of expert business consultancy advice to organizations, many of such organizations still fail. Guess what? One of the major problems would be that the DNA composition was not properly understood and tackled, or if properly understood, it was not properly tackled or aligned with the other key components of the strategic value creation drivers of the organization.

The aforementioned greatly relies on the ability of the entity to see the urgency of preparing itself as a learning organization, capable of incubating radical innovation and absorbing disruptive innovation in the industry in all its ramifications whenever the need arises – and then inject such mindset into its DNA and vigorously cultivate it into its organizational culture.

Notes

1 Ministry of Employment, Immigration and Civil Status. "What Is Productivity." *Government of Seychelles,* http://www.employment.gov.sc/what-is-productivity. Accessed Feb. 2020.
2 Mankins, Michael. "Great Companies Obsess Over Productivity, Not Efficiency." *Harvard Business Review,* 1 Mar. 2017, https://hbr.org/2017/03/great-companies-obsess-over-productivity-not-efficiency?referral=03758&cm_vc=rr_item_page.top_right. Accessed 24 Sep. 2020.
3 Chew, Bruce W. "No-Nonsense Guide to Measuring Productivity." *Harvard Business Review,* Jan. 1988, https://hbr.org/1988/01/no-nonsense-guide-to-measuring-productivity. Accessed 24 Sep. 2020.
4 Mankins, Michael (2017), loc. cit.
5 Mankins, Michael (2017), loc. cit.
6 Study.com. "What Is Profitability? – Definition & Analysis," *Study.com,* https://study.com/academy/lesson/what-is-profitability-definition-analysis-quiz.html. Accessed 4 Feb. 2020.
7 My Accounting Course. "What Is Profitability?" *MyAccountingCourse.com,* https://www.myaccountingcourse.com/accounting-dictionary/profitability. Accessed 4 Feb. 2020.
8 Grant, Mitchell. "Sustainability". *Investopedia,* updated 5 Apr. 2020, https://www.investopedia.com/terms/s/sustainability.asp. Accessed 20 Jun. 2020.
9 Action Inclusion. "Organizational Sustainability." *Actioninclusion.org* https://actioninclusion.org/leadership-diversity-change/what-is-organizational-sustainability. Accessed 10 Jun. 2020.
10 Ibid.
11 Neilson, Gary L., et al. "The Secrets to Successful Strategy Execution." *Harvard Business Review,* Jun. 2008, p. 62, https://hbr.org/2008/06/the-secrets-to-successful-strategy-execution. Accessed 25 May 2020.
12 Neilson et al. (2008), loc. cit.
13 Ibid.
14 Eisenmann, Thomas, et al. "Hypothesis-Driven Entrepreneurship: The Lean Startup." *Harvard Business School Publishing,* Boston, 9-812-095, Rev: 10 Jul. 2013, p. 1, www.hbsp.harvard.edu/educators.
15 Engel, Christoph and Elke U. Weber. "The Impact of Institutions on the Decision How to Decide." *Journal of Institutional Economics: The JOIE Foundation*, vol. 3, no. 3, 2007, p. 334, doi:10.1017/S1744137407000744.
16 Gallouj, Faïz. *Innovation in the Service Economy: The New Wealth of Nations*. Edward Elgar Publishing, 2002, p. 79.
17 Engel and Weber (2007), op. cit., p. 335.
18 Barry, C. and K. Halfmann. "The Effect of Mindset on Decision-Making." *Journal of Integrated Social Sciences*, vol. 6, no. 1, 2016, p. 50. www.JISS.org.
19 As called clarifying *decision rights* in the OrgDNA common bases, and it is usually associated with its OrgDNA synthesized templates called *Norms*

(i.e., what people perceive as being right or wrong, what ought to be done, or what ought not to be done).

20 Barry and Halfmann (2016), op. cit., p. 53. Remember, *information flow* is one of the most dominant formal building blocks of the OrgDNA, with *mindset* as its *informal OrgDNA building block*.
21 Rowe, Glenn W. "Creating Wealth in Organizations: The Role of Strategic Leadership." *Academy of Management Executive,* vol. 15, no. 1, Feb. 2001, p. 81.
22 Course Hero. "Technology & Design: Influences on Product Design." AS LEVEL Section A FACT FILES. *Coursehero.com,* 2011, p. 4, https://www.coursehero.com/file/40838121/A2AS-TECH-Support-10370pdf/.
23 Barry and Halfmann (2016), op. cit. p. 50.
24 As cited by Engel and Weber (2007), op. cit., p. 327.
25 Ibid.
26 Barry and Halfmann (2016), op. cit., p. 50.
27 Nafei, Wageeh. "The Role of Organizational DNA in Improving Organizational Performance: A Study on the Industrial Companies in Egypt." *International Business Research,* vol. 8, 25 Dec. 2014, p. 117, doi: 10.5539/ibr.v8n1p117.
28 YourDictionary. "DNA." *YourDictionary* – LoveToKnow, www.yourdictionary.com/dna. Accessed 14 Jan. 2020.
29 YourDictionary (2020), loc. cit.
30 Gershoni, Jonathan M. "Lesson 2: Main Terms," in *Viruses & How To Beat Them: Cells, Immunity, Vaccines.* TAU Online, Innovative Learning Center, Tel Aviv University in partnership with Edx.org, 2018a, p. 1.
31 U.S. National Library of Medicine. "What Is DNA?" U.S. National Library of Medicine. Published 10 Dec. 2019, https://ghr.nlm.nih.gov/primer/basics/dna.
32 Gershoni (2018a), op. cit., p. 2.
33 Ibid.
34 Thompson, Liam. "The Chemical Structure of DNA." *Andy Brunning/Compound Interest 2018,* www.compoundchem.com, https://www.compoundchem.com/2015/03/24/dna/ (2015). Accessed 5 Jan. 2019.
35 Gershoni, Jonathan M. (2018a), op. cit., p. 1.
36 Compound Interest. "The Chemical Structure of DNA," *Andy Brunning/Compound Interest 2018.* Compoundchem.com, 24 Mar. 2015b, https://www.compoundchem.com/2015/03/24/dna/.
37 Thompson, Liam (2015), loc. cit.
38 U.S. National Library of Medicine (2019), loc. cit.
39 Thompson, Liam (2015), loc. cit.
40 Ibid.
41 Scitable by Nature Education. "Cells Can Replicate Their DNA Precisely." *Nature.com,* 2019, https://www.nature.com/scitable/topicpage/cells-can-replicate-their-dna-precisely-6524830/. Accessed 25 Nov. 2019.
42 Thompson, Liam (2015), loc. cit.
43 Gershoni, Jonathan M. "Lesson 2: Macromolecules – From DNA to Proteins," in *Viruses & How To Beat Them: Cells, Immunity, Vaccines.* TAU Online, Innovative Learning Center, TelAviv University in partnership with Edx.org, 2018c.
44 Compound Interest. "The Chemical Structure of DNA," *Andy Brunning/Compound Interest 2018.* Compoundchem.com, Mar. 2015c, www.compoundchem.com, https://www.compoundchem.com/wp-content/uploads/2015/03/The-Chemical-Structures-of-DNA-RNA-Aug-2018.pdf. Accessed 7 Jan. 2019.

45 Thompson, Liam (2015), loc. cit.
46 Gershoni (2018a), op. cit., p. 2.
47 Ibid.
48 News Medical Life Sciences. "Protein Analysis: Application of Bone Proteomics." *News-Medical,* 22 Jul. 2020, www.news-medical.net.
49 Gershoni (2018a), op. cit., pp. 3–4.
50 Scitable by Nature Education (2019), loc. cit.
51 New Medical Life Sciences (2020), loc. cit.
52 The proteins that make up living organisms are huge molecules that are composed of tinier building blocks, known as *amino acids*. There are over 500 amino acids found in nature, yet, of these, the human genetic code only directly codes for 20. Every protein in your body is made up of some linked combination of these amino acids. Broadly, these 20 amino acids can be sorted into two groups: essential and nonessential. Nonessential amino acids are those which the human body is capable of synthesizing, whereas essential amino acids must be obtained from the diet. See Compound Interest. "A Brief Guide to the Twenty Common Amino Acids." *Compound Interest,* 16 Sep. 2014a, https://www.compoundchem.com/2014/09/16/aminoacids/. Accessed 7 Jan. 2019.
53 Thompson, Liam (2015), loc. cit.
54 Nafei, Wageeh (2014), op. cit., p. 118.
55 Montana State University. "Beautiful Math of Fractals." *Montana State University,* 13 Oct. 2011, https://phys.org/news/2001-10-beautiful-math-fractals.html. Accessed 11 Jul. 2020.
56 Nafei, Wageeh (2014), op. cit., p. 118.
57 Satell, Greg. "How To Manage Innovation." *Forbes Media LLC,* 7 Mar. 2013, https://www.forbes.com/sites/gregsatell/2013/03/07/how-to-manage-innovation-2/#7e6b34784785. Accessed 28 Mar. 2020.
58 Ibid.
59 Satell, Greg. "The Power of Synthesis and the Problem with Experts." *DigitalTonto,* 21 Jun. 2010, https://www.digitaltonto.com/2010/power-of-synthesis/. Accessed 29 Mar. 2020.
60 Ibid.
61 Ibid.
62 Eisenmann et al. (2013), op. cit., p. 16.
63 *Planned serendipity* refers to awaiting expectations that something interesting or pleasant would be happening by chance.
64 Eisenmann et al. (2013), op. cit., p. 16.
65 Mehta, Kumar. "How To Turn An Innovation Failure Into Success." *Forbes Media LLC,* 11 Mar. 2019, https://www.forbes.com/sites/kmehta/2019/03/11/how-to-turn-an-innovation-failure-into-success/#7becbe523fc7. Accessed 24 Mar. 2020.
66 Satell, Greg (2010), loc. cit.
67 Satell, Greg (2010), loc. cit.
68 As cited by Nafei, Wageeh (2014), op. cit., p. 118.
69 Acevedo, Laura. "What Are Ergonomic Products?" *Hearst,* https://smallbusiness.chron.com/ergonomic-products-16880.html. Accessed 10 Jul. 2020.
70 Nibusinessinfo. "User-Centered Design: The Importance of Ergonomics." *Invest Northern Ireland* in partnership with *Nidirect government services,* 2020a, https://www.nibusinessinfo.co.uk/content/importance-ergonomics. Accessed 10 Jul. 2020.
71 Ibid.

72 Acevedo, Laura (2020), loc. cit.
73 Nibusinessinfo (2020a), loc. cit.
74 Marshall, Russell and Steve Summerskill. "Posture and Anthropometry." *DHM and Posturography,* edited by Sofia Scataglini and Paul Gunther, Academic Press, 2019, pp. 333–50, https://doi.org/10.1016/B978-0-12-816713-7.00025-8. Accessed 12 Jul. 2020.
75 Daanen, H.A.M. and P.A. Reffeltrathe. "Function, Fit and Sizing." Sizing in Clothing: Developing Effective Sizing Systems for Ready-to-Wear Clothing," edited by S.P. Ashdown, Woodhead Publishing 2007, pp. 202–09, 1st Edition, https://doi.org/10.1533/9781845692582.202. Accessed 12 Jul. 2020.
76 Skilling, E.J. "Workstation, Work Area, and Console Design." *Human Factors in the Chemical and Process Industries: Making It Work in Practice*, Elsevier, 2016, pp. 205–21, 1st Edition, https://doi.org/10.1016/B978-0-12-803806-2.00012-1. Accessed 12 Jul. 2020.
77 Nibusinessinfo (2020a), loc. cit.
78 Casadei, Kyle and John Kiel. *Anthropometric Measurement.* StatPearls Publishing: Treasure Island (FL), Jan. 2020, https://www.ncbi.nlm.nih.gov/books/NBK537315/#!po=87.9310. Accessed 12 Jul. 2020.
79 Industry Canada. Product Design, Research and Development: A Canadian Manufacturing Perspective. *Publishing and Depository Services Public Works and Government Services*: Canada, Ottawa, 2011, p. 2.
80 Asongu, Januarius J. "Understanding the Importance of International Business to the Rockford Economy." *Rockford College,* Mar. 2011, p. 1, www.rockford.edu.
81 Ibid.
82 Sung, Yun-Wing and Kar-Yiu Wong. *Growth of Hong Kong Before and After Its Reversion to China: The China Factor.* Chinese University of Hong Kong, and University of Washington, 28 Apr. 1998, p. 6.
83 Sung and Wong (1998), op. cit., p. 5.
84 Rowe (2001), op. cit., p. 81.
85 Nyangena, E., et al. "Ethical Leadership for Sustainable Development in Developing Countries," *Editon Cons. Journal of Arts, Humanities, and Social Studies*, vol. 1, no. 1, 2019, p. 1.
86 As cited by Nyangena et al. (2019), op. cit., p. 3.
87 As cited by Nyangena et al. (2019), loc. cit.
88 Mintzberg, Henry. "The Manager's Job: Folklore and Fact." *Harvard Business Review*, 1990 Mar./Apr., p. 3. This article by Professor Henry Mintzberg appeared originally in HBR Jul./Aug. 1975.
89 As cited by Nyangena et al. (2019), op. cit., p. 3.
90 As cited by Lowder, Tim M. "The Best Leadership Model for Organizational Change Management: Transformational Verses Servant Leadership." *Academia.edu,* 2009, p. 17.
91 Eisenmann et al. (2013), op. cit., p. 2.
92 Neilson et al. (2008), op. cit., p. 67.
93 As cited by Ghezzi et al. "A Comparative Study on the Impact of Business Model Design & Lean Startup Approach versus Traditional Business Plan on Mobile Startups Performance." *ResearchGate,* Jan. 2015, p. 4, doi:10.5220/0005337501960203.
94 Lemus-Aguilar et al. "Sustainability Business Models through the Lens of Organizational Design: A Systematic Literature Review." *Sustainability,* 28 Sep. 2019, doi:10.3390/su11195379/www.mdpi.com/journal/sustainability, p. 1.
95 Lemus-Aguilar et al. (2019), loc. cit.

96 Eisenmann et al. (2013), op. cit., p. 20.
97 Eisenmann et al. (2013), op. cit., p. 10.
98 Ries, Innovation Lab presentation at Harvard Business School, 21 Sep. 2011; as cited by Eisenmann et al. (2013), ibid.
99 Satell, Greg (2013), loc. cit.
100 Eisenmann et al. (2013), op. cit., p. 10.
101 Eisenmann et al. (2013), op. cit., pp. 4–5.
102 Eisenmann et al. (2013), op. cit., p. 20.
103 Eisenmann et al. (2013), loc. cit.
104 As cited by Lemus-Aguilar et al. (2019), op. cit., p. 1.
105 As cited Lemus-Aguilar et al. (2019), ibid; pp. 1-2.
106 Ibid.
107 As cited by Lemus-Aguilar et al. (2019), op. cit., p. 2.
108 Ibid.
109 As cited by Ghezzi et al. (2015), op. cit., p. 4.
110 Montague, Monty. "The Amazing Role of Aesthetics in Product Design." *White Paper, Boltgroup.com,* 21 Jun. 2017, p. 3, https://boltgroup.com/aesthetics-in-product-design. Accessed 22 Jan. 2020.
111 Owen, Charles L. "Product Integrity by Design." *Institute of Design,* Illinois Institute of Technology Chicago, Illinois U.S.A, 1991, p. 2. This article was adapted from a paper given at the *Colloque "Design, Matériaux et Environnement" of the* International Design and Industry Forum *held in Toulon, France Sep. 5–7, 1991, and published in the Proceedings of the Deuxièmes Rencontres Internationales du Design et de l'Industrie,* 135–40. Toulon, France: Promo Design, 1991. *Published also in Design/Recherche, no.* 3, (Feb. 1993): 5–10 *and Design Processes Newsletter,* vol. 4, no. 1, 1991, 7–9, 11, https://id.iit.edu/wpcontent/uploads/2015/03/Product-integrity-by-design-Owen_prdinteg-1.pdf/.
112 Mintzberg, Henry (1990), op. cit., p. 18.
113 Owen, Charles L. (1991), op. cit., p. 2.
114 Ibid.
115 Hannon, E., et al. "Developing Products for a Circular Economy." *The Circular Economy: Moving from Theory to Practice*. McKinsey Center for Business and Environment, Special edition, Oct. 2019, p. 24.
116 Owen, Charles L. (1991), op. cit., p. 2.
117 Rowe, Glenn W. (2001), op. cit., pp. 82 & 85.
118 Rowe, Glenn W. (2001), op. cit., p. 86.
119 Prasad, S.P., et al. "Servant Leadership: An Imperative Leadership Style of Managers for Achieving Organizational Change Successfully," 2014, p. 1, academia.edu.

Works Cited

Acevedo, Laura. "What Are Ergonomic Products?" *Hearst Newspapers,* https://smallbusiness.chron.com/ergonomic-products-16880.html. Accessed 11 Oct. 2020.

Action Inclusion. "Organizational Sustainability." *Actioninclusion.org*, https://actioninclusion.org/leadership-diversity-change/what-is-organizational-sustainability.

Asongu, Januarius J. *"Understanding the Importance of International Business to the Rockford Economy." Rockford College*, Rockford, Mar. 2011, pp. 1–2, www.rockford.edu.

Blank, S. "Why the Lean Startup Changes Everything." *Harvard Business Review*, vol. 91, no. 5, 2013, pp. 63–72.

Barry, Carly and Kameko Halfmann. "The Effect of Mindset on Decision-Making." *Journal of Integrated Social Sciences*, vol. 6, no. 1, 2016, pp. 49–74. www.JISS.org.

Casadei, Kyle and John Kiel. *Anthropometric Measurement. StatPearls Publishing*, Jan. 2020, https://www.ncbi.nlm.nih.gov/books/NBK537315/#!po=87.9310.

Casadesus-Masanell, R. and J. E. Ricart. "From Strategy to Business Models and onto Tactics." *Long Range Plan*, vol. 43, 2010, pp. 195–215.

Chew, Bruce W. "No-Nonsense Guide to Measuring Productivity." *Harvard Business Review*, Jan. 1988, https://hbr.org/1988/01/no-nonsense-guide-to-measuring-productivity.

Compound Interest. "A Brief Guide to the Twenty Common Amino Acids." *Compound Interest*, 16 Sep. 2014a, https://www.compoundchem.com/2014/09/16/aminoacids/. Accessed 7 Jan. 2019.

Compound Interest. "The Chemical Structure of DNA," in *Andy Brunning/Compound Interest 2018. Compoundchem. com*, 24 Mar. 2015b, https://www.compoundchem.com/2015/03/24/dna/.

Compound Interest. "The Chemical Structure of DNA," in *Andy Brunning/Compound Interest 2018*. Compoundchem.com, Mar. 2015c, www.compoundchem.com, https://www.compoundchem.com/wp-content/uploads/2015/03/The-Chemical-Structures-of-DNA-RNA-Aug-2018.pdf.

Course Hero. "Technology & Design: Influences on Product Design." AS LEVEL Section A FACT FILES. *Coursehero.com*, 2011, pp. 1–7, https://www.coursehero.com/file/40838121/A2AS-TECH-Support-10370pdf/.

Daanen, H.A.M. and P.A. Reffeltrathe. "Function, Fit and Sizing." *Sizing in Clothing: Developing Effective Sizing Systems for Ready-to-Wear Clothing*, edited by S.P. Ashdown. Woodhead Publishing 2007, pp. 202–09, 1st Edition, https://doi.org/10.1533/9781845692582.202

Davis, J. "Achieving Sustainable Development." *Beyond Leadership: Balancing Economics, Ethics and Ecology*, edited by W. Bennis, J. Parikh, and R. Lessem. Revised Edition. Blackwell Publishers Ltd, Oxford, 1994.

Drucker, P. *The Practice of Management*. Heinemman London, UK, 1955.

Eisenmann, Thomas, et al. *"Hypothesis-Driven Entrepreneurship: The Lean Startup,"* Harvard Business School Publishing, Boston, 9-812-095, Rev: 10 Jul. 2013, pp. 2–26.

Engel, Christoph and Elke U. Weber "The Impact of Institutions on the Decision How to Decide." *Journal of Institutional Economics*: *The JOIE Foundation*, vol. 3, no. 3, 2007, pp. 323–49, doi:10.1017/S1744137407000744.

Fullan, Michael. *Leadership and Sustainability: System Thinkers in Action*. Corwin Press, and Ontario Principals' Council, Thousand Oaks, California, 2005.

Gallouj, Faïz. *Innovation in the Service Economy: The New Wealth of Nations*. Edward Elgar Publishing, Cheltenham, Northampton, 2002, pp. 77–87.

Gebauer, H., et al. "Exploring the Interrelationship Among Patterns of Service Strategy Changes and Organizational Design Elements." *Journal of Service Management*, vol. 21, 2010, pp. 103–29.

Gershoni, Jonathan M. "Lesson 2: Main Terms," in *Viruses & How To Beat Them: Cells, Immunity, Vaccines. TAU Online, Innovative Learning Center,* TelAviv University in partnership with Edx.org, 2018a, pp. 1–4.

Gershoni, Jonathan M. "Lesson 2: Leading Scientists and Experts," in *Viruses & How To Beat Them: Cells, Immunity, Vaccines. TAU Online, Innovative Learning Center,* TelAviv University in partnership with Edx.org, 2018b, pp. 1–6.

Gershoni, Jonathan M. "Lesson 2: Macromolecules – from DNA to Proteins," in *Viruses & How To Beat Them: Cells, Immunity, Vaccines. TAU Online, Innovative Learning Center,* TelAviv University in partnership with Edx.org, 2018c.

Ghezzi, A., et al. "A Comparative Study on the Impact of Business Model Design & Lean Startup Approach versus Traditional Business Plan on Mobile Startups Performance." *ResearchGate*, Jan. 2015, pp. 2–9, doi:10.5220/000533750 1960203.

Grant, Mitchell. "Sustainability". *Investopedia*, updated 5 Apr. 2020, https://www.investopedia.com/terms/s/sustainability.asp.

Hannon, E., et al. "Developing Products for a Circular Economy." *The Circular Economy: Moving from Theory to Practice. McKinsey Center for Business and Environment*, Special edition, Oct. 2019, pp. 23–25.

Hargreaves, A. "Welcome to Sustainable Leadership" [Power Point Slides]. 2006. Retrieved from http://www.minedu.fi/export/sites/default/OPM/Tapahtumakalenteri

Industry Canada. *Product Design, Research and Development: A Canadian Manufacturing Perspective. Publishing and Depository Services Public Works and Government Services*: Canada, Ottawa, 2012, pp. 1–30.

Lemus-Aguilar, I., et al. "Sustainability Business Models through the Lens of Organizational Design: A Systematic Literature Review." *Sustainability*, vol. 11, 28 Sep. 2019, p. 5379, doi:10.3390/su11195379/www.mdpi.com/journal/sustainability.

Lowder, M. Tim. "The Best Leadership Model for Organizational Change Management: Transformational Verses Servant Leadership." *SSRN Electronic Journal*, 14 Jun. 2009, pp. 2–18, doi:10.2139/ssrn.1418796.

Mankins, Michael. "Great Companies Obsess Over Productivity, Not Efficiency." *Harvard Business Review*, 1 Mar. 2017, https://hbr.org/2017/03/great-companies-obsess-over-productivity-not-efficiency?referral=03758&cm_vc=rr_item_page.top_right.

Marshall, Russell and Steve Summerskill. "Posture and Anthropometry." *DHM and Posturography*, edited by Sofia Scataglini and Paul Gunther. Academic Press, 2019, pp. 333–50, https://doi.org/10.1016/B978-0-12-816713-7.00025-8. Accessed 30 Aug. 2019.

Mehta, Kumar. "How To Turn An Innovation Failure Into Success." *Forbes Media LLC*, 11 Mar. 2019, https://www.forbes.com/sites/kmehta/2019/03/11/how-to-turn-an-innovation-failure-into-success/#7becbe523fc7.

Ministry of Employment, Immigration and Civil Status. "What is Productivity." *Government of Seychelles*, http://www.employment.gov.sc/what-is-productivity.

Mintzberg, Henry. "The Manager's Job: Folklore and Fact." *Harvard Business Review*, Mar./Apr. 1990, pp. 12–20.

Mitchell, D. and C. Coles. "The Ultimate Competitive Advantage of Continuing Business Model Innovation." *Journal of Business Strategy*, vol. 24, no. 5, 2003, pp. 15–21.

Mohrman, S. A. and C. G. Worley. "The Organizational Sustainability Journey: Introduction to the Special Issue." *Organizational Dynamics*, 39, 2010, pp. 289–294.

Montague, Monty. "The Amazing Role of Aesthetics in Product Design." *White Paper, Boltgroup.com*, 21 Jun. 2017, pp. 1–4, https://boltgroup.com/aesthetics-in-product-design.

Montana State University. "Beautiful math of fractals." *Montana State University*, 13 Oct. 2011, https://phys.org/news/2001-10-beautiful-math-fractals.html.

My Accounting Course. "What is Profitability?" *MyAccountingCourse.com*, https://www.myaccountingcourse.com/accounting-dictionary/profitability.

Nafei, Wageeh. "The Role of Organizational DNA in Improving Organizational Performance: A Study on the Industrial Companies in Egypt." *International Business Research*, vol. 8, 25 Dec. 2014, pp. 117–30, doi:10.5539/ibr.v8n1p117.

Neilson, Gary L., et al. "The Secrets to Successful Strategy Execution." *Harvard Business Review*, Jun. 2008, pp. 61–70, https://hbr.org/2008/06/the-secrets-to-successful-strategy-execution.

News Medical Life Sciences. "Protein Analysis: Application of Bone Proteomics." *News-Medical*, 22 Jul. 2020, www.news-medical.net.

Nibusinessinfo. "User-Centered Design: The Importance of Ergonomics." *Invest Northern Ireland in partnership with Nidirect government services*, 2020a, https://www.nibusinessinfo.co.uk/content/importance-ergonomics.

Nyangena, E., et al. "Ethical Leadership for Sustainable Development in Developing Countries," *Editon Cons. Journal of Arts, Humanities, and Social Studies*, vol. 1, no. 1, 2019, pp. 1–10.

Owen, Charles L. "Product Integrity by Design." *Institute of Design*. Illinois Institute of Technology Chicago, 1991, pp. 1–5.

Phillips, C. *Sustainable Place: A Place of Sustainable Development*. Wiley-Academy, 2003.

Porter, M. E. and M. R. Kramer. "Creating Shared Value." *Harvard Business Review*, vol. 89, 2011, pp. 62–67.

Prasad, S.P., et al. "*Servant Leadership: An Imperative Leadership Style of Managers for Achieving Organizational Change Successfully.*" *Academia.edu*, 2014, pp. 1–11.

Ries, E. *The Lean Startup: How Today's Entrepreneurs Use Continuous Innovation to Create Radically Successful Businesses*. Random House LLC, 2011.

Rosenberg, Mike. *Strategy and Sustainability: A Hard-Nosed and Clear-Eyed Approach to Environmental Sustainability for Business*. 1st Edition, 27 Sep. 2015a. Springer, https://bookauthority.org. Accessed 23 Jun. 2020.

Rosenberg, Michael. *Strategy and Sustainability: A Hardnosed Clear-Eyed Approach to Environmental Sustainability for Business*. 1st Edition. Palgrave Macmillan, UK, 2015b, doi: 10.1007/978-1-137-50175-2.

Rowe, Glenn W. "Creating Wealth in Organizations: The Role of Strategic Leadership." *Academy of Management Executive*, vol. 15, no. 1, Feb. 2001, pp. 81–94.

Satell, Greg. "How To Manage Innovation." *Forbes Media LLC*, 7 Mar. 2013, https://www.forbes.com/sites/gregsatell/2013/03/07/how-to-manage-innovation-2/#7e6b34784785.

Satell, Greg. "The Power of Synthesis and the Problem with Experts." *DigitalTonto*, 21 Jun. 2010, https://www.digitaltonto.com/2010/power-of-synthesis/.

Scitable by Nature Education. "Cells Can Replicate Their DNA Precisely." *Nature.com*, 2019, https://www.nature.com/scitable/topicpage/cells-can-replicate-their-dna-precisely-6524830/.

Skilling, E.J. "Workstation, Work Area, and Console Design." *Human Factors in the Chemical and Process Industries: Making It Work in Practice*. Elsevier, 2016, pp. 205–21, 1st Edition, https://doi.org/10.1016/B978-0-12-803806-2.00012-1. Accessed 12 Jul. 2020.

Smith, B. N., et al. "Transformational and Servant Leadership: Content and Contextual Comparisons." *Journal of Leadership & Organizational Studies (Baker College)*, vol. 10, no. 4, 2004, pp. 80–91. As cited by Lowder, M. Tim. "The Best Leadership Model for Organizational Change Management: Transformational Verses Servant Leadership." *SSRN Electronic Journal*, 14 Jun. 2009, pp. 2–18, doi: 10.2139/ssrn.1418796.

Soroush, S., et al. "Investigation of Organizational DNA in Esfahan Province Sport and Youth Offices According to Honold and Silverman Model." *International Research Journal of Applied and Basic Sciences*, vol. 4, no. 6, 2013, pp. 1417–25.

Study.com. "What Is Profitability? - Definition & Analysis," *Study.com*, https://study.com/academy/lesson/what-is-profitability-definition-analysis-quiz.html.

Sung, Yun-Wing and Kar-yiu Wong. *Growth of Hong Kong Before and After Its Reversion to China: The China Factor*. Chinese University of Hong Kong, and University of Washington, 1998, pp. 1–26.

Thompson, Liam. "The Chemical Structure of DNA," in Andy Brunning/Compound Interest 2018. *Compoundchem.com*, 24 Mar. 2015, www.compoundchem.com, https://www.compoundchem.com/2015/03/24/dna/

U.S. National Library of Medicine. "What is DNA?" Published: 10 Dec. 2019, https://ghr.nlm.nih.gov/primer/basics/dna

West, Geoffrey. *SCALE: The Universal Laws of Growth, Innovation, Sustainability, and the Pace of Life in Organisms, Cities, Economies, and Companies*. 1st Edition. Penguin Press, 16 May 2017.

YourDictionary. "DNA." *YourDictionary* - LoveToKnow, www.yourdictionary.com/dna.

2 OrgDNA, System Elements, and the Logic of Effective Strategic Alignment: Sustainability Perspective

Introduction

This chapter examines *OrgDNA*, *systems integration*, and the *logic of effective strategic alignment* within the framework of sustainability. This is particularly crucial as businesses of all sizes tend to balance the competing demands of profitability, productivity, and sustainability. As a result, the demands and stresses on companies only grow as executives face a multitude of competing business goals as stakeholders are interested in corporate profits, jobs, business growth, and environmental sustainability.[1] Little wonder why Apte and Sheth (2016) argue that business leaders need to embrace sustainability in order to ensure the lasting success of their organizations.[2]

Indeed, one cannot deny it. But the pertinent issue is that of crafting out a workable synergy between the appropriate organizational framework and the challenges of implementation. To this end, Kuenkel (2016) argues that one of the most important questions facing sustainability and social-change professionals around the world is that, in a world of many silos, how do we get people to work together toward a common goal.[3] In this regard, Sheffi and Blanco (2018) argue in favor of three basic rationales for *corporate sustainability*: cutting costs, reducing risk, and achieving growth. Furthermore, they reasoned that, for companies, sustainability is not a simple case of "profits vs. planet" (i.e., economic vs. environmental factors on a larger scale), but is instead a more subtle issue of (some) people vs. (other) people – those looking for jobs and inexpensive goods vs. those who seek a fresh and clean environment or environment that is preserved in its original or natural condition.

From the aforementioned, this chapter provides comprehensive explanations on key concepts surrounding business thinking that goes beyond the boundaries of traditionally known approaches. This is important as recent trends point out growing interest in the reassessment of the conceptual and empirical relationships that exist between profitability, productivity, and sustainability, and their alignment with organizational behavior and corporate strategies, by both scholars and practitioners alike.

For example, it is now widely agreed by both practitioners and theoreticians alike that the skills needed for leadership have undergone a metamorphic change – and being in a leadership position in the present industrial scenario requires more diverse, complex, and adaptive thinking abilities for survival and growth beyond the frontiers of managerial leadership.

2.1 An Overview of the Crux of the Issue: Where We Stand Today

2.1.1 Beyond the Traditional Concepts of Business Thinking

Antecedents to the Crux of the Issue

What we have always traditionally known in the literature as the manager's job, is appallingly facing increasing challenge and obsoleteness in the 21st century. Mintzberg (1990) in his article titled "The Manager's Job: Folklore and Fact," which won the *McKinsey Award for excellence,* found that the classical view, which says that the manager organizes, coordinates, plans, and controls, suggests otherwise in the real sense of it.[4] Undeniably, this increasing challenge is partly due to the increasing complexity, volatility and unpredictability of the social environment. To this end, Karthikeyan (2017) found that the social environment has changed the natural atmosphere and has become more complex, volatile, and unpredictable. As a result, the skills needed for leadership has undergone a metamorphic change – and being in a leadership position in the present industrial scenario requires more diverse, complex and adaptive thinking abilities for survival and growth[5] beyond the province of managerial leadership.

In the same strand, Karthikeyan (2017) maintains that the methods being used to develop leaders have not changed (much); supposedly as the majority of the leaders are developed from on-the-job experiences, training, and coaching/ mentoring. He contends that while these are all still important, leaders are no longer developing fast enough or in the right ways to match the new environment.[6] Leaders must develop other leaders to be ready and relevant for what organizations will confront over the next five to ten years and beyond – which Karthikeyan calls vertical leadership development.[7] In response, Mintzberg (1990) argues that the manager's job is enormously complicated and difficult – as they are overburdened with obligations, and yet cannot easily delegate their tasks. As a result, they are driven to overwork and forced to do many tasks superficially. Put in another way, their work is characterized by brevity, fragmentation, and verbal communication. It is these characteristics of managerial work that have impeded scientific attempts to improve it.[8] These kinds of dichotomy inherent in typical managerial thinking versus scientific thinking, is giving rise to different leadership theories in an attempt to align organizational challenges.

LEADERSHIP THEORIES RELEVANT TO ORGANIZATIONAL ALIGNMENTS

Visionary, Managerial, and Strategic Leadership With regards to visionary leadership, Rowe (2001) argues that it is the hardest style of leadership to assess regarding performance, as there is the bigger danger that visionaries may achieve below-normal performance much more quickly than managerial leaders. He contends that visionaries coupled with managerial leaders may achieve above normal performance,[9] but believes that a strategic leader will probably create more wealth than a combination of a visionary leader and a managerial leader.[10]

Servant Leadership versus Transformational Leadership In the reasoning of Prasad *et al.* (2014), they contend that the world is desperately in need of ethical and effective leadership that serves others, invests in their development and fulfills a shared vision – known as servant leadership. Put in another way, *servant leadership is an approach to corporate goals by making organization members' individual growth needs a priority;*[11] especially as existing leadership styles are challenged by socio, cultural and people expectations changes in organizations. As such, servant leadership will have a potential value as alternative leadership style to achieve organizational excellence through human excellence.[12]

On the part of Lowder (2009), he maintains that transformational leadership is more effective in a *dynamic environment* – with a stronger focus on intellectual stimulation by emphasizing the enhancement of employees' innovation and creativity. While, on the contrary, servant leadership is more effective in a *static environment* – by emphasizing on developing their followers' personal potential and facilitating their personal growth. However, on a comparable scale, Lowder (2009) concludes that the transformational leadership model is the best alternative for developing followership and dealing with change management in today's dynamic business environment.[13]

Leadership and the Mindset and Culture of Tackling Change Strategy Thinking beyond the traditional concepts of business thinking would require the mindset and culture of constantly embracing change, or initiate one, if and when it becomes possible. Change can be triggered by events internal or external to the company. Empirically, although change would potentially or logically put a business entity ahead of its competitors, yet too often, managers would only initiate change if they experience sufficient discomfort with the status quo.[14]

From the foregoing, a sequence of five steps that makes up a change strategy was introduced by Susman, Jansen, Michael *et al.* (2006). In their reasoning, the firm's competitive strategy and leadership, as well as the content of each step tend to shape this sequence of change strategy. The steps are:

- Generating urgency
- Creating a vision
- Developing political support
- Managing the transition
- Sustaining momentum.[15]

In a related development, Mintzberg (1990) argues that the manager plays the major role in the unit's decision making system. As its formal authority, only the manager can commit the unit to important new courses of action; and as its nerve center, only the manager has full and current information to make the set of decisions that determines the unit's strategy.[16] But for proper managerial and effective strategic alignment, he however cautions that the aforementioned sequence of five steps that make up a change strategy need to be weighed with the following self-study questions for managers:

- What pace of change am I asking my organization to tolerate?
- Is this change balanced, so that our operations are neither excessively static nor overly disrupted?
- Have we sufficiently analyzed the impact of this change on the future of our organization?[17]

In the same direction, Carper (2014) found that successful chief executive officers of multinational enterprises (MNEs) invariably have two overriding objectives as relates to the long-range success of their respective firms: (1) add value to stakeholders of the firm; and (2) create and maintain a competitive economic advantage. But observed that neither of the two overriding objectives is an easy task to accomplish. Also, given their at times conflicting nature, it renders the two objectives even more difficult to simultaneously accomplish.[18] According to Adler (1994), it is at the point where *business* and *culture intersect* that constitutes the most important criterion for selecting an approach in order to maximize an opportunity to excel.[19]

On this line of reasoning, Mintzberg (1990) found that chief executives face incredibly complex choices, as they have to consider the impact of each decision and their impact on the organization's strategy. They have to ensure that the decision would be acceptable to those who influence the organization, ensure that resources would not be overextended, understand the various costs and benefits as well as the feasibility of the proposed decision on the other choices, and lastly they also have to consider questions of timing.[20] He however contends that at the same time, delay could lose time to make good use of the opportunity at hand; where quick approval could be ill-considered, whereas quick rejection might discourage the subordinate who had spent months developing a project.[21]

In addition, Mintzberg (1990) argues that for the most part, managerial logjams, notably; the dilemma of delegating functions, the issue of database being centralized in one brain, the problems of working with the management scientist – all revolve around the verbal nature of the manager's information. As a result, subordinates are at an informational disadvantage when they are out of convenient verbal reach of the manager. And that it is a great danger in centralizing the organization's data bank in the minds of its managers; because when the managers leave, they take their memory with them.[22]

From the foregoing, one of the primary or dominant tools through which intergenerational spillovers can be realized in the 21st century is through *big data* and *predictive analytics*.Singh (2018) describes Predictive Analytics as a term that prescribes the use of past data to develop informed guesses about future outcomes. As such, many business corporations have been using this advanced tool for many years to assess risk and detect frauds.[23] So too, many marketing companies do make use of these predictive analytical skills to predict the demand for their products or services, personalize their content and increase conversion.[24]

Besides Big Data and Predictive Analytics, there are other major tools such as Business Analytics, Business Intelligence, Data Science, and Machine Learning.

MATERIALS SCIENCE AND ENGINEERING (MSE)

Business thinking has equally been greatly influenced by the materials we use at a given point in time, while the existence and use of these materials have further accelerated the search for better and superior materials and processes. Sinke (2019b) found that the performance of a product depends highly on its design, the selected production method and the material used. In other words, there are interrelations between these three entities.[25] This falls within a framework of Materials Science and Engineering (MSE). Mukasyan (2019) defines MSE as the sequential overlapping of the science of processing (methods of design), science of structures (manufacturing technology), and science of properties (materials) which altogether come to the desired performance (optimal solution).[26]

Recently, the trend is increasingly tilting toward manufacturing design of lightweight structures and material-oriented development processes in terms of cost, performance, quality, and aesthetics. In this regard, Miltenović *et al.* (2014) found that in the most part, the application of lightweight construction is present in spacecraft, in wagon construction, shipbuilding, and especially in making car body.[27] They define the manufacturing of lightweight structure, or lightweight design as an interdisciplinary engineering approach which aims to develop a system of minimum weight, which in the given conditions, successfully fulfill the desired function with optimal utilization of available resources.[28]

In a related development, Mukasyan (2019) found that MSE is especially crucial in the classification of the human being, as all the ages do have names which are related to material. For instance, the Stone Age, the Iron Age, the Bronze Age, et cetera. That said; 85% *of discoveries in mankind's history were made based on the discovery in materials.* Meanwhile, engineers from any kind of areas are dealing with materials for more than 75% of their work.[29]

PRODUCT, PROCESS/SERVICE AND THE CUSTOMER-CENTRIC APPROACH

In another development, King (2015) found that manufacturing already generates more data than any other sector in terms of value assets.[30] For example, 1980s, Quality was the major driver, and it made use of Total Productive Maintenance (TPM). In the 1990s, Lean Management Six Sigma became the major driver that made use of Data Centric processes to drive continuous improvements. The *Six Sigma* is a disciplined, statistical-based approach improvement methodology for *eliminating defects* in a product, process or service. It was developed by Motorola and Bill Smith in the early 1980s based on quality management fundamentals, and then became a popular management approach at General Electric (GE) with Jack Welch in the early 1990s.[31]

Like Six Sigma, Lean Management is used by businesses to streamline manufacturing and production processes. However, the main emphasis of *Lean* management is on *cutting out unnecessary and wasteful steps in the creation of a product so that only steps that directly add value to the product are taken.* Put in another way, as far as Lean methodology is concerned, the only way to determine if something has value or not is to consider whether a customer would be willing to pay for it.[32] Thus, any part of the production that does not add value is simply removed from the equation, leaving a highly streamlined and profitable process in place that that will flow smoothly and efficiently.[33]

In a nutshell, Lean practitioners believe that waste comes *from unnecessary steps in the production process that do not add value to the finished product,* while Six Sigma proponents assert that waste results from *variation within the process.* Of course, there is truth in both of these assessments, which is why both Lean and Six Sigma methodologies have been so successful in improving overall business performance in a variety of fields. In this regard, these two disciplines have proven to be especially successful when working in tandem – hence the creation of Lean Six Sigma.[34]

Closely associated with the Lean Six Sigma is the Condition-based Maintenance (CBM), which is a maintenance strategy that monitors the actual condition of an asset to decide what maintenance needs to be done. CBM dictates that maintenance should only be performed when certain indicators show signs of decreasing performance or upcoming failures. CBM can be applied to mission critical and non-mission critical assets.

There are various types of condition-based maintenance CBM) monitoring techniques, some common examples include: oil analysis, infrared, electrical, operational performance, ultrasonic, acoustic, and vibration analysis.[35] Thus, unlike in planned maintenance (PM), where maintenance is performed based upon predefined scheduled intervals, CBM is performed only after a decrease in the condition of the equipment has been observed.[36] Meanwhile, preventive maintenance (or preventative maintenance) is maintenance that is regularly performed while the equipment is still working so that it does not break down unexpectedly. There are two types of preventive maintenance: time-based preventive maintenance, and usage-based preventive maintenance.[37]

That notwithstanding, Six Sigma remains one of today's practical problem solving methodologies also known as DMAIC, which stands for *Define, Measure, Analyze, Improve, and Control* – and has for many years, been used by companies to tackle problems associated with variation and defects. Some scholars argue that today, it is now being improved upon by the *Plan, Do, Check, or Act cycle,* or the PDCA Cycle.[38]

Also from 2000, came the use of predictive tools such as Population Health Management (PHM), and Product Lifecycle Management (PLM). In addition, from 2000 extending to 2010, more companies increasingly began to focus on Predictive Analytics – for a Customer Centric value creation. One aspect of a customer-centric culture is the *customer experience,* which is to create the best possible *customer experience (CX)* you can by placing the customer in the heart of the company's marketing, product development, and operations. While CX "summarizes" all customer perceptions created during interactions with your brand across various channels, customer-centricity stands for a wider commitment to ensuring the absolute success of every customer heading your way.[39]

Customer-centricity appeared as a stark contrast to previously dominant product-centricity – an approach where a company tries to sell as many products as possible, by every means necessary with the hope that more people will buy from them. But this works at the expense of cultivating long-term profitable relationships with the existing customers. However, while product-centricity has been around for much longer than customer-centricity, the former practice is gradually losing its viability.[40]

The aforementioned has been closely followed by the Best-in-Class (BiC) Analysis. The BiC firms are characterized by an increasing demand for IP protection resulting from Product, Design, Research and Development (PDR&D) initiatives. Industry Canada (2012) found that protecting design specifications is an important aspect of safeguarding product information generated during *product innovation* performed both *within a firm* and in *open innovation partnerships.* They argue that overall; Best-in-Class (BiC) firms are in a better position to protect IP resulting from their PDR&D initiatives. More especially as BiC firms are the top 20% performers in the following three metrics: percentage of products launched/delivered on time;

increase in product revenue since engaging in a global PDR&D initiative; and decrease in PDR&D costs. Laggards represent the bottom 30% of firms benchmarked to the same metric.[41]

In addition, in *open innovation partnerships,* BiC firms are more likely to limit the information (e.g., product specifications and design data) shared with external partners to the level required for the portion of the product those partners are developing.[42] Meanwhile, at the level of *innovation within the firm,* firstly, Industry Canada (2012) found that to ensure the level of access to product design specifications (i.e., whether a user can view the specifications), is defined according to functional roles in the enterprise – and BiC firms are twice as likely to implement such a solution, compared to laggards.[43] Secondly, BiC firms also distinguish themselves by the implementation of defined standards for providing product design data to other business units. Sharing the visual representation of a product design instead of a complete data file is an example.[44]

With regards to Robotics, Tzafestas (2018) found that many recent studies predicted there will be an enormous increase in the number of robots (industrial, service/social, intelligent/autonomous) in the future. As robots are directly involved in human life, notably; industrial robots, household robots, medical robots, assistive robots, sociable/entertainment robots, and war robots – all play important roles in human life, and they tend to raise crucial ethical problems for our society.[45] With regards to Artificial intelligence (AI), Taddeo and Floridi (2018) argue that AI is not just a new technology that requires regulation. It is a powerful force that is reshaping daily practices, personal and professional interactions, and environments.[46] For the well-being of humanity, it is crucial that this power is used as a force of good. Ethics plays a key role in this process by ensuring that regulations of AI harness its potential while mitigating its risks.

That being said, predictive analytics, including the Internet of Things (IoTs), machine-to-machine learning, the cyber physical system, and much more are today's technology. So, by using these technologies, we clearly see a shift in the future of manufacturing – that is using predictive data, and not just data analytics. In a related development, Hausmann, Hidalgo *et al.* (2011) reveal that the secret of modern societies is not that each person holds much more productive knowledge than those in a more traditional society. Rather, the secret to modernity is that, we collectively use large volumes of knowledge, while each one of us holds only a few bits of it. Thus, a modern society functions at a higher level of vibration because its members form webs that allow them to specialize and share their knowledge with others.[47] This is especially true with industries such as the aircraft manufacturing and aviation industry, electronics manufacturing, and the health industry – that are experiencing some of the fastest speed of innovations in the world today.

From the foregoing, transcending the boundaries of the traditionally known concepts of value creation requires managing the future actively.

Tucker (1991) argues that by managing the future actively, you take a positive approach to where your company will be in the future; and that no sustainably prosperous business stands still. That said, you either take an active role in managing the future, or face the risk of being left behind by changes now occurring in the marketplace.[48] So arguably, the future is not a place we go to, but one which we create – and while things happen that we cannot predict, we can still be prepared for them.[49]

An Analytical Review of Robert Kiyosaki's "Cash Flow Quadrant"

While this is not new to many, but it is worthwhile to throw some light on Kiyosaki's four ways of producing income – at least to refresh your knowledge before delving into the crux of this chapter's business. The Cash Flow Quadrant is an important diagram presented and explained by Robert Kiyosaki. The Quadrant is made of four different people who make up the business world, which correspond to 4 different ways they generate incomes. On the left, you will find Employee (E) and Self-Employed (S). On the right, you will find Big Business Owner (B) and Investor (I). That said, people in each quadrant have different core values, and that is what separates them into the different quadrants.[50] As a result, Fig. 2.1 shows the 4 primary ways to produce income as per the research findings of Kiyosaki.

THE LEFT- AND RIGHT-HAND SIDES OF THE QUADRANT

The Left-Hand Side of the Quadrant As mentioned earlier, Kiyosaki and Letcher (2016) argues that in the business world, the left hand side of his cash flow quadrant harbors the "E" and the "S" quadrants. The "E" stands for "EMPLOYEE" and "S" stands for "SELF-EMPLOYED." He

"E" EMPLOYEE (HAVE A JOB) This group is estimated at controlling 5% of total wealth	"B" BUSINESS OWNER (OWN A SYSTEM) This group is estimated at controlling 95% of total wealth
"S" SELF-EMPLOYED (OWN A JOB) This group constitutes about 95% of the population	"I" INVESTOR (OWN INVESTMENTS) This group constitutes just about 5% of the population

Figure 2.1 Description of Kiyosaki's Cash Flow Quadrant.
Source: Adapted from Kiyosaki and Letcher (2016).

argues that you can always tell who they are by their core values. For employees, an "EMPLOYEE" will always say the same words – the words are, "I'm looking for a safe, secure job with benefits." That's what makes them employees because their core value is security." To this end, Barry and Halfmann (2016) found that almost every choice we make traverses time and involves intertemporal tradeoffs (choices). They define intertemporal choices as decisions with effects that unfold over time.[51]

They maintain that a common intertemporal tradeoff we experience is the choice between *immediate gratification* or temporal discounting and *delayed gratification*. Thus, the more proximate an option is; the more it is generally ephemeral or immediately satisfying and short lived. This is the case with the option of immediate gratification. Meanwhile, the delayed gratification option often matches our long-term goals and has greater overall benefits.[52] That notwithstanding, they also found that whether it is immediate gratification, or delayed gratification; the choices about spending money and investing, insurance, marriage, diet and exercise, drug use, education, work and play, and procreating – you name the rest, are all intertemporal decisions.[53]

With regards to Kiyosaki's "S" quadrant, where "S" stands for "SELF-EMPLOYED" and located at the left hand side of the quadrant, it is dominated by the small business owner or the self-employed. Similar to what obtains in the "E" quadrant, he argues that the core values of the "S" quadrant will cause them to use words such as, *"If you want it done right, do it by yourself."* On this strand of reasoning, Kiyosaki found that too often, these are generally one person act – as they tend to operate by themselves.

The Right Hand Side of the Quadrant Regarding the right hand side of Kiyosaki's Cash Flow Quadrant, he denotes it as "B"s which stands for "BIG BUSINESS OWNERS" such as Bill Gates. He recounts that peculiar to this quadrant the proponents would too often say, *"I'm looking for good system, good network, and the smartest people I know to help run my business."* As a result, Kiyosaki argues that unlike the "S"s, the "B"s wouldn't want to run the company by themselves – they would want smart people to run the company for them.

Finally, the fourth of the Cash Flow Quadrant is the "I". The "I" stands for "INVESTORS." As Kiyosaki simply puts it, those people in the "I" Quadrant have *money* work hard for them. Meanwhile, those in the "B" Quadrant have *people* work hard for them. Consequently, the people in the "E" & "S" Quadrants (located on the left hand side of the Quadrant) are the people who work hard for the rich who are located on the right hand side of the Cash Flow Quadrant (that is, for the "B"s and "I"s). With regards to the components of the right hand side of the Quadrant, Tang and

Greenwald (2016) posit that the investment value chain has three key participants: corporations, asset owners, and asset managers.[54]

From the aforementioned, Barry and Halfmann (2016) found that there is a causal relationship between (1): an abstract mindset, which involves *more general, context-independent* mental processing, and *delayed gratification* on the one hand; and (2) a concrete mindset, which involves *specific, context-dependent* mental processing, and *immediate gratification,* on the other hand. The propensity to lean more on immediate gratification is referred to as present-bias. In other words, present-bias refers to how much an individual over weights more *temporally proximate* events compared to *later events.*[55] In a similar vein, Freitas *et al.* (2004) found that an *abstract mindset* led participants to consider information that affected long-term goals (e.g., accurate self-knowledge), whereas a *concrete mindset* led participants to consider more immediately gratifying information (e.g., positive self-evaluations).[56]

On this strand of reasoning, Engel and Weber (2007) argue that by attempting to influence someone's decision about *how to decide* only makes sense if decision-makers possess more than one *mental tool* for the purpose.[57] That being said, one of the mental tools is *delaying gratification,* while the other mental tool is *foregoing immediate gratification.* Both of them are embedded in a *decision-making process,* which is alternatively referred to as the *dual-process theories.* Engel and Weber (2007) equally found that a large body of behavioral decision research has documented a broad range of qualitatively different ways in which people have been shown to decide on a course of action.[58] Especially as the intangible outcomes were more future-oriented outcomes, and moreover, as the effect of mindset on choices persists over time and tasks.[59]

According to Fehr (2002), these findings are very crucial as optimal decision-making involves at least – occasionally delaying gratification and forgoing immediate gratification in pursuit of long-term goals.[60] Furthermore, the idea of immediate gratification and delayed gratification (Barry and Halfmann, 2016), has also been captured by a broad range of recent dual-process theories (Evans and Over, 1997; Chaiken and Trope, 1999; Stanovich and West, 2000; Bohner, 2001). They hypothesize that the human mind has two processing modes; one of them is more analytic and reflective (i.e., delayed gratification), and the other is more automatic and impulsive (i.e., immediate gratification) – that operate in parallel, and can both compete and cooperate with each other (Strack and Deutsch, 2004).[61]

In addition, Engel and Weber (2007), in the *taxonomy of decision modes* or deciding on how to decide (the dual-process theories), also distinguishes between three classes of decision modes: *Calculation-based, affect-based,* and *recognition-based* ways of making decisions – captured colloquially as decisions made by the head, by the heart, and by the book respectively.[62]

THE CORE VALUES: SECURITY OR FREEDOM?

On the left side of the Cash Flow Quadrant, people work for SECURITY, they work for MONEY also. On the right hand side of the Cash flow Quadrant, what they want is Freedom, financial liberty. They don't want to have to work in a job anymore. So for those who want freedom, the beauty of building a business and learning how to invest simply arises out of the mind, and subsequently transforms to the culture of building and maintaining a growing passive income stream.

Interestingly, Malkoc, Zauberman, and Bettman (2010) found that manipulating mindset (abstract versus concrete) affects participants' present bias in a series of experiments. In this regard, they found that individuals tend to demonstrate a present bias by selecting the "*sooner*" when both options are close in time, but showing a preference reversal and selecting the "*later*" when both options are farther away in time. For example, if you were to choose between $10 tomorrow and $15 in 30 days, you might choose $10 tomorrow. But if you were asked to choose between $10 in 90 days and $15 in 120 days, you might choose $15 in 120 days; even though each choice involves a 30-day span.[63]

In Millie Leung's analysis of Kiyosaki's Cash Flow Quadrants, she found that the most successful Business Owners "B"s and Investors "I"s are innately curious, knowledge-thirsty and uncompromising in the pursuit of their goals. They chose to learn through mentors – reading voraciously, attending training courses and educational seminars – and converting this knowledge into action.[64]

Hypotheses of the Inner and the Outer Worlds of Value Creation

A critical look at the "Cashflow Quadrant" as explained by Robert Kiyosaki on the 4 ways to generate income helps in a way to reveal the existence of the inner and outer worlds of value creation. On a similar note, David Mattin (2017), who is the Global Head of Trends & Insights at *TrendWatching* argues that today; we are at the beginnings of a radical shift, where a newly-emerging techno-consumerism will target the final frontier when it comes to humans – and that the "angle of attack" of this radical shift is not the world around us, but the world *inside* us.[65] In a similar vein, Engel and Weber (2007) argue that technical progress has not left a single internal resource without an external substitute,[66] especially as internal and external resources normally have their comparative strengths and weaknesses. They noted, for example, that a computer may have higher storage capacity than human memory, but the former is worse at reconfiguring its stock of knowledge according to changes in interest or in the environment.[67]

THE MISSING LINKS BETWEEN THE INNER AND OUTER WORLDS OF VALUE CREATION

From the foregoing, we can begin to guess that there are missing links between the inner world and outer world of value creation. Sondhe (2010), for instance, argues that when a country is financially weak, it stems from two broad categories of problems: (1) Because its people are not prospering; and (2) the economic engine is not growing. As such, it would culminate too often to a stronger tendency to focus only on affordability of products and services in terms of price, rather than what is of the highest value.[68] Little wonder, why Schumpeter identified the entrepreneur as an essential element of the dynamic theory of economic change, and that the major role of the entrepreneur is to realize new combinations or innovations that ensure economic change.[69]

In the same direction, Satell (2010) argues that as the world becomes more complex, the business world is increasingly specialized, but such specialization can only stand the test of time as long as functions remain separate, but contends that the real problem lies not between people, but within people.[70] For instance, in marketing, we have people who specialize in planning, digital media, social media, TV buying, print buying, experiential marketing, et cetera. But very few of these people are prepared to integrate their specialties because so few have done more than one thing.[71] In addition, Satell (2010) argues that as technology changes, the problem is becoming more acute. For example, those who have toiled for decades using traditional marketing channels are amazingly daft when it comes to new media, while digital specialists suffer from ignorance of decades of accumulated wisdom (and are often even dafter).[72]

To this end, Eker (2005) argues that we live in at least four different realms at once. These four quadrants are the *physical world,* the *mental world,* the *emotional world,* and the *spiritual world.*[73] And that most people hardly realize that the physical realm is merely a "printout" of the other three.[74] In this regard, it would be difficult to deny the fact that value creation of individuals resides both in the combination of the inner world (the toolbox) and the outer world (the tools).[75] And that a larger slice of this consciousness lies beyond the outer game of wealth. Therefore, just as there are "outer" laws of money, there must be "inner" laws too. The outer laws include essential skills like business knowledge, money management, and investment strategies.[76]

In this regard, we can talk of financial sustainability, which is part of organizational sustainability. It has to do with the ongoing ability of the organization to generate enough resources to work toward its vision. This is similar to what we saw earlier in *Chapter 1,* where Rowe (2001) argued that organizations led by visionaries who are not properly supported by strong managerial leadership, may destroy wealth even more quickly than organizations led by managerial leaders.[77]

THE OUTER GAME (THE TOOLS)

From the foregoing, there is evidence that much of what guides the outer game value creation is the managerial job. Mintzberg's description of managerial work suggests a number of important managerial skills – developing peer relationships, carrying out negotiations, motivating subordinates, resolving conflicts, establishing information networks and subsequently disseminating information, making decisions in conditions of extreme ambiguity, and allocating resources. Above all, the manager needs to be introspective in order to continue to learn on the job.[78] He argues that, no job is more vital to our society than that of the manager. The manager determines whether our social institutions will serve us well or whether they will squander our talents and resources.[79]

In the same direction, Page (2005) posited that a corporation exercises the ultimate power when it allocates resources, which it must do efficiently if it hopes to create value.[80] As a result, the organization must acquire the best resources, such as financial, material, and human at the best possible price, and it must use them as productively as possible.[81] Besides a good mastery of the job of a manager as distinct from management science, Rowe (2001) argues that executives in such organizations should start thinking of themselves as strategic leaders who have to accept and merge the visionaries and managerial leaders in their organizations. They should fight against the constraining influence of financial controls and fight for the exercise of strategic and financial controls, with the emphasis on strategic controls.[82]

Arguably, what makes an organization sustainable, and what makes an organization financially sustainable – is not mutually exclusive. So, *what makes an organization sustainable?* For an organization to be sustainable, the following factors are deemed critical – in that, an organization should have, or better still, an organization must:

- have a clear strategic direction;
- be able to scan its environment or context to identify opportunities for its work;
- be able to attract, manage and retain competent staff;
- have an adequate administrative and financial infrastructure;
- be able to demonstrate its effectiveness and impact in order to leverage further resources; and
- get community support for, and involvement in its work.

That said, our next concern is, *what makes an organization financially sustainable?* To be financially sustainable, the following steps appear to be imperative to an organization:

- have more than one source of income;
- have more than one way of generating income;
- match strategic action with financial planning regularly;
- have adequate financial systems;
- have a good public image;
- be clear about its values (value clarity); and
- have some considerable degree of financial autonomy.

From the foregoing, Tsui (2018a) is strongly of the opinion that it is important for the resources to be heterogeneous – comprised of varied combinations that support the organization's activities and goals.[83] In addition, he opines that such typical resources possessed by an organization needs to be *immobile,* in the sense that it cannot not easily be lost, transferred or copied by another organization.[84] Rowe (2001) argues that by influencing employees to voluntarily make decisions that enhance the organization is the most important part of strategic leadership.[85] In a similar vein, Ticky and Cohen (1997) argue that leaders have to be sure that the people they are trusting, have values that are going to elicit the decisions and actions that they want.[86]

THE INNER WORLD (THE TOOLBOX)

As we saw earlier in the outer game, the *inner world* is just as important, and comprises of the subconscious mind. Eker (2005) contends that if your subconscious mind – which embodies your "financial blueprint," is not "set" for success; nothing you learn, nothing you know, and nothing you do will make much of a difference.[87] Similarly, Engel and Weber (2007) found that it is more difficult to enhance internal resources by outside intervention, but contends that skill development is one way to do so.[88]

FREQUENTLY MISUNDERSTOOD ASPECTS OF THE INTANGIBLES OF VALUE CREATION

Remember, earlier on we made mention of Eker's four quadrants of wealth creation, which are the physical world, the mental world, the emotional world, and the spiritual world, and that most people hardly realize that the physical realm is merely a "printout" of the other three (Eker, 2005). So let's see how we can align all the possible options of the inner world and the outer game of value creation with Eker's four quadrants to find out what we can make out of it (see Fig. 2.2).

As shown on Fig. 2.2, in our first quadrant in relation*to the inner world of value creation,* we can identify three items – the "mind," "will", and "emotions." As you can see, it is primarily dominated by *spiritually-inclined forces*. The second quadrant, "*the outer game of value creation,*" constitute the *human and health related behavioral patterns, productive knowledge*

The Inner World of Value Creation

The Inner World of Value Creation	The Outer Game of Value Creation
Spiritually-Inclined Forces **(Mind, Will, and Emotions)**	Manager's job , Productive Knowledge Acquisitions and the Physical World **(Dominated by evolutions in materials science engineering, and other innovation-related breakthroughs)**
The Intermediary to Both Worlds	**The White Space**
Spiritually-inclined forces vs.the manager's job, productive knowledge acquisitions, and the physical world **(dominated by continuously sequential interplay between the inner world and the outer game of value creation)**	Set in motion by the ever increasing demand for productive knowledge arising out of the rapid and widespread accumulation of productive knowledge **(these demands tend to go beyond the boundaries of an organization's core activities and its adjacencies)**

The Intermediary to Both Worlds | The Outer Game of Value Creation

Figure 2.2 Aligning the Inner World with the Outer Game of Value.
Source: Author created.

acquisitions and the physical world, and which is dominated primarily by the evolutions in materials science and engineering, and other innovation-related breakthroughs arising out of the rapid and widespread accumulation of productive knowledge. The third quadrant is the intermediary to both worlds; comprised of *spiritually-inclined forces vs. manager's job, productive knowledge acquisitions and the physical world,* and is primarily dominated by a continuously sequential and concomitant interplay between the inner world and the outer game of value creation. Lastly, the fourth quadrant is the *white space*, which is propelled by the ever increasing demand for productive knowledge – that goes beyond the boundaries of an organization's core activities and its adjacencies.

Arguably, a proper combination of all these four quadrants would provide reliable answers to a sizeable slice of questions related to organizational value creation imperatives and their sustainability concerns.

2.1.2 Leadership, and Strategic and Adaptive Influencing: The Dynamics

Leadership and the Dynamics of Influencing

In the reasoning of Lowder (2009), the development and evolution in *management theory* during the past several decades can be illustrated from the perspective of the paradigmatic shifts from an *analytical approach* (design, planning, and positioning schools), to a *systems approach* (entrepreneurial, cognitive, learning, and political schools) to an *"actors" approach* (cultural, environmental, and configurational schools).[89]

Meanwhile, current research in the *leadership field* is context bound – as it focuses on mutual power and influence, emphasizes collective and collaborative relationships, promotes learning, empowerment, change, and is process oriented.[90] Schermerhorn, Hunt, and Osborn (2002) view leadership as a type of interpersonal influence, by which an individual leads another individual or group to perform the task that he/she wants – so as to attain a desired result.[91] As a start-off point, and with regards to leadership, French and Raven (1959) posited that[92] leaders have access to five distinct sources of power:

1. Legitimate. This source of power comes from a belief that the leader has the authority to make demands and can expect compliance from others.
2. Reward. This source of power stems from a leader's ability to provide rewards or inducements to employees.
3. Expert. This source of power is acquired from the knowledge and skills possessed by a leader.
4. Referent. This source of power results from the leader's perceived attractiveness, charisma or likeability.
5. Coercive. This source of power is based on fear of the leader and the belief that the leader can punish others for noncompliance.

According to Elias (2008), while French and Raven's taxonomy remains a popular and frequently utilized conceptualization of power, a number of other taxonomies and further refinements of the model have been developed over the past years.[93] However, Randall (2012) further argues that all these sources of power generally fall into two broad dimensions: positional power (power originating from the position) and personal power (power originating from within the person).[94]

In a related development, to strategically influence adaptively, Johnson (2010) argues that the starting place of every business is a powerful customer proposition, which is the answer to the question as to why anyone should want to buy anything from you? In his submission, he observed that when most people describe the company they work for, they talk about them in terms of products and services they sell – and that what successful companies really do is something more basic, in that, they fulfill some important "need," or "job" to a customer at a certain price. That said, the more important the "job," the better the match between the "job" and the "offering." Also, the lower the offering price generally, the more powerful the customer value proposition – and by extension, the greater the growth potential for the company.[95]

In concurrence, Rowe (2001) found that Konosuke Matsushita, the founder and former CEO of Matsushita Electric concentrated on creating products for his customers that created value in their minds that was greater than they expected.[96] Meanwhile, Earl (2005) found that buying routines can make consumers vulnerable to seller manipulation.[97] From the foregoing, Johnson (2010) argues that *every successful company is operating according to a successful business model,* whether it explicitly knows what that business model consist of or not – and strangely, many companies are not aware.[98]

However, having a good insight as to when your company wishes to catch an existing wave, for example, through incremental innovation, or even create a new wave, for example, through radical or disruptive innovation – is critical to successful companies. For the latter, this would require strategy formulation at different levels of gradation in the company. This means that the opportunity is a move into their white space – requiring a new model. Johnson (2010) describes the white space as opportunities that a company wishes to pursue that can only be addressed using a different business model than the one it is currently using.[99] Put in another way, this means the company has to go beyond its core activities or adjacencies. In this regard, Patrick (2012) argues that today's managers need to make a transition from guiding and leading, to shaping and influencing growth – by the ways in which they approach their work and interact with one another.[100]

According to Kilpi (2017), Management has historically been seen as a collection of tasks involving planning, organizing, controlling and incentivizing. A competent manager is believed to be able to analyze organizational and task requirements and also the emotionally loaded human motivations. In this case, a successful management has to be able to significantly mitigate conflict and uncertainty[101] so as to attain their predetermined goals and performance targets. In other words, the role of management is to control the movement into a chosen future.[102] This should be within the framework of the predetermined goals and targets – especially as managerial leaders are sensitive to the past – and are concerned with and more comfortable in functional areas of responsibilities.[103] Furthermore managers have been noted to engage in, and support, short-term, least-cost behavior activities, to enhance financial performance figures in the short term.[104] At this juncture, Patrick (2012) argues that the key point in differentiating leadership and management is the idea that employees willingly follow leaders because they want to, not because they have to.[105]

Nowadays, however, this process is experiencing a shift in paradigm from the conventional approach, notably; the challenges surrounding the development of new models, the way its various parts have to work together, and the strength and weaknesses in pursuit of new growths are shifting to new grounds[106] toward fundamentally strategic decisions – and which can only be made at the highest level[107] of individual leadership capabilities. This now poses a somewhat entirely new challenge, by taking us into the province of *leadership, strategic and adaptive influence.* That notwithstanding, since most organizations make extensive use of managerial leadership in their day-to-day activities, it worthwhile to find out what the manager's job really is (see Fig. 2.3).

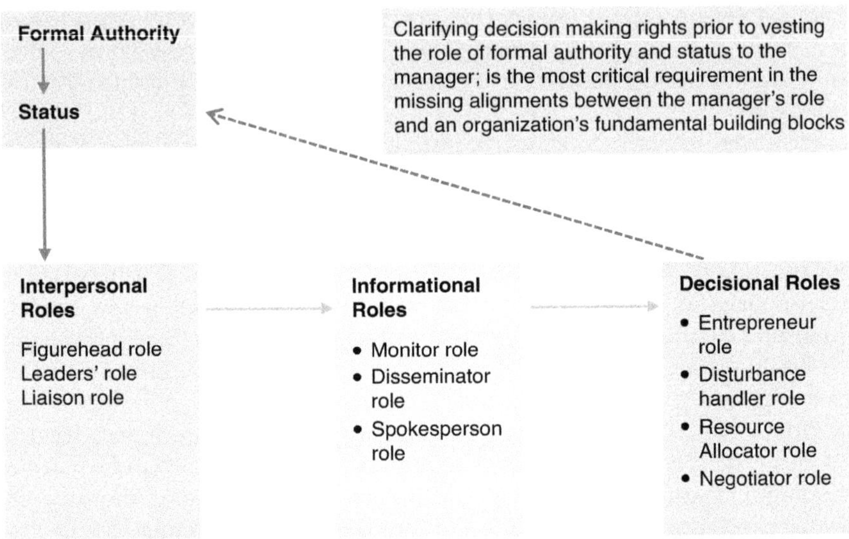

Figure 2.3 Manager's Role and the Most Critical Requirement for Successful Strategy Execution.
Source: Adapted from Mintzberg (1990), p. 15.

Power Bases and Review of Mintzberg's Job of the Manager

Going through the lenses of the OrgDNA building blocks, Neilson *et al.* (2008), argues that for there to be effective strategy execution, you first take steps to address *decision rights* and *information flows,* which would then enable you, design the necessary changes to *motivators* and *structure* to support the new strategy intend to execute.[108] But strangely, if we go by the arguments put forward by Mintzberg (1990) concerning the role of the manager in the process of organizing for strategy execution, the situation becomes a bit difficult to comprehend.

That being said, Mintzberg (1990) defines the manager as that person in charge of an organization or subunit. He contends that besides being a Chief Executive Officer (CEO), this definition would include vice presidents, bishops, foremen, hockey coaches, and prime ministers, et cetera. All these "managers" are vested with *formal authority* over an organizational unit. From *formal authority* comes *status,* which leads to various *interpersonal relations* (interpersonal roles), and from these comes access to *information* (informational roles). Information, in turn, enables the manager to make *decisions* and strategies (decisional roles) for the unit.[109]

As shown on Fig. 2.3, the manager's job can be described in terms of various "roles," or organized sets of behaviors identified with a position. "The Manager's Roles," comprises ten roles. This starts with formal authority which is naturally accompanied by status. This gives rise to *three* interpersonal roles, which in turn give rise to *three* informational roles. These two sets of roles enable the manager to play *four* decisional roles: entrepreneur, disturbance handler, resource allocator, and negotiator.

But strangely, within the framework of successful strategy execution, the role of the manager appears to work somewhat in opposite direction with what should normally obtain in the fundamental building blocks of the organization. For instance, if we go by the logic of the fundamental building blocks of an organization, decision rights have to be clarified prior to vesting the role of formal authority to the manager, et cetera. This partly explains why successful strategy execution in organizations is quite difficult to come by due to this lack of alignment. That being said, companies that can successfully align these factors inevitably turn out to be industry leaders. However, most companies who succeed in aligning these factors – almost always do it unconsciously, or by gambling their way through (see Chapter 6 for more discussions).

FORMAL AUTHORITY

We saw earlier according to Mintzberg (1990), the manager's role starts with formal authority, which is naturally accompanied by status. This gives rise to *three* interpersonal roles, which in turn give rise to *three* informational roles. These two sets of roles enable the manager to play *four* decisional roles: entrepreneur, disturbance handler, resource allocator, and negotiator.

INTERPERSONAL ROLES

First is the figurehead role. As the head of an organizational unit, every manager need to perform some ceremonial duties, which may sometimes be routine, involving little serious communication and no important decision making. Nevertheless, they are important to the smooth functioning of an organization and cannot be ignored.

Second is the leader role. The influence of managers is most clearly seen in the leader role; as formal authority vests them with great potential power to be responsible for the work of the people of their unit. Some of these actions involve leadership directly – for example, in most organizations the managers are normally responsible for hiring and training their own staff. In addition, there is the indirect exercise of the leader role. For instance, it's imperative for every manager to motivate and encourage employees – somehow reconciling their individual needs with the goals of the organization.[110] Thompson and Strictland (2003) argues that balancing between positive (financial and non-financial) and negative (punishment) motivational considerations is one of the critical issues for managers to attend.[111] This functional attribute constitutes some elements of servant leadership functions in the job of a manager.

Third is the liaison role. Mintzberg (1990) found that the literature of management has always recognized the leader role, particularly those aspects of it related to *motivation*. In comparison, until recently it has hardly mentioned the liaison role, in which the manager makes contacts outside the vertical chain of command. This is remarkable in light of the finding of virtually every study of managerial work that managers spend as much time with peers and other people outside their units as they do with their own subordinates – and, surprisingly, very little time with their own superiors.[112]

INFORMATIONAL ROLES

Regarding Informational Roles, the first is the monitor role. The manager is perpetually scanning the environment for information, interrogating liaison contacts and subordinates, and receiving unsolicited information, with much of it as a result of the network of personal contacts. Mintzberg (1990) found that a good part of the information the manager collects in the monitor role arrives in verbal form, often as gossip, hearsay, and speculation. Managers tend to cherish gossip because experience has shown that today's gossip may be tomorrow's fact. The other two roles are the *disseminator* role and the *spokesman* role.[113]

Therefore, informational roles is the mover of activities at the organization and may be employed to measure employees' performance – as bad information may contaminate the remaining components of the OrgDNA, especially decision rights and motivators. Consequently, without accurate information, decision makers cannot take decisive steps and seize available market opportunities. Also, employees would not be able to gain the appreciation they deserve.[114]

DECISIONAL ROLES

With regards to Decisional Roles, the first is entrepreneur role. As entrepreneur, the manager seeks to improve the unit, to adapt it to changing conditions in the environment. In *the monitor role* within the framework of the entrepreneurial role, the manager is constantly on the lookout for new ideas. When a good one appears, he initiates a development project that he may supervise himself or delegate to an employee (perhaps with the stipulation that he must approve the final proposal).[115]

The second is *disturbance handler* role. Mintzberg (1990) contends that while the *entrepreneur* role describes the manager as the voluntary initiator of change, the *disturbance handler* role depicts the manager as involuntarily responding to pressures – here change is beyond the manager's control. The pressures of a situation are too severe to be ignored – for example, a strike looms, a major customer has gone bankrupt – so the manager must act.[116] He further found that every manager must spend a considerable amount of time responding to high-pressure disturbances. And that no organization can be so well run, and so standardized in such a way that it can accurately consider every contingency in the uncertain environment in advance. As a result, disturbances arise not only because poor managers ignore situations until they reach crisis proportions but also because good managers cannot possibly anticipate all the consequences of the actions they take.[117] This empirical evidence strongly leverages strategic foresight as being a crucial element for managers who hope to emerge as champions in their industries.

The third decisional role is that of *resource allocator*. This has much to do with decision rights. Who decides what? How many people are involved in a decision process? Where does one person's decision-making authority end and another's begin?[118] Mintzberg (1990) found that the manager is responsible for deciding who will get what. In this regard, the manager is also charged with designing the unit's *structure* – that pattern of formal relationships that determines how work is to be divided and coordinated. Also, as *resource allocator,* the manager authorizes the important decisions of the unit before they are implemented. As result, by retaining this power, the manager can ensure that decisions are interrelated. Mintzberg (1990) argues that by attempting to fragment this power, it could negatively encourage discontinuous decision making and a disjointed strategy[119] – especially as *decision rights* are the basic task that should be tackled by organizations that suffer functional imbalance – as they are the cornerstone of efficient development.[120] This sends a powerful signal across the board, in concurrence with the compelling argument why it is important for a visionary leader to work closely with the managerial leader to ensure proper alignment of strategic choices.

Strategic and Adaptive Influencing in Leadership: Perspectives and Issues

Before proceeding to examine some technicalities in leadership, strategic and adaptive influence, it is worth the effort to remember that an important component of *power* is leadership. This means that no manager can be efficient without understanding and using power in an appropriate manner.[121] Consequently, using power in an appropriate manner requires good leadership skills. In the same vein, Payne (2012) makes us to believe that leadership can be broadly construed as the ability to persuade others to behave in certain ways, to shape their interests, and to influence their thinking toward achieving particular objectives. This means that at the foundation of leadership *lays the domain of influence* – which is the ability of a leader to get others to follow.[122]

On this strand, Dellaert and Davydov (2017) stress the need of distinguishing *influencing* from *manipulation*. In their assessment, *influencing* is a process and is characterized by a *positive intention* in the interest of the persons being influenced and of the organization. According to Patrick

(2012), Trust is at the core of the relationship between the influencer and the people being influenced. Therefore, effective leaders express their need for power and influence in ways that create value to the organization.[123] For example, the servant leader actively recruits exemplary followers and is open to input from them, which enhances leader-follower trust.[124] However, Mintzberg (1990) noted that managing insightfully depends on the direct experience and personal knowledge that come from intimate contact. But in organizations that have grown larger and more diversified, that becomes difficult to achieve.[125]

That being said, the leader or person who exercises influence needs to build trustful relations – by being transparent about the goals, the purpose, and his or her values.[126] But Mintzberg (1990) cautions that managers would be well advised to weigh the risks of exposing privileged information against having subordinates who can make effective decisions.[127] According to Gawler (2005), transparent connections in building trust relations can take two approaches:

1. The why approach? or the bottom-top approach – that iterates from activities, outputs, targets, goal, and ends at vision.
2. The how approach? or the top-bottom approach – that takes the reverse iterative order, starting from vision, goal, targets, output, and ends at activities.[128]

From the foregoing, "influencing affects, shapes, or transforms opinions, behaviors, and actions"[129] for the good of the influencer and those that are being influenced. These are rare qualities that could be attributed to great leaders. To this end, Dickson (2015) argues that *"great leaders base their behavior and decisions on the power of moral principles."*[130] Obviously, this requires some degree of wisdom, which is the foundation upon which the life of the dynamic personality is built.[131]

Undeniably, power plays a major role in the interactions occurring in organizational life.[132] On the one hand, positional power is often associated with control in hierarchical organizations; where leaders at all levels in the organization can leverage different bases of power to influence others.[133] On the other hand, horizontal organizations frequently use personal power, which is critical to positive and effective influence, and generally results in alignment and commitment. Consequently, power over others is intertwined with an understanding of leadership processes.[134] To balance the equation in both instances, Mintzberg (1990) suggests that managerial leadership would need to be guided by the following questions:

- How do my subordinates react to my managerial style?
- Am I sufficiently sensitive to the powerful influence of my actions?
- Do I fully understand their reactions to my actions?
- Do I find an appropriate balance between encouragement and pressure?

- Do I stifle their initiative?[135]

On this strand of reasoning, Moye (2018) is strongly of the opinion that, the current and future challenge for high impact leaders is the ability to lead and influence others toward a common goal, by being able to design effective influence strategies to accomplish goals, even without formal authority. In other words, they should be capable to develop the skills to motivate and inspire others in such a way that they can confidently lead their organizations to success.[136] Moye (2018) suggests that to accomplish this task, you must develop your own toolbox of strategies – that would enable you to maintain engagement, to build collaborative support and to master conflict while remaining true to your authentic self.[137] Kilpi (2017) argues that the fundamental dynamics of the evolution in effective strategic influencing in the new economic dispensation – is not *competitive selection,* but *interactive cooperation.*[138]

In a related development, Payne (2012) holds that leadership can be structural, institutional, or situational.[139] To him, structural leadership requires structural power. Patrick (2012) describes structural power as the production and reproduction of internally related positions of *super* and *subordination domination.*[140] In addition, he argues that structural leadership is often augmented by institutional leadership; which is the ability to determine the rules, principles, procedures, and practices that guide the behavior of members of an organization, or a community. For this reason, institutions provide order and predictability and allow the dominant power to exercise control. Undeniably, managerial leadership would thrive in this kind of positional power base.

This is quite close to Mintzberg's description of the roles of the manager, which comprises of ten roles. Wherein formal authority gives rise to three interpersonal roles (figure head, leader, and liaison), which in turn give rise to three informational roles (monitor, disseminator, spokesman); and these two sets of roles enable the manager to play the four decisional roles (entrepreneur, disturbance handler, resource allocator, and negotiator.[141]*It is largely due to these attributes that makes managerial leadership more inclined to positional power.*

But as Rowe (2001) notes, managerial leaders will at best maintain the level of wealth that has been created in the past, but over time may cause wealth to be slowly destroyed.[142] As a result, Engel and Weber (2007) found that the use of formal authority, precisely that of *institutional powers* have not really performed well in adaptive leadership and influence – reason being that institutional designers are not necessarily interested in the processes by which people generate behavior, but care more about the resulting behavior.[143] Finally, keeping aside the distribution of power and the building of institutions, situational leadership is primarily the ability to seize opportunities to build or reorient an organizational system. As noted by Payne (2012), often, this kind of leadership is associated with a specific individual.[144] Situational leaders use the most appropriate approach to match their particular situation and/or environment that can encompass one or more leadership styles.[145] However, different types of leadership styles, including but not limited to visionary leadership, servant leadership, strategic leadership, transformational leadership, and above all sustainability leadership are equipped with these capabilities, though with a varying degree of success comparably.

Meanwhile, among the aforementioned three types of leadership, notably; structural leadership, institutional leadership, and situational leadership, Moye (2018) tends to give priority of place to situational leadership – since it closely relates to *influencing* that could be attained through logical appeals (i.e., that which taps into people's rational and intellectual positions), emotional appeals (i.e., connect your message, goal, or project to individual goals and values), and cooperative appeals (i.e., involve collaboration, consultation, and alliances).[146] On this strand, Moye (2018) argues that the foundation for the core capability of leaders is more prevalent in situational leadership (i.e., individual leadership skills) than in the other two attributes of leadership – that is, structural leadership and institutional leadership (positional power).[147] On this basis, she maintains that the ultimate outcome of influence in a leader is maximizing his capacity to influence people toward a shared goal.

That being said, the aforementioned argument is also built around the premise that influence isn't a one-size-fits-all approach, but that the most effective leaders match their approach to the challenge at hand. In other words, the most effective leaders are adaptive; they diagnose the situation and choose the behavior best suited for it.[148] It is within the context of this framework that Moye (2018) defines leadership as a process of social influence that maximizes sustained effort of others toward a shared goal.[149] To concur, Festré and Garrouste (2008) maintain that the success of the process does not only depend on a leader's intrinsic characteristics, but also on their social leadership (that is, on leadership ability to make novelty being accepted by the community of followers or imitators).[150]

2.2 The Compatibility of OrgDNA and High Performance

2.2.1 Overview

High Performance and the Science of Complexity

Remember, we saw earlier that *management* has historically been seen as a collection of tasks involving planning, organizing, coordinating and controlling. This makes sense within the framework of management science. However, we will see later in this chapter that the actual job of a manager essentially spans beyond these demarcations, and in most cases the tasks tend to intertwine across these historical collections, as well as across different disciplines not mentioned here.

In concurrence, Kilpi (2007) argues that the idealistic view of a manager as someone who is in control is not consistent with our practical experience, or with modern science. He further argues that from the point of view of the sciences of complexity, an organization is not even a system, but should be understood as a pattern or as interconnected patterns in time. As such, by looking toward the future, we can create what happens next without actually knowing what will happen next.[151] In the same vein, Schumpeter identifies a major characteristic of leaders' behavior as those which do not follow the logic of prevailing rules in order to reach a given objective – as leaders would have to invent new rules to reach new objectives.[152]

Robert Goizueta, a former CEO of Coca-Cola Company argues that if you are number one or two in your industry, you can have a lot of say in what the future is going to be like by what you do. For instance, if you can take actions that create the future, or at least shape it, you can benefit from it – and that the belief in strategic choice is about creating what can be, as opposed to what is.[153]

DNA Testing and Organizational Dysfunctions

In a related development, Bruderlein (2018) found that organizations are like biological organisms; they live in an environment, they need a level of communication, and the interdependencies to grow and operate; just as organizations need staff, resources, and funding.[154] Again, just as biological organisms need to have processes within their cells that process and maintain a sense of direction, and a sense of priorities – and that these mechanisms have to be physical, organizations too, do need to establish certain communication and interdependency with the organization's environment simultaneously.[155]

Similarly; Neilson, Pasternack, and Mendes (2003) believe that DNA testing can be as valuable to corporate health as it has become to human health care.[156] As a result, *an analysis of a company's "genetic material"* can isolate the underlying causes of and potential solutions to organizational dysfunctions – and even head off problems before they start."[157] Bordia, Kronenberg, Neely, Hamilton, *et al.* (2005), argue that just as nature's DNA spells out the exact instructions required to create a unique organism, OrgDNA determines how an organization will function.[158]

2.2.2 Dynamics of High Performance: A Broad-Based Perspective

To begin addressing issues relating to the dynamics of high performance, organizations should look internally to locate and organize these resources, but imperatively, they must equally align internal resources with the exigencies of the competitive environment if they have to be sustainable. To this end, Tsui (2018a) found that in the perspective of a *resource-based view* (RBV) of the firm, it functions on the logic that the existence and appropriate use of resources are critical to generating competitive advantage – and, with proper protection, it can lead to sustained superior performance by an organization.[159] Some typical resources possessed by an organization in this regard include the following: people or networks, physical assets, processes, cash and other types of equity, software and data (Tsui, 2018a).

Finding and Working with the Right People

It is well established that the vast majority of businesses start small. But the challenge to growing it, is finding the right people. For any organization to grow, improve, and most especially stay ahead, or even beat the competition; it needs to have the best, smartest, and most-skilled people suitable for the organization's business model.

As a result, hiring the right people is vital to the success of any entrepreneur. Hiring a wrong person is not only a waste of resources, but it also creates a negative work environment which is not a good sign for your company.[160] For example, Watson (2018) suggests that instead of regretting a lousy hire, take a wise move to replace it with a right one.[161] In a similar vein, *CB Insights* found that NOT pivoting away or quickly enough from a bad product, a bad hire or a bad decision quickly enough was cited as a reason for failure in 7% of 101 start-up venture failure post-mortems.[162] In this regard, successful entrepreneurs surround themselves with people that will help their business grow. It can be a mentor or an adviser. It can also be other successful entrepreneurs or business owners. It can be suppliers and influencers to boost their marketing.[163]

Furthermore, Nelson (2019) contends that successful entrepreneurs already know that in order to grow they need to grow their network in the industry as well. That said, if you have the right connection and network, it is easy to penetrate the market.[164] It must surround itself with people it can't afford to miss. Kim and Mauborgne (2014) call them the "pioneers." These are businesses that offer unprecedented value.[165] Maximizing talent by way of attracting, retaining, developing, and promoting outstanding talent – is one of the critical capabilities that will distinguish a successful organization now and in the future. Consequently, it is imperative for leaders to keep their eyes on the horizon, so as to anticipate potential change and ensure that they have the right talent with the right skill sets in place when and where it is likely to be needed.[166] This is no doubt, one of the key attributes of sustainable leadership. Nyangena, Akujah, and Okanga (2019) argue that sustainable leaders are rare today, and they are essential for sustainable development of a society.[167]

In concurrence, Carper (2014) found that all top MNE executives seem to agree that ultimately what sets their firms apart from other firms in the increasingly competitive global marketplace – is their people, their ideas, expertise, and ability to solve problems creatively, and flexibility.[168] Further, he argues that nowhere are these attributes more important than in today's global marketplace.[169] Therefore, winning the war for talent today will determine whether an organization will be positioned to win in the dynamic business environment of tomorrow.[170] But then, how do you get these people on board? Sondhe (2010) suggests that you give them a stake in the company.[171]

Attracting them by giving them a stake in that company applies not to just anybody, but the best people within your reach. In this regard, Peter Drucker (1966) argues that every knowledge worker in modern organization is an executive – if, by virtue of his position or knowledge, he is responsible for a contribution that materially affects the capacity of the organization to perform and to obtain results.[172] Therefore to attract and acquire the right talent, organizations will have to *translate new market demands into skill requirements* – and as the talent playing field gets more and more competitive, it will become ever more difficult.[173] In addition, attracting them would require that some mechanism needs to be put in place to make their lives better than they would be, if they choose to work elsewhere.[174]

In the reasoning of Sondhe (2010), the employee's status as stakeholder begins with a job, and then builds the employee relationship, establishing trust; with trust, employee loyalty can be built by rewarding them with ownership.[175] In a similar vein, Bhalla, Caye, Dyer *et al.* (2011) maintain that while many companies boast particular strengths in recruiting, training, or performance management, high-performance organizations are effective at translating their business strategy into a compelling people strategy.[176] As it goes, supervisors often translate messages from senior executives and make those messages real, through interaction with employees and by setting daily expectations.[177] To this end, Kilpi (2017) contends that what an organization becomes; emerges from the relationships of its members rather than being chosen by some individuals.[178] Bhalla *et al.* (2011) found that at these organizations, the HR function acts as a strong advisor to business units on both operational and strategic people issues. And they tend to have short-term and long-term plans for identifying, attracting, developing, and retaining the right people with the right capabilities.[179]

According to Ireland and Hitt (1999), accomplishing the aforementioned tasks would require effective strategic leadership. Without effective strategic leadership, the probability that a firm can achieve superior or even satisfactory performance when confronting the challenges of the global economy, will be greatly reduced.[180] To this end, effective strategic leadership tactfully reconciles the visionary leadership orientations for those willing to take risks, with the managerial leadership orientation for those with a rational way of looking at the world.[181]

Leadership as a Scarce Resource

Leaders are accountable to assemble teams and lead them to optimal performance outcomes. In this regard, an effective leader recognizes the importance of embracing differences in people and knows how to connect the dots among those differences to get the best outcomes from the team.[182] Great leaders inspire their employees by empowering them to generate ideas for solving pressing problems and making process improvements – and encourage them to take the lead in putting their ideas into action.[183] Karthikeyan (2017) maintains that a truly authentic leader relates well to others, is open to new ideas, and can inspire high levels of performance in tough times.[184] This is what cultivates a workplace environment of continuous improvements, innovation and initiative.[185]

Bhalla *et al.* (2011) found that effective leaders think strategically – set the pace, allocate resources, build engagement, drive accountability, and deliver results – and that leadership may start at the top of the pyramid, but does not stop at the top of the pyramid.[186] As a result, the key management capability is not being in control, but participating and influencing the formation of sense making and meaning. It is about creating a context that enables connectedness, interaction and trust between people.[187] In a similar vein, Llopis (2014) argues that leaders must foster a commitment from the team to embrace an innovation mindset where each employee learns to apply the differences that exist in one another for their own success and that of the organization.[188]

From the foregoing, Bhalla *et al.* (2011) contend that high-performance organizations create leaders at every level through three primary levers:

1. That high-performance teams of leaders drive urgency and direction
2. That the pipeline is stocked with future leaders whose skills are matched to future needs
3. That middle managers embrace and translate strategy.[189]

HIGH-PERFORMANCE TEAMS OF LEADERS DRIVE URGENCY AND DIRECTION

Nafei (2014) suggests that performance in its simplest form is the desired results which the organization seeks to achieve efficiently and effectively.[190] Bhalla *et al.* (2011) found that high performance leaders are comfortable with complexity, volatility, and change. In the face of ambiguity, they are able to mobilize the organization. However, they need to work cooperatively with their peers and recognize the collective strength generated through collaboration.[191]

In this regard, Darroch (2003) found that there exists a relationship between the organization's fundamental building blocks (OrgDNA) as an *independent* organizational variable and organizational performance (OP) as a *dependent* variable that functions on two performance segments – i.e., *comparative performance* and *internal performance.*[192] That said, the fundamental organizational building blocks is said to be an independent organizational variable because it is made of the genetic material of the organization, which contains its DNA. So it cannot be changed, but can undergo some form of an *organizational gene transfer,* or in a less effective way, an *organizational gene editing* – as in gene therapy in medicine. And in some cases, overwhelmingly powerful external forces – powerful enough to make an organization to completely lose control of its adjacencies and sometimes its core activities, can lead to a *mutation* in the *organization's genetic material* or its *OrgDNA.* On this strand of reasoning, while the organization's fundamental building blocks can be construed as an *independent variable,* its variability as being *independent* can only be understood by understanding the functional *interdependence* of each of the bases of its organizational formal building blocks in tandem with its organizational informal building blocks.

STOCKING THE PIPELINE WITH FUTURE LEADERS

According to Hodge and Anthony (1991) and Daft (2001), organizational structure is the sum total of the ways in which the organization divides its labor into distinct tasks to ensure effective communication, coordination, and integration of efforts across departments.[193] Consequently, there is the strategic need to continue nurturing future leaders in the backyard. In this regard, as the pipeline is stocked with future leaders whose skills are matched to future needs, these organizations identify potential leaders early in their careers – and cultivate in them the skills and competences that will be required in the future.[194]

Similarly, Rowe (2001) contends that when organizations restore strategic control and allow the development of a critical mass of strategic leaders, these leaders will be a source of above-average returns. The result will be wealth creation for the employees, customers, suppliers, and shareholders of entrepreneurial and established organizations.[195] This would mean to some firms, a trade-off between their agenda to meet up with short-term profit maximization and those of long-term sustainability. By using talented employees just to maximize profit in the short run is arguably, exploitative, while making efforts to strategically mold employees to take on future leadership positions in the organization is an exploratory measure by the firm. In the latter case, it makes much sense for a firm to trade-off some slice of its short-term profits in favor of future viability.[196] As it would have the advantage of providing the firm with long-term growth in shareholder value.[197] In a similar vein, Nyangena *et al.* (2019) found that nurturing ethical leaders is essential and will determine the transformation speed in overall development.[198]

Along this strand, Gibson and Birkinshaw (2004) argue that another potential avenue for future studies is the way firms can mitigate exploration versus exploitation tension at their individual levels. According to Katila and Ahuja (2002), exploratory activities are mainly related to the development of new knowledge and capabilities, while exploitative operations are more concerned with the utilization of current capabilities and existing stock of knowledge. In the same vein, March (1991) and Van de Ven and Engleman (2004) argue that a basic tension that firms face is whether to attend to their employees toward *exploratory activities for future viability* or in *exploitative activities to ensure existing viability*.Burgelman and Valikangas (2005) and Burgelman (1983) also confirm that these activities are competing with each other for organizational attention.[199]

According to Raisch *et al.* (2009) and Jansen *et al.* (2005), firms need both exploratory and exploitative activities for higher performance and innovative activities – they are called ambidextrous firms. Similarly, Gupta *et al.* (2006) hold that exploration and exploitation can be viewed as tradeoffs for firms. Finally, according to Hill and Birkinshaw (2014), the dominant view is that such activities are distinct, yet complementary modes of activity.[200]

HOW MIDDLE MANAGERS EMBRACE AND TRANSLATE STRATEGY

Middle managers oversee the vast majority of employees, translating the strategy and vision endorsed by senior leaders into concrete plans for their teams. They also select and elevate the key issues from the frontline that needs senior management's attention. However, Bhalla *et al.* (2011) argue that despite the pivotal and difficult role middle managers play; they often get lost in the shuffle and receive insufficient development, support, and attention from senior leadership.[201]

In another development, Kilpi (2017) argues that most people believe the role of leaders is to choose strategic directions and then persuade others to follow them, but contends that a modern view of strategy is about exploration and experiments – a search process of trial and error, and openness to what is possible through the search process.[202] In this regard, leading organizations that recognize the importance of middle managers, invest in their success, and actively monitor and work to strengthen their engagement and skills.[203]

DIGITAL-ERA LEADERSHIP AND THE SOCIAL MEDIA

With regards to marketing and leading in the digital age, Dettmann, Canwell, and Wellins (2018) found that 50% of the 2006 Fortune 500 companies no longer exist. Competition rains in from every direction. Looking ahead, technologies such as robotics and artificial intelligence (AI) are projected to affect two billion jobs over the next decade. These trends represent both a threat and an opportunity. Organizations with digitally savvy leaders (the pioneers), are outperforming those organizations with less digitally capable leaders (the laggards) – and as our work world is becoming increasingly digital, that performance gap will only grow.[204]

The question now is, are there some other hidden issues underpinning this mass exit from the industry? Obviously, a firm's inability to competitively cope with emerging *digital era-leadership* challenges would definitely face a double dose of leadership problems, when confronted with an additional burden coming in from another invading front – which is, the social networking environment.

As companies grapple with how to transform and innovate better and faster, the population of leaders guiding these decisions is changing dramatically (see Table 2.1). Most popular discussions about the next generational shift has centered on the mass of Baby Boomers (people born before 1965) retiring, or the eager ascension of Millennials into leadership.[205] Millennials are "digital natives" – the generation born between 1982 and 2000. They grew up in a digital environment and seem to embrace technology in all aspects of their lives.[206]

Table 2.1 Leader Assessment of Effectiveness at Three Digital-Leadership Skills

Digital-Leadership Skills	*Ratings on 1–5 Point Scale**	*Ranking on Overall Effectiveness*	
Digital Literacy		Rank	Average Points
Millennials	3.6/5	First Place	
Generation X	3.5/5	Millennials	3.40/5
Baby Boomers	3.3/5	Second Place	
Leading with Digitization		Generation X	3.37/5
Millennials	3.4/5	Third Place	
Generation X	3.3/5	Baby Boomers	3.30/5
Baby Boomers	3.2/5		
Leading Virtual Teams			
Millennials	3.2/5		
Generation X	3.3/5		
Baby Boomers	3.4/5		

Source: Author created, but data was extracted from Ddiworld.com, 2018. As cited by Neal, Stephanie (2018), op. cit., p. 31.

Note

* Ratings on a five-point scale, where "1" is not at all effective and "5" is very highly effective.

Often overlooked is the next generation to leadership, Generation X, which is leading the way in a time of great change with technology advancement – on how jobs are automated and created, and how businesses are designed and transformed.[207] Born between 1965 and 1981 and with an average of 20 years' experience in the workplace, members of "Gen X" are primed to take on nearly every important leadership role in organizations. They already hold 51% of leadership roles globally and will continue to grow into more senior positions. Yet, little is commonly known about what defines the Gen X leadership experience and style.[208]

Also of equal importance, Professor Barbara Bickart (2018) observed that social media is an integral part of our lives. We use social media to discuss world events, to keep up with friends and family, to consult online reviews, and for fun. While social media may seem essential to our personal lives, can it also help us to meet our marketing objectives? As social media technologies are transforming the way consumers interact with each other and with firms – these definitely need answers. As Bickart contends, these changes constitute a fundamental shift in the marketplace, as consumers increasingly tend to have greater opportunities to voice their opinions and connect with their peers, as well as increased influence over brand meaning and messaging.[209] But for an organization to successfully manage its social media outlets, the leadership must be digitally savvy.

Change Management

Change Management is a natural complement to Effective Leadership. "*To improve is to change; to be perfect is to change often*" – *Winston Churchill.* Many scholars have agreed that in today's fast-paced changing world, the ability to change comes in two fundamental ways, notably; the *planned* and *unplanned* change. In the same vein, McMahon (2013) maintains that there are really only two kinds of change in the world: *planned* and *unplanned* change.[210] Obviously, a well craft out mechanism to manage change in an organization can incredibly tend to generate sustained competitive advantage.

Similar, Engel and Weber (2007) argue that it is not always necessary that behavior be changed ad hoc – i.e., by a single act of intervention – as society sometimes tolerates temporary deviations from the social optimum.[211] Given these favorable conditions, they suggest that institutional designers may pursue one of two strategies – the more intrusive or the less intrusive strategy. The *more intrusive strategy* aims at endowing the intended recipients with additional problem-solving modes. While the *less intrusive strategy*increases the availability of a previously existing problem-solving mode in a new area.[212] As a result, in the interest of reaching long-term goals, interventions may be more or less direct.[213]

In reality, however, the change process would sometimes need to accommodate *unplanned* elements in a *planned* change and vice versa. Firstly, with regards to planned change – companies need to have a *disciplined approach* to drive shifts in focus, strategy, direction, structure, and culture. Secondly, with unplanned change – companies need to have the *ability to adapt* to rapidly changing developments in the market.[214] Also, in relation to unplanned change, Bhalla *et al.* (2011) observed that *high performance organizations* are *inherently evolutionary* in character. In this sense, they are adaptive – by continually detecting changes in the market and making strategic adjustments. And in particular, they reveal that this evolutionary approach *supplements* rather than *replaces* the broad strokes of classic strategy.[215]

In any case, be it a planned change or unplanned change, the basis of change management requires that it has to have a clear process which everyone understands. Although in reality, it becomes near impossible for everyone to digest its dynamics at the same wave length, largely due to variations in the insight of individuals and sometimes due to cultural differences, et cetera. That said; basic elements of a change process are:

- What is under change control and what is excluded?
- How are changes requested?
- Who has the authority to approve or reject changes?
- How are decisions upon approval or rejection documented and disseminated?
- How changes are implemented and their implementation recorded?

The process should be widely understood and accepted and should be effective without necessarily being bureaucratic or prescriptive. To this end, Susman, Jansen, Michael *et al.* (2006) argue that regardless of which of the many triggers has initiated the change process – critical to change management, are several key activities that can facilitate a successful change implementation. These activities can be organized into a five-step change process in descending order, as follows:

- The need to generate urgency,
- the need create a vision,
- the need to develop political support,
- the need to manage the transition, and
- the need to sustain the momentum of change.[216]

Furthermore, they opine that these step-wise models still provide a useful organizing framework, even if all the steps are not necessary, or even if the order varies depending on the company or the change initiatives of the actors.[217]

Organizational Design/Structure

Organizational design is a well-established field of business research. Waterman *et al.* (1980) found that although the first contributions on organizational design dates from the 1960s, recent years have shown a growing interest in the topic, leading to the development of models that struggle to represent the complexity and variety of environmental and organizational factors.[218] According to Mohrman and Worley (2010), organizational design elements include the routines and work activities encompassed in different processes to deliver value for customers and other stakeholders. This involves (1) structures to provide decision-making, and communication, as well as the decision settings to these processes; (2) processes to attract and motivate talents with the skills they need; (3) and the alignment of all these processes to the firm's strategy.[219]

In this regard, Bhalla *et al.* (2011) maintain that structure and resource allocation reflects strategic tradeoffs – and a well-designed structure should emphasize what matters most to an organization; because in the real world, it is impossible to accommodate all dimensions equally.[220] Nafei (2014) found that organizational *structure* constitute the following parameters:

- What the organizational hierarchy looks like,
- how are lines and boxes in the organization chart connected,
- how many layers are in the hierarchy, and
- how many direct reports each layer has.

That said, he argues that *structure* is the clearest of the four components of OrgDNA, as it is *the launching pad of organizational change programs.*[221] Emphatically, Govindarajan and Trimble (2006) posited that structure should not be the starting point, but the logical outcome of the options relating to the other three determinants; clarifying *decision rights,* designing *information flow,* and *aligning motivators.* In this regard, making changes to *structure* is seen as the climax or *outgrowth* of reorganizational change efforts, and not the *basis* of the efforts of reorganization.[222]

Another interesting finding from Bhalla *et al.* (2011) is that an organization's structure should also be dynamic – oriented around current and future, rather than legacy priorities. This implies that when strategy, performance, or the competitive environment changes, an organization's structure may need adjustment.[223] This is particularly crucial in that, a typical managerial function may not be a good fit to respond appropriately to the adjustment of an organization's structure when it becomes imperative to do so in a process of transition. In a similar vein, Rowe (2001) argues that if an organization is in a transition phase – driven by a vision of what it should be to maintain and enhance long-term viability, it is very hard on those who are managerial leaders.[224] On this strand of reasoning, he contends that organizations need visionary leadership to ensure their long-term viability; but however notes that organizations that are led by visionaries without the constraining influence of managerial leaders are probably more in danger of failing in the short term than those led by managerial leaders. Thus, on the one hand, visionary leaders are willing to risk all, and in doing so may create wealth. On the other hand, they may however stand a high risk of investing more in their vision than the warranted returns, and without the constraining influence of managerial leaders, it could instead, turn to destroy wealth.[225]

Another important observation is that high performance is usually characterized by few layers that separate the CEO and the frontline, and spans of control are wide. As such, these kind of lean structures allow organizations to focus on meaningful work, rather than coordination – where activities that don't deliver value are eliminated.[226] In this regard, the *Council for Advancement and Support of Education (2012)* suggests that new employees can be paired with successful and well – engaged employees – who live and breathe the organization's values. In this way, such new employees will tend to imitate those feelings and behaviors.[227] Therefore, mentoring programs to expose new hires to employees who reflect values of the organization would likely create more value.[228]

Thus, with fewer organizational layers, communication and decision making are faster, and senior leaders have a better view of day-to-day operations and customer interactions. With wider spans of control, managers become more ambitious in applying their leadership skills. To this end, high-performance organizations have clearly defined roles that are carefully assembled to form a highly efficient organization. To enhance shared accountability – people should understand clearly – what is expected of them and which decisions are theirs to make, when to make it, and with whom they need to collaborate.[229] Randall (2012) suggests the putting in place of orientation sessions to convey values of the firm, and training opportunities to reinforce basic values.[230] To this end, frequent reinforcement of organizational values by the leader is important;[231] by articulating them at every opportunity – from all-staff meetings to culture-specific training sessions.[232]

A glaring manifestation of high performance organization is that individual capabilities are matched to role requirements. Roles need to be staffed by the right people with the right skills depending on its needs.

Culture and Employee Engagement

According to Bhalla *et al.* (2011), *culture* is the way things get done in an organization – and reflects employees' behaviors and attitudes toward work. Meanwhile, *employee engagement* is the willingness of employees to go the extra mile for an organization; not merely out of obligation or for a paycheck, but because work matters both personally and professionally to them.[233]

CULTURE

According to Adler (1994), culture can be defined as an acquired behavioral aspect assigned to a person and his group – by which the individual is identified, expressed and transmitted through symbols, distinguishing mark, its values and beliefs.[234] Research has shown that a strong corporate culture can give a company a powerful advantage over its competitors, especially in highly competitive and commodity-like markets. On the strength of this reasoning, Susman *et al.* (2006) maintains that, perhaps the most important component of the informal organization is the firm's culture.[235] According to Mittal (2015), culture signifies the basic values and belief systems of individuals that are expected to impact managerial processes and leadership mechanisms.[236] To this end, Lorsch (1986) argues that culture pervades every level of a company, including the shared beliefs held by top managers regarding how they should manage themselves, their subordinates, and the company.[237]

Finally, Schein (1992) defines organizational culture as a set of basic assumptions – that have been invented, discovered or developed by a group dealing with problems of *external adaptation* and *internal integration.*[238] In this regard, Carper (2014) suggests that senior executives working across cultures must be able to earn the respect and trust of others quickly – in order to acquire timely information that is valid and reliable for decision-making purposes.[239] In addition, for innovative efforts to succeed, the firm's culture should be supportive of innovation.[240]

The task of integrating these different cultures is primarily the noble task of the leader, who is the ultimate architect and the builder of the organizational culture.[241] Sultana *et al.* (2013) consider the management of cultural *diversity* as a process with a set of interrelated stages to create sustainable competitive advantages.[242] On this strand of reasoning, Gardenswartz and Lowe (1995) argue that diversity can be understood as a scale at three levels: (1) *internal dimensions,* (2) *external dimensions,* and (3) *organizational dimensions.* That said, the *internal dimensions* are essentially within the person and are very much intrinsic (and in most parts, they are inherently unchangeable). This denotes the age, gender, race, ethnicity, sexual orientation, et cetera. The *external dimensions,* in turn, refer to religion, education, personal habits, experience, marital status, parental status and so on.[243] The *organizational dimensions* refer to the function of the individual in the organization, professional affiliation, its unity, division or department, type of management and so on.[244]

In a similar vein, Sultana *et al.* (2013) argue that there exist two principal *synergistic relationships* in an organization: *the dual role of organizational culture,* and *three dimensions of diversity.* First, *the dual role of organizational culture* is made of *external adaptation* which comprises of the mission, core objectives, and means of the organization; and *internal adjustment* that is being carried out through the collective mobilization and cohesion of the members of that organization.[245] Second, *the three dimensions of diversity* comprises of the *internal dimension,* the *external dimension,* and the *organization dimension.* Fig. 2.4 suggests a synergistic

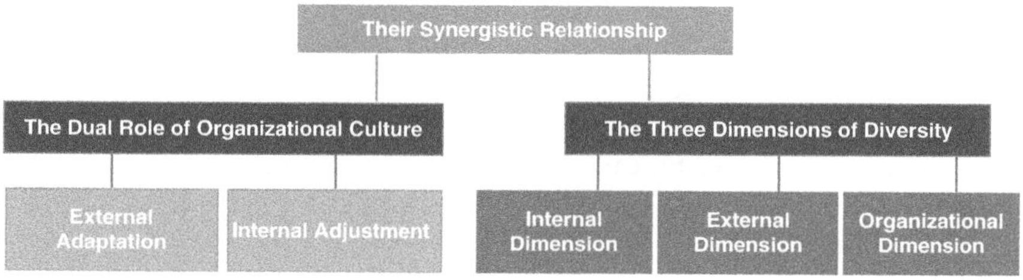

Figure 2.4 The Dual Role of Organizational Culture vs. the Three Dimensions of Diversity.

Source: Author created, but drew inspiration from data by Sultana *et al.* (2013), pp. 137–38.

relationship between the *dual role of organizational culture,* and the *three dimensions of diversity.*

As shown on Fig. 2.4, a dynamic construct of this synergistic relationship for competitive advantage, effectiveness and performance is a noble task of the leader.

Following the logic and exigencies of cultural diversity management, it becomes imperative that global executives should readily ADAPT to other cultures – not necessarily ADOPT them,[246] especially as innovation-supportive culture is one that values creativity and cooperation.[247]Zahra (1995) argues that this is mainly because firms in international markets are faced with the liability of foreignness – arising from constraints, lack of knowledge of the target markets' institutional and business environments, and lack of legitimacy in foreign markets.[248] To this end, Carper argues that Cultural ADAPTATION is not cultural ADOPTION; since culture is not an abstraction, but a powerful human reality that is an integral part of what it means to be a human being, in a specific place at a given point in time.[249]

Interestingly, Bhalla *et al.* (2011) argue that culture and employee engagement are different from leadership, design, people, and change management. In particular, they contend that a culture either works for a given enterprise – or it doesn't at a given point in time. This argument is based on the premise that as strategic priorities change, so should culture. This equally implies that culture accelerates strategic objectives.[250] In a related vein, Schein (1990) noted that many organizational change programs failed probably because they ignored the cultural forces in the organizations in which change programs were to be installed.[251] As a result, the cultural diversity management of an organization provides benefits if and only if, it is well managed.[252] In this regard, Trevino and Brown (2005) argue that ethical codes of conduct would not be effective unless those codes are consistent with the organizational culture and are a being enforced.[253] In a similar vein, Sultana *et al.* (2013) opine that if cultural diversity is mismanaged, it can be the source of negative impact because many people would feel threatened to work with other people in the organization – for example, different age groups, sex or cultural backgrounds, et cetera.[254]

Consequently, it is vital for a manager to identify the cultural specificity of a group, so as to understand the way to react and solve the problems it faces – as this insecurity can have a negative impact on overall productivity.[255]

EMPLOYEE ENGAGEMENT

According to *Harvard Business Review Analytic Services (2020),* engagement is what employers want from their workers. Well-being, on the other hand is what workers want for themselves – and what enlightened employers want for their workers.[256] Furthermore, they argue there is a wide agreement that engagement and happiness are driven by the same dimensions.[257] In the same vein, Wildermuth (2008) and Kahn (1990) maintain that employee engagement is a strong bond between oneself and the job responsibility – a sort of multidimensional construct where employees could fully express themselves emotionally, cognitively and physically.[258]

Vazirani (2007) defines employee engagement as the level of involvement and commitment an employee has toward the organization and its value.[259] This means that when an employee is properly engaged, it ignites a positive reaction and feeling toward the organization, which in turn leads to high level of commitment that influences others to increase the productivity of work; which in turn, improves the image of the organization and accelerate profit.[260] Meanwhile, in the *Harvard Business Review Analytic Services (2020),* recent survey of 1,073 US executives reveals that 79% of the survey respondents agree that unhappiness among some of their workforce is hurting productivity, and 75% agree that it is leading to unwanted turnover, while 87% of survey respondents believe workforce well-being can give their companies a competitive edge.[261]

2.3 OrgDNA Common Bases and Their Intangibles

As we saw earlier, Neilson *et al.* (2008) argued that execution is as the result of thousands of decisions made every day by employees acting according to the information they have and their own interest. In the process, they identified four fundamental building blocks executives can use to influence those actions, notably; clarifying decision rights, designing information flows, aligning motivators, and making changes to structure. These are commonly referred to as decision rights, information, motivators, and structure.[262] However, their corresponding informal building blocks, notably; norms, mindsets, commitments, and networks respectively, are powerful forces that are critical in the life of an organization. That being said, it is common practice for most people to see OrgDNA mainly from the perspective of formal building blocks – the tangibles, as opposed to the informal building blocks – the intangibles.

Within the framework of strategy execution in relation to the four fundamental building blocks executives can use to influence successful strategy execution, Neilson *et al.* (2008) identified 17 fundamental traits of organizational effectiveness. Ranking in the traits show that clarifying *decision rights* and designing *information flows* are most effective to strategy execution. To this end, the first eight traits map directly to *decision rights* and *information flow*. Four of the 17 traits relate to *motivators,* and none of these ranked higher than 9th position. Meanwhile, only three of the 17 traits relate to *structure,* and none of these ranks higher than 13th position.[263]

2.3.1 Common Bases of OrgDNA: The Tangibles

The nomenclature of FORMAL OrgDNA building blocks has been described by Lozano, Gomez, and Rositas (2011) as a series of orderly interlinked elements that constitute its OrgDNA.[264] And that these four elements are not mutually independent – rather, they depend on, and must be consistent with, each other.[265]

OrgDNA Profiles (Organizational Personality Types)

While OrgDNA is also known as an organization's genetic material, Estupiñán and Neilson (2014) use the term OrgDNA for defining an organization's personality and determines whether it is strong or weak in executing strategy.[266] As shown on Table 2.2, they equally found that although every company may seem unique, but in their enterprise-wide behavior, they fall into *seven behavioral patterns.* That said, in the order from least to most effective at execution, they range from: passive-aggressive, over-managed, outgrown, fits-and-starts, just-in-time, military-precision, and the resilient organization.[267]

Similarly, Dehoff *et al.* (2005) refer to it as the *seven bases of OrgDNA profiles,* and further argue that, just as in the natural case, OrgDNA can lead to healthy or unhealthy or dysfunctional outcomes.[268]

THE HEALTHY AND RESILIENT ORGANIZATION (HERO)

As you can see from Table 2.2, of the seven profiles, the three on the left hand side of the Table, especially the resilient organization, represent what can be considered healthy and effective organizations.[269] According to Llorens, Salanova, Torrente, and Acosta (2013), a Healthy and Resilient Organization (HERO) is conceptualized as an organization that makes systematic, planned, and proactive efforts to

Table 2.2 OrgDNA Profiles

Healthy Organizational Profile		*Unhealthy Organizational Profile*	
The Resilient Organization	The resilient organization, which is also known as Healthy and Resilient Organizations (HERO); is flexible enough to adapt quickly to external market shifts, yet steadfastly focused on and aligned to a coherent business strategy. They can react nimbly (quickly and easily) to challenges and also recover quickly from those they cannot dodge.	The Outgrown Organization	Too large and complex to be effectively controlled by a small team, but has yet to democratize decision-making authority.
		The Over-managed Organization	Multiple layers of management create analysis paralysis in a frequently bureaucratic and highly political environment.
The Just-in-Time Organization	Inconsistently prepared for change, but can turn on the focal point when necessary, without losing sight of the big picture.	The Fits-and-Starts Organization	Contains scores of smart, motivated, and talented people, who rarely pull in the same direction at the same time.
The Military Organization	It is often driven by a small, involved senior team, and succeeds primarily through the will and foresight of its leaders.	The Passive-Aggressive Organization	This category takes its name from the organization's quiet but tenacious resistance, in all its ramifications, but is open to corporate directives. However, those people pay lip service to corporate directives by putting in only enough effort to appear compliant.

Sources: Adapted from Booz Allen Hamilton: as cited by Dehoff *et al.* (2005), p. 1; Llorens, Salanova, Torrente, and Acosta (2013), p. 1; and Neilson *et al.* (2005).

improve employees' and organizational processes and outcomes. These efforts involve fostering healthy organizational resources and practices intended to improve the work environment at the task, interpersonal, and organizational levels – especially during times of change and crisis.[270]

In a similar vein, Neilson, Pasternack, and Van Nuys (2005) maintain that healthy companies are hard to make mistakes. This is obvious, as their managers have access to good, timely information, the authority to make informed decisions, and the incentives to make them on behalf of the organization – which promptly and capably carries them out.[271] That said, a good term for the healthiest of such organizations is "resilient," since they can react nimbly (quickly and easily) to challenges and also recover quickly from those they cannot dodge.[272]

UNHEALTHY OR DYSFUNCTIONAL ORGANIZATIONS

Again, as shown in Table 2.2, the four profiles on the right hand side of the Table comprise of what can be called unhealthy or dysfunctional organizations.[273] Most prominent in this group is the passive-aggressive organization. According to Neilson, Pasternack and Van Nuys (2005), the category takes its name from the organization's quiet but tenacious resistance, in all its ramifications, but is open to corporate directives. However, those people pay lip service to corporate directives by putting in only enough effort to appear compliant.[274] In this regard, they argue that when employees' healthy impulses, such as to learn, to share, to achieve – are not encouraged, other harmful but adaptive conduct gradually takes over.[275]

Finally, Neilson *et al.* (2005) maintain that as a general rule, companies that are not healthy suffer from *either too much control at the top, or not enough control* – either can cripple performance. That said, in such organizations, people with authority lack the information to exercise control wisely, or lack the incentives to serve the company's strategy and interests, or may lack the personnel that will carry out their directives. Conversely, *people with the incentives and information necessary to make good decisions lack the authority to execute them or oversee their execution by others.* As a result, many in senior positions operate under the false impression that they control things they actually do not. At the same time, many think they cannot control what they actually can (Neilson *et al.* 2005).

2.3.2 *The Tangibles, Intangibles, and OrgDNA Replication*

Remember, we saw earlier that the DNA, or deoxyribonucleic acid, is the hereditary material in humans and almost all other organisms. Most DNA is located in the cell nucleus (where it is called nuclear DNA), but a small amount of DNA can also be found in the mitochondria (where it is called mitochondrial DNA or mtDNA). Mitochondria are structures within cells that convert the energy from food into a form that cells can use.[276]

At this juncture, if we can accept the argument that there is a striking similarity between the microbiological process of DNA with that of an Organizational behavior, then it would not be out of order to equally accept that since there is a DNA replication, which is a biological process of producing two identical replicas from one original DNA molecule – it can produce a mirror imaging effect similar to a typical organizational platform.

Estupiñán and Neilson (2014) argue that formal OrgDNA elements are attractive to companies because they are tangible – as they can be easily defined and measured. But they are only half the story as the intangible elements also matter in the life of an organization. Supposedly as companies often realize this after they've made significant changes – reassigned decision rights, reworked the organization chart, established new incentives, or set up knowledge-sharing systems – yet don't see the results they expect. That's because they ignored the informal, intangible elements.[277] These include norms (what people think is the right way to behave), commitments (the promises people feel motivated to keep) mind-sets (deeply held attitudes and beliefs), and networks (connections among employees outside the formal structure). All these add up to influence the ways people think, feel, communicate, and behave. From the foregoing, Estupiñán and Neilson (2014) hold that until we learn to influence these factors, our efforts to build performance will be unbalanced.[278]

In addition, most prominent on Table 2.3 is the interesting research findings from Neilson *et al.* (2008), which reveal that among the common bases of OrgDNA building blocks – *decision rights* and *information* flows traits are twice as powerful as *structure* and *motivators* in driving organizational effectiveness. In this direction, they analyzed dozens of strong-execution companies and discovered that *information* had the strongest correlation to execution, at 54%, and *decision rights* correlated at 50%. *Motivators* came in with 26%, and finally *structure* came in at 25%.[279] In parity with the findings of Neilson *et al.* (2008) on *decision rights,* Robinson *et al.* (2004) found that committed employees perform better. In the same vein, Perrin (2003) contends that the strongest driver is a sense of feeling valued and involved, especially in decision making.[280]"

2.4 Empowering People and Unlocking Organizations' Potentials: The Precepts

Going beyond an existing business model is an uphill task for any organization, especially the ones that are less dynamic to change. Consequently, empowering people and unlocking organizations' potentials is one of the strategic options in crossing the frontiers of execution based on an organization's current model. As a result, understanding the requirements for

Table 2.3 OrgDNA Bases and Their Synthesized Templates

FORMAL (Common DNA Bases)		*INFORMAL (Synthesized Templates)*	
Formal Organizational Building Blocks	*Power Traits Coefficient*	*Informal Organizational building Blocks (Synthesized Templates)*	*Power Traits Coefficient*
Information How the organization formally processes data and information • What metrics are used to measure performance? • How are activities coordinated, and how is knowledge transferred? • How are expectations and progress communicated? • Who knows what? • Who needs to know what? • How information is transferred from the people who have it to the people who require it?	2	**Mind-Sets** How pivotal are deeply held attitudes and beliefs • Identity, shared language, and beliefs • Assumptions and biases • Mental models	2
Decision Rights How decisions are made • Who decides what? • How many people are involved in a decision process? • Where does one person's decision-making authority end and another's begin?	2	**Norms** what people think is the right way to behave) • Expectations and "unwritten rules" • Values and standards • Behaviors	2

(*Continued*)

Table 2.3 (Continued)

FORMAL (Common DNA Bases)		*INFORMAL (Synthesized Templates)*	
Formal Organizational Building Blocks	*Power Traits Coefficient*	*Informal Organizational building Blocks (Synthesized Templates)*	*Power Traits Coefficient*
Structures How work and responsibilities get divided • What does the organizational hierarchy look like? • How are the lines and boxes in the organization chart connected? • How many layers are in the hierarchy, and how many direct reports does each layer have?	1	**Networks** How connections among employees outside the formal structure goes on • Organizational influence • Teams and other working units • Relationships and collaboration	1
Motivators How people are compelled to perform • What objectives, incentives, and career alternatives do people have? • How are people rewarded – financially and non-financially, for what they achieve? • What are they encouraged to care about, by whatever means, explicit or implicit?	1	**Commitments** How people are inspired to contribute • Individual goals and aspirations • Sources of pride in individual and collective achievements • Shared vision and objectives	1

Sources: Adapted from multiple sources, some examples include; Neilson *et al.* (2003), op. cit., pp. 3 & 4; Estupiñán and Neilson (2014), op. cit., pp. 2 & 3; and other sources.

effective and positive influence as an essential part of leadership becomes imperative for successful organizations.[281]

On the path to becoming high-performance organizations, Bhalla *et al.* (2011) observed that surprisingly, *executives* tend to have well developed tools for *financial and operational performance,* but these tools are not well developed for *driving organizational and people capabilities.*[282] In concurrence, Mintzberg (1990) argues that in practice, management has to be two-faced: the *cerebral face* and the *insightful face* – and that there has to be a balance between them. According to him, the *long-dominant professional* or *cerebral face* operates with the words and numbers of rationality; while the *insightful face* is rooted in the images and feel of a manager's integrity.[283]

Furthermore, he argues that contrary to the cerebral face of management, managing insightfully depends on the direct experience and personal knowledge that come from *intimate contact.* However, in organizations that have grown larger and more diversified, that becomes difficult to achieve. As a result, managers turn increasingly to the cerebral face, and the delicate balance between the two faces is lost.[284] Consequently, to overcome the challenges in managing insightfully, Mintzberg (1990) contends that managers need more ways to convey the images and impressions they carry inside of them – this would help renew employees' interest in the organization and in the *strategic vision* of management as well.[285]

From the foregoing, in spite of the turbulence of changing business environment and personnel, some scholars have successfully identified ten useful precepts that have stood the test of time for empowering people and unlocking the potentials of organizations. The ten precepts are:

1. That there are only a few organizational personality types.
2. That most companies contain a mix of personalities.
3. That the connection between the organization's personality type and how well the organization executes on strategy is always strong.
4. That strong execution is not self-sustaining (for example, leaders in organizations should relentlessly seek feedback from those closest to the market, encouraging and acting on criticism from customers and frontline employees, and taking action to address minor issues before they become bigger problems).
5. That performance is based on interdependent factors (as a result, it is crucial, then, for companies that want to improve their execution to consider organizational building blocks as a whole and not individually.
6. That the organizational chart is not the solution. Estupiñán and Neilson (2014) and *Neilson et al.* (2008) found that many company leaders frequently fall into a common trap; in thinking that by changing their organization's structure it will solve their problems. As such, they may remove significant management layers and temporarily reduce

costs along the line of structural change – but all too soon, the layers creep back in and the short-term efficiencies disappear. Consequently, they see *structure* as the capstone, and not the cornerstone.

7. That intangibles matter – as they add up to influence the ways people think, feel, communicate, and behave. This is a vital tool to correct unbalanced performance.
8. That decision rights and information flows are twice as powerful as structure.
9. That informal factors change when you focus on what works. Estupiñán and Neilson (2014) suggest that the best approach for improving intangibles like *norms* and *commitments* is to use them as a force for *transformation.*
10. That high performance of certain business units can't be isolated from the rest of the organization.[286]

2.4.1 Proper Alignment of Effective Power Bases

In the reasoning of Patrick (2012), *leadership behavior* and *power processes* are closely related, especially as leaders use power as a means of attaining group goals. In other words, leaders achieve their organizational goals with the use of power as a facilitator to goal achievement,[287] and not just the use of power for the sake of retaining power. Therefore, the borderlines between leadership and power can be *delineated* on the bases of the *absence* or the *presence* of *goal compatibility.* By implication therefore, Patrick maintains that *power* does not require goal compatibility, but merely depends on *power* to achieve its goal,[288] but acknowledges that leadership requires some *congruence* between the goals of the leader and the goals of those being led.[289] Simply put, leadership requires goal compatibility to achieve its goal, whereas power does not necessarily require goal compatibility to achieve its goal.

By some measures, it could be partly for this reason that Moye (2018) sees *leadership* as a social process of *influencing* others to maximize efforts toward a shared goal. She argues that such *influence is rooted in different types of power, which in turn indicates the most effective influence tactics when leading others.*[290] In this regard, for proper alignment of effective power bases, an employer needs to facilitate or enable the employee to cultivate his or her personal power bases, and then align it with the employer's positional power bases. Meanwhile, Coomber (2018) refers to the process of influencing others as making use of *effective power bases.*[291] As shown on Fig. 2.5, power bases can be both effective and ineffective, depending on the nature and extent of alignment between personal power bases (individual leadership) and positional power bases (institutional and structural leadership).

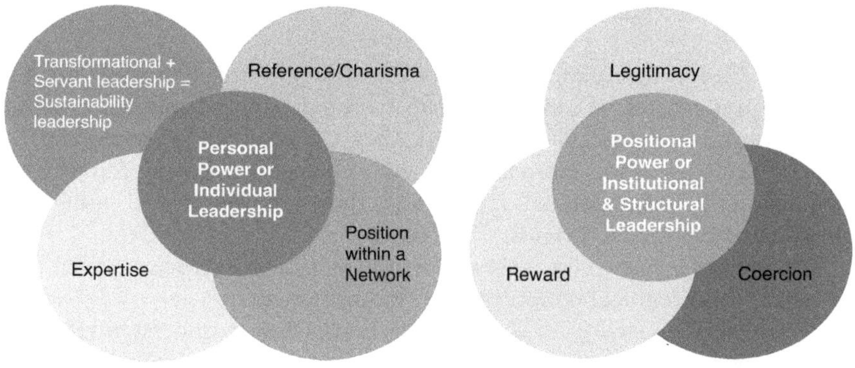

Figure 2.5 Personal Power Bases vs. Positional Power Bases.
Sources: Adapted from the works of Coomber (2018); Payne (2012), p. 16; Mittal (2015); and among others.

Leadership Styles and Their Alignment with Effective Power Bases

Individual leadership or personal power is traditionally comprised of charisma, expertise, and position within a network. Mittal (2015) defines *charismatic leadership* as that which arouse enthusiasm and commitment in followers by articulating a compelling vision and increasing follower confidence about achieving it.[292] According to Hoogh *et al.* (2004) and Mannarelli (2006), charismatic leaders exemplify extraordinarily powerful leadership characteristics that inspire and direct followers by building their commitment to a shared vision.[293]

Under *visionary leadership,* organizational control is maintained through socialization and the sharing of, and compliance with a commonly held set of norms, values, and shared beliefs.[294] Nyangena *et al.* (2019) argues that it gives a lot of autonomy to junior leaders on how they can achieve their objectives. In this regard, it is ideal for institutions or organizations that are lacking direction; but however contend that it has similar downsides as the case of *laissez-faire* leadership style.[295] To Rowe (2001), *visionary leadership* is being future oriented, concerned with risk-taking, and are not dependent on their organizations for their sense of who they are.[296] To this end, Rowe identifies some subtle distinctions between *visionary leadership* and *managerial leadership* as follows:

1. While managerial leaders usually have expertise in their functional areas, visionary leaders tend to know less than their functional area experts – as they focus on tacit knowledge, and then develop strategies on such tacit knowledge which helps promote the acceptance of their vision.

2. Visionary leadership usually utilize nonlinear thinking, while managerial leadership use linear thinking.[297]

Strategic leaders formulate and implement strategies for immediate impact and the preservation of long-term goals to enhance organizational growth, survival, and viability. In this regard, they use strategic controls and financial controls, they interchange tacit and explicit knowledge on individual and organizational levels, and they use linear and nonlinear thinking patterns concurrently,[298] et cetera.

The *servant leader* makes every effort to create a workplace environment in which followers feel comfortable to be themselves.[299]

The *vertical leadership* – Henley (2020) argues that to understand *vertical leadership development,* it would be helpful to contrast it with *horizontal leadership development,* which is what we typically think of when it comes to leadership development in general. *Horizontal development* is about *expanding your toolkit by adding to the tools you already have,* such as gaining more skills, expanding your knowledge and becoming more competent – think of communications training, dealing with conflict, developing a more strategic approach to growing the enterprise, et cetera.[300] In other words, horizontal leadership development means expanding your outer world of value creation - the tools. *Vertical leadership development,* on the other hand, is about *expanding your mindset – changing the way you think and behave.* Your mindset refers to the mental models you engage when you are thinking, as well as your sense of identity. Put in another way, vertical leadership development means deepening your inner world of value creation – the toolbox. Thus, in vertical leadership development, you pay attention to becoming more adaptable, more self-aware, more collaborative and able to span boundaries and networks.[301]

In the same direction, Petrie (2014) maintains that *vertical leadership* rests on the premise that *leadership development* is all about *living at the intersection of preparation and opportunity.*[302] As such, leaders need to develop other leaders to be ready and relevant for what organizations will confront, perhaps, over the next five to ten years and even beyond.[303]

In a similar vein, the result of a study of 15 organizations by Jones, Chesley, and Egan (2020) show that the degree to which an organization implemented vertical development depends largely on the *organization's leadership development mindset* as well as upon a number of secondary factors, such as: senior leader engagement, space for openness and vulnerability, capability and experience of practitioners, alignment in business processes, and expanded understanding of risk-taking.[304] In addition, the results of their research illustrate that accelerating leadership capacity of an organization through the implementation of vertical development requires *significant organizational commitment and change.*[305] Especially as organizational factors that have long impeded leadership development are still present for those integrating vertical development, and still pose a challenge to the success of vertical development practices at the systemic and cultural levels.[306]

Transformational leadership focuses on developing followers and incorporating their abilities into every aspects of organizational change management process.[307] Finally, after transformational leadership, we can get to *sustainability leadership*. Remember, we said earlier that transformational leadership qualities plus servant leadership qualities will amount to sustainability leadership. In addition, by some measures, strategic leadership can conveniently fit itself within this framework as a subset of sustainability leadership.

Leadership Styles and Their Alignment with Influence Styles

A careful observation of the characteristics of visionary leadership and charismatic leadership would reveal a striking compatibility with one of the four major influence styles – known as the *"ingratiator" approach*. The latter occurs in situations where someone relies more heavily on friendliness, making the other person look good, and by building relationships to get things done. The other three basic influence styles are; the *"shortgun" approach*, the *"tactician"approach*, and the *"bystander" approach* (Coomber, 2018).

ASSESSMENT OF CHARISMATIC, TRANSFORMATIONAL, AND VISIONARY LEADERSHIP

There have been lots of interests lately in the scientific world as to the role played by charismatic leadership, transformational leadership, and visionary styles in influencing; that can create sustainably more value to an organization.

With regards to *transformational leadership*, Mittal (2015) argues it make followers more aware of the importance and value of their work, thereby inducing them to transcend self-interest for the sake of the organization.[308] In this direction, we can observe that transformational leadership tends to flow seemingly well with one of the four influence styles – known as the *"tactician" approach*. According to Coomber (2018), the tactician approach, it generally relies on reason and expertise to convince others to take a particular course of action.[309]

According to Mittal (2015), *charismatic leadership* would be the preferred leadership style in individualistic and loose societies, as charismatic leaders' influence stems from the power bases of expert and referent power,[310] whereas the *transformational leadership* style would be more acceptable in collectivistic and tight societies – and these insights have practical implications for design of leadership intervention programs for businesses spanning more than one culture.[311] On the contrary, Nyangena *et al.* (2019) argue that the charismatic style of leadership is mainly focused on the leader's traits and usually his or her own ambitions. As such, it does not emphasize the qualities relevant to the development of his or her follower's expertise.[312] In concurrence with the argument of Nyangena et al. (2019), often, the charismatic leader's influence may not primarily stem from the power bases of expert power, but from referent power.

So at this juncture, at least there are two things you should remember; that charismatic leaders arouse *enthusiasm and commitment* in followers, while transformational leaders make followers *more aware of the importance and value of their work*. As you can see, transformational leadership extends the frontiers of individual leadership or personal power - to incorporate transformational value added processes in the organization. So it would not be out of order to conclude at this juncture that individual leadership now has four elements, instead of the traditionally known three elements which have been; charisma, expertise, and position within a network. Thus, this fourth element is the awareness of the importance of productive knowledge and value of work, which extends the frontiers of individual leadership.

Again, between transformational leadership and charismatic leadership, it appears transformational leadership would be a better option when compared to charismatic leaders, owing to the former's potentials for transformational reciprocity between the leader and followers – especially as individuals are encouraged to acquire knowledge, expertise and skills to develop themselves in the process of transformational reciprocity. In the same line of reasoning, the *Social Exchange Theory (SET)* suggests that employees reciprocate leaders' behavior toward them with their own matched behaviors on a pro quo (mutual reciprocity) basis – as part of a social exchange relationship development process.[313]

The main reason for this exchange is to maximize benefits and minimize costs. In accordance with this theory, people measure the potential benefits and risks of social relationships, and will terminate or disregard the relationship when the risks outbalance the rewards. That said, social exchange relationships between leaders and their subordinates develop from such interactions, and are motivated by the mutual benefits derived from the exchanges.[314] This process can sometimes be referred to as reverse mentoring. The traditional notion of mentoring usually involves a more experienced mentor developing a junior mentee. *Reverse mentoring* recognizes that junior employees also have insights which more senior employees can benefit from. Using this approach, a multicultural workforce with its collective intelligence and knowledge can for instance, produce higher quality goods to meet customer needs more satisfactorily.[315] This kind of workforce environment contributes to internal team work; by transforming the workplace into a place of learning, practice of new ideas, behavioral testing, the application of new rules and organizational processes for greater competitive advantage of the company.[316]

If we can settle on the argument that transformational leadership does not only inspire followers to share a vision, but also empowers them to attain the vision by providing the necessary resources to develop their full personal potential,[317] then one can guess that transformational leadership, and more preferably, sustainability leadership is closely associated with what Rowe (2001) refers to as *effective strategic leadership*. He defines *effective strategic leadership* as the ability to influence others to voluntarily make day-to-day decisions that enhance the long-term viability of the organization, while at the same time maintaining its short-term financial stability.[318]

Charismatic leaders tend to arouse enthusiasm among followers, as the leader is attributed larger than life qualities, and hence worthy to be emulated and followed,[319] it however runs the risk of having organizational innovative capacity being constraint by the personal agenda, creative and reflective ability of the charismatic leader. Additionally, the influence process is one-way; as the personal inputs of the followers are dwarfed by the highly disproportionate lording of the charismatic leader's referent power, and where applicable, the leader's expertise. In a similar vein, Mittal (2015) argues that charismatic influence processes are primarily intended to align followers' vision with that of the leader – which makes it a one-way influence process. Meanwhile, in transformational leadership, there is mutuality in the leader-follower relationship that has the implications of both leader and follower being simultaneously "transformed."[320] To a certain extent, under *visionary leadership*, there is mutual transformation between the leader and those being led – especially as organizational control are maintained through socialization and the sharing of, as well as compliance with a commonly held set of norms, values, and shared beliefs.[321] Interestingly, these kinds of mutual transformation also exist in servant leadership. The servant leader believes in people, serves other's needs before their own, is receptive and nonjudgmental, and listens intently to followers.[322]

From the foregoing, Sultana, Rashid, Mohiuddin, and Mazumder (2013) posit that leadership is one of the leading determinants of the management of cultural diversity. And it's also necessary to have a transformative leadership position to bring the seeds of cultural diversity, which can provide a competitive advantage to the company.[323]

PERSONAL POWER VS. POSITIONAL POWER

Role of Networks, Information Flow, and Decision Rights Again, as we saw earlier in Table 2.3, since *information flow* and *decision rights* in the organizational buildings blocks are twice as powerful as *structure* and *motivators* in driving organizational effectiveness, the alignment scale in the balance for effective power bases should logically be tilted toward individual leadership qualities or personal power. Reason being that the ability to effectively manage *information flow* and *decision rights* are building blocks that are closely associated to the attributes of personal power or individual leadership, while *structure* has much in common with positional power (i.e., structural and institutional leadership).

Arguably, one of the main reasons for the reduction of Structural Power in the formal building block of the OrgDNA is the overwhelming strength of its synthesized template, referred to as Networks. Filled with varied connections and agendas of agents in the same network, and the conflicting constraints of agents arising out of the differences in the network; Kilpi (2017) maintains that no one agent chooses the number and strength of connections for other agents in the network. In this regard, it holds true that no agent can be in control of a complex system in the network – as it is partly dictated by the conflicting constraints arising out of the differences in the network. This is why the goal of networks is not primarily to reach consensus.[324] But to level the playing-field for balanced, productive, and sustainable socialization to thrive in the organization. To this end, Kim and Mauborgne (2014) suggest that by probably balancing the extremes, or by focusing on transforming the extremes in organizational collaboration networks - it would provide some kind of a check and balance to the people; in relation to actions and activities that exercise a disproportionate influence on performance in the organization. Clearly, structural power would suffer great limitations in effectively influencing followers in the face of such complex networks – that is, where there is a widening gap between network and structure.

Role of Motivators Interestingly, *motivators* appear to find itself at mid-way between personal power and positional power – since *motivators* such as reward are tools that is variably used by both personal power and positional power to achieve different goals at different points in time. In this regard, some scholars argue that awards and recognition reinforce positive attitudes and behaviors by recognizing exemplary leaders in creating an *inclusive and harmonious workplace.* On this strand of reasoning, they maintain that Organizations which already have employee awards in place can consider including values and behavior that foster inclusive and harmonious workplaces as part of the award criteria. On this keynote, some are the following *Tips* for achieving effectiveness in implementing awards and recognition:

- Be clear about the context and expectations
- The recognition should demonstrate to employees the specific behaviors or actions which are being recognized by the organization

- Team-based recognition or rewards can encourage teams to work toward a common goal and foster greater bonding.

However, historically, blending *motivators* with positional power to achieve certain goals have proven to produce positive results only in the short run, but can hardly be sustainable in the long run – since these are only changes on the surface – which goes with the ideas the leader has suggested, but without the employees believing in it, due to lack of effective power alignment. This is a common attribute with *pacesetting leadership* approach, where the core of pacesetting leadership style is high standards and achievement of objectives. The leadership puts short term goal at the center of its focus and uses them to drive up the performance of the organization.[325] At this level, it has some common characteristics identical to the *Tactician Approach* influence styles, but only focuses on the short-term aspects of it. In concurrence, Nyangena *et al.* (2019) argues this leadership style usually uses an element of rewards to motivate juniors to act and make quick returns. As a result, this style is effective in the short-run,[326] but some scholars believe it's among the influence styles that can be potentially having the most negative impact in an organization.[327]

Remember, we saw earlier that, for proper alignment of effective power bases, an employer needs to facilitate or enable the employee to cultivate his/her personal power bases and align it with the employer's positional power. But it would be unwise to hastily dismiss the virtues of reward in the context of positional power. The right thing to do will be to delve into the distinction of rewards in the context of *positional power* and rewards in the context of *personal power*.

Arguably, reward initiated through the use personal power or individual leadership in mind, and those initiated with the mindset of positional power would likely produce two vastly different outcomes; *as they would largely depend on the motive, and how they are systematically deployed for the benefit of the employee concerned and the organization as a whole.* In other words, it is imperative for reward schemes to be scaled along the lines of, or weighed against its potential performance – in terms of immediate and future prospects for employee engagement, employee commitment, and its positive relational alignment with organizational sustainability in the middle and long-terms.

As shown on Fig. 2.5, the effective ability to transform people in an organization that would have long-term sustainable impact has little to do with positional power, but has everything to do with personal power – that is, charisma, expertise, and position within a network, plus servant and transformational leadership skills. As transformational leadership embraces a deep rooted conviction on the part of employees, it logically makes the element of transformation an element of personal power. Exercising personal sources of power are more likely to result in commitment, while *reward power* and *legitimate power* are more likely to create a feeling of compliance in followers. Meanwhile, resistance often results from acting from a *coercive base of power.*[328] Failure to align personal power and positional power by the boss will only amount to *creating compliance*, but not necessarily an internal change on the part of the employee; and which amounts to ineffective power bases.

In a nutshell, since leadership involves the exercise of influence by one person over others, the quality of leadership is a critical determinant of organizational and managerial behavior.[329] As noted by the *Chief Financial Officer (retired) of a Global Airline, influencing* is selling ideas internally. The leader inspires, motivates and engages individuals, teams, and the whole organization. Recognizing talent and creating a climate of security for the group are essential.[330] To this end, with highly confirming results, Ghafoor *et al.* (2011) found that among the leadership styles, the association of *employee engagement* and *transformational leadership* tend to increase the level of employee engagement.[331]

2.4.2 Balancing the Hurdles to Execution and the White Space

Definition and Classification of Problems

One of the first key considerations in balancing the hurdles to execution and the white space is that of adopting a practical problem solving approach – as it turns out to be a powerful tool. Pereira (2015) defines a *problem as any deviation from the standard. It can also be defined as a gap between actual and desired conditions. Finally, a problem can also be defined as an unfulfilled customer need.*[332] From this perspective, Pereira (2015) argues we are often able to classify problems into one of three types, notably: (1) where standard is not achieved; (2) where standard is achieved, but a higher standard is required; and finally, (3) where performance standard varies:

1. Standard not achieved. For example, the standard = 100% on-time delivery and, we actually experience 83% a month on-time delivery. Therefore our actual performance doesn't meet the standard.
2. Standard is achieved, but a higher standard is required. For instance, actual on-time delivery is = 100% at 2 weeks lead-time. However, our customers may very well ask us to reduce our lead time to 1 week, while still maintaining 100% on-time delivery.
3. Performance standard varies. The third classification to problems occurs when performance standard varies. In other words, standard is not consistently achieved, or that unevenness is transforming the course of your value stream.[333]

Issues and Perspectives on Problem-Solving Approach

ISSUES

Johnson (2010) argues that every successful company is already fulfilling a real customer job with an effective business model, but only few organizations can explicitly articulate what that model really is.[334] Furthermore, without an explicit understanding of their business model, it makes it quite complex and complicated, notably; the premise behind its development, the way its various parts work together, and its strengths and weaknesses when in pursuit of new growth. Put in another way, organizations that are unable to explicitly articulate what their business model is, end up not knowing whether they can use their existing customer job to deliver on a new customer opportunity, or if that opportunity is a move into their *white space* requiring a new model.[335] This undoubtedly poses a serious challenge to execution.

Also, ideas may not be implemented because of a lack of human capital. The more a company is able to create product differentiation through strong branding, the more it reduces the chances of its products being substitutable by those of its competitors, and the more likely it will be willing to bear the risks associated with introducing innovative new products (Schwab, Sala-i-Martin, Samans, Blanke *et al.*, 2015–2016).

Still, the commercialization of ideas may be held back by inadequate internal processes and misalignment of different departments (Schwab *et al.*, 2015–2016). This is a phenomenon very common with firms in the developing world – especially in low-income countries.

While there are varying interpretations of the term "white space," Johnson (2010) sees white space as opportunities that are particularly useful for strategy formulation. That is, the opportunities that your company wishes to pursue that can only be addressed by *using a different business model than the one it is currently using.* Alternatively, a *white space* might present itself as a strategic imperative to address a competitive threat – such as the threat the Internet poses for newspapers' advertising-supported print-publishing business.[336]

Of course, the challenge of execution exists for any strategy, irrespective of whether it is a move into the white space requiring a new model or not. Additionally, companies, like individuals, often have a tough time translating thought into action irrespective of the type of business strategy in place. Undeniably, however, a move into the white space requiring a new model would theoretically pose greater challenges.

PERSPECTIVES

As we said, the challenge of execution exists for any strategy, irrespective of whether it is a move into the white space requiring a new model or not –

so this requires a practical problem solving approach among other variables. In this regard, Peirera (2015) identifies three arguments why practical problem solving approach is powerful, notably: (1) it enables organizations to have common understanding and definition of a problem; (2) it creates a workable framework for a standard problem solving approach; and finally, (3) it enhances and strengthens root-cause planning.[337]

With regards to the latter, planning root-cause analysis and implementation of mistake-proofing ensures that problems don't reoccur, as it becomes so disheartening to see a problem reappear a few months after it was thought to be solved. He argues that by using the logic of the PDCA Cycle (Plan, Do, Check, and Act) as illustrated in Fig. 2.6, the failure to plan properly almost always result in longer times to resolve problems.[338]

As shown on Fig. 2.6, the failure to plan properly almost always results in longer times to resolve the problem. In other words, disorganization rushes through the *planning phase* only turns out to pay for its hastiness in the *check* and *act phases*. On the other hand, when an organization takes the time to do slow, thorough planning solving approach, it is far more likely to solve their problems faster and more efficiently (Pereira, 2015).

This should be true to a significantly larger extent as errors in disorganization rush at the planning phase can only be mitigated by a highly efficient leadership. But even with a highly efficient team, solving errors arising out of disorganization rush at the planning phase often address problems at the superficial level, and subsequently, these problems tend to resurface in the future with even greater complexity - that is, by carrying alongside other problems which were not initially seen as problems that required prompt and special attention. That said, as leadership is a scare resource, only few organizations can lay hands on such leadership qualities or even nurture one - that can successful tackle such problems. However, if there should be any leadership that is easily adaptable to this impasse, then preferably, a sustainability leader is best placed to tackle

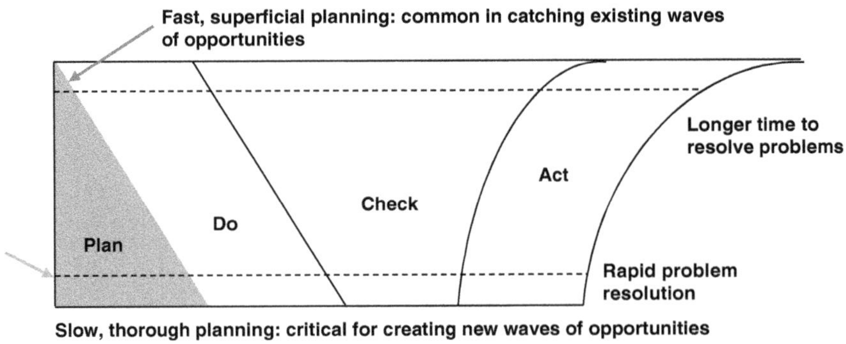

Figure 2.6 Merits of Proper Planning Phase Prior the Action Phase.
Source: Adapted from Pereira (2015).

these kinds of issues - by making use of early deployment of pre-emptive strategies that requires appropriate strategic foresight. From the foregoing, common sense requires preventive strategic measures in the form of proper planning - which is less expensive, reassuring and sustainable - rather than taking unnecessarily high risks that can only necessitate curative measures, which does not provide any insurance in terms of future value creation and sustainability – a risk that could be avoided in the planning phase in the first place.

Translating Thought into Action: The Hurdles to Strategy Execution

Neilson *et al.* (2008) found that unclear decision rights not only paralyze decision making but also impede information flow – blocking information flow results in poor decisions, limited career development, and a reinforcement of structural misalignments.[339] Engel and Weber (2007) argue that having made a decision to do something is not the same as actually doing it, which makes execution a separate element of the problem-solving cycle.[340] However, proper planning will significantly narrow the gap between execution and the problem solving cycle as we saw earlier. That said, Kim and Mauborgne (2014) argue that companies may face all or a subset of the following four hurdles: cognitive hurdle, resource hurdle, motivational hurdle, and political hurdle.[341]

COGNITIVE HURDLE

Cognitive Hurdle exists in a situation where an organization is wedded to the status quo that may have served the organization historically and employees have grown comfortable with them, and they are still making profits. But it may not be the paths to future profitable growth. As such, Kim and Mauborgne (2014) suggest that waking employees up to the need for a strategic shift, so as to ensure future profitable growth is crucial.

THE RESOURCE HURDLE

The Resource Hurdle is based on the notion of the limited resources, it is assumed that the greater the shift in strategy, the greater the resources it requires for execution. In this regard, Tsui (2018b) argues that *people* and *data* are pivotal to the success of an organization in terms of the Resource-based view of the firm (RBV).[342] He defines the RBV as referring to some resources typically possessed by organizations. They include physical assets; processes, cash and other types of equity; software and data; and *networks* – where the latter is mainly comprised of *people* (i.e., know-how, analytical, collaborative, and decision making.[343]

Additionally, the RBV works in synergy with the concept which he referred to as the VRIO (Value, Rarity, Imitability, and Organization). To him, *Organization* pertains to two things:

1. The ability to organize the necessary resources and deliver the value in a cost effective manner
2. The agility to be able to sense, adapt, respond, measure and continuously improve performance.[344]

Furthermore, he argues the pivotal role of people to the success of an organization can be perceived from three angles:

1. The skills and competencies that help to identify and generate the "value" for customers
2. The research that is carried out by people to generate new knowledge (which in turn leads to the development of new tools, systems, solutions, et cetera)
3. The protection of the firm's resource. It should be extremely very difficult to imitate a firm's resource, especially where loyal staff is a well-guarded resource for such an organization.[345]

In addition to the logic of the resource-based view (RBV) of the firm, Jay Barney argues that the appropriate use of valuable and rare resources possessed by firms, will lead to competitive advantage. And that if a firm can protect against *resource imitation, substitution or transfer,* the competitive advantage can even be sustained over long period.[346]

THE MOTIVATIONAL HURDLE

The Motivational Hurdle witnesses a situation where almost every organization faces the challenge of unmotivated staff at varying degrees. So the question is how do you motivate key players to move fast and tenaciously to carry out a break from the status quo? In concurrence, HBRAS (2020) found that most executives recognize that their organization has great influence over the happiness and well-being of their workforce, their survey shows that senior executives seldom takes the lead in crafting the policies and priorities to create a happier workplace. To this end, they argue that making workforce well-being a *priority* and then developing a strategy to *manage* it are two initial steps to driving workforce happiness[347] as follows:

- Make workforce well-being a priority
- Develop a strategy to listen and act on worker needs and concerns
- Establish mutual responsibility between individuals and the organization

- Maintain trust through transparency and honest communication
- Incentivize managers to prioritize their workers' well-being.[348]

THE POLITICAL HURDLE

The Political Hurdle arises predominantly out of opposition from powerful vested interests. As recounted by Kim and Mauborgne (2014), one manager commented that, "In our organization you get shot down before you stand up."[349]

In concurrence with the aforementioned, Nafei (2014) found that a structure with multiple organizational layers and narrow span of control often result in excess bureaucracy and bottlenecked decision making.[350] In this regard, Bordia *et al.* (2005) proposed two key remedies for solving excess bureaucracy and bottlenecked decision making. First, rooting out and eliminating or redeploying shadow staff-people performing tasks that duplicate what is performed elsewhere in the organization are a key to improve OP. Second, managing the career path and ensuring rotations in different geographies, functions, and roles – is important to the development of well-rounded senior managers.[351]

Gaining Support in Strategy Execution: Exercising Power

Arguably, some of the most common features encountered in the process of gaining support in strategy execution are; exercising power through influence styles and influence tactics. Exercising power can create reactions that are not always positive. It is hoped that it will have the most positive reaction, which is *commitment*. Remember! We saw earlier that *Commitment* is a synthesized template of *Motivators*. The latter is one of the common bases of the OrgDNA formal building blocks.

Firstly, in Exercising Personal Power we did raise the question earlier as to what happens when power is not exercised effectively. In response, Coomber (2018) argues that power is not exercised effectively in situations where someone makes a change only on the "surface" (the subordinate, for example) by going along with the idea the leader has suggested, but without believing in it. She goes further to argue that it can even get worse, as individuals can sometimes resist the request, which then creates problems for the leader in gaining support and getting things done. That being said, she settles on the position that the process of *commitment* starts by individuals internalizing the request, believing it is necessary and will be effective, and then identifying with the leader, and finally experiencing satisfaction with working with the leader who has placed the request.[352]

Secondly, the Exercise of Reward and Legitimate Power is more likely to create a feeling of compliance in followers. The challenge presented by the use of reward power is that some of the rewards may have limited perceived value to the employee, consequently igniting just a feeling of compliance and not commitment.[353] While, resistance often results from acting from a *coercive base of power;*[354] as opposed to the exercise of personal sources of power that are more likely to result in commitment.

Influence Styles and Influence Tactics

As mentioned, some of the most common features encountered in the process of gaining support in strategy execution are; exercising power, influence styles and influence tactics. In relation to influence, in his article titled "*7 Ways to Build Influence in the Workplace,*" Jayson DeMers who is the Founder and CEO of AudienceBloom argues that *influence has countless benefits, and is a particularly lucrative asset in the business world.* As such, no matter who you are, where you work, or what your professional goals are, achieving more influence in the workplace is critical for success in the following ways:

- Gaining influence on a team can help you work together more effectively.
- Gaining influence in a supervisory position can make you more respected and appreciated.
- Gaining influence in a meeting can make your voice more likely to be heard and acknowledged.[355]

In line with the aforementioned, Mittal (2015) holds that since the conceptualization of leadership revolves around influence and influencing, it is inherently culture-sensitive.[356]

On the bases of these arguments, DeMers (2015) suggests seven ways to build your influence, and these suggestions tend to cut across the traditional boundaries that spans through both the influence styles and influence tactics: (1) Build trust with your co-workers; (2) cultivate reliability through consistency; (3) assertiveness, and not aggressiveness in the way you get to sell your ideas; (4) work actively to show your flexibility while holding firm on your beliefs – negotiations and compromises are often the best ways to do this – that is, stay rigid in your beliefs when someone contradicts you, but work with them to find a mutually acceptable solution; (5) be personal – that is, avoid the temptation of trying to build your perceived authority by distancing yourself from the others, as this might only serve to alienate you and put you in a position where you are viewed with distrust or even resentment; (6) focus on actions rather than argument – for instance, if you're going to build influence in the workplace, you need to speak through your actions, and part of this comes into play when you build consistency; and (7) listen to others – remember that influence is a two-way street – the more you believe in the people around you and incorporate their ideas into your vision, the more they'll believe in your ideas and incorporate them into their work habits.[357]

INFLUENCE STYLES

In her reasoning, Coomber (2018) argues that when you need to get something done, but lacks the formal authority to do so; first, you must rely on your personal bases of power, which includes your likability or reference power; your network; and your expertise. Furthermore, as we saw earlier, when looking at styles of influence in general, Coomber (2018) identifies four basic methods that people can use, namely; the shortgun approach, the ingratiatory approach, the tactician approach, and the bystander approach.

Shortgun Approach The first, often called the "shortgun approach," happen in scenarios where someone is persistent and uses many different tactics of influence to get things done (Coomber, 2018). The risk involved here is that team members or colleagues at the workplace might interpret this kind of approach with high level of unpredictability. And as such, the subordinates or team members may increasingly grow suspicious of that person, which has the ultimate effect of eroding trust between the "shortgunner" and those who are being influenced or are supposed to be influenced.

The "shortgun approach" influence style seems to have some similar characteristics with those of *situational leadership*. In that, situational leadership style can be effective because it recognizes that not all junior staff and situations are similar.[358] However, Nyangena *et al.* (2019) found that this style is often considered more of a management style and can lead to confusion within the workplace if the leader keeps on changing from one approach to another.[359] To this end, it should be worth noting that situational leadership is neither synonymous to personal /individual leadership, nor is it fundamentally an integral component of personal bases of power, but a temporally optional leadership style that is occasionally available for use, alongside the exercise of personal power. That is, when it becomes absolutely necessary to do so for purposes of operational and tactical maneuvers, to the strategic benefit of the organization as a whole.

Ingratiator Approach The second, the "ingratiator" approach, occurs in situations where someone relies more heavily on friendliness, making the other person look good, and by building relationships to get things done (Coomber, 2018). Remember, we saw earlier that the "ingratiator" approach works apparently well with *charismatic leadership*. However, Rowe (2001) seem to extend this frontier to also include visionary leadership, where organizational control is maintained through socialization, and the sharing of, and compliance with a commonly held set of norms, values, and shared beliefs.[360] In addition, the "ingratiator" approach influence style seems to have many common attributes also identical to democratic leadership style.

To concur, Nyangena *et al.* (2019) found that democratic leadership style encourages and promotes engagement between the leader and the juniors; but the leader is still in charge of the final decisions. Nevertheless, the junior staff is involved with the tasks or causes of action, even though they might not have powers to make any decision. This type of leadership style removes the issues of low staff morale, and high employees turn over through the participatory approach involved.[361] In addition, they found that it can be effective in innovation and can boost employees' morale. However, the style does not necessarily create the most efficient systems that respond to issues swiftly enough.[362]

Tactician Approach People in the third strategic level, labeled the "tactician," generally rely on reason and expertise to convince others to take a particular course of action (Coomber, 2018). On this strand of reasoning, we can observe that the "tactician approach" influence style shares many common characteristics with *sustainable leadership* – as sustainable leaders lead by example.[363]

Bystander Approach The "bystander approach" is passive and does very little to exercise influence over others. Managers and subordinates can use all these styles when influencing others. From our discussion of power bases, it is clear that the ingratiator and the tactician approaches use the most effective power bases, and out of all four styles, Coomber (2018) argues that *the tacticians have the most favorable outcome* – perhaps because it explores the most of individual leadership skills or personal power. Yet most people fall into the bystander category, which suggests that many of us have more power to influence others than we are currently exercising (Coomber, 2018).

The "Bystander Approach" influence style seems to work well with *laissez-faire leadership styles.* To concur with this reasoning, Nyangena *et al.* (2019) found that with laissez-faire leadership, junior staffs are given the ultimate power to decide how they want to achieve their vision as set out by the leader. As such, the main work of the leader is to provide resources and advice to the subordinates when necessary.[364] This style helps to increase job satisfaction, although lack of structural restraints on the extent of ultimate power accorded to employees can be a source of challenge within the organization. Therefore, this approach of leadership requires well experienced, trained and enthusiastic employees to work efficiently.[365]

In a nutshell, the most favorable influence style is the *tactician approach,* but for maximum results, it needs to be almost always accompanied by some elements of the *ingratiator approach.* Meanwhile, in highly unstable and competitive business environments, the occasional inclusion of some vital elements of the *shortgun approach* could be an asset. Finally, the bystander approach would be most relevant for team members who are especially in the early phases of a new product innovation decision – as they will require greater flexibility to explore their creative potentials in the process of brainstorming for the best product ideas.

INFLUENCE TACTICS

In the research findings of Dellaert and Davydov (2017), they identify three broad categories of different tactics that a leader can influence the behaviors and opinions of others, notably: through facts and logic (logical appeals – the Head), through appeals to values and beliefs (emotional appeals – the Heart), or through support of them (cooperative appeals – the Hands). They argue that leaders use these influence tactics to implement decisions and to gain support for ideas and their vision.[366]

However, two other categories we might be missing out is the use of coercive persuasion and coercive abuse, which arise too often out of the excessive use of legitimate power (i.e., coercive persuasion) or the outright abuse of legitimate power (i.e., coercive abuse).] A study on retail sales managers' bases of *social power* indicated that non coercive sources of power were generally related to higher overall job satisfaction and satisfaction with the supervisor, whereas coercive power produced inverse effects on satisfaction and with the supervisor.[367]

The Five Broad Categories of Influence Tactics As mentioned, Dellaert and Davydov (2017) identified three broad categories of influence tactics, these are: logical appeals, emotional appeals, and cooperative appeals. In addition to these, there is also the use of coercive persuasion and coercive abuse.

1. Logical Appeals – involves tapping into people's rational and intellectual positions. Alternatively referred to as logical influencing tactics (the Head), it address people in a rational or intellectual way. Consequently, arguments and information such as facts and figures are brought forward in the best interest of the organization, the team, or the person.[368]
2. Emotional Appeals – connect your message, goal, or project to individual goals and values. Also known as emotional influencing tactics (the Heart) – it connects the communication or decision to a person's feelings of well-being or sense of belonging. The leader appeals to attitudes, values, a common purpose, ideals, and beliefs through inspiration or enthusiasm.[369]
3. Cooperative Appeals – involve collaboration, consultation, and alliances. Cooperative influencing tactics (the Hands) involve seeking advice and offering assistance. The leader reinforces the connection that he or she has with the others. Put in another way, in order to accomplish a mutually important goal, the leader extends a hand to others.[370]

4. Coercive persuasion - involves the excessive use of legitimate power in persuading others to do what they would normally don't want to do, by using force or threatening to use force. Remember! Coercive persuasion is different from rational persuasion. In rational persuasion, you present logical arguments and factual evidence to demonstrate that a request is reasonable.
5. Coercive abuse – involves the excessive use of force or threat of force which usually surpasses the boundaries of legitimate power, or it can be an outright abuse of legitimate power.

So let's proceed to fill the segments of influence tactics into their five broad categories of influence tactics as in Table 2.4. As mentioned, people respond in generally three ways to the exercise of power: *Commitment*, which is ideal; *compliance,* which is Okay; and

Table 2.4 Key Influence Tactics, Specific Segments, and Their Corresponding Reactions

Broad Categories of Influence Tactics	*Specific Power Segments*	*Corresponding Reactions in the Exercise of Power*
Logical Appeals	Rational Persuasion	Commitment
Emotional Appeals	Inspirational and or Personal Appeal	Compliance
Cooperative Appeals	• Bargaining • Building Coalition • Consultation • Just Ask! (a direct request) • Legitimacy backed by Rational Persuasion (this can be termed legitimate rational persuasion)	Compliance
Coercive Persuasion	• Legitimacy backed by the use of force or threat of force, or threat of exposure from lower level staff (that can be termed legitimate coercive persuasion)	"Cold War" Resistance
Coercive Abuse	• Coercive Abuse. This one is usually associated with excessive use of persuasive power outside the boundaries of legitimate power, or it can be an outright abuse of legitimate power	"Hot War" Resistance

Source: Author created.

resistance, which is undesirable. However, as we will see, there are intermittent reactions that can possibly pup up in between these response reactions.

Fitting the Specific Power Segments into their Broad Categories of Influence Tactics

Logical Appeals: Rational Persuasion The core characteristic of logical appeals is the *rational persuasion,* which explores the strongest arm of personal power. Remember, we said, personal power leverages the use of expertise, likeability, and peer or professional networks. Among which, *expertise* is the most powerful. In this regard, Coomber (2018) argues that rational persuasion is the preferred tactic of the tactician – as they resort to present logical arguments and factual evidence to demonstrate that a request is reasonable. Recall again that the "tactician" generally relies on reason and expertise to convince others to take a particular course of action. As you can already guess, rational persuasion would inevitably lead to *commitment* – every other thing being equal. Because, in addition to rational persuasion, you still need to acquire and retain power which aids you in achieving your goals. But to acquire and retain power, a leader must skillfully use organizational politics – that is, informal approaches to gaining power through means other than merit or luck.[371]

Again, we say rational persuasion would inevitably lead to *commitment* – granted every other thing being equal. Because in almost all organizations there are maliciously slippery individuals who would stop at nothing to push through their personal agenda, even if it's detrimental to the long term growth of other team members and the organization itself. And in situations where these individuals happen to form a clique; they would be as dangerous as lonely hyenas that have just teamed-up. With such vigor stemming from that coalition, they can harness superior psychological manipulative power – strong enough to suppress even the most powerful opponents.

This explains why no matter how transparent, productive, profitable and promising your ideas are as a leader; you should as a matter of necessity, also learn the inns-and-outs of organizational politics – else, even at the apex of your achievements, you might easily be rooted out by the forces of the "unknown" "unknowns" or genuine unknowns. One of the strategies to ensure lasting commitment through rational persuasion is by putting in place preventive measures that are: sufficiently subtle; constantly changing depending on the organizational dynamics; and should be inexhaustibly recyclable - so as to continually deter the recurrent possibilities of malicious organizational detractors from forming powerful alliances. But this can only be sustainable if it's done with utmost good faith. That is, by putting in place a sustainable scale balance, which rallies the concerns of employee wellbeing in alignment with those of the organization in the right strategic direction.

Emotional Appeals As mentioned, inspirational and or personal appeals are the main segments of emotional appeals. Besides connecting your message, goal, or project to individual goals and values; you might as well talk about how complying with your request will help them get job satisfaction, get promoted or benefit their clients. The response is usually that of *compliance.*

Cooperative Appeals Apparently this category is the home of the largest number of specific segments of leadership tactics among the five broad categories. While we might be looking too far away, it's interesting to begin with one kind of cooperative appeal that can be within reach of everyone – that is, just ask! or direct appeal.

Just ask! One of the most commonly used tactics in getting others to work with you – is *just asking*! This semantic[372] is sometimes known as the *low-hanging fruits initiatives* due to its high frequency of use, especially in addressing "small problems." Usually, a direct request is associated with compliance. As recounted by Coomber (2018), in a study of 370 different influence tactics, a direct request was second only to rational persuasion in frequency of use. Pereira (2015) also found that many companies utilize the "JUST-DO-IT" as the simplest problem solving approaches today.

Bargaining In bargaining, you offer the person you are influencing with benefits or favors in exchange for helping you out. Sometimes, people will invoke previous favors the person has done for them, or compromise in another area. You might offer specific public praise, or additional benefits (Coomber, 2018). As you can guess again, bargaining leads to *compliance.*

Building coalitions Another tactic is by building coalitions. Under this segment you can obtain support from co-workers, supervisors, or subordinates to convince the individual they need to do something. You might even make formal appeals to a higher level manager to encourage the person to comply with your request (Coomber, 2018). Building coalitions too, leads to *compliance.*

Consultation In consultation, you consult the person you are hoping to influence to get their feedback on the idea, with the hope that if they are involved in creating it, they will be more likely to participate. Sometimes, you might involve them in the training on how to do the job as part of the convincing process (Coomber, 2018). Obviously, consultation leads to *compliance.*

Coercive Persuasion – Legitimate Coercive Persuasion A mentioned, coercive persuasion is the exercise of legitimacy backed by the use or threat of force (that can be termed legitimate coercive persuasion). As Coomber (2018) observes, coercive persuasion might begin from lower-level tactics such as "being annoying" in asking and reminding the person, to threatening to report the individual to others, to withholding salary increases, et cetera. As noted, coercive persuasion is a tactic that unfortunately is used more often than it should be. As we can agree, coercive persuasion results in *resistance.* One can talk of *"cold war" resistance* to distinguish it from *"hot war" resistance* as in coercive abuse. In essence, coercive persuasion is not persuasion in the true sense of the word. It is in fact, using legitimate power to compel someone to act from without, rather than actually persuading someone to act from within as in rational persuasion.

Our use of the term *"cold war" resistance* presupposes that, much of the resistance seen under this power segment usually take the form of silent warfare and resentment, as opposed to hostile attacks and all-out war as in the reaction to coercive abuse.

Coercive Abuse As we saw on Table 2.4, coercive abuse is usually associated with excessive use or abuse of legitimate power (which can be termed outright abuse of legitimate power). This kind of abuse does not really have any real legitimate power that backs its execution. So it's just like hiding behind the canopy of a shadow legitimacy to inflict havoc on others. Coercive abuse is a subtle form of illegitimacy purporting to be legitimacy, and by extension, a subtle form of illegality purporting to be legality.

Consequently, with the absence of any real legitimate power to justify such excessive use of power, a situation of near anarchy is automatically established, and the playing-field is rife for a *"hot war" resistance* – an all-round war, filled with hostile attacks. Where the central referee becomes the player and the player becomes the central referee.

In concurrence with the aforementioned, Harris (2007) argues that leadership position should be seen as a central establishment, which acts as a source and center of unity. Therefore, it must take actions which hold the entire establishment together, addressing both the individual as well as group concerns;[373] such that the leader and the controlled team come to function as two sides of the same coin.[374]

The White Space and Strategic Action

The white space is new opportunities that could not be captured by a firm's existing business model. So such a firm would need to create a new business model to grab such new opportunities. However, what could be considered white space to one firm might not necessarily be white space to another firm.

EXPLORING OPPORTUNITIES BY FORMULATING APPROPRIATE BUSINESS MODELS

For a firm to enter the white space, it needs to understand two theoretical frameworks: strategic influencing, and strategic action. According Dellaert and Davydov (2017), *strategic influencing* requires mobilizing commitment to the organization's strategic direction – by inviting others into the strategic process, forging relationships inside and outside the organization, and utilizing organizational culture and systems of influence. While *strategic action* requires taking decisive and timely action consistent with the strategic direction of the organization, in spite of the ambiguity, complexity, and chaos inherent in organizational life.[375]

From the foregoing, Johnson (2010) argues that when formulating strategy to enter the white space, firms need to understand the following two conceptual limitations: (1) the need to acknowledge the limitations of their existing business model; and (2) the need to understand that one company's white space maybe another company's core competence.

The Need to Acknowledge the Limitations of their Existing Business Model Many companies have failed to enter their white space because they have not understood that the new opportunity could not be captured by their existing business model. Arguably, such new opportunities could as well be captured if they had formulated a different model. That said, due to the lack of exposure and mastery of such strategic foresighted needs, companies traditionally tend to retreat to their core operations and adjacencies, and unnecessarily limit themselves to only those strategic moves they could execute with their current models.[376]

One Company's White Space Maybe Another Company's Core Competence Companies also have to understand that one company's white space may be another company's core competence,[377] and failure to comprehend this reality makes the competitive threat greater. Alternatively, some competitor's white space may be a perfect fit with another company's current business model.[378]

So why is it so hard for a company to move beyond its core competence? In response, Johnson (2010) argues that it is very difficult and challenging for a business unit optimized to do one thing and at the same time optimized to do something else.[379] This becomes especially crucial, if you take into consideration the elements of the profit formula, as some of them are really very difficult to adjust. For instance, once a company has mastery of a winning way to sell a certain number of items at a specific price, using a specific process that involves a particular overhead expense, and operates at a certain velocity to produce a profit at a specific margin; it is hard to change any part of that without threatening the whole.[380] To this end, Johnson (2010) believes that another way to implement a new business model is the need to really do it in a separate unit.[381] This makes some business sense – implementing a new business model by using *a separate and dedicated unit* for it – will liberate the team's task force from the regular administrative or bureaucratic hurdles involved in corporate management. This new unit dedicated to implement a new business model is known as corporate entrepreneurship. Simply, corporate entrepreneurship refers to the efforts on the part of companies to foster entrepreneurs, innovation and new ventures in the corporate setting.[382]

NEW STRATEGY EXECUTION THROUGH "TIPPING POINT LEADERSHIP"

Confronted with the dilemma of executing new strategy, Kim and Mauborgne (2014) maintain that the conventional theory of organizational change rests on transforming the mass – requiring enormous resources and long time frames – which they argue, are luxuries that only few executives can afford.[383] On the contrary, *tipping point leadership* takes a reverse course. In this regard, to change the mass, it focuses on *transforming the extremes:* the people, acts, and activities that exercise a *disproportionate influence on performance.* By transforming the extremes, tipping point leaders are able to change the core, faster and at lower cost to execute their new strategy,[384] instead of navigating through the entire process of changing the mass.[385]

CORE COMPETENCES AND THEIR DIMENSIONS

A competence is said to be core if it creates competitive advantage, it is sustainable and not imitable in the short to medium term. It may be an asset or an intangible that creates value to a firm, and must be measurable. It is argued that firms enjoy the advantages of enhancing development where diversification can be possible, by reducing excess capacity of factors that are subject to market failure.[386] But core competences do have their own disadvantages, especially where they tend to inhibit development – referred to as core rigidities.

From the foregoing, *core rigidities* are core capacities that served the corporation well in the past, and are at a given time in the future they tend to present themselves as unproductive or inappropriate set of knowledge for an evolving environment. Consequently, clinging to such previous core capabilities does more harm than good and are actively creating problems. Simply put, *core competences* of the past can become *core liabilities* as the business environment changes – especially with the aggressive invasion of powerful competitors into the existing market. The situation can be further compounded by the increasing complexity of consumer choices. In this regard, Baumgartner (2009) argues that when doing the core competency analysis, it is important to map the core competences to the strategic question – *why is this profitably sustainable?* In response, he opines that the sustainability of a core competency may be found in bundles of competences rather than in individual competences – which calls for creative collaboration as an essential element of organizational innovation.[387]

Mastering Conflict in Strategy Execution

The achievement and stability of an organization depends on the ability of conflict recognition and the competency of managers in managing conflict at workplaces.[388] In this regard, Engel and Weber (2007) found that while novel problem-solving modes can be constructed on the spot, this probably does not happen very often. Instead, most people most of the time will select between existing, tried-and-true problem solving modes for the present task and available resources, and employ the problem-solving mode that provides the best match.[389]

On the same platform, Soieb *et al.* (2013) argue that disengaged employees are more likely to have some extent of controversy with their superiors, while an engaged workforce means less conflict.[390]*Patrick Lencioni argues* that it's not finance, not strategy, not technology, but teamwork that remains the ultimate competitive advantage, both because it is so powerful and so rare.[391]

But, before delving into this idea of teamwork, Carper (2014) cautions that it is not only important that people understand their differences with others and try to adapt accordingly, but also important for people to recognize their boundaries.[392] In a similar vein, a survey carried out by Atsan (2016) revealed that many entrepreneurial failures were largely due to unfavorable interpersonal relationships which can be linked to lack of trust as a contextual factor,[393] and that interpersonal trust is a must for a sustainable business.[394]

However, Carper (2014) contends that although it is important to attempt to pursue open lines of communication, including mutual understanding, it is not a rule of thumb that one should adopt the value orientations of the other person. As it goes, sometimes, there are situations in which it is easy to adapt and even adopt a cultural practice of someone else that makes sense. On the contrary, there are situations in which one feels there is a line which one cannot cross. Such situations tend to represent value orientations, which are closer to the core of who you are; and therefore, should not be compromised. This should also be the case with the shared values of one's company.[395] This is also a critical point for self-scrutiny in deciding one's own adaptability prior to accepting an assignment especially in someone else's country.[396]

Characteristics of Dysfunctional and Cohesive Teams

Essentially two types of teams have been identified in the management literature. These are the cohesive team and the dysfunctional team. But the starting point for understanding the characteristics of dysfunctional and cohesive teams is by understanding the essential ingredients of collaboration. According to Emergency Management Institute - EMI (2021), collaboration is the process of shared creation that occurs when people produce something by combining efforts, sharing ownership of the outcome, making joint decisions, and exchanging expertise, information, and resources.i As a result, they argue that on any effective team, people working together can accomplish more than individuals working separately. Put in another way, significant results can be achieved through collaboration, and that there is nothing routine about this process. Because when it occurs, there is something new that wasn't there before.ii

The Dysfunctional Team

In their analysis of a dysfunctional team, Cameron et al. (2017) found that it is being dominated by the following characteristics, notably:

- Focus on personal goals rather than the team goals (i.e., "ME" focused);
- unhealthy competition;
- not being open or honest;
- poor results;
- lack of trust (finger-pointing);
- pessimistic (blame is rife); and
- no collective accountability (few opportunities to learn, meetings are dreaded).[397]

In addition, they found that these dominant characteristics in turn throw some light on five behaviors of a *dysfunctional team,* namely:

1. inattention to results;
2. avoidance of accountability;
3. lack of commitment;
4. fear of conflict; and
5. absence of trust.[398]

From the five critical issues earmarked above, it is clear that dysfunctional teams are counterproductive to any organization, and can potentially corrode any ingenious business initiative – be it at the level of business strategy, innovation, and the portfolio management of innovation. Meanwhile, a cohesive team does the exact opposite.

The Cohesive Team

With regards to *cohesive teams,*Patrick (2012) reveals five behaviors model and describes them as follows:

1. Trust – Trust one another. When team members are genuinely open and honest with each other, it forms a safe environment that creates and builds vulnerability-based trust.
2. Conflict – engage in conflict around ideas. When there is trust, team members engage in unfiltered, constructive debate of ideas.
3. Commitment – commit to decisions. When team members are able to offer opinions and actively debate ideas, they feel heard and respected, and will be more likely to commit to decisions.
4. Accountability – hold one another accountable. When everyone is committed to a clear plan of action, they will hold each other accountable.
5. Results – focusing on achieving collective results. The ultimate goal is the achievement of results, unlocked through implementing the five behavior model's principles of Trust, Conflict, Commitment, and Accountability. Furthermore, ideally, for a team to excel, all members must put team goals ahead of their goals.[399]

However, we should understand that what Lencioni (2002) suggests as characteristics of a cohesive team are practically ideal scenarios. For example, from an *internal perspective,* it would be practically very rare to see a scenario where all team members could put team goals ahead of their goals. In such a situation, while a vast majority would want to do so, some team member might be hypocritical by having their own personal agenda in the making, while others would be passive participants to the team activities. These kinds of people must always exist in an organization, but the challenge of management is to reduce to the lowest possible level, the overall potential negative impact on team dysfunctions in an organization. That being said, every resilient organizations would strive for the best, and not for the better.

Furthermore, from an *external perspective,* cross-cultural issues must be taken into consideration, as the five behaviors model may not be advantageous in its entirety, all the time in certain cultures. For example, in some developing countries especially in Africa and Latin America, a frequent open debate of ideas might likely be wrongly interpreted by employees, and could lure these employees to thinking that Management is incompetent – or lacks a sense of direction. As in some of these cultures, there is the general belief that a manager is simply there to give direction and not really to openly solicit employees' opinions on critical issues. That said, while open debate should be encouraged, the culture of the environment where the business operates should be carefully calibrated and weighed before advancing open debates on certain issues in the organization.

From the foregoing, putting together a reliable cohesive team requires high level of collaboration. But attaining and preserving such status quo isn't always easy. That being said, the Emergency Management Institute – EMI (2021) argues that among the greatest challenges to collaboration are turf concerns and mistrust. Turf Concerns. For collaboration to work with regards to turf concerns, EMI (2021) argues that the parties need to be assured that they have everything to gain and nothing to lose. In this direction, they have identified four turf concerns. But three out of the four turf concerns are of much relevance to our context. These include: (1) Conflicting goals and measures; (2) Need for power; and (3) Competition for resources.(1) Conflicting goals and measures. Parties often disagree about what should be accomplished and how to measure success. (2) Need for power. People with the need for power are likely to feel threatened by collaboration. An individual's need for power may be derived from; (1) a perceived need to control in order to achieve high standards for the organization or oneself; (2) personal satisfaction from having control over others; and (3) desire for recognition and status from others.(3) Competition for resources. Collaboration works best when the parties are not competing for the same resources. In this regard, each party should be seen as contributing something of value (e.g., resources, enthusiasm, influence, expertise, et cetera) to the collaborative process.Mistrust. Finally, as common sense will let us know, mistrust, which is the opposite of trust of fellow team members, can get in the way of collaboration.

In conclusion, one of the best approaches is to properly master the OrgDNA informal building blocks. It is essentially from this angle that leadership can have tips as to when there is a green light, red light or yellow light in the process of incorporating the five behaviors model in the life of the organization.

Trust

Essentially, what we mean by trust is that teammates need to get comfortable *being vulnerable* with one another.[400] In this regard, the expected trust behaviors could look like the following:

a. Team members openly admit their weaknesses and mistakes
b. Team members quickly and genuinely apologize to one another when they say or do something inappropriate or possibly damaging to the team
c. Team members know about one another's personal lives to a considerable extent, and are comfortable and/or interested in discussing them.[401]

Conflict and their Characteristics

Resolving conflict and disagreement at the workplace seem to share much in common with *affiliate leadership* style. To this end, Nyangena *et al.* (2019) found that the objective of *affiliate leadership* style is to bring harmony in the workplace and ensure there is a healthy relationship in the organization. As a result, this leadership style is applied in conflict resolution and is effective in overcoming disagreements.[402]

Good Conflict and Bad Conflict

When we talk of conflict in an organization we make a distinction between *good conflict* and *bad conflict*.Good conflict or productive conflict would manifest the following characteristics:

- Productive conflict is focused on ideas and concepts
- It is not about mean-spirited personal attacks
- No one holds back, no one is afraid to speak up because they TRUST one another. However, cultures differ greatly and vary in what we understand as trust. The best idea is to understand clearly how "TRUST" is perceived in the culture of the people.
- People engage in passionate debates, although it can sometimes be uncomfortable.
- During team meetings, the most important and most difficult issues are put on the table to be resolved; and it is in pursuit of the best possible and most creative solution or answer.

Bad conflict is seen as the one that is destructive in nature. In this sense, conflict is said to be destructive when it undermines information sharing, motivation or engagement in group discussion or even trust. Essentially, any synthesized template of the OrgDNA common bases that is undermined is a potential ground for destructive conflict – notably; norms, mindsets, commitments, and networks.

Cold and Hot Conflicts

Out of control emotions (or personal mean-spirited attacks): Based on the perspective of team dynamics, Moye (2018) observes that in deciphering teams with "bad" conflict, most people tend to limit their understanding of it as the "heated" kind; where people are not listening to each other, talking to each other, or maybe, even emotionally out of control (by responding to differences with open personal attacks). Clearly, these are signs of what is known as amygdala hijack - which is characterized primarily by "fight" or "flight" responses.

Artificial harmony (cold conflicts): In the observation of Moye (2018), another type of "bad" or "destructive" conflict takes the form of what is referred to as *artificial harmony*. And the observable behavior looks like this: A group of people sitting around a table, arms crossed, maybe looking at their watches, simply nodding their heads to whomever is speaking, even when they disagree with that speaker. Obviously, that's a pretty cold meeting, as it's a team that avoids revealing differences, and shows they are avoiding conflict. It is just as detrimental as one at all-out war.

Consequently, both versions – that is, *out of control emotions* (hot conflicts) and *artificial harmony* (cold conflicts) tends to have the same outcome. In this sense, where differences are not deliberated, and people are not engaged and motivated to work through differences – turns to implant mistrust, which is a silent element of conflict.

The Conflict Sweet Spot

As the descriptions of both good and bad conflict behavior is characterized by each of the team missing out to create a convenient forum so as to iron out their differences through reasoning, there is the need to pull people in each side of the teams who are in hot or cold conflict toward the center. This center is known as the "conflict sweet spot" as shown on Fig. 2.7.

Featuring in the conflict sweet spot is open, active, energizing discussions and deliberations of differences; where individuals feel comfortable in revealing different perspectives about tasks, processes, and decisions – and such differences are considered, listened to, and resolved through reasoning (Moye, 2018).

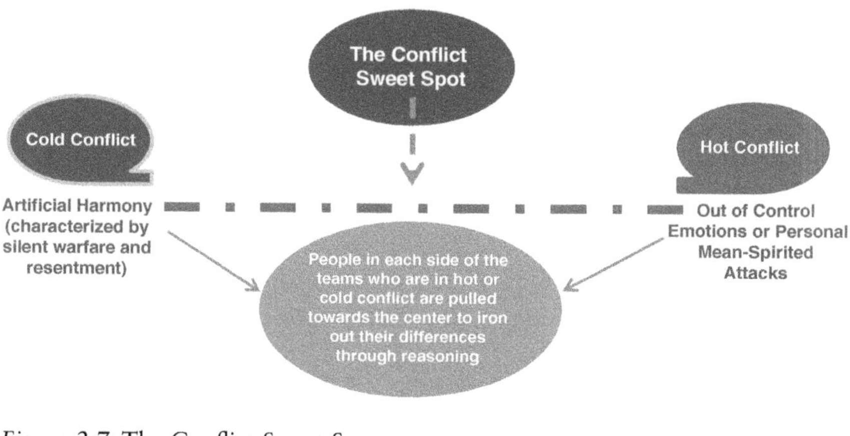

Figure 2.7 The Conflict Sweet Spot.
Source: Adapted from Moye (2018).

How to Get To the Conflict Sweet Spot – General Perspective

Knight (2013) found that there is a vast amount of research that highlights the importance of giving time and space for divergent thinking, diverse opinions and challenge, creating an innovative organization and for creative problem solving. But the reality is that, will disagreeing with someone really help sharpen both of your thinking and get a better result?[403] That said, she contends that in its most extreme form, conflict can make employees feel they have done a bad job even when they have not.[404]

On this keynote, Knight (2013) further reveals that traditionally, conflict within teams can be categorized as either "relationship conflict" (for example, personal taste, preference, values, style) or "task conflict" (for example, procedures, policies, interpretation of facts). Low levels of *task conflict* can aid creative activity and divergent thinking, while even the smallest levels of *relationship conflict* have been found to have a profoundly negative effect on team dynamics, productivity, and satisfaction.[405] In this regard, Viki (2018) believes that a good process should allow teams to change direction based on learning, and stop the project if they need to, without negative consequences for them.[406] In the same line of reasoning, Knight (2013) contends that *unless a team has pre-existing high levels of trust, openness and feelings of psychological safety, task conflict can lead to relationship conflict.*[407]

From observation, "relationship conflict" is usually closely associated with "out of control emotion or personal mean-spirited attacks" – and could be quite devastating (a "bad" or "destructive conflict"). Meanwhile, "task conflict" is usually more closely related to "artificial harmony" – where team members usually avoid revealing differences (this is another version of "bad" conflict). And if not addressed quickly enough, it can degenerate into a "relationship conflict" – even to an all-round war, which is an extreme situation in a "relationship conflict." That said, Moye (2018) suggests three main points to get to the conflict sweet spot: (1) diagnose hot and cold behavior in self and others; (2) remedy behaviors in individuals; and (3) guide teams toward the sweet spot.

In guiding teams toward the sweet spot, Moye (2018) suggests you lead with a balance of *Inquiry* and *Advocacy,* and proposes the following useful tips:

- Advocacy. She sees advocacy in this context as championing your idea or opinion because you believe in it;
    - Because it is "most right" – and as such, your idea must win
    - Because it is downplaying weaknesses (i.e., when you advocate your idea, you are downplaying its weaknesses)
    - Because it is defending your position (i.e., your effort is focused on defending your position).

- Inquiry. She sees inquiry a as viable tool that can bring the desired effect of pulling people who are in hot and cold conflict toward the middle of the conflict sweet spot;
  - Because it promotes collaborative problem solving
  - Because it promotes critical thinking
  - Because it focuses on listening and building dialogue around conflicting ideas.

In response to the question as to when should you use inquiry versus advocacy? Moye (2018) opines that, whenever conflict is anywhere other than the sweet spot you should use inquiry (ask questions). As we saw earlier, this can have the desired effect of pulling people who are in hot and cold conflict toward the middle of the conflict sweet spot. On the contrary, by implication, if the conflict is within the sweet spot, then advocacy is the preferred choice.

Coming back to inquiry, Moye (2018) argues that if you have a team that was built on *good conflict norms* and *psychological safety,*inquiry should be enough to get the best ideas on the table. In this regard, Knight (2013) reasons that, commonly shared values and goals can help organizations pull in the same direction, set objectives and give a sense of purpose for the championing of best ideas. In addition, by setting out *the types of behaviors that are valued before solving a problem,* a manger can help set the tone for a meeting and affect the outcome.

Managing Conflict in a Cross-Functional Team – Integrating Strategic User Experience Design into Creating Value

In his article, "*Creating business value through strategic user experience design,*"Kreitzberg (2019) argues that interactive products are developed by cross-functional teams. This means that individuals on the team come to the table with different perspectives and priorities. Inevitably, this will lead to conflict that must be resolved. Lack of alignment among team members is one of the most serious problems leading to disappointing project results.[408] He believes that at a minimum, cross-functional teams have a *business lead* and a *technical lead.* Usually missing from this minimal team is someone representing the *end user* or customer (the UX person).[409] Thus, ignoring end users is a tried and true way to fail.[410]

The role of the end user in product design is known as co-creation. Gustafsson, Kristensson, and Wittel (2012) argue that co-creation is largely about communicating with customers in order to understand their future needs. As a result, co-creation is becoming increasingly popular among companies, and that intensive communication with customers is generally seen as a determinant of the success of a new service or product.[411] In order to understand the value of customer co-creation in service innovation, they analyzed customer co-creation based on four dimensions of communication

– frequency, direction, modality, and content.[412] The findings also suggested that companies should create dialogues with customers during the value creation process and meet and communicate with customers in the customers' own environment or through various media, such as social media.[413] Meanwhile, the role of the *business lead* is to represent the interests of a variety of business stakeholders, and role of the *technical lead* is to represent a variety of technical participants such as developers, architects, and quality assurance.[414]

In a further development, Kreitzberg (2019) argues that although the players on each dimension share the common goal of producing a high-quality product, there are inherent conflicts among them. These conflicts come from different world views and priorities as follows:

- Typically, the business players (business lead) are interested in such element as costs, revenue, market share, and time to market.
- Technology players (technology lead) are concerned with such elements as ease of development or configuration, maintainability, and reliability.
- End users (customers) are interested in extreme usability – products that deliver the functionality they envision in an efficient and easy to use package.[415] Gustafsson *et al.* (2012) argue that this finding also corroborate those of previous studies – as the results of the analysis point toward the need for increased understanding of the circumstances surrounding the customers' value-creation processes.[416]

Consequently, creating and maintaining alignment among the three sets of players – business lead, technical lead, and end user – is essential to a successful project (Kreitzberg, 2019). Because every time there is a decision to be made, these priorities are likely to clash as team members will favor their own priorities. This may not be in either the best interests of the project as a whole or the product being developed.[417]

Now the question is; *how do you find the sweet spot?* The sweet spot balances the three priorities: business, technical and user experience. This means that the decision-making process needs to take into account that which is most important for major decisions. But there is the usual tendency for team members to look at decisions through their own particular lens. For instance, a development team will tend to support decisions that make development easier or less risky, while the business team will focus on business goals and ROI.[418] So to solve the problem, there is need for balance between *business, technical and the end-user experience.*Kreitzberg (2019) suggests three ways to achieve better balance[419] between the three priorities:

1. Treat end user or customer (UX design) as strategic rather than operational.

2. Maintain alignment among team members around a common vision.
3. Agree as a team on how decisions will be made (clarifying decision rights).

On these keynotes, Kreitzberg (2019) argues that treating the *end user* or customer as *strategic rather than operational is critical,* as they are often treated as a purely tactical need in which a designer's job is to lay out the prescriptions on behalf of customers.[420] This has often proven to be a fatal mistake. To concur, Gustafsson *et al.* (2012) argue that employees, whether frontline or elsewhere in the organization, *must communicate with the customers in order to understand the experiences that create value for them;*[421] otherwise they will *lose their capacity to generate ideas for the next generation of offerings that will serve their customers.*[422] Kreitzberg (2019) argues that for the end user's role to be strategic, it means listening to customer needs and translating those needs into a conceptual approach that the technical and business teams can use to guide their thinking and decision-making.[423] Similarly, according to *VoterTide,* it is easy to get tricked into thinking your product design is cool, so you have to pay attention to your customers and adapt to their needs.[424]

Finally, Kreitzberg (2019) arrives at a conclusion that the conflict in a cross-functional team can be a positive or negative force. If conflict results in churn (often disapproving) and the inability to make good decisions, it will bring the project down. Or, at least, impair its outcome. On the other hand, if conflict is positioned as problem solving that incorporates diverse perspectives, the team dynamics will be more positive. This will set the stage for a much better, shared understanding of the problem and agreement on a more robust, higher quality solution.[425]

Tips and Strategies for Managing Conflicts within Your Team

Even when teams are effective in working well together, conflicts can arise. Within diverse teams, conflicts often result from differences in values, social norms and languages – these are common characteristics in *"relationship conflict."* It is important to resolve matters quickly so that they do not spiral downwards to affect team cohesion.

The following are some tips on resolving workplace conflicts arising from differences in team members' backgrounds, values and communication styles:

1. Identify the root of the problem and clarify each party's position to avoid ambiguity
2. Facilitate understanding of the other party
3. Involve a neutral mediator
4. Commit to the solution

5. Resolve conflicts quickly.

Understanding Amygdala Hijack and the Fight or Flight Response

According to Cuncic (2018), the term "amygdala hijack" was coined by psychologist Daniel Goleman in his 1995 book, titled *Emotional Intelligence: Why It Can Matter More Than IQ*. Goleman used the term to recognize that although we have evolved as humans, we retain an ancient structure in our brain that is designed to respond swiftly to a threat. That said, while this ancient structure was designed to protect us, it can interfere with our functioning in the modern world where threats are often more subtle in nature.[426]

Definition and Functions of the Amygdala

The *Oxford Advanced Learners Dictionary of Current English* defines the amygdala as either of the two areas in the human brain that are linked to *memory, the emotions,* and the *sense of smell.*[427] Among other functions, this structure is involved in the fear circuit of the brain, responsible for the fight-or-flight response that causes you to respond to threats (Cuncic, 2018). Put in another way, amygdala turns on fight or flight, and stores memories of the event in the human brain.[428] Therefore the role of fear is very crucial. For some people, their biggest fear may be death. For others, it may be public speaking. In fact, most humans will have at least one or more things that they fear in life, no matter how dangerous or innocent the object of that fear may be.[429] But there is a reason for that. Fear often helps us with self-preservation. We feel fear, as well as related emotions, in order to protect ourselves from danger and to heighten our awareness. This awareness is thought to be controlled by a section of the brain known as the amygdala.[430]

That being said, the amygdala is responsible for the perception of emotions such as anger, fear, and sadness, as well as the controlling of aggression. The amygdala helps to store memories of events and emotions so that an individual may be able to recognize similar events in the future. For example, if you have ever suffered a dog bite, then the amygdalae may help in processing that event and, therefore, increase your fear or alertness around dogs. The size of the amygdala is positively correlated with increased aggression and physical behavior.[431]

Preventing Amygdala Hijack

In the reasoning of Cuncic (2018), the best way to overcome amygdala hijack is to prevent it from happening in the first place. Managing the functioning of your amygdala is part of developing emotional intelligence, and it is something that fortunately may improve with age.

Emotional intelligence is the opposite of an amygdala hijack. A person who is emotionally intelligent has strong connections between the *emotional center* of his or her brain and the *executive (thinking) center.* Emotionally intelligent people know how to de-escalate their own emotions as well as those of others by becoming engaged, focused, and attentive to their thoughts and feelings (Cuncic, 2018).

Coping with Amigdala Hijack

It can take up to three to four hours to return to a normal state after an attack. However, Cuncic (2018) argues that there are things you can do to speed up that process and get control of your emotional state as follows:

- Name your emotions as you experience them. This helps to engage the thinking part of your brain and trigger mindfulness.
- Take deep breaths from your abdomen. Breathing deeply will help to bring oxygen to the brain and slow you down.
- Draw on mindfulness. Look around you and notice things in the environment. This will help you to move out of your head and back into the situation.
- Take a timeout. If you are truly feeling out of control, excuse yourself from the situation you are in to get a hold of your emotions.

2.4.3 "I Exist, and Then I Understand, I Understand and Then I Exist"!

The Psyche of Change Management

Many people have often asked, and are still asking why change management is so difficult to understand and implement? Engel and Weber (2007) contend that the human mind is not a general problem-solving machine. As a result, instead of deliberately and analytically processing all available information to calculate which action will provide the greatest expected utility, people can and do rely on routines, rules, roles, or effects when deciding what to do in a given situation. They can also bring in information technology or experts to provide advice.[432]

From the foregoing, Mintzberg (1990) maintains that although effective managers have to adapt at responding quickly to numerous and varying problems. But the danger in managerial work is that managers will respond to every issue equally – and too often abruptly. This means that managers would rarely ever work the tangible bits and pieces of information into a comprehensive picture of their world.[433] Atsan (2016) perceives this as one of the internal causes that can be attributed to *managerial incompetence or poor management.* He refers to internal causes as those decisions/actions that are under management's control, while external causes are events that are outside of management's control, and that in most cases, a complex mixture of causes contribute to business failure.[434] Meanwhile, *poor management* is referred to the failure of the management to be able to ensure that problems are identified promptly and the correct solutions applied, so as to give the company the best possible chance of survival and growth.[435]

In a related vein, Mintzberg (1990) suggests that to create a comprehensive picture of their world, managers can supplement their own models with those of specialists. For example, economists would describe the functioning of markets, operations researchers would simulate financial flow processes, and behavioral scientists would explain the needs and goals of people – the best of these models can be searched out and learned.[436] Again, he suggested that in dealing with complex issues, the senior manager has much to gain from a close relationship with the organization's own management scientists (management analysts) – especially as management scientists tend to have something important that the manager lacks. Guess what! Managers lack the time to probe complex issues.[437]

In this regard, managers have the information and the authority, while analysts have the time and the technology.[438] Therefore a successful working relationship between the two will be effectively handled when the *manager learns to share information* and the *analyst or management scientist learns to adapt to the manager's needs.*[439] This works in synergy with the argument that alternative processes used to arrive at a decision would not be of much general interest if the outcome of such decisions were not influenced by the mode in which the decisions were arrive at.[440] To concur, Engel and Weber (2007) argue that there is indisputable evidence to the effect that - how we decide, often determines what we decide.[441] Engel and Weber believe this is the reason why institutional designers frequently attempt to influence the choice of the problem-solving or decision-making mode.[442]

Based on the observation that all humans first come into existence before understanding change, what to be changed, and how to implement change – provides an initial clue to the answer to the question why change is so difficult to understand and manage? Table 2.5 provides some information about the eight stages man. This is prima facie, a good foundation to appreciate the understanding of change and managing change.

But to tackle the challenges of change, it is primordial to understand that change itself needs to be first and foremost, understood as a big picture by the problem solver, from there he/she can progress to examine the specifics of the problem before the appropriate action comes into existence. From the foregoing, "humans" and "change" function at opposite directions to each other – this is the underlying mystery behind change and change management.

Table 2.5 Eight Stages of Man

Psychological Stage		*Approximate Age*	*Crisis*
Infancy:	Oral-sensory	Birth to 18 months	Trust/mistrust
	Anal-muscular	18 months to 3 years	Antonomy/shame, self-doubt
Start of formal education with naivety:	Genital-locomotor control	3 to 5 years	Initiative/guilt
Early stages of formal education:	Latency	5 to 13 years	Industry, competence/inferiority, failure
Teenager	Puberty	13 to 21 years	Identity/role confusion
Young man/woman:	Genitality (young adulthood)	21 to 40 years	Intimacy/isolation
Middle aged	Productivity (adulthood)	40 to 60 years	Generativity/self-absorption, stagnation
Old age:	Maturity	60 years to death	Integrity, self-worth/despair

Sources: Adapted from "Ericson's Eight Stages of Man" in Albert, D., Block, A. M., Bruce, B. B. et al. Dorland's Illustrated Medical Dictionary, 32nd Edition, Philadelphia: Elsevier – Saunders, 2012, p. 1759; No Sweat Shakespeare. "The Seven Ages of Man." 2020, *Nosweatshakespeare.com;* and other sources.

As shown in Fig. 2.8, the *existence* of the human species is ascertained from birth, from that stage he/she starts *understanding* nature and other things around him before progressing to learn why and how other complex mechanisms surrounding life do operate. On the contrary, successfully designing change management strategies begins with understanding and mastering strategic foresight. This means that the change initiator should have the ability to see a clear picture with some commensurate level of accuracy, about how the end of the tunnel would look like if the change is implemented. This helps to properly guide management decision along a time-proven organizational problem solving mode. This is critical to *understanding* the inherent challenges in the change management process, such as: what is going to be changed? Who will be impacted by the change and to what extent? What's the degree of willingness/resistance to change? And above all, what has triggered such refusal to change (if applicable)? These are essential questions to be solved before one begins to take action.

Once the action to be taken, follows a logical and realizable pattern toward its desired results, then change is said to *exist*.

Furthermore, as shown on Fig. 2.8, the process of understanding change in humans begin from birth (human existence), and progresses to the understanding of the complex mechanisms surrounding the essence of life. Meanwhile, the process of organizational change management instead begins by tapping from the wisdom of an accurate long-term view of the problem. This provides better or accurate insight into understanding the critical issues inherent in the change management and how to control the change process, before progressing to *invoking the implementation of change action* via a thorough understanding and itemizing of the specific challenges involved. This shows that the natural tendency for change in humans – as an individual, and the inherent characteristics of the change management process in organizations as a collectivity of individuals; tend to function in opposite direction. The situation even becomes more complicated when it involves more individuals whose perceptions about organizations and culture are widely divergent.

Strategic Foresight and the Business of Shaping the Future

The Center for Strategic Excellence (2009) maintained that foresight is concerned with long-term futures, as well as the production of knowledge about alternative futures. As such, foresight is *intended to empower decision makers to consciously expand the boundaries of their own perception with regard to future challenges.*[443]

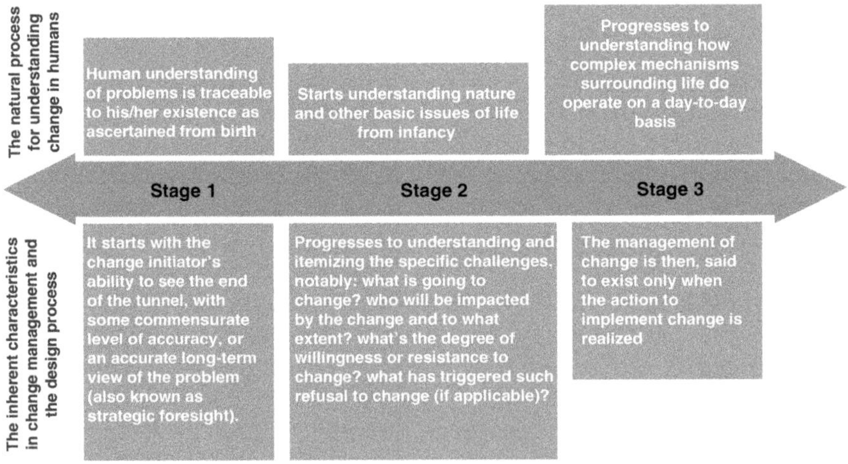

Figure 2.8 How "Humans" and "Change" Function at Opposite Directions to Each Other.
Source: Author created.

In the same direction, but from a different platform, Taddeo and Floridi (2018) found that foresight methodologies can never map the entire spectrum of opportunities, risks, and unintended consequences of systems, but may identify preferable alternatives, valuable courses of action, likely risks, and mitigating strategies.[444] They argue that this perspective has a dual advantage. Firstly, as an *opportunity strategy*, foresight methodologies can help leverage ethical solutions. Secondly, as a *form of risk management*, they can help prevent or mitigate costly mistakes, by avoiding decisions or actions that are ethically unacceptable. This will lower the opportunity costs of choices not made or options not seized for lack of clarity or fear of backlash.[445]

Futures Studies vs. Foresight

The difference between "futures" and "foresight" is subtle. Futures Studies consist of pondering possible, plausible, probable and preferable futures. *"The future starts today, not tomorrow" – Pope John Paul II.* Foresight is about strategizing how to navigate a course in the face of uncertainty. Both processes encompass many techniques that think about or use the future as a strategic planning tool. Futures Studies is not an exercise concerned with getting it right or wrong; it is about using imagination to escape from the present and drive innovation by thinking about different ways of doing things. The ultimate aim of Futures Studies is to inform decision-making by exploring future trends and potential discontinuities. Furthermore, the techniques employed in Futures Studies span a wide range, from visioning and backcasting to technically sophisticated trend analyses and statistical projections.[446]

To sum it up, a distinction between Futures studies and foresight is made because not all futures techniques fall into the foresight toolkit (Petrus van de Pol *et al.*, 2014).

Vision versus Foresight

It is argued that vision and foresight are non-interchangeable ideas, and are not products of the same mental processes. In this regard, vision tends to be a fixed image of the future, while foresight is based on assumptions that are always understood to be in flux.[447] Nevertheless, vision is required to ignite the spirit of foresightedness. That said, it was noted that "Our lives begin to end the day we become silent about things that matter" - Martin Luther King, Jr." As a result,

> There are times when a leader must move out ahead of the flock, go off in a new direction, confident that he is leading his people the right way.
>
> – Nelson Mandela

Undeniably, while visioning has its benefits as a long-term planning tool, it fails to anticipate the breadth of possible forces that may come into play at any point in the future to assist or detract from a desired outcome. It is this sense of preparedness that strategic foresight aims to foster (Petrus van de Pol *et al.*, 2014).

Strategic Foresight vs. Forecasting

Strategic foresight should not be confused with forecasting, especially as the latter can create a narrow view of the future. In concurrence, Berkhout and Hertin (2002) found that long-term forecasting has increasingly become discredited, because more often than not predictions have proved to be incorrect. In the same light, it was noted that *"it is always wise to look ahead, but difficult to look further than you can see" – Winston Churchill,* the former British prime minister. To concur, Bland and Westlake (2013); Berkhout and Hertin (2002); and Fuerth (2009) maintain that rather than making predictions based on extrapolation of current trends or frequency of similar past events, foresight cultivates the capacity to anticipate alternative futures and an ability to visualize multiple possible outcomes and their consequences.[448]

This implies that strategic foresight is an imperative virtue for any organization striving to outperform its competitors, or even beat the competition and sustain leadership in the industry.

Foresight and Policymaking

As a factor in governance, the purpose of foresight is to enhance the ability of decision-makers to engage and shape events at a longer range and, therefore, to the best advantage of the citizens they serve.[449] The biggest difficulty however, is to get the message across to decision makers, so that they can most effectively use the foresight results. One way policy-oriented foresight practitioners can overcome the gap between themselves and decision makers; is to align their work with national political agendas and ongoing administrative processes, which allows them to more effectively feed their results into the appropriate political channels.

But in a critically vast majority of cases, the aforementioned kind of congruence between foresight and policymaking can only be sustainable under two conditions:That there is sufficient political will on the part of the government as a community of policy makers, and on the part of its leadership as a collectivity of individual capabilities.That the regime in power will not for selfish reasons, exploit the advantages arising out of the foresight results to extent its political mandate beyond the conventionally accepted timeframe. Supposedly, as substituting self-seeking political agenda with critical strategic matters, can only be counterproductive in the long run.

Complexity and Wicked Problems – "BHAGS"

Ceru (2018) opines that sometimes the best way to learn how to solve everyday challenges is by thinking about large, seemingly unsolvable problems. What consultants sometimes refer to as "BHAGs" – Big Hairy Audacious Goals,[450] also known as wicked problems. Petrus van de Pol *et al.* (2014) describe wicked problems as large and intractable issues that have no immediate or obvious solutions, and whose causes and influencing factors are not easily determined. Ceru (2018) defines it as unresolved issues that are common to every industry, city, and society, for which conventional methods and wisdom have not yet been able to overcome.[451]

In this regard, organizations may sometimes be blindsided by the said impediments in the likes of the following: "black swans," "unknown unknowns" and "wildcards." As has been noted, these scenarios usually arise because traditional forecasting methods are based primarily on linear extrapolation;[452] which ultimately generate what the political scientist, Horst Rittel, called "*wicked problems.*"

"Black swan events" – *a black swan is an event or occurrence that deviates beyond what is normally expected of a situation and is extremely difficult to predict.* Black swan events are typically random and unexpected. The term was popularized by Nassim Nicholas Taleb after the results of the 2008 financial crisis.[453] Nassim Nicholas Taleb, a finance professor, writer, and former Wall Street trader; argued that black swan events are impossible to predict, and yet have catastrophic ramifications. Therefore, it is important for people to always assume a black swan event is a possibility, whatever it may be, and to plan accordingly.[454] As expressed by Will Kenton (2017), Taleb states that a black swan event depends on the observer. For example, what may be a black swan surprise for a turkey is not a black swan surprise to its butcher; hence the objective should be to "avoid being the turkey" by identifying areas of vulnerability in order to "turn the Black Swans white."[455]

There are also the "unknowns," the "unknown unknowns" alternatively known as the *genuine "unknowns;"* refer to situations that *planners are unaware that they do not know about, and are beyond rational fact-based forecasting.*[456] But there are "unknowns" that can be more easily included in strategic calculation, and through imaginative extrapolation from what is anticipated.[457] Many unknowns have a low probability of occurring, but coping well with them can produce a very high gain, especially for military planners. Addressing these unknowns should be pursued against the odds.[458]

Meanwhile, "Wild cards" *refer to low-probability and high-impact events.*Aaltonen and Sanders (2006) argue that wild cards occur because traditional forecasting methods are based primarily on *linear extrapolation.*[459] However, according to Ho (2012), because today's global environment, events and trends in various spheres interact with one another in complex and sometimes mystifying ways, foresight practitioners are more comfortable with a *non-linear* world.[460] Ramos *et al.* (2012) argue that most of the pressing threats to global civilization fall into this class of wicked problems.[461] As "wicked problems" often have many agents interacting with each other in often mystifying ways, and many stakeholders with different perspectives and goals; Da Costa, Warnke, Cagnin and Scapolo (2008) argue that the growing complexity of the system which a particular policy is trying to affect, becomes impossible to steer directly without facing the risk of unintended consequences.[462]

But foresight practitioners still use this logic to try and build new urns and devise new games all the time. To this end, Dunn III (1992) sees the business of shaping the future from the perspective of *evolution vs revolution.* In evolutionary change, progress is made by improving on the last generation of something – a tool, a process, a thought, a weapon, whatever. Sometimes progress can be very impressive, but continuity still exists between generations. While in revolutionary change, almost no continuity exists between generations – here we are looking at something entirely new.[463]

Conclusion

It has now become a gospel truth that a basic tension that firms face is whether to attend to their employees toward exploratory activities for future viability, or in exploitative activities to ensure existing viability.

We saw that in the reasoning of Darroch (2003), there exists a relationship between the organization's fundamental building blocks (OrgDNA) as an *independent organizational variable* and organizational performance (OP) as a *dependent variable* that functions on two performance segments – i.e., comparative performance and internal performance.[464] That said, the fundamental organizational building block is said to be an *independent organizational variable* because it is made of the *genetic material of the organization,* which contains its DNA. So it cannot be changed but can undergo some form of an *organizational gene transfer,* or in a less effective way, an *organizational gene editing* – as in gene therapy in medicine. And in some cases, overwhelmingly powerful external forces, powerful enough to make an organization completely lose control of its adjacencies and sometimes its core activities, can lead to a *mutation* in the *organization's genetic material* or its *OrgDNA.*

On this strand of reasoning, there is a somewhat subtly complex transformative effect between the organization's genetic material (OrgDNA) and organizational performance (OP). That said, the organization's fundamental building blocks (OrgDNA) are considered an *independent variable* because its components are *hereditary* in nature. Also, they are considered *interdependent* building blocks because, at the functional level, the formal building blocks need to function in tandem with its informal building blocks to enhance organizational performance, by transforming OP *dependent variables* into OP *interdependent factors.*

Arguably, the main reason we can buy the argument that decision rights and information flow are twice as powerful as structure and motivators is based on the assumption that the underlying rationale for decision rights and information flows is to bring about greater synergy and consistency between emergent strategies and the organizational vision (alternatively referred to as shared vision in this context), and which are the core tenets of strategic leadership. To concur, Rowe (2001) reasons that strategic leaders understand and use this process to ensure the future viability of their organizations; especially as strategic leadership presumes a shared vision of what an organization is to be, so that the day-to-day decision-making, or emergent strategy process, is consistent with this vision.[465]

Meanwhile, *motivators* could be having a weaker correlation to execution, partly because reward power, which is a major component of motivators, does have some major limitations. As noted by Randall (2012), the challenge presented by the use of reward power is that some of the rewards may have limited perceived value to the employee.[466] To this end, Murray (2019) found that understanding the motives of employees and their preferred rewards should have a positive influence on job satisfaction and tenure of workers.[467] Little wonder why Murray (2019) argues that if you really want to facilitate the motivation of a particular individual, ask them what they want.[468] As a result, managers who possess an understanding of the preferred motivators have better chances to engage their workforce, tapping into the willingness and volition of employees to behave in certain ways and ultimately influence job performance.[469]

Notes

1 Sheffi, Yossi and Edgar Blanco. "Balancing Green: When to Embrace Sustainability in Business (and When Not To)." *The MIT Press*, 18 March 2018, *Bookauthority.org*, https://bookauthority.org. Accessed 23 June 2020.
2 Apte, Suhas and Jagdish N. Sheth. *The Sustainability Edge: How to Drive Top-Line Growth with Triple-Bottom-Line Thinking*. Rotman – UTP Publishing, 1st Edition, 5 Dec. 2016, *Bookauthority.org*,https://bookauthority.org. Accessed 23 June 2020.
3 Kuenkel, Petra. *The Art of Leading Collectively: Co-Creating a Sustainable, Socially Just Future*. Chelsea Green Publishing, 20 Jan. 2016, *Bookauthority.org*, https://bookauthority.org. Accessed 23 June 2020.
4 Mintzberg, Henry (1990), op. cit., p. 12.
5 Karthikeyan, C. "A Predictive Analysis on Future of Vertical Leadership Development; A Leadership Perspective." *International Journal of Research in Social Sciences*, vol. 7 no. 4, April, 2017, p. 468, http://www.ijmra.us.
6 Ibid.
7 Karthikeyan, C. (2017), op. cit., p. 469.
8 Mintzberg, Henry (1990), op. cit., p. 15.

9 Rowe, W. Glenn (2001), op. cit., p. 90.
10 Rowe, W. Glenn (2001), op. cit., p. 86.
11 Prasad et al. (2014), op. cit., pp. 1&10.
12 Prasad et al. (2014), op. cit., pp. 11.
13 Lowder, M. Tim. "The Best Leadership Model for Organizational Change Management: Transformational Verses Servant Leadership," *SSRN Electronic Journal,* 14 June 2009, pp. 2&17–18. DOI: 10.2139/ssrn.1418796.
14 Susman, G., Jansen, K., Michael, J. et al. "Innovation and Change Management in Small and Medium-Sized Manufacturing Companies," *Sponsored Research Prepared for: United States Department of Commerce, the National Institute of Standards and Technology Manufacturing Extension Partnership,* Prepared by Smeal College of Business, The Pennsylvania State University. Final Report of Task 4 RFP 05-480-5823, Contract No. SB1341-03-Z-0015/65364, June 30, 2006, p. 3, https://www.bpir.com/images/PDFs/BPInnovation/ds4_innovation_and_change_management.pdf.
15 Ibid.
16 Mintzberg, Henry (1990), op. cit., p. 16.
17 Mintzberg, Henry (1990), op. cit., p. 18.
18 Carper, B. William. "Global Business: A Cultural Perspective." *Journal of Applied Business and Economics,* vol. 16, no. 6, 2014, p. 109, http://www.na-businesspress.com/JABE/CarperWB_Web16_6_.pdf.
19 As cited by Carper, B. William (2014), op. cit., p. 118.
20 Mintzberg, Henry (1990), op. cit., p. 18.
21 Mintzberg, Henry (1990), loc. cit.
22 Mintzberg, Henry (1990), op. cit., p. 19.
23 Singh, Yogesh. "Importance of Predictive Analytics: What it is & Why it's Important?" *Edupristine.com,* 1 Nov. 2018, https://www.edupristine.com/blog/importance-of-predictive-analytics/.
24 Ibid.
25 Sinke, Jos. "Text Lecture 8c – Production." Introduction to Aeronautical Engineering. *MOOC Learning Materials,* course excerpt from Delft University of Technology, in partnership with edx.org, 2019b, p. 1.
26 Mukasyan, Alexander. Materials Science and Engineering. *MOOC Learning Materials* – course excerpts, University of Notre dame, Indiana, and Moscow Institute of Steel and Alloy, in partnership with edx.org, 2019.
27 Miltenović, A., et al. "Role and Importance of Lightweight Design in the Product Development." *COMET a 2014: 2nd International Scientific Conference;* University of East Sarajevo, 2 – 5 Dec. 2014, p. 529.
28 Miltenović et al. (2014), op. cit., p. 530.
29 Mukasyan, Alexander (2019), loc. cit.
30 King, P. Williams. "Digital Manufacturing." *UI LABS Collaboration,* Digital Manufacturing and Design Innovation Institute (DMDII), University of Illinois, June 2015, pp. 2–13, https://www.naefrontiers.org/File.aspx?id=49924.
31 Lean Six Sigma Definition. "Six Sigma." Leansixsigmadefinition.com/glossary/six-sigma. Accessed 30 July 2020.
32 Villanova University. "Six Sigma vs. Lean Six Sigma." *Villanova University,*https://www.villanovau.com/resources/six-sigma/six-sigma-vs-lean-six-sigma. Accessed 30 July 2020.
33 Ibid.
34 Villanova University (2020), loc. cit.
35 Fiix. "Condition based maintenance and monitoring software." *Fiixsoftware.com,* 2020a, https://www.fiixsoftware.com/condition-based-maintenance. Accessed 6 Aug. 2020.

36 Fiix (2020a), loc. cit.
37 Fiix. "Preventive maintenance." *Fiixsoftware.com,* 2020b, https://www.fiixsoftware.com/maintenance-strategies/preventative-maintenance. Accessed 6 Aug. 2020.
38 Pereira, Rom. "Toyota's 8 Steps Practical Problem Solving Methodology." *Gembaacademy.com,* 3 Dec. 2015, https://www.youtube.com/watch?v=gd3uUl2fFPA. Accessed 1 Oct. 2019.
39 SlideModel. "Why Customer Centricity Will Win You More Business (in 2020)." *SlideModel.com,* 14 May 2020a, https://slidemodel.com. Accessed 20 July 2020.
40 Ibid.
41 Industry Canada (2012), op. cit., p. 13.
42 Industry Canada (2012), loc. cit.
43 Aberdeen Group. *Design Anywhere,* 2009. As cited by Industry Canada (2012), op. cit., p. 14.
44 Aberdeen Group (2009); as cited by Industry Canada (2012), ibid.
45 Tzafestas, G. Spyros. "Roboethics: Fundamental Concepts and Future Prospects." *Information,* 10 June 2018: Basel, 9, 148, p. 1, DOI: 10.3390/info9060148.
46 Taddeo, Mariarosaria and Floridi, Luciano. "How AI can be a force for good," *Science,*361 (6404), pp. 751–752, 24, Aug. 2018, vol. 361, no. 6404: AAAS, p. 1, DOI: 10.1126/science.aat5991.
47 Hausmann and Hidalgo et al. "The atlas of economic complexity: Mapping paths to prosperity." Harvard University, Harvard Kennedy School and MIT Media Lab, 2011, pp. 15–16, http://atlas.cid.harvard.edu/media/atlas/pdf/HarvardMIT_ AtlasOfEconomicComplexity_Part_I.pdf, 2011/.
48 Tucker, B. Robert. "Managing the Future: 10 Driving Forces of Change for the '90s." *Internet Delivered Business Book Summaries,* 1 Dec. 1991, p. 1, http://www.mainstreetmagazines.com/ebooks/manage-future.pdf.
49 See Rendell, Michael: in Pepper, S., Nordqvist, C., Blakstad, M. et al. "Managing Tomorrow's People: The Future of Work to 2020." *Connectedthinking,* PricewaterhouseCoopers LLP, 2007, p. 1, https://www.pwc.com/gx/en/managing-tomorrows-people/future-of-work/pdf/mtp-future-of-work.pdf.
50 Kiyosaki, T. Robert with Sharon L. Letcher. Rich Dad Poor Dad: What The Rich Teach Their Kids About Money That the Poor and Middle Class Do Not! *Warner Books in association with CASHFLOW Technologies Inc. Mass Market Paperback,* 16 Aug. 2016. These are excerpts of commentaries from Robert T. Kiyosaki. This book was initially published in 1998, https://www.knowledgebringsmoney.com/cash-flow-quadrant.html/. Accessed 7 March 2019.
51 Barry, C. and Halfmann, K. (2016), op. cit., p. 50.
52 Barry, C. and Halfmann, K. (2016), op. cit., p. 51.
53 Ibid.
54 Tang, Kelly and Greenwald, Christopher. "Long-Termism versus Short-Termism: Time for the Pendulum to Shift?" *Research,* S&P Dow Jones Indices LLC, a division of S&P Global, April 2016, p. 1, http://integratedreporting.org/wp-content/uploads/2017/03/Splodge-TermismversusShort-termism.pdf.
55 Barry, C. and Halfmann, K. (2016), op. cit., pp. 53&54.
56 As cited by Barry, C. and Halfmann, K. (2016), loc. cit.
57 Engel, C. and Weber, E. U. (2007), op. cit., p. 323.
58 Ibid.

59 As cited by Barry, C. and Halfmann, K. (2016), op. cit., p. 54.
60 As cited by Barry, C. and Halfmann, K. (2016), op. cit., p. 51.
61 As cited by Engel, C. and Weber, E. U. (2007), op. cit., p. 325.
62 Engel, C. and Weber, E. U. (2007), loc. cit.
63 As cited by Barry, C. and Halfmann, K. (2016), op. cit., pp. 53–54.
64 Leung, Millie. "Cashflow Quadrant." *Millieleung.com,* https://millieleung.com/cashflow-quadrant/. Accessed 7 March 2019.
65 Mattin, David. "Welcome to Augmented Modernity." *Newco Shift,* 10 Sept. 2017, https://shift.newco.co/2017/09/10/welcome-to-augmented-modernity/ retrieved. Accessed 16 Jan. 2019.
66 Engel, C. and Weber, E.U. (2007), op. cit., p. 330.
67 Engel, C. and Weber, E.U. (2007), op. cit., p. 331.
68 Sondhe, S. Ratanjit. "Wealth Creation vs. Job Creation: Why Creating Jobs Isn't the Real Answer to Our Economic Problems." *Probizwriters.com,* 2010, p. 6.
69 As cited by Basılgan, Müslüm. "The Creative Destruction of Economic Development: The Schumpeterian Entrepreneur." *TODAİE's Review of Public Administration,* Volume 5 No 3, Sept. 2011, p. 35, https://www.academia.edu.
70 Satell, Greg (2010), loc. cit.
71 Ibid.
72 Ibid.
73 Eker, T. Harv. Secrets of the Millionaire Mind: Mastering the Inner Game of Wealth. *Library of Congress Cataloging-in-Publication Data;* Pymble, Toronto, Auckland, London, New York: HarperCollins Publishers, Adobe Acrobat e-book Reader Feb. 2005, pp. 13–14.
74 Ibid; p. 14.
75 Please, take note that the "outer game" (the tools) and the "outer world" (the tools) are used interchangeably; and they mean one and the same thing.
76 Eker, T. Harry (2005), op. cit., p. 9.
77 Rowe, W. Glenn (2001), op. cit., p. 81.
78 Mintzberg, Henry (1990), op. cit., p. 20.
79 Ibid.
80 Page, Jean-Paul. Corporate Governance and Value Creation. *The CFA Institute Research Foundation, Volume 2005 Issue 1,* 1 March 2005, p. 2, https://www.cfainstitute.org/en/research/foundation/2005/corporate-governance-and-value-creation.
81 Ibid.
82 Rowe, W. Glenn. (2001), op. cit., p. 92.
83 Tsui, Eric. "Resource-based view (RBV) of a firm: What is RBV?." MOOC Learning Materials, course excerpts from The Hong Kong Polytechnic University, in partnership with edx.org, 2018a, p. 10.
84 Ibid.
85 Rowe, W. Glenn (2001), loc. cit. Please note that the term strategic leadership comprises both elements of strategic thinking and strategic foresight.
86 Tichy, N. M., and Cohen, E. The leadership engine: How winning companies build leaders at every level. New York: HarperCollins, 1997, p. 106; as cited by Rowe, W. Glenn (2001), ibid.
87 Eker, H. T. (2005), op. cit., p. 2.
88 Engel, C. and Weber, E.U. (2007), op. cit., p. 338.
89 Lowder, M. Tim (2009), op. cit., p. 3.
90 Kezar et al. (2006); and B. N. Smith et al. (2004). As cited by Lowder, M. Tim (2009), ibid; pp. 3–4.

91 Schermerhorn, J. R., et al. (2002). *Comportement humain et organisation* (2nd ed.).Village Mondial; as cited by Sultana, M. A., Rashid, M., Mohiuddin, M. and Mazumder, M. N. H. "Cross-Cultural Management and Organizational Performance: A Content Analysis Perspective." *International Journal of Business and Management,* vol. 8, no. 8, 2013, Published by Canadian Center of Science and Education, March 26, 2013, p. 138.

92 As cited by Randall, M. Donna. "Leadership and the Use of Power: Shaping an Ethical Climate." *The Journal of Applied Christian Leadership,* Vol. 6, No. 1 Spring, April 2012, p. 29, https://www.andrews.edu/services/jacl/article_archive/6_1_spring_2012/04-featurearticles/jacl_6-1_randall.pdf/.

93 Elias, S. "Fifty Years of Influence in the Workplace: The Evolution of the French and Raven Power Taxonomy." *Journal of Management History,* vol. 14, no. 3, 2018, pp. 267–283; as cited by Randall, M. Donna (2012), op. cit., p. 3.

94 Ibid.

95 Johnson, W. Mark. "Seizing the White Space." Featured Interview, *Emerald Group Publishing Limited,* April 2010, p. 4.

96 Rowe, W. Gleen (2001), op. cit., p. 90.

97 As cited by Engel, C. and Weber, E.U. (2007), op. cit., p. 329.

98 Johnson, W. Mark (2010), op. cit., p. 3.

99 Johnson, W. Mark (2010), op. cit., p. 2.

100 Patrick, A. Harold. "Influence of Power Bases on Leadership Strategies Adopted by Managers' in Information Technology Organizations." *European Journal of Business and Management,* vol. 4, no. 11, 2012, p. 101, www.iiste.org.

101 Kilpi, Esko. "The Future of Management." *Shift.newco.co,* 9 Sept. 2017, https://shift.newco.co/2017/09/09/the-future-of-management. Accessed 16 Jan. 2019.

102 Ibid.

103 Rowe, W. Glenn (2001), op. cit., p. 84.

104 See Hill, C. W. L. and Hoskisson, R, E. (1987), and Hoskisson, R. E. and Hitt. M. A. (1994); as cited by Rowe, W. Glenn (2001), op. cit., p. 85.

105 Patrick, A. Harold. (2012), op. cit., p. 101.

106 Johnson, W. Mark (2010), op. cit., p. 1.

107 Johnson, W. Mark (2010), op. cit., p. 5.

108 Neilson et al. (2008), op. cit., p. 67.

109 Mintzberg, Henry (1990), op. cit., p. 15.

110 Mintzberg, Henry (1990), op. cit., p. 15.

111 As cited by Nafei, Wageeh (2014), op. cit., p. 119.

112 Mintzberg, Henry (1990), op. cit., p. 15.

113 Mintzberg, Henry (1990), op. cit., pp. 13&16.

114 Nafei, Wageeh (2014), op. cit., p. 119.

115 Mintzberg, Henry (1990), op. cit., p. 16.

116 Mintzberg, Henry (1990), op. cit., p. 17.

117 Ibid.

118 Nafei, Wageeh (2014), op. cit., p. 119.

119 Mintzberg, Henry (1990), op. cit., p. 17.

120 Nafei, Wageeh (2014), op. cit., p. 118.

121 Patrick, A. Harold (2012), op. cit., p. 101.

122 Payne, J. Richard. "The Struggle for Primacy in a Global Society." Chapter 2, *Global Issues,* Boston: Pearson Education (US), 4th edition, 2012, p. 16.

123 Patrick, A. Harold (2012), op. cit., p. 101.

124 See Banutu-Gomez, M. B. (2004) and Pepper, A. (2003); as cited by Lowder, M. Tim (2009), op. cit., p. 12.
125 Mintzberg, Henry (1990), op. cit., p. 17.
126 Dellaert, Marc and Davydov, Sergey. "Influencing: The Skill of Persuasion – Building Commitment and Getting Results." *White Paper,* Center for Creative Leadership, 2017, p. 8, https://www.ccl.org/wp-content/uploads/2017/01/Influencing-the-skill-of-persuasion.pdf/.
127 Mintzberg, Henry (1990), op. cit., p. 19.
128 Gawler, Meg. "Project Design in the Context of Project Cycle Management – Sourcebook." *WWF Introductory Course,* Prévessin-Moëns: ARTEMIS Services for Nature Conservation and Development, Feb. 2005, p. 7, http://www.artemis-services.com.
129 Ibid.
130 Dickson, E. Roger. Dickson Biblical Research Library. Revised and Expanded Edition, Hutchinson & Cape Town: Africa International Missions, 2015, p. 1079, www.africainternational.org/.
131 Dickson, E. Roger (2015), op. cit., p. 1078.
132 Patrick, A. Harold (2012), op. cit., p. 102.
133 Dickson, E. Roger (2015), op. cit., p. 1079.
134 Patrick, A. Harold (2012), op. cit., p. 102.
135 Mintzberg, Henry (1990), op. cit., p. 17.
136 Moye, Neta. "Expanding Your Capacity to Lead;" an excerpt from MOOC Learning Materials on *Leadership and Influence,* Robert H. Smith School of Business, University of Maryland, in partnership with edx.org, 2018, https://www.edx.org/course/usmx-leadership-and-influence/.
137 Moye, Neta (2018), loc. cit.
138 Kilpi, Esko. (2017), loc. cit.
139 Payne, J. Richard (2012), op. cit., p. 16.
140 Patrick, A. Harold (2012), op. cit., p. 102.
141 Mintzberg, Henry (1990), op. cit., p. 15.
142 Rowe, W. Glenn (2001), op. cit., p. 89.
143 Engel, C. and Weber, E.U. (2007), op. cit., p. 329.
144 Payne, J. Richard (2012), op. cit., p. 16.
145 See Baum and Locke (2004), Leahy, K. T. (1997), and Weick, K. E. (2002); as cited by Lowder, T. M. (2009), op. cit., p. 6.
146 Dellaert, M. and Davydov, S. (2017), op. cit., p. 3.
147 IMPORTANT NOTE: For purposes of clarification; situational leadership, personal power, individual leadership skills, specific individual skills mean one and the same thing – and commonly called personal power (i.e., exercising power). Meanwhile, institutional leadership and structural leadership are usually grouped under positional power (i.e., exercising the bases for power).
148 Moye, Neta (2018), loc. cit.
149 Moye, Neta (2018), loc. cit.
150 Festré, Agnès – Garrouste, Pierre. "Rationality, Behavior, Institutional, and Economic Change in Schumpeter." *Journal of Economic Methodology,* vol. 15, no. 4, Dec. 2008, p. 383; as cited by Basılgan, Müslüm (2011), op. cit., p. 44.
151 Kilpi Esko, (2017), loc. cit.
152 As cited by Basılgan, Müslüm (2011), op. cit., p. 46.
153 Rowe, W. Glenn (2001), op. cit., p. 90
154 See Bruderlein, Claude. Humanitarian Response to Conflicts and Disaster. *MOOC Learning Materials,* course excerpts from Harvard University, in partnership with edx.org, 2018.

155 Ibid.
156 Neilson, G., et al. "The Four Bases of Organizational DNA." Organizational DNA Reading Materials, strategy+business issue 33, Booz Allen Hamilton Inc., 2003, p. 5, www.boozallen.com.
157 Ibid.
158 Bordia, R., Kronenberg, E., Neely, D., Hamilton, B. A. et al. "Innovation's OrgDNA," *Booz & Company Inc.,* 2005, p. 1, www.booz.com/.
159 Tsui, Eric (2018a), op. cit., p. 3.
160 Watson, Jessica. "Top 10 Reasons for Entrepreneurs Failure in 2018." *Mercy – CBNation,* 21 March 2018,https://rescue.ceoblognation.com/2018/03/21/top-10-reasons-for-entrepreneurs-failure-in-2018. Accessed 28 Feb. 2020.
161 Ibid.
162 CB Insights. "The Top 20 Reasons Startups Fail." *Cbinsights.com,* 2020, p. 4, https://s3-us-west-2.amazonaws.com/cbi-content/research-reports/The-20-Reasons-Startups-Fail.pdf. Accessed 28 Feb. 2020.
163 Nelson, Gabe. "10 Reasons Why Most Entrepreneurs Succeed in Their Business." *Ingeniumweb.com,* 13 March 2019,https://www.ingeniumweb.com/blog/post/10-reasons-why-most-entrepreneurs-succeed-in-their-business/4232/. Accessed 28 Feb. 2020.
164 Ibid.
165 Kim and Mauborgne. "Blue Ocean Strategy: Blue Ocean Strategy Tools and Frameworks." *Blueoceanstrategy.com,* 2014, p. 15.
166 Karthikeyan, C. (2017), op. cit., p. 485.
167 Nyangena, E., et al. "Ethical leadership for sustainable development in developing countries." *Editon Cons. J. Arts., Humanit. S. Stud.,* vol. 1, no. 1, 2019, p. 1.
168 Carper, B. William. "Global Business: A Cultural Perspective." *Journal of Applied Business and Economics,* vol. 16, no. 6, 2014, p. 109.
169 Ibid.
170 Karthikeyan, C. (2017), op. cit., p. 485.
171 Sondhe, S. Ratanjit (2010), op. cit., p. 13.
172 As cited by Patrick, A. Harold (2012), op. cit., p. 107.
173 Karthikeyan, C. (2017), op. cit., p. 485.
174 Sondhe, R. Ratanjit (2010), op. cit., p. 13.
175 Sondhe, R. Ratanjit (2010), loc. cit.
176 Bhalla, V., Caye, J-M., Dyer, A. et al. "High-Performance Organizations: The Secrets of Their Success." *The Boston Consulting Group (BCG),* Sept. 2011, pp. 3–13, www.bcg.com.
177 See Trevino, L. K., and Brown, M. E. (2005), The role of leaders in influencing unethical behavior in the workplace. In R. E. Kidwell and C. L. Martin (Eds.), Managing organizational deviance (pp. 69–87). Thousand Oaks, CA: Sage; as cited by Randall, M. Donna (2012), op. cit., p. 33.
178 Kilpi, E. (2017), loc. cit.
179 Bhalla et al. (2011), op. cit., pp. 7–8.
180 See Ireland, R. D. and Hitt, M. A. 1999, Achieving and maintaining strategic competitiveness in the 21st century: The role of strategic leadership. *The Academy of Management Executive,* vol. 13, no. 1, 43-57; as cited by Rowe, W. Glenn (2001), op. cit., p. 81.
181 Rowe, W. Glenn (2001), op. cit., p. 84.
182 Llopis, Glenn. "5 Ways Leaders Enable Innovation In their Teams." *Forbes.com,* 7 April 2014, https://www.forbes.com/sites/glennllopis/2014/04/07/5-ways-leaders-enable-innovation-in-their-teams/#4843aad88c4c. Accessed 15 May 2020.

183 Harvard Business Publishing. "Employee Engagement." Leading the Way, *Harvard Business Publishing – Corporate Learning,* 13 Feb. 2020.
184 Karthikeyan, C. (2017), op. cit., p. 485.
185 Llopis, Glenn (2014), loc. cit.
186 Bhalla et al. (2011), op. cit., p. 4.
187 Kilpi, Esko. (2017), loc. cit.
188 Llopis, Glenn (2014), loc. cit.
189 Bhalla et al. (2011), op. cit., pp. 4–6.
190 Nafei, Wageeh (2014), op. cit., p. 120.
191 Bhalla et al. (2011), op. cit., p. 4-5.
192 As cited by Nafei, Wageeh (2014), op. cit., p. 120.
193 As cited by Nafei, Wageeh (2014), op. cit., p. 120.
194 Bhalla et al. (2011), op. cit., pp. 5–6.
195 Rowe, W. Glenn (2001), op. cit., p. 81.
196 See Mintzberg, H., et al. J. 1998, *Strategy safaii.* New York: The Free Press; as cited by Rowe, W. Glenn (2001), op. cit., p. 81.
197 As cited by Rowe, W. Glenn (2001), loc. cit.
198 Nyangena et al. (2019), op. cit., p. 1.
199 As cited by Sakhdari, Kamal. "Corporate Entrepreneurship: A Review and Future Research Agenda." *Technology Innovation Management Review,* vol. 6 no. 8, Aug. 2016, p. 11, https://timreview.ca/sites/default/files/article_PDF/Sakhdari_TIMReview_August2016.pdf /.
200 As cited by Sakhdari, Kamal (2016), loc. cit.
201 Bhalla et al. (2011), op. cit., p. 6.
202 Kilpi, Esko (2017), loc. cit.
203 Bhalla et al. (2011), op. cit., p.
204 Dettmann, Joe, et al. "Digital-Era Leadership: Ready Or Not, Digital Competence Is Already Differentiating Winners From Losers." Global Leadership Forecast 2018: 25 Research Insights to Fuel Your People Strategy. *Ddiworld.com,* 2018, p. 12, www.ddiworld.com/glf2018.
205 Neal, Stephanie. "Generation X-Change: Don't Underestimate the Powerful Influence of Gen X Leaders." Global Leadership Forecast 2018: 25 Research Insights to Fuel Your People Strategy, *Ddiworld.com,* 2018, p. 32, www.ddiworld.com/glf2018.
206 Popiela, Amanda. "The Rise of Digital Natives: Are Millennials Ready to Lead?." Global Leadership Forecast 2018: 25 Research Insights to Fuel Your People Strategy. *Ddiworld.com,* 2018, p. 30, www.ddiworld.com/glf2018.
207 Neal, Stephanie (2018), op. cit., p. 32.
208 Ibid.
209 Bickart, Barbara. "Strategic Social Media Marketing." *Micromasters in Digital Product Management* program, an excerpt from online learning materials – Questrom School of Business at Boston University, in partnership with ed-x.org, 2018.
210 McMahon, T. Edward. "The Secrets of Successful Communities." *Burlington: PlannersWeb.com,* 29 July 2013, p. 4.
211 Engel, C. and Weber, E. U. (2007), op. cit., p. 342.
212 Ibid.
213 Ibid.
214 Bhalla et al. (2011), op. cit., p. 8.
215 Bhalla et al. (2011), op. cit., p. 10.
216 Susman, G., Jansen, K., Michael, J. et al. "Innovation and Change Management in Small and Medium-Sized Manufacturing Companies." *Sponsored Research Prepared for: United States Department of Commerce,*

the National Institute of Standards and Technology Manufacturing Extension Partnership – by Smeal College of Business, The Pennsylvania State University. Final Report of Task 4 RFP 05-480-5823, Contract No. SB1341-03-Z-0015/ 65364, June 30 2006, p. 29.
217 Susman et al. (2006), loc. cit.
218 As cited by Lemus-Aguilar et al (2019), op. cit., p. 4.
219 As cited by Lemus-Aguilar et al (2019) loc. cit.
220 Bhalla et al. (2011), op. cit., p. 6.
221 Nafei, Wageeh (2014), op. cit., p. 120.
222 As cited by Nafei, Wageeh (2014); ibid.
223 Bhalla et al. (2011), op. cit., p. 6.
224 Rowe, W. Glenn (2001), op. cit., p. 86.
225 Rowe, W. Glenn (2001), op. cit., p. 85.
226 Bhalla et al. (2011), op. cit., p. 6.
227 See Council for Advancement and Support of Education (CASE) (2012), Teaching new employees how to fit in, *Advancement Weekly,* vol. 38, no. 1, p. 1. As cited by Randall, M. Donna. "Leadership and the Use of Power: Shaping an Ethical Climate." *The Journal of Applied Christian Leadership,* vol. 6, no. 1 Spring, 2012, p. 30, https://www.andrews.edu/services/jacl/article_archive/6_1_spring_2012/04-featurearticles/jacl_6-1_randall.pdf/.
228 Randall, M. Donna (2012); ibid.
229 Bhalla et al. (2011), op. cit., pp. 6–7.
230 As cited by Randall, M. Donna (2012), op. cit., p. 30.
231 Randal, M. Donna (2012), op. cit., p. 30.
232 See the Council for Advancement and Support of Education, 2012, op. cit., p. 1. As cited by Randall, M. Donna (2012), op. cit., p. 30.
233 Bhalla et al. (2011), op. cit., p. 7.
234 See Adler, N. J. (1994). Comportement organisationnel: une approche multiculturelle. Éditions Reynald Goulet,Université McGill, Canada; as cited by Sultana, M. A., Rashid, M., Mohiuddin, M. and Mazumder, M. N. H. "Cross-Cultural Management and Organizational Performance: A Content Analysis Perspective." *International Journal of Business and Management;* Vol. 8, No. 8; 2013, Published by Canadian Center of Science and Education, 26 March 2013, p. 134.
235 Susman et al. (2006), op. cit., p. 26.
236 Mittal, Rakesh. "Charismatic and Transformational Leadership Styles: A Cross-Cultural Perspective." *International Journal of Business and Management,* vol. 10, no. 3; 2015, 27 Feb. 2015, p. 26. DOI:10.5539/ijbm.v10n3p26.Mittal, Rakesh (2015), op. cit., p. 26.
237 See Lorsch, J. W. "Managing Culture: The Invisible Barrier to Strategic Change." *CaliforniaManagement Review,* vol. 28, no. 2, 1986, pp. 95–109; as cited by Susman, G., Jansen, K., Michael, J. et al. (2006), op. cit., p. 26.
238 Schein, E. *Organisational culture and leadership,* (2nd Ed.), Jossey Bass, California, 1992; as cited by Sultana et al. (2013), op. cit., p. 138.
239 Carper, B. William (2014), op. cit., p. 109.
240 Susman et al. (2006), op. cit., p. 26.
241 Sultana et al. (2013), op. cit., p. 138.
242 Sultana et al. (2013), op. cit., p. 139.
243 See Gardenswartz, L. and Rowe, A. (1995). *Diverse Teams at Work.* New York: Irwin; as cited by Sultana et al. (2013), op. cit., pp. 137–138.
244 Ibid; p. 138.
245 Sultana et al. (2013), op. cit., p. 135.
246 Carper, B. William (2014), op. cit., p. 109.

247 Susman et al. (2006), op. cit., p. 26.
248 As cited by Sakhdari, Kamal (2016), op. cit., p. 7.
249 Carper, B. William (2014), op. cit., p. 118.
250 Bhalla et al. (2011), op. cit., pp. 10–11.
251 See Schein, E. H. (1990), Organizational culture, *American Psychologist,* p. 118; as cited by Randall, M. Donna (2012), op. cit., p. 30.
252 See the classic studies of (Hall, 1959 &1960); Lawrence and Lorch, 1967; Hofstede, 1980); as cited by Sultana, et al. (2013), op. cit., p. 135.
253 See Trevino, L. K. "Ethical Decision Making in Organizations: A Person-situation Interactionist Model." *Academy of Management*, vol. 11, no. 3, 1986, pp. 601–617; as cited by Randall, M. Donna (2012), op. cit., p. 118.
254 Sultana et al. (2013), op. cit., p. 135.
255 See Trompenaars, F. (1993), *L'entreprise multiculturelle*, Éditions Maxima; as cited by Sultana et al. (2013), ibid.
256 Harvard Business Analytic Services. "Cultivating Workforce Well-Being to Drive Business Value." *Harvard Business Review Group,* 2020, p. 7.
257 Harvard Business Analytic Services (2020), op. cit., p. 8.
258 As cited by Soieb, A. Z., et al. "The Effects of Perceived Leadership Styles and Organizational Citizenship Behaviour on Employee Engagement: The Mediating Role of Conflict Management." *International Journal of Business and Management,* vol. 8, no. 8, 22 March 2013, p. 92, http://dx.doi.org/10.5539/ijbm.v8n8p91.
259 See Vazirani, N. (2007), Employee engagement. *Working paper series 05/07.* College of management studies, Nerul, India, p. 2. As cited by Soieb et al. (2013), op. cit., p. 96.
260 Soieb et al. (2013), op. cit., p. 91.
261 Harvard Business Analytic Services (2020), op. cit., p. 1.
262 Neilson et al. (2008), op. cit., p. 62.
263 Neilson et al. (2008), op. cit., p. 63.
264 Lozano, O., et al. "Organizational DNA: Customer & Operations Strategy." *Sintec,* Mexico City, Monterrey, Bogota, Sao Paulo: Sistemas Interactivos de Consultoría, S.A. de C.V., 2011, p. 2, www.sintec.com/.
265 Ibid.
266 Estupiñán, Jaime and Neilson, L. Gary. "The 10 Principles of Organizational DNA." *Strategy-business.com,* 27 Oct. 2014, p. 1.
267 Estupiñán, Jaime and Neilson, L. Gary (2014), loc. cit.
268 Dehoff, K., et al. "Innovation's OrgDNA." Booz & Company, 2005, p. 2, www.orgdna.com.
269 Dehoff et al. (2005), loc. cit.
270 Llorens, S., Salanova, M., Torrente, P., and Acosta, H. "Chapter 6: Interventions to Promote Healthy & Resilient Organizations (HERO) from Positive Psychology." The Concepts Behind Organizational Health Intervention Research. *Springer Science+Business Media Dordrecht,* 2013. p. 1. DOI: 10.1007/978-94-007-6470-5_6.
271 Neilson, L. Gary, et al. "The Passive-Aggressive Organization." *Harvard Business Review,* From the Oct. 2005 Issue, https://hbr.org/2005/10/the-passive-aggressive-organization. Accessed 21 Oct. 2020.
272 Ibid.
273 Dehoff et al. (2005), op. cit., p. 2.
274 Neilson et al. (2005), loc. cit.
275 Neilson et al. (2005), loc. cit.
276 U.S. National Library of Medicine (2019), loc. cit.
277 Estupiñán, Jaime and Neilson, L. Gary (2014), op. cit., p. 3.

278 Estupiñán, Jaime and Neilson, L. Gary (2014), loc. cit.
279 Neilson et al. (2008), op. cit., p. 62.
280 As cited by Soieb et al. (2013), op. cit., p. 92.
281 Dellaert, M. and Davydov, S. (2017), op. cit., p. 2.
282 As cited by Bhalla et al. (2011), op. cit., p. 3.
283 Mintzberg, Henry (1990), op. cit., p. 17.
284 Mintzberg, Henry (1990), loc. cit.
285 Mintzberg, Henry (1990), loc. cit.
286 Sources: Part of the data is an excerpt from Estupiñán, Jaime and Neilson, L. Gary (2014), op. cit., pp. 1–3; Neilson et al. (2008); and others – with a review, complementary analysis and supplementary inputs from the author.
287 Patrick, A. Harold (2012), op. cit., p. 102.
288 Patrick, A. Harold (2012), loc. cit.
289 Patrick, A. Harold (2012), loc. cit.
290 Moye, Neta (2018), loc. cit.
291 Coomber, Nicole. "Gaining Support," in Leadership and Influence. *MOOC Learning Materials*, a course excerpt from Robert H. Smith School of Business, University of Maryland, in partnership with edx.org, 2018, https://www.edx.org/course/usmx-leadership-and-influence/.
292 Mittal, Rakesh (2015), op. cit., p. 27.
293 As cited by Lowder, M. Tim (2009), op. cit., p. 6.
294 Rowe, W. Glenn 2001), op. cit., p. 82.
295 Nyangena et al. (2019), loc. cit.
296 Rowe, W. Glenn (2001), op. cit., p. 82.
297 Rowe, W. Glenn (2001), op. cit., p. 82.
298 Rowe, W. Glenn (2001), op. cit., pp. 82&89.
299 Lowder, M. Tim (2009), op. cit., p. 15.
300 Henley, Dede. "Research Says Vertical Development Can Make You A Better Leader." *Henleyleadership.com*, 14 Feb. 2020, https://www.henleyleadership.com/blog/blog/resources/research-says-vertical-development-can-make-you-a-better-leader. Accessed 24 Oct. 2020.
301 Henley, Dede (2020), loc. cit.
302 Petrie, Nick. "Vertical Leadership Development–Part 1: Developing Leaders for a Complex World." *Center for Creative Leadership*, 2014, p. 6, https://www.ccl.org/wp-content/uploads/2015/04/VerticalLeadersPart1.pdf. Accessed 24 Oct. 2020.
303 Karthikeyan, C. (2017), op. cit., p. 2.
304 Jones, H. E., et al. "Helping Leaders Grow Up: Vertical Leadership Development in Practice." *The Journal of Values-Based Leadership*, vol. 13, no. 1, Article 8, 2020, p. 6, http://dx.doi.org/10.22543/0733.131.1275.
305 Ibid.
306 Jones et al. (2020), op. cit., p. 13.
307 Lowder, M. Tim (2009), op. cit., p. 11.
308 Mittal, Rakesh (2015), op. cit., p. 27.
309 Coomber, Nicole (2018), loc. cit.
310 See French and Raven, 1959; Lunenburg, 2012; as cited in Mittal, Rakesh (2015), op. cit., p. 29.
311 Mittal, Rakesh (2015), op. cit., p. 26.
312 Nyangena et al. (2019), op. cit., p. 5.
313 Soieb et al. (2013), op. cit., p. 93.
314 See Hansen, S. D. (2010). Ethical leadership: A multifocal social exchange perspective. *The Journal of Business Inquiry*. Washington University, USA. As

cited by Soieb et al. (2013), ibid; p. 93. The term Social Exchange Theory (SET) was initiated by Hormans in 1958 (Devan, 2006).
315 Sultana et al. (2013), op. cit., p. 138.
316 Ibid.
317 Lowder, M. Tim (2009), op. cit., p. 6.
318 Rowe, W. Glenn (2001), op. cit., pp. 81–82.
319 Mittal, Rakesh (2015), op. cit., p. 29.
320 Mittal, Rakesh (2015), op. cit., p. 26.
321 Rowe, W. Glenn 2001), op. cit., p. 82.
322 Lowder, M. Tim (2009), op. cit., p. 12.
323 Sultana et al. (2013), op. cit., p. 135.
324 Kilpi, Esko (2017), loc. cit.
325 Nyangena et al. (2019), op. cit., p. 5.
326 Ibid.
327 Ibid.
328 Coomber, Nicole (2018), loc. cit.
329 Patrick, A. Harold (2012), op. cit., p. 101.
330 As cited by Dellaert, M. and Davydov, S. (2017), op. cit., p. 2.
331 As cited by Soieb et al. (2013), op. cit., p. 91.
332 Pereira, Rom. "Toyota's 8 Steps Practical Problem Solving Methodology." *Gembaacademy.com*, 3 Dec. 2015, https://www.youtube.com/watch?v=gd3uUl2fFPA.
333 Pereira, Rump (2015), loc. cit.
334 Johnson, W. Mark (2010), op. cit., p. 1.
335 Johnson, W. Mark (2010), loc. cit.
336 Johnson, W. Mark (2010), op. cit., p. 2.
337 Pereira, Rump (2015), loc. cit.
338 Ibid.
339 Neilson et al. (2008), op. cit., p. 67.
340 Engel, C. and Weber, E. U. (2007), op. cit., p. 333.
341 See Kim and Mauborngе (2014), op. cit., pp. 23&24.
342 Tsui, Eric. "Resource-based view (RBV) of a firm: The VRIO Framework." *The Hong Kong Polytechnic University*, 2018b, pp. 2&7.
343 Tsui, Eric (2018a), op. cit., pp. 5–9.
344 Ibid; pp. 5–6.
345 Tsui, Eric (2018b), op. cit., p. 8.
346 As cited by Tsui, Eric (2018a), op. cit., p. 2.
347 HBRAS (2020), op. cit., p. 12.
348 HBRAS (2020), op. cit., p. 11.
349 Kim and Mauborngе (2014), op. cit., p. 23.
350 Nafei, Wageeh (2014), op. cit., p. 120.
351 Bordia et al. (2005), as cited by Nafei, Wageeh (2014); ibid.
352 Coomber, Nicole (2018), loc. cit.
353 Randall, M. Donna (2012), op. cit., p. 31.
354 Coomber, Nicole (2018), loc. cit.
355 DeMers, Jayson. "7 Ways to Build Influence in the Workplace." *Inc.com*, 15 Jan. 2015, https://www.inc.com/jayson-demers/7-ways-to-build-influence-in-the-workplace.html/. Accessed 8 Feb. 2019.
356 Mittal, Rakesh (2015), op. cit., p. 26.
357 DeMers, Jayson (2019), loc. cit.
358 Nyangena et al (2019), op. cit., p. 6.
359 Ibid.
360 Rowe, W. Glenn (2001), op. cit., p. 82.

361 Nyangena et al. (2019), op. cit., p. 4.
362 Nyangena et al. (2019), loc. cit.
363 As cited by Nyangena et al. (2019), op. cit., p. 6.
364 Nyangena et al. (2019), op. cit., p. 4.
365 Ibid; pp. 4–5.
366 Dellaert, M. and Davydov, S. (2017), op. cit., p. 3.
367 Patrick, A. Harold (2012), op. cit., p. 102.
368 Dellaert, M. and Davydov, S. (2017), op. cit., p. 3.
369 Ibid.
370 Ibid.
371 Patrick, A. Harold (2012), op. cit., p. 101.
372 Semantics is the "right" interpretation of words in a language.
373 As cited by Nyangena et al. (2019), op. cit., p. 7.
374 As cited by Nyangena et al. (2019), ibid.
375 Dellaert, M. and Davydov, S. (2017), op. cit., p. 8.
376 Johnson, W. Mark (2010), op. cit., p. 2.
377 This will be discussed in detail later in this chapter under "Core competences and their dimensions."
378 Johnson, W. Mark (2010), op. cit., p. 2.
379 Johnson, W. Mark (2010), op. cit., p. 3.
380 Johnson, W. Mark (2010), op. cit., pp. 3&4.
381 Johnson, W. Mark (2010), op. cit., p. 4.
382 Tan, Wee Liang and Tan, Teck Meng. "The Impact of Corporate Governance on Value Creation in Entrepreneurial Firms." *Rencontres de St-Gall 2004, Appenzell.* Research Collection Lee Kong Chian School of Business, 2004, p. 5, https://ink.library.smu.edu.sg/lkcsb_research/2349.
383 Kim and Mauborgne (2014), op. cit., p. 25.
384 Ibid.
385 Kim and Mauborgne (2014), op. cit., p. 23.
386 Bouchard, Véronique. "Exploring Corporate Entrepreneurship: A Corporate Strategy Perspective." *European Entrepreneurial Learning,* EM Lyon, Dec. 2001, p. 8.
387 Baumgartner, Jeffrey. "The Corporate Innovation Machine: A Model for Implementing Idea Management Based Innovation Strategy in Your Firm." *Creativejeffrey.com,* 2009, p. 5.
388 See Doherty, N. and Guyler, M. (2008). *The Essential Guide to Workplace Mediation and Conflict Resolution:Rebuilding Working Relationships.* Kogan page limited, London, UK and Philadephia, USA. As cited by Soieb et al. (2013), op. cit., p. 95.
389 Engel, C. and Weber, E. U. (2007), op. cit., p. 334.
390 Soieb et al (2013), op. cit., p. 95.
391 As cited by Cameron, F., et al. "5 Behaviours of a Cohesive Team." *StickyChange: Experts in Fostering Change that Sticks.* Feb. 2017, p. 9, stickychange.com.
392 Carper, B. William (2014), op. cit., p. 118.
393 Atsan, Nuray. "Failure Experiences of Entrepreneurs: Causes and Learning Outcomes." *12th International Strategic Management Conference, ISMC 2016,* 28-30 Oct. 2016, Antalya, Turkey: Elservier, *Procedia – Social and Behavioral Sciences 235, 2016,* p. 441, www.sciencedirect.com.
394 Carper, B. William (2014), op. cit., p. 118.
395 Ibid.
396 Ibid.

397 Cameron, F., et al. "5 Behaviours of a Cohesive Team," in StickyChange: Experts in Fostering Change that Sticks, *Stickychange.com*, Feb. 2017, p. 6.
398 See Patrick Lencioni's description of five behaviours of a dysfunctional team. As cited by Cameron, F., et al. (2017), op. cit., p. 7. Also see The Five Behaviors. "State of Teams." *The Five Behaviors – A Wiley Brand,* 2020, p. 13, https://www.fivebehaviors.com/Home.aspx. Accessed 1 Nov. 2020.
399 See Patrick Lencioni's description of five behaviours of a coecive team. As cited byCameron et al. (2017), op. cit., p. 8.
400 Cameron et al. (2017), op. cit., p. 11.
401 Cameron et al. (2017), op. cit., p. 12.
402 Nyangena et al. (2019), op. cit., p. 5.
403 Knight, Joanna. "How to hit the sweet spot between conflict and new ideas." *Hrzone.com,* 4 Oct. 2013, https://www.hrzone.com/perform/business/how-to-hit-the-sweet-spot-between-conflict-and-new-ideas/. Accessed 21 Feb. 2019.
404 Ibid.
405 Ibid.
406 Viki, Tendayi. "Six Principles For Creating A Good Corporate Innovation Process," *Forbes Media LLC,* 26 March 2018, https://www.forbes.com/sites/tendayiviki/2018/03/26/six-principles-corporate-innovation-process/#4ba5a45544f4. Accessed 22 Feb. 2020.
407 Ibid.
408 This is an excerpt from Kreitzberg, B. Charles. "Creating Business Value through Strategic User Experience Design." *Icharlie.me,* 2020, http://www.icharlie.me/sweetspot/. Accessed 21 Feb. 2019.
409 Kreitzberg, B. Charles (2019), loc. cit.
410 CB Insights (2020), op. cit., p. 8.
411 Gustafsson, A., et al. "Customer co-creation in service innovation: A matter of communication?" *Journal of Service Management,* vol. 23, no. 3, June 2012, p. 4.
412 Ibid.
413 Gustafsson et al. (2012), op. cit., p. 20.
414 Kreitzberg, B. Charles (2019), loc. cit.
415 Kreitzberg, B. Charles (2019), loc. cit.
416 Gustafsson et al. (2012), op. cit., p. 20.
417 Kreitzberg, B. Charles (2019), loc. cit.
418 Kreitzberg, B. Charles (2019), loc. cit.
419 Ibid.
420 Kreitzberg, B. Charles C. B. (2019), loc. cit.
421 Gustafsson et al. (2012), op. cit., p. 20.
422 Ibid; p. 21.
423 Kreitzberg, B. Charles C. B. (2019), loc. cit.
424 As cited by CB Insights. "The Top 20 Reasons Startups Fail." *Cbinsights.com,* p. 8, https://s3-us-west-2.amazonaws.com/cbi-content/research-reports/The-20-Reasons-Startups-Fail.pdf. Accessed 28 Feb. 2020.
425 Kreitzberg, B. Charles (2019), loc. cit.
426 Cuncic, Arlin. "Amygdala Hijack and the Fight or Flight Response," *Verywellmind.com,* 26 Oct. 2018, https://www.verywellmind.com/what-happens-during-an-amygdala-hijack-4165944/. Accessed 19 Jan. 2018.
427 Hornby, A. S. Oxford Advanced Learners Dictionary of Current English, 8th Edition, New York: Oxford University Press, 2010-2015, p. 46.
428 Cameron et al. (2017), op. cit., p. 41.
429 Study.com. "The Amygdala: Definition, Role & Function." *Study.com,* https://

study.com/academy/lesson/the-amygdala-definition-role-function.html/. Accessed 6 Feb. 2019.

430 Ibid.
431 Ibid.
432 Engel, C. and Weber, E.U. (2007), op. cit., p. 323.
433 Mintzberg, Henry (1990), op. cit., p. 19.
434 Atsan, Nuray (2016), op. cit., p. 436.
435 Ibid.
436 Mintzberg, Henry (1990), op. cit., p. 19.
437 Ibid.
438 Ibid.
439 Ibid.
440 Engel, C. and Weber, E.U. (2007), op. cit., p. 323.
441 As cited by Engel, C. and Weber, E.U. (2007); ibid.
442 Engel, C. and Weber, E.U. (2007); ibid.
443 Centre for Security Studies. "Strategic foresight: anticipation and capacity to act." *CSS Analyses in Security Policy no. 52*, ETH Zurich, April 2009; as cited by Petrus van de Pol, Sweeney, J., Oprunenco, A., Richardson, J., Lum, K.C., Desker, T. and Goh, Z. "Foresight as a Strategic Long-Term Planning Tool for Developing Countries." Singapore: Global Center for Public Service Excellence (GCPSE), UNDP, 2014, p. 7.
444 Taddeo, Mariarosaria and Floridi, Luciano (2018), op. cit., p. 2.
445 Ibid.
446 See Bland (2013), Berkhout and Hertin (2002), & Nandy (1996); as cited by Petrus van de Pol et al. (2014), op. cit., p. 6.
447 See Fuerth (2009), as cited by Petrus van de Pol et al. (2014), ibid.
448 As cited by Petrus van de Pol et al. (2014), ibid.
449 Leon S. Fuerth (2009). "Foresight and anticipatory governance." *Foresight* 11, no. 4: 17; as cited by Petrus van de Pol et al. (2014), op. cit., p. 10.
450 Ceru, J. Dennis. Mindset of the Entrepreneur. *MOOC Learning Materials*, course excerpts from Babson College of Entrepreneurship, in partnership with edx.org, 2018.
451 Ceru, J. Dennis (2018), loc. cit.
452 *Linear extrapolation* generally involves inferring or estimating by extending or projecting known information beyond the specific range of given variable. It might be below or above the given values. Interpolation provides an estimation between the given data or observations. See http://math.tutorvista.com/calculus/extrapolation.html. Accessed 11 Oct. 2016.
453 Taleb, N. Nicholas. "Black Swan," reviewed by Will Kenton, updated 13 Dec. 2017, https://www.investopedia.com/terms/b/blackswan.asp/. Accessed 25 Jan. 2019.
454 Ibid.
455 Ibid.
456 Rousseau, Richard. "Modern Warfare and Its Evolving Weapons – Assumptions and Inherent Contradictions." *Khazar Journal of Humanities and Social Sciences,* Khazar University, Konstitutcii: Khazar University Press, 2011, p. 13.
457 Ibid.
458 Ibid.
459 As cited by Petrus van de Pol et al. (2014), op. cit., p. 10.
460 As cited by Petrus van de Pol et al. (2014), ibid.
461 Ramos, J., et al. "Foresight in a network era: Peer producing alternative

futures." *Journal of Futures Studies* vol. 17, no. 1: 72, 2012; as cited by Petrus van de Pol, Sweeney, J. et al. (2014), op. cit., p. 10.

462 Da Costa, O., et al. "The impact of foresight on policy-making: Insights from the FORLEARN mutual learning process." *Technology Analysis & Strategic Management* (Institute for Prospective Technological Studies Joint Research Centre / European Commission), 2008, p. 2.

463 Dunn III, J. Richard. From Gettysburg to the Gulf and Beyond: Coping with Revolutionary Technological change in Land Warfare. *The Institute for National Strategic Studies,* Mc Nair Papers, Number 13, March 1992, p. 3.

464 As cited by Nafei, Wageeh (2014), op. cit., p. 120.

465 Rowe, W. Glenn (2001), op. cit., p. 83.

466 Randall, M. Donna (2012), op. cit., p. 31.

467 See Simons, T., and Enz, C. "Motivating hotel employees: Beyond the carrot and the stick." *CornellHotel and Restaurant Administration Quarterly, 36,* 1995, p. 27; as cited by Murray, W. C. "Motivational Dynamics: Understanding the Perceptions of Self and Others in the Canadian Lodging Industry," *Workplace Review,* April 2019 Issue, p. 17.

468 Murray, W. C. (2019), op. cit., p. 19.

469 Murray, W. C. (2019), op. cit., p. 18.

Works Cited

Aaltonen, M. and Irene Sanders, T. "Identifying Systems' New Initial Conditions as Influence Points for the Future." *Foresight,* vol. 8 no. 3, 2006, pp. 28–35. https://doi.org/10.1108/14636680610668054.

Adler, N. J. *Comportement organisationnel: une approche multiculturelle.* Éditions Reynald Goulet, Université McGill, Canada, 1994.

Albert, D., et al. *Dorland's Illustrated Medical Dictionary,* 32nd Edition, Philadelphia: Elsevier – Saunders, 2012, p. 1759.

Apte, Suhas and Jagdish N. Sheth. *The Sustainability Edge: How to Drive Top-Line Growth with Triple-Bottom-Line Thinking.* Rotman – UTP Publishing, 1st Edition, 5 Dec. 2016, *Bookauthority.org,* https://bookauthority.org.

Atsan, Nuray. "Failure Experiences of Entrepreneurs: Causes and Learning Outcomes." *12th International Strategic Management Conference, ISMC 2016,* 28-30 Oct. 2016, Antalya, Turkey: Elservier, *Procedia – Social and Behavioral Sciences 235,* 2016, pp. 435–442.

Barry, C. & Halfmann, K. "The Effect of Mindset on Decision-Making." *Journal of Integrated Social Sciences,* www.JISS.org, vol. 6, no. 1, 2016, pp. 49–74.

Basılgan, Müslüm. "The Creative Destruction of Economic Development: The Schumpeterian Entrepreneur." *TODAİE's Review of Public Administration,* vol. 5, no 3, Sept. 2011, pp. 35–76.

Baumgartner, Jeffrey. "The Corporate Innovation Machine: A Model for Implementing Idea Management Based Innovation Strategy in Your Firm." *Creativejeffrey.com,* 2009, pp. 1-16.

Berkhout, Frans and Hertin, Julia. "Foresight futures scenarios: Developing and applying a participative strategic planning tool." *Greener Management International,* vol. 2002, 1 Mar. 2002, pp. 37-52. DOI: 10.9774/GLEAF.3062.2002.sp.00005.

Bhalla, V., et al. "High-Performance Organizations: The Secrets of Their Success." *The Boston Consulting Group (BCG),* Sept. 2011, pp. 7–8, www.bcg.com.

Bickart, Barbara. "Strategic Social Media Marketing." *Micromasters in Digital Product Management program*, an excerpt from online learning materials – Questrom School of Business at Boston University, in partnership with edx.org, 2018.

Bohner, G. "Attitudes," in Miles Hewstone and Wolfgang Stroebe (eds). *Introduction to Social Psychology*, Oxford: Blackwell, 2001, pp. 239–282.

Bland, Jessica and Westlake Stian. "Don't Stop Thinking About Tomorrow: A Modest Defence of Futurology." Nesta.org.uk, 2013, https://www.nesta.org.uk/report/dont-stop-thinking-about-tomorrow-a-modest-defence-of-futurology/.

Bordia, R., et al. "Innovation's OrgDNA," *Booz & Company Inc.*, 2005, pp. 1-10, www.booz.com/.

Bouchard, Véronique. "Exploring Corporate Entrepreneurship: A Corporate Strategy Perspective." *European Entrepreneurial Learning*, No. 2001/12: Dec. 2001, EM Lyon, pp. 1-30.

Bruderlein, Claude. Humanitarian Response to Conflicts and Disaster. *MOOC Learning Materials*, course excerpts from Harvard University, in partnership with edx.org, 2018.

Burgelman, R. A. "A Process Model of Internal Corporate Venturing in the Diversified Major Firm." *Administrative Science Quarterly*, vol. 28, no. 2, 1983, pp. 223-244, http://dx.doi.org/10.2307/2392619.

Burgelman, R. A. and Valikangas, L. "Venturing Cycles." *MIT Sloan Management Review*, vol. 46, no. 4, 2005, pp. 26-34.

Cameron, F., et al. "5 Behaviours of a Cohesive Team," in StickyChange: Experts in Fostering Change that Sticks, *Stickychange.com*, Feb. 2017, pp. 5–46.

Carper, B. William. "Global Business: A Cultural Perspective." *Journal of Applied Business and Economics*, vol. 16, no. 6, 2014, pp. 109–118.

CB Insights. "The Top 20 Reasons Startups Fail." *Cbinsights.com*, 2020, pp. 2–11.

Centre for Security Studies. "Strategic foresight: anticipation and capacity to act." *CSS Analyses in Security Policy no. 52*, ETH Zurich, Apr. 2009.

Ceru, J. Dennis. Mindset of the Entrepreneur. *MOOC Learning Materials*, course excerpts from Babson College of Entrepreneurship, in partnership with edx.org, 2018.

Chaiken, S. and Y. Trope. *Dual-process Theories in Social Psychology*. New York: Guilford Press, 1999.

Coomber, Nicole. "Gaining Support," in *Leadership and Influence*. *MOOC Learning Materials*, a course excerpt from Robert H. Smith School of Business, University of Maryland, in partnership with edx.org, 2018, https://www.edx.org/course/usmx-leadership-and-influence/.

Cuncic, Arlin. "Amygdala Hijack and the Fight or Flight Response," *Verywellmind.com*, 26 Oct. 2018, https://www.verywellmind.com/what-happens-during-an-amygdala-hijack-4165944/.

Da Costa, O., et al. "The impact of foresight on policy-making: Insights from the FORLEARN mutual learning process." *Technology Analysis & Strategic*

Management (Institute for Prospective Technological Studies Joint Research Centre / European Commission), 2008.

Daft, R. *Organization Theory & Design*. South-Western College Publishing, 2001.

Darroch, J. "Developing A Measure of Knowledge Management Behaviors and Practices." *Journal of Knowledge Management*, vol. 7, no. 5, 2003, pp. 41-54, http://dx.doi.org/10.1108/13673270310505377754.

Dehoff, K., et al. "*Innovation's OrgDNA.*" *Booz & Company*, 2005, pp. 1–10, www.orgdna.com.

Dellaert, Marc and Davydov, Sergey. "Influencing: The Skill of Persuasion – Building Commitment and Getting Results." *White Paper*, Center for Creative Leadership, 2017, pp. 1-12.

DeMers, Jayson. "7 Ways to Build Influence in the Workplace." *Inc.com*, 15 Jan. 2015, https://www.inc.com/jayson-demers/7-ways-to-build-influence-in-the-workplace.html/.

Dettmann, Joe, et al. "Digital-Era Leadership: Ready Or Not, Digital Competence Is Already Differentiating Winners From Losers." Global Leadership Forecast 2018: 25 Research Insights to Fuel Your People Strategy. *Ddiworld.com*, 2018, pp. 12–13.

Dickson, E. Roger. *Dickson Biblical Research Library*. Revised and Expanded Edition, Hutchinson & Cape Town: Africa International Missions, 2015, p. 1079.

Dunn III, J. Richard. *From Gettysburg to the Gulf and Beyond: Coping with Revolutionary Technological change in Land Warfare. The Institute for National Strategic Studies*, Mc Nair Papers, Number 13, Mar., 1992, pp. 1–98.

Earl, P. E. Behavioral Economics and the Economics of Regulation, 2005, http://eprint.uq.edu.au/archive/00003308/

Eker, T. Harv. Secrets of the Millionaire Mind: Mastering the Inner Game of Wealth. *Library of Congress Cataloging-in-Publication Data*; Pymble, Toronto, Auckland, London, New York: HarperCollins Publishers, Adobe Acrobat e-book Reader Feb. 2005, pp. 1–47.

Elias, Steven. "Fifty Years of Influence in the Workplace: The Evolution of the French and Raven Power Taxonomy." *Journal of Management History*, vol. 14, no. 3, 2008, pp. 267-283

Engel, C. and Weber, E. U. "The impact of institutions on the decision how to decide." *Journal of Institutional Economics: The JOIE Foundation*, vol. 3, no. 3, 2007, pp. 323-349. DOI: 10.1017/S1744137407000744.

Estupiñán, Jaime and Neilson, L. Gary. "The 10 Principles of Organizational DNA." *Strategy-business.com*, 27 Oct. 2014, pp. 1–3.

Evans, J. S. B. T. and D. E. Over. "Are People Rational? Yes, No, and Sometimes." *Psychologist*, 1997, pp. 403-406.

Fehr, E. "The Economics of Impatience." *Nature*, vol. 17, 2002, pp. 269-272. DOI: 10.1038/415269a

Festré, Agnès and Garrouste, Pierre. "Rationality, Behavior, Institutional, and Economic Change in Schumpeter." *Journal of Economic Methodology*, vol. 15, no. 4, December 2008.

Fiix. "Condition based maintenance and monitoring software." *Fiixsoftware.com*, 2020a, https://www.fiixsoftware.com/condition-based-maintenance.

Fiix. "Preventive maintenance." *Fiixsoftware.com*, 2020b, https://www.fiixsoftware.com/maintenance-strategies/preventative-maintenance.

Freitas, A. L., et al. "The Influence of Abstract and Concrete Mindsets on Anticipating and Guiding Others' Self-regulatory Efforts." *Journal of Experimental Social Psychology*, vol. 40, 2004, pp. 739-752.

French, J. R. P. and Raven, B. The Basis of Power. In Cartwright, D. (Ed.), *Studies in Social Power*. Ann Arbor, MI: University of Michigan Press, 1959, pp. 529-569.

Fuerth, Leon S. "Foresight and Anticipatory Governance." *Foresight*, vol. 11, no. 4, 2009, 14-32. http://www.altfutures.com/pubs/propoor/Anticipatory_Governance.pdf

Gardenswartz, L. and Rowe, A. *Diverse Teams at Work*. Irwin, 1995, New York.

Gawler, Meg. "Project Design in the Context of Project Cycle Management – Sourcebook." *WWF Introductory Course*, Prévessin-Moëns: ARTEMIS Services for Nature Conservation and Development, Feb. 2005, pp. 1–56, http://www.artemis-services.com.

Gershoni, M. Jonathan. "Lesson 2: Main Terms," in *Viruses & How To Beat Them: Cells, Immunity, Vaccines. TAU Online, Innovative Learning Center*, TelAviv University in partnership with Edx.org, 2018a, pp. 1–4.

Gershoni, M. Jonathan. "Lesson 2: Leading Scientists and Experts," in *Viruses & How To Beat Them: Cells, Immunity, Vaccines. TAU Online, Innovative Learning Center*, TelAviv University in partnership with Edx.org, 2018b, pp. 1–6.

Ghafoor, A., et al. "Transformational Leadership, Employee Engagement and Performance: Mediating Effect of Psychological Ownership." *African Journal of Business Management*, vol. 5, 2011, pp. 7391–7403, University of Central Punjabi, Pakistan.

Gibson, C. B. and Birkinshaw, J. "The Antecedents, Consequences, and Mediating Role of Organizational Ambidexterity." *Academy of Management Journal*, vol. 47, no. 2, 2004, pp. 209–226, http://dx.doi.org/10.2307/20159573.

Govindarajan, V. and Trimble, C. *Organizational DNA for Structure Innovation, Management Span and Layers*, 2006, http://www.Orgdna.com.

Gupta, A., et al. "The Interplay Between Exploration and Exploitation." *Academy of Management Journal*, vol. 49, no. 4, 2006, pp. 693–706, http://dx.doi.org/10.5465/AMJ.2006.22083026

Gustafsson, A., et al. "Customer co-creation in service innovation: A matter of communication?" *Journal of Service Management*, vol. 23, no. 3, Jun. 2012, pp. 4–32.

Harris, Neils. "Corporate Engagement in Processes for Planetary Sustainability: Understanding Corporate Capacity in Non-Renewable Resource Extractive Sector, Australia." *Business Strategy and the Environment*, vol. 16, 1 Nov. 2007, pp. 538–553.

Harvard Business Analytic Services. "*Cultivating Workforce Well-Being to Drive Business Value.*" *Harvard Business Review Group*, 2020, pp. 1–12.

Harvard Business Review Analytic Services (HBRA). "Cultivating Workforce Well-Being to Drive Business Value," Research Report. Harvard Business School Publishing – sponsored by Indeed.com, 28 Jul. 2020, pp. 1-12. https://bg.hbr.org/sponsored/2020/07/cultivating-workforce-well-being-to-drive-business-value.

Harvard Business Publishing. "*Employee Engagement.*" Leading the Way, *Harvard Business Publishing – Corporate Learning*, 13 Feb. 2020.

Hausmann and Hidalgo. "*The atlas of economic complexity: Mapping paths to prosperity.*" Harvard University, Harvard Kennedy School and MIT Media Lab, 2011, pp. 6-91.

Henley, Dede. "Research Says Vertical Development Can Make You A Better Leader." *Henleyleadership.com*, 14 Feb. 2020.

Hill, S. A. and Birkinshaw, J. "Ambidexterity and Survival in Corporate Venture Units." *Journal of Management*, vol. 40, no. 7, 2014, pp. 1899-1931, http://dx.doi.org/10.1177/0149206312445925

Ho, Peter. "Coping with complexity," In *Government Designed for New Times: A Global Conversation.* McKinsey & Company, 2012 pp. 84-86, http://www.mckinsey.com/features/government_ designed_for_new_times

Hodge, B. and Anthony, W. *Organization Theory: A Strategic Approach.* Allyn & Bacon, Inc., 1991.

Hoogh, A., et al. "Charismatic Leadership, Environmental Dynamism, and Performance." *European Journal of Work & Organizational Psychology*, vol. 13, no. 4, 2004, pp. 447-471.

Hornby, A. S. *Oxford Advanced Learners Dictionary of Current English*, 8th Edition, New York: Oxford University Press, 2010-2015.

Industry Canada. *Product Design, Research and Development: A Canadian Manufacturing Perspective. Publishing and Depository Services*, Public Works and Government Services Canada, Catalogue number: Iu44-60/2012, Ottawa, 26 Sept. 2012, pp. 1-30. https://www.fightspam.gc.ca/eic/site/iccat.nsf/eng/07076_1.html.

Ireland, R. D. and Hitt, M. A. "Achieving and Maintaining Strategic Competitiveness In the 21st Century: The Role of Strategic Leadership." *The Academy of Management Executive*, vol. 13, no. 1, 1999, pp. 43-57.

Jansen, J. J., et al. "Managing Potential and Realized Absorptive Capacity: How Do Organizational Antecedents Matter?" *The Academy of Management Journal*, vol. 48, no. 6, 2005, pp. 999-1015, http://dx.doi.org/10.5465/AMJ.2005.19573106

Johnson, W. Mark, "Seizing the White Space." *Featured Interview, Emerald Group Publishing Limited*, Apr. 2010, pp. 1-6.

Jones, H. E., et al. "Helping Leaders Grow Up: Vertical Leadership Development in Practice." *The Journal of Values-Based Leadership*, vol. 13, Iss. 1, Article 8, 2020, pp. 1-16, http://dx.doi.org/10.22543/0733.131.1275.

Karthikeyan, C. "A Predictive Analysis on Future of Vertical Leadership Development; A Leadership Perspective." *International Journal of Research in Social Sciences*, vol. 7, Issue 4, Apr., 2017, pp. 468-487, http://www.ijmra.us.

Katila, R. and Ahuja, G. "Something Old, Something New: A Longitudinal Study of Search Behavior and New Product Introduction." *Academy of Management Journal*, vol. 45, no. 6, 2002, pp. 1183-1195, http://dx.doi.org/10.2307/3069433.

Khan, W. A. "Psychological Conditions of Personal Engagement and Disengagement of Work." *Academy of Management Journal*, vol. 33, 1990, pp. 692-724. http://dx.doi.org/10.2307/256287.

Kilpi, Esko. "The Future of Management." *Shift.newco.co*, 9 Sept. 2017, https://shift.newco.co/2017/09/09/the-future-of-management.

Kim and Mauborgne. "Blue Ocean Strategy: Blue Ocean Strategy Tools and Frameworks." *Blueoceanstrategy.com*, 2014.

King, P. Williams. "*Digital Manufacturing.*" UI LABS Collaboration, Digital Manufacturing and Design Innovation Institute (DMDII), University of Illinois, June 2015, pp. 2-13.

Kiyosaki, T. Robert with Sharon L. Letcher. *Rich Dad Poor Dad: What The Rich Teach Their Kids About Money That the Poor and Middle Class Do Not! Warner Books in association with CASHFLOW Technologies Inc. Mass Market Paperback*, 16 Aug. 2016.

Knight, Joanna. "How to hit the sweet spot between conflict and new ideas." *Hrzone.com*, 4 Oct. 2013, https://www.hrzone.com/perform/business/how-to-hit-the-sweet-spot-between-conflict-and-new-ideas/.

Kreitzberg, B. Charles. "Creating Business Value through Strategic User Experience Design." *Icharlie.me*, 2019, http://www.icharlie.me/sweetspot/.

Kuenkel, Petra. *The Art of Leading Collectively: Co-Creating a Sustainable, Socially Just Future*. Chelsea Green Publishing, 20 Jan. 2016, *Bookauthority.org*, https://bookauthority.org.

Lean Six Sigma Definition. "Six Sigma." Leansixsigmadefinition.com/glossary/six-sigma. Accessed 30 Jul. 2020.

Leung, Millie. "Cashflow Quadrant." *Millieleung.com*, https://millieleung.com/cashflow-quadrant/. Accessed 7 Mar. 2019.

Llopis, Glenn. "5 Ways Leaders Enable Innovation In their Teams." *Forbes.com*, 7 Apr. 2014, https://www.forbes.com/sites/glennllopis/2014/04/07/5-ways-leaders-enable-innovation-in-their-teams/#4843aad88c4c.

Llorens, S., et al. "*Chapter 6: Interventions to Promote Healthy & Resilient Organizations (HERO) from Positive Psychology.*" The Concepts Behind Organizational Health Intervention Research. *Springer Science+Business Media Dordrecht*, 2013. pp. 1-13. DOI: 10.1007/978-94-007-6470-5_6.

Lorsch, J. W. "Managing Culture: The Invisible Barrier to Strategic Change." *California Management Review*, vol. 28, no. 2, 1986, pp. 95-109.

Lowder, M. Tim. "The Best Leadership Model for Organizational Change Management: Transformational Verses Servant Leadership," *SSRN Electronic Journal*, 14 Jun. 2009, pp. 2-18. DOI: 10.2139/ssrn.1418796.

Lozano, O., et al. "Organizational DNA: Customer & Operations Strategy." *Sintec*, Mexico City, Monterrey, Bogota, Sao Paulo: Sistemas Interactivos de Consultoría, S.A. de C.V., 2011, pp. 1-5.

Mannarelli, T. "Accounting for Leadership: Charismatic, Transformational Leadership Through Reflection and Self-awareness." *Accountancy Ireland*, vol. 38, no. 6, 2006, pp. 46-48.

March, J. G. "Exploration and Exploitation in Organizational Learning." *Organization Science*, vol. 2, no. 1, 1991, pp. 71-87, http://dx.doi.org/10.1287/orsc.2.1.71

Mattin, David. "Welcome to Augmented Modernity." *Newco Shift*, 10 Sept. 2017, https://shift.newco.co/2017/09/10/welcome-to-augmented-modernity/ retrieved.

McMahon, T. Edward. "*The Secrets of Successful Communities." Burlington: PlannersWeb.com*, 29 Jul. 2013, pp. 1-15.

Miltenović, A., et al. "Role and Importance of Lightweight Design in the Product Development." *COMET a 2014*: 2nd International Scientific Conference; University of East Sarajevo, 2-5 Dec. 2014, pp. 529-538.

Mintzberg, Henry. "The Manager's Job: Folklore and Fact." *Harvard Business Review*, Reference no. 75409: 1990 March/April, pp. 12-20. This article was originally published in July-August 1975 and was republished in March-April 1990 as an Harvard Business Review (HBR) "Classic," https://www.thecasecentre.org/main/products/view?id=46983.

Mittal, Rakesh. "Charismatic and Transformational Leadership Styles: A Cross-Cultural Perspective." *International Journal of Business and Management*, vol. 10, no. 3, 2015, 27 Feb. 2015, pp. 26-30, doi:10.5539/ijbm.v10n3p26.

Mohrman, S. A. and Worley, C. G. "The Organizational Sustainability Journey: Introduction to the Special Issue." *Organizational Dynamics*, vol. 39, 2010, pp. 289-294.

Moye, Neta. "Expanding Your Capacity to Lead," in Leadership and Influence. *MOOC Learning Materials*, a course excerpt from Robert H. Smith School of Business, University of Maryland, in partnership with edx.org, 2018, https://www.edx.org/course/usmx-leadership-and-influence/.

Mukasyan, Alexander. Materials Science and Engineering. *MOOC Learning Materials* – course excerpts, University of Notre dame, Indiana, and Moscow Institute of Steel and Alloy, in partnership with edx.org, 2019.

Murray, W. C. "Motivational Dynamics: Understanding the Perceptions of Self and Others in the Canadian Lodging Industry," *Workplace Review*, Apr. 2019 Issue, pp. 16-30.

Nafei, Wageeh. "The Role of Organizational DNA in Improving Organizational Performance: A Study on the Industrial Companies in Egypt." *International Business Research*, vol. 8, 25 Dec. 2014, pp. 117-130. DOI: 10.5539/ibr.v8n1p117.

Neal, Stephanie. "Generation X-Change: Don't Underestimate the Powerful Influence of Gen X Leaders." Global Leadership Forecast 2018: 25 Research Insights to Fuel Your People Strategy, *Ddiworld.com*, 2018, pp. 32-33.

Neilson, L. Gary, et al. "The Secrets to Successful Strategy Execution." *Harvard Business Review*, June 2008, pp. 61-70, https://hbr.org/2008/06/the-secrets-to-successful-strategy-execution.

Neilson, L. Gary, et al. "The Passive-Aggressive Organization." *Harvard Business Review*, From the Oct. 2005 Issue, https://hbr.org/2005/10/the-passive-aggressive-organization.

Neilson, G., et al. "The Four Bases of Organizational DNA." *Organizational DNA Reading Materials, strategy+business issue 33*, Booz Allen Hamilton Inc., 2003, p. 5, www.boozallen.com.

Nelson, Gabe. "10 Reasons Why Most Entrepreneurs Succeed in Their Business." *Ingeniumweb.com*, 13 Mar. 2019.

No Sweat Shakespeare. "The Seven Ages of Man." 2020, *Nosweatshakespeare.com*.

Nyangena, E., et al. "Ethical leadership for sustainable development in developing countries." *Editon Cons. J. Arts., Humanit. S. Stud.*, vol. 1, no. 1, 2019, pp. 1-10.

Owen, L. Charles. *"Insight and Ideas." Institute of Design – Illinois Institute of Technology*, a web article written for: The Business Process Management Institute. Web site: www.BPMInstitute.org, Feb. 2008, pp. 3-5.

Owen, L. Charles. "Design, Advanced Planning and Product Development." 3o Congresso Brasileiro de Pesquisa e Desenvolvimento em Design, Rio de Janeiro, Brazil: 26 Oct. 1998. International Symposium: Nuevos Metodos & Tecnologias para el Diseño de Productos, Santiago, Chile: Nov. 12, 1998, pp. 1-13.

Owen, L. Charles, *"Product Integrity by Design,"* Institute of Design, Illinois Institute of Technology Chicago, Illinois U.S.A, 1991, pp. 1-5.

Page, Jean-Paul. Corporate Governance and Value Creation. *The CFA Institute Research Foundation*, vol. 2005, no. 1, 1 Mar. 2005, pp. 1-75.

Patrick, A. Harold (2012). "Influence of Power Bases on Leadership Strategies Adopted by Managers' in Information Technology Organizations." *European Journal of Business and Management*, vol. 4, no. 11, pp. 101-107.

Payne, J. Richard. "The Struggle for Primacy in a Global Society." Chapter 2, *Global Issues*, Boston: Pearson Education (US), 4th edition, 2012, pp. 16-25.

Pepper, S., et al. "Managing Tomorrow's People: The Future of Work to 2020." *Connectedthinking*, PricewaterhouseCoopers LLP, 2007, pp. 1-31.

Pereira, Rom. "Toyota's 8 Steps Practical Problem Solving Methodology." *Gembaacademy.com*, 3 Dec. 2015, https://www.youtube.com/watch?v=gd3uUl2fFPA.

Petrie, Nick. "Vertical Leadership Development–Part 1: Developing Leaders for a Complex World." White Paper, *Center for Creative Leadership*, 2014, pp. 1-16.

Petrus van de Pol, et al. *"Foresight as a Strategic Long-Term Planning Tool for Developing Countries."* Singapore: Global Center for Public Service Excellence (GCPSE), UNDP, 2014, pp. 4-18.

Popiela, Amanda. "The Rise of Digital Natives: Are Millennials Ready to Lead?." Global Leadership Forecast 2018: 25 Research Insights to Fuel Your People Strategy. *Ddiworld.com*, 2018, pp. 30-31.

Prasad, S. P., et al. "Servant Leadership: An Imperative Leadership Style of Managers for Achieving Organizational Change Successfully." *Academia.edu*, 2014, pp. 1-11.

Raisch, S., et al. "Organizational Ambidexterity: Balancing Exploitation and Exploration for Sustained Performance." *Organization Science*, vol. 20, no. 4, 2009, pp. 685-695, http://dx.doi.org/10.1287/orsc.1090.0428

Ramos, J., et al., "Foresight in a Network Era: Peer Producing Alternative Futures." *Journal of Futures Studies*, 7, no. 1, Sept. 2012, pp. 71-90.

Randall, M. Donna. "Leadership and the Use of Power: Shaping an Ethical Climate." *The Journal of Applied Christian Leadership*, vol. 6, no. 1, Spring, Apr. 2012, pp. 28-35.

Robinson, D., et al. *The Drives of Employee Engagement. Institute for Employement Studies*, 2004, Birighton, UK.

Rousseau, Richard. "Modern Warfare and Its Evolving Weapons – Assumptions and Inherent Contradictions." *Khazar Journal of Humanities and Social Sciences*, Khazar University, Konstitutcii: Khazar University Press, 2011.

Rowe, W. Glenn. "Creating wealth in organizations: The role of strategic

leadership." *Academy of Management Executive*, vol. 15, no. 1, Feb., 2001, pp. 81-94.
Sakhdari, Kamal. "Corporate Entrepreneurship: A Review and Future Research Agenda." *Technology Innovation Management Review*, vol. 6, no. 8, Aug. 2016, pp. 1-11.
Satell, Greg. "The Power of Synthesis and the Problem with Experts." *DigitalTonto*, 21 June 2010, https://www.digitaltonto.com/2010/power-of-synthesis/.
Schein, E. *Organizational Culture and Leadership*. 2nd Ed., Jossey Bass, 1992, California.
Schein, E. H. "Organizational Culture." *American Psychologist*, vol. 45, 1990, pp. 109-119.
Schermerhorn, John R., et al. Comportément Humain ét Organisation. *Adaptation française de Claire de Billy*, 2ème édition, ERPI 2002, pp. 1-90.
Schwab, K., et al. *The Global Competitiveness Report (GCI). Insight Report, Geneva: World Economic Forum*, 2015-2016, pp. 3-84.
Sheffi, Yossi and Edgar Blanco. *Balancing Green: When to Embrace Sustainability in Business (and When Not To)*. The MIT Press, 18 March 2018, *Bookauthority.org*, https://bookauthority.org.
Singh, Yogesh. "Importance of Predictive Analytics: What it is & why it's Important?" *Edupristine.com*, 1 Nov. 2018, https://www.edupristine.com/blog/importance-of-predictive-analytics/.
Sinke, Jos. "Text Lecture 8c – Production." Introduction to Aeronautical Engineering. *MOOC Learning Materials*, course excerpt from Delft University of Technology, in partnership with edx.org, 2019b, pp. 1-2.
Skidmore, Paul. "11 Tips for Good Ergonomic Product Design and Development." *Cadcrowd.com*, 12 Dec. 2018, https://www.cadcrowd.com/blog/11-tips-for-good-ergonomic-product-design-and-development.
SlideModel. "Why Customer Centricity Will Win You More Business (in 2020)." *SlideModel.com*, 14 May 2020a, https://slidemodel.com.
Soieb, A. Z. M., et al. "The Effects of Perceived Leadership Styles and Organizational Citizenship Behaviour on Employee Engagement: The Mediating Role of Conflict Management." *International Journal of Business and Management*, vol. 8, no. 8, 22 March 2013, pp. 91-96.
Sondhe, S. Ratanjit. "Wealth Creation vs. Job Creation: Why Creating Jobs Isn't the Real Answer to Our Economic Problems." *Probizwriters.com*, 2010, pp. 1-18.
Stanovich, K. E. and West, R. F. "Individual Differences in Reasoning: Implications for the Rationality Debate?" *Behavioral and Brain Sciences*, vol. 23, 2000, pp. 645-665.
Strack, F. and Deutsch, R. "Reflective and Impulsive Determinants of Social Behaviour." *Personality and Social Psychology Review*, vol. 8, 2004, pp. 220-247.
Study.com. "The Amygdala: Definition, Role & Function." *Study.com*, https://study.com/academy/lesson/the-amygdala-definition-role-function.html/.
Sultana, M. A., et al. "Cross-Cultural Management and Organizational Performance: A Content Analysis Perspective." *International Journal of*

Business and Management, vol. 8, no. 8, 2013, Published by Canadian Center of Science and Education, 26 Mar. 2013, pp. 133-146.

Susman, G., et al. "Innovation and Change Management in Small and Medium-Sized Manufacturing Companies," *Sponsored Research Prepared for: United States Department of Commerce, the National Institute of Standards and Technology Manufacturing Extension Partnership*, Prepared by Smeal College of Business, The Pennsylvania State University. Final Report of Task 4 RFP 05-480-5823, Contract No. SB1341-03-Z-0015/65364, Jun. 30, 2006, pp. 3-49.

Taddeo, Mariarosaria and Floridi, Luciano. "How AI can be a force for good," *Science*, vol. 361, no. 6404, 24 Aug. 2018, pp. 751-752, vol. 361, no. 6404: AAAS, pp. 1-3. DOI: 10.1126/science.aat5991.

Taleb, N. Nicholas. "Black Swan," reviewed by Will Kenton, updated 13 Dec. 2017, https://www.investopedia.com/terms/b/blackswan.asp/.

Tan, Wee Liang and Tan, Teck Meng. "The Impact of Corporate Governance on Value Creation in Entrepreneurial Firms." *Rencontres de St-Gall 2004, Appenzell*. Research Collection Lee Kong Chian School of Business, 2004, pp. 1-10.

Tang, Kelly & Greenwald, Christopher. "Long-Termism versus Short-Termism: Time for the Pendulum to Shift?" *Research*, S&P Dow Jones Indices LLC, a division of S&P Global, Apr. 2016, pp. 1-13.

The Five Behaviors. "State of Teams." *The Five Behaviors – A Wiley Brand*, 2020, pp. 2-16, https://www.fivebehaviors.com/Home.aspx.

Thompson, A. and Strickland, A. *Strategic Management: Concepts and Cases*. McGraw-Hill /Irwin, 2003.

Tichy, N. M., and Cohen, E. *The Leadership Engine: How Winning Companies Build Leaders at Every Level*. New York: HarperCollins, 1997.

Trevino, L. K. "Ethical Decision Making in Organizations: A Person-situation Interactionist Model." *Academy of Management*, vol. 11, no. 3, 1986, pp. 601-617.

Trevino, L. K. and Brown, M. E. "The Role of Leaders in Influencing Unethical Behavior in the Workplace. In Kidwell, R. E. & Martin, C. L. (Eds.), *Managing Organizational Deviance*. Thousand Oaks: Sage, 2005, pp. 69-87, CA.

Tsui, Eric. "Resource-based view (RBV) of a firm: What is RBV?." MOOC Learning Materials, course excerpts from The Hong Kong Polytechnic University, in partnership with edx.org, 2018a, pp. 1-10.

Tsui, Eric. "Resource-based view (RBV) of a firm: The VRIO Framework." *MOOC Learning Materials*, course excerpts from The Hong Kong Polytechnic University, 2018b, pp. 1-9.

Tucker, B. Robert. "Managing the Future: 10 Driving Forces of Change for the '90s." *Internet Delivered Business Book Summaries*, 1 Dec. 1991, pp. 1-7.

Tzafestas, G. Spyros. "Roboethics: Fundamental Concepts and Future Prospects." *Information*, Basel, vol. 9, no. 148, 10 Jun. 2018, pp. 1-25. DOI: 10.3390/info9060148.

Van de Ven, A. H. and Engleman, R. Central Problems in Managing Corporate Innovation and Entrepreneurship. In J. Katz & A. C. Corbett (Eds.), *Advances in Entrepreneurship, Firm Emergence and Growth*. Bingley, United Kingdom:

Emerald Group Publishing Limited. Volume 7, 2004, pp. 47-72, http://dx.doi.org/10.1016/S1074-7540%2804%2907003-5

Vazirani, N. *Employee Engagement.* Working paper series 05/07. College of Management Studies, 2007, Nerul, India.

Viki, Tendayi. *"Six Principles for Creating a Good Corporate Innovation Process," Forbes Media LLC*, 26 Mar. 2018, https://www.forbes.com.

Villanova University. *"Six Sigma vs. Lean Six Sigma." Villanova University*, https://www.villanovau.com/resources/six-sigma/six-sigma-vs-lean-six-sigma.

Waterman, R. H., et al. "Structure is Not Organization." *Business Horizons*, vol. 23, 1980, pp. 14-26.

Watson, Jessica. "Top 10 Reasons for Entrepreneurs Failure in 2018," *Mercy – CBNation*, 21 Mar. 2018, https://rescue.ceoblognation.com/2018/03/21/top-10-reasons-for-entrepreneurs-failure-in-2018/

Zahra, S. A. "Corporate Entrepreneurship and Financial Performance: The Case of Management Leveraged Buyouts." *Journal of Business Venturing*, vol. 10, no. 3, 1995, pp. 225-247. http://dx.doi.org/10.1016/0883-9026(94)00024-O.

3 Entrepreneurship, Management, and Their Strategic Organizational Value Creation Imperatives: Profitability Perspective

Introduction

1. Empirical Foundation: Getting the Basics Right!

Arguably, starting an entirely new business is uncharted territory for most people. It offers great rewards, but equally high risks – around 80% of all new small businesses fail within the first five years. Wanting to be your own boss is not enough to make you successful. That said, before you set up a new venture, you need to think hard about whether you have the right temperament, leadership skills, support system, and dedication to be an entrepreneur.

From the foregoing, before delving into this "unchartered territory," it is imperative to objectively evaluate your strengths and weaknesses – by honestly answering the following questions:

1. Are you a self-starter? You need to be able to develop and drive projects, manage your time and follow through on details.
2. Are you willing to work long hours? When you own a business you're committed to it 24 hours a day, seven days a week – particularly during the first few years.
3. Are you good at making decisions? As a sole owner, you will have to make decisions quickly, under pressure, and on your own.
4. Do you plan well? Research indicates that many business failures could have been avoided through better planning. Good organization of financials, inventory, schedules, and production is the oil that keeps any business engine running smoothly.
5. Do you have the strength to stay motivated (sustaining the momentum)? Running a business can wear you down, especially when all the responsibility is on your shoulders. It takes strong motivation and passion to survive a slump in business or periods of burnout.
6. Are you willing to invest? True entrepreneurs put their money where their mouths are, and this might mean using personal savings or property.

7. Have you considered the possible impact on your family? Starting a business can be hard on family life. For example, the strain of a spouse who isn't behind you 100% may be hard to balance against your new business demands. There may also be financial difficulties until the business becomes profitable, which could necessitate lowering your standard of living.
8. Do you have a network of friends or associates who could provide outside financing? Insufficient capital is a key cause of small business failure. If you are not able to obtain enough funds from a bank, you may need to rely on funds from friends and family. Most start-up businesses are funded this way.
9. The people issue: How well do you get along with different personalities? Business owners need to develop working relationships with a variety of people including customers, vendors, staff, bankers, and professionals such as lawyers, accountants, or consultants. Can you deal with a demanding client, an unreliable vendor, or a cranky employee in the best interest of your business?

Note! If you can answer YES to most of the above questions, then you may have the potential to join the ranks of successful small enterprise owners. If you can't, you need to consider whether starting a small business is the best solution for you.

2. Theoretical Foundation: Getting the Concepts Right!

As we saw earlier, getting the basics rights in the world of entrepreneurship – prior to exploring the entrepreneurial literature is of prime and paramount importance. That said, Slywotzky (2003) argues that in the past, companies taught their employees about quality, but in today's unstable economy, employees must stress the importance of profitability.[1] According to Gibbons *et al.* (1994), wealth creation increasingly depends on the generation and exploitation of knowledge involving not only science and technology, but also knowledge of practice required to create economic value.[2] To this end, new firms excel at detecting opportunities and resourcing ventures, but matching these up is a delicate process. This is reflected in the highly nonlinear growth paths of new firms and high exit rates. Therefore, new firms have to create a resource base in order to commercialize knowledge on a scale that can make an impact. Whether or not opportunities are taken up successfully, it however, depends on entrepreneurial behavior in an economy, and the way in which new businesses are managed.[3]

3.1 The Entrepreneurial Landscape

3.1.1 Types and Stages of Entrepreneurial Start-ups

Yunus (2018) defines an entrepreneur as basically someone who takes initiatives. In this regard, an entrepreneur sees something, probably a vacuum to be filled or a problem that needs to be attended to – and wants to do something to fill that vacuum and solve that problem. So you become an entrepreneur by initiating such a business venture to make money for yourself.[4] Consequently, the entrepreneurial process is not only for start-ups, but it is also a comprehensive mindset that identifies, assess, shape, and act on opportunities in a variety of contexts, settings, and organizations.[5]

Types of Entrepreneurial Start-ups

THE MAJOR CATEGORIES OF VENTURES

With regards to a typology of start-ups, Davidsson (2005) argues that entrepreneurs create ventures that take many different forms, suggesting a very heterogeneous landscape.[6] In concurrence, Morris *et al.* (2015) argue that if we consider the entire range of possibilities, by focusing on the for-profit sector, at least four major categories of ventures can be identified; these include survival, lifestyle, managed growth, and aggressive or high growth (HG) ventures.[7]

The four categories are distinguished based on their relative emphasis on growth, innovation, and reinvestment in the business, their means of extracting income or returns, the principal kinds of stakeholders involved with the business, and the primary managerial challenges confronting the founder. Each is further explained below:

- *Survival ventures* – Provide basic subsistence for the entrepreneur and his or her family, in effect, allowing little more than a hand-to-mouth type of existence. These ventures may or may not be formally registered, they typically have no premises, very few assets, and no business banking relationship, and they operate on a cash or barter basis. As these businesses exist to provide for basic personal financial needs, once costs are covered there is generally no capacity to reinvest into these ventures. The launch of these ventures is often necessity-driven or motivated by "push" factors, and the businesses typically operate in highly competitive, price-based, and largely undifferentiated markets.[8]
- *Lifestyle ventures* – Provide a relatively stable income stream for owners based on a workable business model and a maintenance approach to management. Relatively modest reinvestments are made to maintain competitiveness in a local market where these firms are embedded. These ventures typically have premises, usually a single

location, and do not seek expansion or meaningful growth. The numbers of employees remain relatively constant. Given limited capacity, it is difficult for these ventures to achieve economies of scale.

- *Managed growth ventures* – Have a workable business model and seek stable growth over time, as reflected in occasional new product launches; periodic entry into new markets; steady expansion of facilities, locations, and staff; and development of a strong local and regional brand. There is continuous ongoing reinvestment in these businesses, but the ongoing business development is of moderate regional growth standards.[9]
- *Aggressive/high-growth ventures* – Referred to as *gazelles*, these are often technology-based ventures with strong innovation capabilities that seek exponential growth and are funded by equity capital. The launch of these ventures is opportunity-driven, with the founders (often a team) seeking to create new markets. Their market focus is typically national or international, and they often become candidates for initial public offerings or acquisition.[10]

Stages of Entrepreneurial Start-Ups

A start-up has typically *three stages* for the purpose of calculating start-up costs, namely: the pre-seed stage, the seed stage, and the early stage.

- The pre-seed stage – i.e., expenses before the starting date. This includes, but is not limited to the following: market research, registration fees, legal fees, office stationery, design and printing of corporate identity (business cards and letterheads), registration of a domain name and creation of a website, installations, and utility connections (if moving into a new property).
- The seed stage – comprises expenses from the starting date and during the early months before sales reach break-even levels. This typically embodies two things: (1) *start-up inventory* (if yours is a product-based business; (2) *cash reserve* to support the company during the early months before sales reach break-even levels.
- The early stage – spans between the periods when sales reach breakeven levels and some small profits start accruing. Common cost features can be typically grouped under two stages: (1) *current assets*, such as fixtures and signage, office furniture, and vehicles (either purchase price or down payments); and (2) *long-term or fixed assets*, such as property and equipment.

3.1.2 Understanding Cognitive Biases

Cognitive biases play a decisive role in entrepreneurial start-up ventures, as well as in established businesses. Cherry (2020a), defines *cognitive bias* as a systematic error in thinking that occurs when people are processing and interpreting information in the world around them, and affects the decisions and judgments they have.[11] Furthermore, people sometimes confuse *cognitive biases* with *logical fallacies*, but the two are not the same. A *logical fallacy* stems from an error in *logical argument*, while a *cognitive bias* is rooted in *thought processing errors* often arising from problems with memory, attention, attribution, and other mental mistakes.[12]

Rationale for Cognitive Biases

The concept of cognitive bias was first introduced by researchers Amos Tversky and Daniel Kahneman in 1972. Since then, researchers have described a number of different biases that affect decision-making in a wide range of areas including social behavior, cognition, behavioral economics, education, management, healthcare, business, and finance.[13] That said, Cherry (2020a) argues that the causes of cognitive biases arise due to the fact that if you have to think about every possible option when making a decision, it would take a lot of time to make even the simplest choice. And because of the sheer complexity of the world around you and the amount of information in the environment, it is necessary sometimes to rely on some mental shortcuts that would allow you to act quickly.[14] Consequently, while we cannot eliminate these biases, we can mitigate their impact by understanding them and employing strategies to combat them.

Cherry (2020a) argues that although cognitive biases can be caused by a number of different things, however, it is the mental shortcuts, known as *heuristics* (availability bias) that often play a major contributing role. Thus, while they can often be surprisingly accurate, they can also lead to errors in thinking. Other factors that can also contribute to these biases include:

- Emotions
- Individual motivations
- Limits on the mind's ability to process information
- Social pressures.[15]

Wilson *et al.* (2018) found that cognitive bias may also increase as people get older due to decrease cognitive flexibility; as older adults are often worse than younger adults at adapting to changing situational demands, and this difference is commonly attributed to an age-related decline in acquiring and updating information.[16]

That being said, the following cognitive biases are especially relevant for early-stage entrepreneurs: availability heuristics, anchoring bias, confirmation bias, attentional bias, functional fixedness, the Dunning-

Kruger effect, false consensus effect, optimism bias, the planning fallacy, the sunk cost fallacy, and the halo effect.

Other biases include actor-observer bias (this is the tendency to attribute your own actions to external causes while attributing other people's behaviors to internal causes), misinformation effect (the tendency for post-event information to interfere with the memory of the event at hand), and self-serving effect (the tendency to blame external forces when bad things happen and give yourself credit when good things happen).[17]

The aforementioned notwithstanding, Cherry (2020a) argues that at times, multiple biases may play a role in influencing your decisions and thinking. And some of the tips for overcoming them include being aware of biases, frequently considering the factors that influence your decisions, and challenging your biases.

Types of Biases Relevant to Early-Stage Entrepreneurial Ventures

Understanding these biases at the early stages of the entrepreneurial venture plays a critical role in enhancing the ability of the entrepreneurial team selection and team dynamics. This is an indispensable tool to ensure short-term and long-term entrepreneurial venture success. To facilitate a better understanding, the biases will be categorized under four distinct groups.

GROUP 1 SET OF BIASES

Interestingly, the following five biases seem to work in tandem and tend to follow some logical patterns in their occurrence, notably; availability heuristics, anchoring bias, confirmation bias, attentional bias, and functional fixedness. For instance, the availability heuristics (or availability bias) is that bias occasioned by placing greater value on information that comes to your mind quickly. This works in tandem with the anchoring bias, which is the tendency to rely too heavily on the very first piece of information you learn. For example, if you learn that the average price for a car is a certain value; you will think any amount below that is a good deal, perhaps making you not to search for better deals. That said, Cherry (2020a) suggests that you can use the anchoring bias to set the expectations of others - by putting your very first piece of priority information on the table for consideration.

The next is the *confirmation bias*. This bias is favoring information that conforms to your existing beliefs and discounting evidence that does not conform. This type of bias provides a breeding ground for *attentional bias*. Cherry (2020a), argues that attentional bias is the tendency to pay attention to some things, while simultaneously ignoring others.

For instance, when making a decision on which car to buy, you may pay attention to the look and feel of the exterior and interior, but ignore the safety record and gas mileage. In a similar vein, Ghezzi *et al.* (2015) found that entrepreneurial start-ups tend not to take stock of existing strategy analysis models, and are seldom employed in the early phases of the new venture activity.[18] Again, the *attentional bias* appears to set the stage for the *functional fixedness bias.* This type of bias is the tendency to see objects as only working in a particular way. For instance, if you don't have a hammer, you never consider that a big wrench can also be used to drive a nail into the wall (Cherry, 2020a).

GROUP 2 SET OF BIASES

The three next sets of biases that work in tandem and also appear to follow a logical sequence in their occurrence are *the Dunning-Kruger effect, false consensus effect*, and the *optimism bias.* According to Cherry (2019), *the Dunning-Kruger effect* is a type of cognitive bias in which people believe that they are smarter and more capable than they are. And that essentially, low ability people do not possess the skills needed to recognize their incompetence. In this regard, the combination of *poor self-awareness* and *low cognitive ability* leads them to overestimate their own capability.[19] This would likely lead to another cognitive bias, the *false consensus effect*, which according to Cherry (2020a), it is the tendency to overestimate how much people agree with you.

Finally, the *false consensus effect* would likely take you to the *optimism bias.* This bias leads us to believe that we are less likely to suffer from misfortune and more likely to attain success than our peers or than reality would suggest. Sharot (2011) defines optimism bias as the difference between a person's expectation and the outcome that follows. If expectations are better than reality, the bias is optimistic; if reality is better than expected, the bias is pessimistic.[20] The extent of the optimism bias is thus, measured empirically by recording an individual's expectations before an event unfolds, and contrasting those with the outcomes that transpire.[21]

Another type of cognitive bias in this category is the *planning fallacy.* According to iResearchNet (2020), the *planning fallacy* refers to a specific form of *optimism bias* wherein people underestimate the time that it will take to complete an upcoming task, even though they are fully aware that similar tasks have taken longer in the past.[22] An intriguing aspect of this phenomenon is that people simultaneously hold both optimistic beliefs (concerning the specific future task) as well as more realistic beliefs (concerning relevant past experiences). So when it comes to planning the future, people can know the past and yet be doomed to repeat.[23] Kahneman and Tversky describe the *planning fallacy* as a combination of optimistic prediction about a particular case in the face of more general knowledge that would suggest otherwise.[24]

iResearchNet (2020) argues that the major causes have been that when people focus narrowly on a plan for successful task completion, they tend to neglect other sources of information – such as past completion times, competing priorities, and factors that may delay their progress – that could lead to more realistic predictions.[25] In this regard, the following three tips to avoid becoming a planning fallacy victim could be helpful:

1. Use the data from past projects to predict your future project timelines
2. Curb down enthusiasm by approaching planning from a conservative, risk management standpoint
3. Ask an unbiased party to gut-check your plan.[26]

GROUP 3 SET OF BIASES: THE SUNK-COST AND SUNK-COST FALLACY

Olivola (2018) describes the *sunk-cost fallacy* as the general tendency for people to continue an endeavor, or continue consuming or pursuing an option, which of course, is an inferior alternative, merely because they have previously invested significant time or money or some resource in it. He argues that this approach represents a striking violation of rational decision making.[27] In economics, there is the concept of *sunk-costs,* which are costs that have already been incurred, but which cannot be recouped. Meanwhile, the *sunk-cost fallacy* refers to the fallacy of honoring such costs, which theoretically, rational decision making would suggest that it should be ignored.[28] According to *Toggl track (2020)*, the sunk-cost fallacy is a trap most people fall into. More especially as it's hard to abandon a project once you've invested so much of your time and money in the cause. They argue that by falling for the trap, we risk losing much more than our initial investment in an anxious attempt to recoup the loss.[29] The sunk cost fallacy goes by a number of aliases, including:

- Sunk cost effect
- Sunk cost heuristic
- Concorde fallacy
- Argument from waste
- Investment trap
- Escalation of commitment
- Irrational escalation
- Escalation bias.[30]

That being said, Olivola (2018) also found that while theoretical accounts and empirical examinations of the sunk-cost effect have generally been based on the assumption that it is a purely intrapersonal phenomenon (i.e., solely driven by one's own past investments), the present research demonstrates that it is also an interpersonal effect (i.e., people will alter their choices in response to other people's past investments). This finding was documented across eight experiments (*N* = 6,076) covering diverse scenarios when the sunk-cost effects are borne by someone other than the decision-maker.[31] Moreover, he also found that the interpersonal sunk-cost effect is not moderated by social closeness or whether other people observe their sunk costs being "honored." Consequently, the sunk-cost effect is a much broader phenomenon than previously thought and poses interesting challenges,[32] especially as it is not just a trap that only companies fall into. It affects any area of life, career or business where impactful decisions are involved.[33]

Finally, although it's not easy to let go a significant loss, it is argued that a rational approach to sunk costs is to say that money you can't get back should have no influence on decisions about what you do next. As a result, only additional future costs should matter.[34]

GROUP 4 SET OF BIASES: HALO BIASES

In the reasoning of Cherry (2020b), the *halo effect* is a type of cognitive bias in which our overall impression of a person influences how we feel and think about their character. Also, the halo effect is sometimes referred to as the "physical attractiveness stereotype" and the "what is beautiful is also good" principle. That being said, several different studies have found that when we rate people as good-looking, we also tend to believe that they have positive personality traits and that they are more intelligent.[35] However, this attractiveness stereotype can also be a double-edged sword. As other studies have found that while people are more likely to ascribe a host of positive qualities to attractive people, they are also more likely to believe that good-looking individuals are vain, dishonest, and likely to use their attractiveness to manipulate others.

Put simply, the halo effect makes it such that the perceptions of one quality - leads to biased judgments of other qualities.[36]

The halo effect may have an impact on a number of real-world settings, such as in education, in the workplace, and in marketing, et cetera. In the *workplace*, for example, experts suggest that the halo effect is one of the most common biases affecting performance appraisals and reviews. In that, supervisors may rate subordinates based on the perception of a single character, rather than the whole of their performance and contribution. For instance, a worker's enthusiasm or positive attitude may overshadow their lack of knowledge or skill, causing co-workers to rate them more highly than their actual performance justifies.[37] In a similar vein, Parrett (2015) finds that attractive servers earn approximately $1261 more per year in tips than unattractive servers, the primary driver of which is female customers tipping attractive females more than unattractive females.[38] Cherry (2020b) argues that job applicants are also likely to feel the impact of the halo effect. For example, if a prospective employer views the applicant as attractive or likable, they are more likely to also rate the individual as intelligent, competent, and qualified.

In *education*, the halo effect can influence how teachers treat students, but it can also impact how students perceive teachers. In the experiment by Clifford and Walster (1973), teachers were given objective information, presumably about a student's scholastic and social potential, accompanied by a photograph of an attractive or an unattractive boy or girl. It was found that the student's attractiveness was significantly associated with the teacher's expectations about how intelligent the student was, how interested in education his parents were, how far he/she was likely to progress in school, and how popular he would be with his peers.[39] In one other study, researchers found that when an instructor was viewed as warm and friendly, students also rated them as more attractive, appealing, and likable.[40]

Finally, in *marketing*, marketers take advantage of the halo effect to sell products and services. For example, when a celebrity spokesperson endorses a particular item, our positive evaluations of that individual can spread to our perceptions of the product itself.[41]

3.2 Mindset, Resilience, and the Culture of Value Creation

Our mindset can determine how we mentally represent a decision. In other words, our mindset is an approach or manner of understanding information.[42] However, it's been a difficult task to draw a clear borderline between the *mindset of value creation* and the *culture of value creation*.

That being said, the *mindset of value creation* can be defined as the mental aspects of the foundational plan and design of *value creation* activities; especially applicable to the sub-conscious mind and its corresponding match in the outer world. The *culture of value creation* requires the effective and continuous linking of the *mindset of value creation* (the intangibles) with the requisite levels of implementation in the form of *value-added* activities in a tangible form.

3.2.1 The Mindset of Value Creation

In the arguments of Eker (2005), rich people really do think differently not only from poor people, but from even middle-class people as well.

He maintains further that uniquely, it has been observed that rich people tend to keep their commitments.[43] Also, to enhance the value creation mindset, one trick is to use the attractive force of nature. To this end, Stuart Wilde argues that the key to success is to raise your own energy; when you do, people will naturally be attracted to you – and when they show up, you bill them.[44]

This holds true, even in the world of atomic physics where an increase in the energy level of the atom through heating, can enable an insulator (a non-conductor) to conduct electricity and light bulb. In a similar direction, Leung (2019) also argues that your passion is contagious – and if you love what you do, your passion will ignite the same intensity in others, who are likely to join you as you build a team to succeed in the said endeavor. And with the same passion, both your team and your customers are more likely to see your vision and be excited to be part of your journey.[45]

The Psychology of Money: Your Financial/Money Blueprint

We can define financial or money blueprint as a combination of your thoughts, feelings, and actions in the arena of money – primarily from the *information or "programming"* you received in the past (or verbal programming/information – i.e., what did you *hear* when you were young?), as well as *modeling* (i.e., what did you see when you were young?), and finally the *specific incidents* you encountered especially as a young child (or what did you *experience* when you were young?). These are subconscious conditioning that determines your thinking.

To that end, many, if not most of us have heard or noticed how some people have a lot of money and then lose it, or have excellent opportunities and start well at the beginning, but then go down the drainage with them. Eker (2005) found that to many, on the outside, it looks like bad luck, or some kind of a downturn in the economy, or blame it on a lousy partner, whatever; while on the inside, however, it's a different ballgame altogether. On the strength of this observation, he argues that that's why, if you come into big money when you're not ready for it on the inside, the chances are that your wealth will be short-lived and you will lose it.[46] On this strand, he goes further to argue that the vast majority of people simply do not have the internal capacity to create and hold on to large amounts of money, and the increased challenges that go with more money and success. For instance, a perfect example is lottery winners.[47]

To this end, Eker argues that regardless of the size of their winnings, *most lottery winners* eventually return to their original financial state – the amount they can comfortably handle. On the contrary, when *self-made millionaires* lose their money, they usually have it back within a relatively short time. He cites Donald Trump as a good example. Trump was worth billions, lost everything, and then a couple of years later, got it all back again and more. He attributes this to Trump's financial "thermostat."[48] In this sense the "thermostat" provides the rules of engagement in the inner game of wealth (the toolbox), which then paves the way for this inner game of wealth to dictate, guide or dominate the outer game of wealth (the tools), and then wealth is created.

The Mindset of Decision-Making Power and Persistence

One of the common intertemporal tradeoff we experience is the choice between immediate gratification (temporal discount) and delayed gratification. The more proximate an option is; the more it is generally ephemeral and more immediately satisfying. Meanwhile delayed gratification option often matches our long-term goals and has greater overall benefits.[49] We equally saw that according to Fehr (2002), optimal decision-making involves at least occasionally delaying gratification and forgoing immediate gratification in pursuit of long-term goals.[50]

Another subtle underpinning surrounding the mindset of decision making power and persistence is the strongly-rooted argument that; the better approach to convince your target audience to buy your products or ideas is to sell through comparisons. Of course, this is based on the argument that people make decisions based on comparisons. People don't just look at one product and think to themselves, "that the product is right for me." Instead, they look at different options, and then they make their decision. For example, when they look at an option, they ask themselves, "this option is better compared to what?" That's how they determine value.[51] As such, *decisions* are comparative by nature – wherein we're always asking ourselves, "compared to what?" So give them that comparison. This is how you sell.[52]

THE MINDSET OF DECISION-MAKING POWER

Drawing inspiration from the aforementioned explanations, two schools of thought has emerged: the *"hot-cool"* perspective, and the *construal level* perspective. They come in with their own ramifications as follows:

The *first* scenario is the *"hot-cool" perspective.* In this regard, Barry and Halfmann (2016) found that sometimes we use our gut instinct to make a decision, while other times we use rational thinking.[53] In a similar vein, Kahneman (2011) suggests that we have two systems of thinking, an *intuitive, automatic* system that is accountable for many of our everyday decisions (denominated as System 1) and a *deliberate, logical* part of the mind that is able to rationally analyze and solve problems (denominated as System 2). He argues that although *System 1*, is adaptive in many situations, it is however more likely to make mistakes in judgment; by contrast, *System 2* takes more mental effort. As a result,

System 1 is often referred to as a "hot" system and *System 2* is often described as a "cool" system.[54]

Meanwhile, Tversky and Kahneman (1973) found that by operating in one or the other system, we more readily access memories and ideas available to that system. This has to do with the phenomenon known as the "availability bias." The availability bias relies on how easily information comes to mind. They argue that more salient, frequent, and recent information tends to be more accessible. For instance, if an event is frequently advertised in media or highly emotional, it will more readily come to mind.[55]

The *second* scenario is the ***construal level*** **perspective** – alternatively referred to as Construal-Level Theory (CLT). Barry and Halfmann argue that the availability bias and ease of cognitive access also relates to Construal-Level Theory (CLT).[56] For example, Trope and Liberman (2010) found that objects, events, and decision options exist at different psychological distances and this affects how we think or construe them. Earlier on in Liberman and Trope (2003), they found that the greater the psychological distance between the individual and the object or event, the more abstract the object or event. Put in another way, closer psychological distances tend to activate a more concrete mindset. For example, temporal distance (now or in a few years), spatial distance (here or miles away), and social distance (me or you) – all contribute to psychological distance.[57]

THE MINDSET OF PERSISTENCE – THE POWER OF WILL

Trump (2008) holds the opinion that, when we hear the word "No," it becomes a challenge to us. He argues that the so-called impossible is actually very often possible, provided one is willing to work very hard – sooner or later those problems can turn out to become opportunities. And by maintaining this kind of resilience, it can potentially harness the power to conquer obstacles and succeed in the face of long odds.[58] In a related development, Hill (2009) identified four simple steps which can lead to the habit of persistence:

1. A definite purpose backed by burning desire for its fulfillment.
2. A definite purpose, backed by the burning desire for its fulfillment.
3. A mind closed tightly against all negative and discouraging influences, including negative suggestions of relatives, friends, and acquaintances.
4. A friendly alliance with one or more persons who will encourage one to follow through with both plan and purpose.[59]

On the strength of Hill's proposed four steps that can lead to the habit of persistence, he concluded that poverty is attracted to the one whose mind is favorable to it, as money is attracted to him whose mind has been deliberately prepared to attract it. And through the same laws, poverty consciousness will voluntarily seize the mind which is not occupied with money consciousness.[60]

3.2.2 Core Issues in Value Creation and Entrepreneurial Resilience

Entrepreneurial resilience stems from the belief that there is a subconscious mindset inside people, especially entrepreneurs, which are inherently driven by what they can do. It is further consolidated by the belief that, no one knows you more than you know yourself. To this end, Trump (2008) opines that, having confidence in yourself is key to being resilient and staring adversity in the face.[61] In the same strand of reasoning, Goldstein (2018) argues that the idea of resilience is something that is inside you, which effectively pushes the burden of challenge upon you to solve your own problems, rather than constantly looking and saying to someone else or believing that the answer is coming from outside. To him, this puts you in a position of weakness when the reality is that the answer is inside you.[62] In the same direction, Trump (2008) reasons that discouragement should not be tolerated for very long.[63]

According to Goldstein (2018), if we take the standpoint that the answer to entrepreneurial resilience is inside you, the logical question that will follow is; are you in a position to solve your own problems? This logically takes us to the next point, which is, do you value, and do you know what it is that you are really good at? Or "what is it that you do very easily?"[64] Obviously, there are many things you can do – and do very well. But then, even what you can do very well have their own challenges, and we have to be mentally prepared for that. In this regard, Trump (2008) argues that every project comes with its own set of major challenges, and we should learn to expect them.[65]

Again, Goldstein (2018) reveals that a lot of people have trouble answering this question: What is it that I am really good at – "strength spotting"? In response, he asserts that each of us has a God-given gift – something located inside each of us that we are very good at. However, we have the tendency not to value our own assets. For instance, *if something comes very easily to you, you can easily hastily conclude that anybody can do that, whereas this could be your greatest asset, and a rarity to others.*[66] That said, when you take responsibility over what you can do really well and do it, then you positively create a forum for like minds to be discovered by you – people that are really good at doing it. It is from this pool of resources that you harness and pick out like minds and make them your valuable partners with whom you can together create a competitive edge. In other words, *it is this inner resilience, combined with people around you who understand, value, and respect your own inside natural gifts, that leads to resilience over the long run in entrepreneurship.*[67]

In a related sense, Rowe (2001) found that this lack of self-confidence is most common in managerially led organizations, where only financial controls are exercised. This leads to a stifling of creativity and innovation and to below-normal performance in the long term. However, he agrees that there are also creative and innovative people in such organizations, but it is harder for them to be creative and innovative in such circumstances.[68] In a similar direction, Trump (2008) observed that one is not entirely free from up-and-downs; both the foreseeable and the unforeseeable ones. In spite of this, we have to be stubbornly and yet patiently in subtle ways, to become masters of the situation.[69]

The next question is, *outside the strict confines of what you can do really well, how do you handle the situation of things you are unable to do really well?* Common sense will require that you would have to pick out partners from among those who are not in essence, your peers. So how do you understand and measure their talents, and then merge them into an effective strategic alignment? It is at this decisive point where the likelihood of a venture success or failure can really occur, among other factors (*see* Fig. 3.1). This would require the alignment of the entrepreneurial "*inner*" resilience with missing competences in the entrepreneurial "*external*" environment, and then transmute them into a continuous iteration of value creation that spans across the short term, middle term, and long term portfolio horizons.

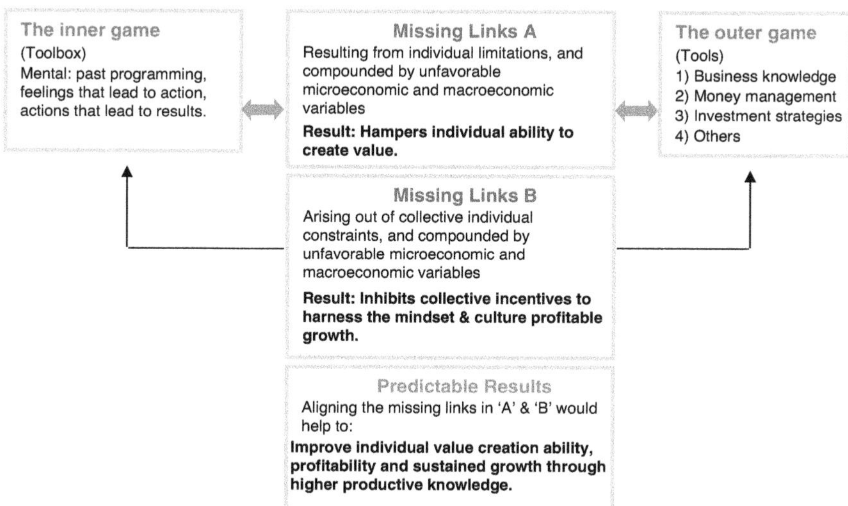

Figure 3.1 Aligning Entrepreneurial "Inner" Resilience with the "External" Environment
Source: Author created.

As shown on Fig. 3.1, aligning the missing links "A" would more likely result to value creation at the individual level. Sustaining this value would largely depend on the continuous mastery of the dynamics of the inner and outer games of wealth, and to a certain extent, the accompanying microeconomic variables. Obviously, individuals in advanced economies or industrialized nations would usually enjoy a greater advantage over those from middle income and low income economies, largely due to the relatively favorable combinations of microeconomic variables in advanced economies.

Focusing on the missing links "B" would ensure a level playing field for economic growth to thrive. The alignment of the missing links "A" and "B" has a strong preponderance to level the playing field for profitable growth. The more organized and advanced the economy is, the greater the chance of reconciling the alignment in the missing links "A" and "B".

To concur, Barrowclough and Kozul-Wright (2018) argue that no country has achieved industrial and postindustrial transformation without the use of *targeted* and *selective government* policies to shift the production structure toward activities and sectors with higher productivity, better paid jobs, and greater technological potential. Moreover, those countries that have succeeded in such transformation, tend to share a broadly common geometry in institutions within government and within business.[70] From the foregoing, these are the institutions that make mature markets to work, namely:

1. The institutions that define how market information is being conveyed;
2. the institutions that define how to bridge the information gap between buyers and sellers;
3. the institutions that define property rights; and
4. the institutions that define the enforcement of contract.

Consequently, the requirements for mature markets to work, vary with the level of economic development in terms of manufacturing and products complexity.

3.2.3 Employees' Ownership Mindset and the Scarcity Mentality

In the reasoning of Sondhe (2010), the more responsible stewards of wealth we create by allowing participation in the wealth-creation process, the more people that can give back to society, make a positive difference, and help the world to eliminate much of its ills; by dominating the subsequently fewer people that will misuse wealth for evil purposes.[71]

In this regard, Newey (2018) argues that employees become entrusted with more resources when they demonstrate their expertise to invest resources wisely and innovate with a level of strategic coherence. Using this thinking, employees can gain strategic coherence and therefore be better stewards of the resources entrusted to them. This has the potential to put their organization on a path toward getting the right results from their innovation investments.[72] In a the same vein, Rowe (2001) points out that relying on managers and employees to voluntarily make decisions that benefit the organization means that senior management will not have to expend as much effort on monitoring and controlling employees, and will have more capacity to examine what the organization needs to do in both the short and long terms.[73]

The Scarcity Mentality and Consumer-Centered Mentality

While it is acknowledged that many studies have shown compelling evidence that allowing employees to participate in profits or ownership (giving them a stake in outcomes) is beneficial for companies, but most employers tend to have a "scarcity mentality." *This is a kind of consistent and persistent mindset and culture of wealth-oriented monopoly, which is rooted in the "ownership" and the "protection of wealth" by the employer, to the exclusion of the employees.* To this end, Sondhe (2010) observed that the employer scarcity mentality exhibits the following characteristics:

1. Rooted in an "ownership" and a "protection of wealth" mindset;
2. Human frailties – jealousy and ego;
3. Employers are focused on "bottom line," (i.e., business profit); and
4. Many employers and business managers feel threatened by hard working, intelligent, capable employees. They often maneuver such employees by diminishing and frustrating them – all for the sake of protecting the manager's fragile ego, and their fear of being made to look bad themselves by an earnest, diligent, up-and-coming new hire.[74]

Coincidentally, this is one of the main problem with corporate entrepreneurship, and one of the critical underlying factors that hinders productivity. And when transformed into a macro-scale – it remains a pervasive force that is prevalent in underdevelopment and economic stagnation. And the situation becomes more confusing and complicated when associated with a high degree of *consumer-centered mentality* – that is, the near complete absence of the mindset of manufacturing and value added in an economy, in favor of a heavy and continuous reliance on imported products including basic commodities.

Arguably, it is against this backdrop of confusion in scaling the balance between *scarcity mentality* on the one hand, and *consumer-centered mentality* on the other hand, that most likely prompted the Nobel Laureate, Prof. Muhammad Yunus to introduce his concept of *social business* – that sets to distinguish on the one hand, *conventional or traditional business*, which he considers a selfish-driven business with the main goal of profit maximization, and on the other hand, *social business*, which he believes is a selflessness-driven business.[75]

In a practical sense, Yunus' concept of *social business* resides on the logic of charging higher prices on goods and services supplied to the rich, in order to cross-subsidize the purchases of goods and services supplied to the poor in the form of lower prices, and yet, maintain overall equilibrium in the performance of the social business (Yunus, 2018).

Further, he goes ahead to make distinctions and similarities between *social business* and *social entrepreneurship* as follows. That *social entrepreneurship* is about someone taking an initiative to solve a problem people are facing. These initiatives could be taken in a variety of ways. *Firstly*, for example, it could be a charity program where people do it without charging any money – where everything is free. *Secondly*, it could as well be business programs where you solve a pressing social problem while at the same time you make money.[76] In a similar direction, Stenn (2017) perceives social entrepreneurship as an innovative and creative model for building justice and sustainability.[77]

Meanwhile, *social business* stands right at the middle of them, that is, it stands in between the *charity* aspects of social entrepreneurship and the personal profit-making aspects of social entrepreneurship. So, *social business* is neither charity, nor personal profit-making business. In other words, it remains a business, but a non-dividend business, meaning that the entrepreneur who started this business does not want to make personal money out of it. A zero dividend – what he gets is the return of the money he has invested, and not more, because the whole business is devoted to solving human problems.[78]

Added to the ranks of *social entrepreneurship* and *social business*, is what is known as *social innovation*. This stems from the historical observations that the "Government" is too slow to come up with creative solutions to social problems, which creates a vacuum to be filled by *social entrepreneurship*, and the more robustness of *social business* and other initiatives that would evolve over time.

Facilitating Employees' Ownership Mindset

It should be remembered that when employees are usually trained to do certain limited things, in one way, it poses a problem to corporate entrepreneurship. As such, people trained just to be specialists have limited adaptation skills, and they don't think outside of their specialty. This is even more pronounced as the advent of the fourth industrial revolution requires certain categories of employees to be trans-disciplinary in order for the firm to remain competitive. Obviously, the lack of a 'T' shaped orientation of employees, do constrain, and can potentially constrain their problem-solving capabilities, and their propensity for innovative entrepreneurial thinking; consequently, hampering their wealth-creating potential. Therefore, it is critical for employers to re-orientate employees toward "value-adding mindset" by focusing on re-training these employees not as job seekers, but as owners, as value adders, as problem solvers – this implies that what is needed is a "creative workforce."[79]

Well, now that creativity does not essentially arise out of performing repetitive task on a daily basis or strictly specializing in a particle line of activity, many experts have suggested that building and sustaining a creative workforce requires training employees to be generalists first, especially as too many specialists know only their specialty. To this end, Bhalla *et al.* (2011) suggested that some necessary additions needs to be made to the views of Adam Smith, which opines that beyond specialization, high-performance organizations need to invest in employee development through training and by rotating people through roles and responsibilities.[80]

In a similar vein, Gronau (2018) stresses the importance of nine types of *competences* and their *attributes* that must not be neglected in the Industry 4.0, namely:

- Professional Competence – knowledge, capabilities
- Personal Competence – stress management, information procurement, reflection, critical faculties, reliability
- Cultural Competence – intercultural competence, professional cultural competence
- Methodological Competence – technical, non-technical
- Leadership Competence
- Social Competence – capacity for teamwork, context-appropriate behavior, integrity and honesty, respect another one's rights, and conflict management ability
- Organizational Competence
- Process Competence – technical and operational process assurance, process sequences, process engineering, identify faults and checking automated executed actions
- Interaction Competence – ability to collaborate or cooperate with humans and smart technical entities to purposely use media and technical equipment. For instance, employees have to be able to work in a group to achieve a mutual holistic result and to be able to work by themselves on results. Further, they need to able to use and apply communication technologies and devices.[81]

The "Entreployee"

André Ullrich, in his presentation tilted the "Change of Work," posited that the concept of the "entreployee" describes the employees' self-responsibility for the development of their own capabilities, and their own employment simultaneously. Hence, every employee has to act as an entrepreneur. He argues that the entreployee can be identified by three main characteristics:[82]

Firstly – increased self-organization and self-regulation. This process begins with the tendency to tilt toward goal orientation. This tilting process toward goal orientation tends to tip the scale balance of the entreployees' mindset and culture toward the direction of self-organization and self-regulation. This can result to a higher level of self-assessment, and might as well, eventually lead to an increase in performance, or at least scale up the pressure for increased performance. *Secondly – extended self-economization.* Essentially, this refers to the strategic handling of their individual labor needs. To this end, the employees tend to have a larger burden to permanently develop and produce their own labor schedule, as well as conduct self-marketing. *Thirdly – self-rationalization.* Essentially, the employees are tasked to plan and design not just their own work life, but the entire living environment due to the progressive dissolution of the boundaries between work and life balance.

From the foregoing, it was said many years ago that:

> "We cannot teach people anything; we can only help them discover it within themselves"
>
> —*Galileo Galilei*

However, much easily said than done, the concept of entreployee needs to be accompanied by some minimum level of *attitude acceptance* to usher this kind of transformation process. As Ullrich (2018) puts it, this can be influenced by addressing the *employees' willingness* and their *capability to change* – and that adequate sensitization and appropriate measures to assess the required qualifications are necessary for a successful transformation.[83]

This is particularly critical as Rowe (2001) points out that if managers and employees do not know the strategic direction of the organization, they may erroneously make decisions that damage the organization. Still, if they know the strategic direction and want to do damage to the organization in some small way, they may voluntarily make decisions that hurt the organization.[84] As we saw earlier, trust is critical. That means leaders have to be sure that the people they are trusting, have values that are going to elicit the decisions and actions that they want.

3.3 Entrepreneurial and Managerial Leadership, Market Orientation, and the Drive for Value

3.3.1 Expanding the Capacity of Entrepreneurial and Managerial Leadership

As we saw earlier, leadership has everything to do with value creation. Leadership orientation largely depends on whether you are catching existing waves or creating a new wave. Each of these value creation sides of the coin would require different mixes and combinations of leadership. In catching an existing wave of opportunities, managerial leadership might be a good-fit since its main focus is on short-term financial returns with the highest possible profit and the lowest possible cost. However, to guarantee the future financially viability of the company, there is the need to create a new wave of opportunities as opposed to existing waves. But the task of creating a new wave is in a vast majority of cases, technically outside the scope of managerial leadership.[85]

From the foregoing, Ceru (2018) pointed out that the entrepreneurial mindset is about seeing the world as a set of opportunities – not obstacles. It's about seeing problems to be solved, not barriers that limit them. It's about being driven to create value for a broad set of stakeholders and lifting the human condition.[86]

Therefore, by way of comparison, the entrepreneurial mindset and the concerns of the entrepreneur are very different from those of the administrator/manager. The Entrepreneur asks different questions about the environment, and the opportunity. Here the opportunity has a more external and proactive perspective; where capitalizing on the opportunity is the goal. The Administrator/Manager ask questions about the organizational structure and the resources. Here the opportunity has a more internal and reactive perspective; where trying to control resources, and analyze and minimize risk is the goal.

Many scholars are now increasingly identifying the borderlines that differentiate between entrepreneurial thinking, managerial thinking, and strategic thinking. While managerial thinking may or may not involve creative thinking, entrepreneurial thinking on its part, is inherently creative. Managerial thinking tends to focus on the avoidance of surprises as far as possible.[87]

It is important to point out though that the same person can use both managerial and entrepreneurial thinking at different times, depending on what the circumstances call for. The best entrepreneurs combine creativity, innovation and business skills to create high potential ventures. People with an entrepreneurial mindset accept that making mistakes is part of the process. For instance, Ceru (2018) noted that in the United States, a key cultural dimension of the entrepreneurial mindset is the notion that it is easier to fail, to make mistakes, and to recover from them. Thus, making mistakes can be a positive step forward in applying the entrepreneurial mindset to opportunity – provided we learn from these mistakes and use them to better inform our next set of actions.[88]

However, Haycock, Cheadle and Bluestone (2012) reason that some lessons need to be learned from strategic thinking, so as to mitigate the bad side of potential avoidable failures. They maintain that Strategic thinking can be used in any organization seeking to gain a competitive edge.[89] And with a focus on improvement, often through creativity and innovation, *strategic thinking builds a vision for an organization's future prior to the linear process of developing a strategic plan.*[90] A smarter way is for an entrepreneurial thinker to partner with a skilled predictive thinker or a managerial thinker who can help make the creative ideas more orderly and structured – thereby increasing its feasibility prospects and the chances of its commercial realization. A good example of such a combination is the Montgolfier brothers, namely; Joseph-Michael Montgolfier and Jacques-Etienne Montgolfier who designed the first manned balloon flight. In this regard, it was found that one of the Montgolfier brothers was very creative and had many ideas, and the other one more orderly and structured (and trying to see whether the ideas were really possible and realizable) – a combination which often worked very well with them.

3.3.2 Market Orientation and the Entrepreneurial Value Creation Trajectory

The Entrepreneurial Vision

The entrepreneurial vision has been known to embody one or more of the following components or characteristics; pattern for the future, values, mental image, a purpose that can be communicated to inspire others, process, and content. Among these characteristics, the definition of entrepreneurial vision as a pattern for the future appears to be the most outstanding. In other words, a vision allows you to see the future in the present.[91] In a similar vein, just as the central vision and peripheral vision in the human eye sight can be seen as being comprised of two main functions: *central* and *peripheral;*[92] so too in understanding entrepreneurial vision as a pattern for the future, we can split it into *core vision* and *peripheral vision.*

With regards to the human eye sight, Yun (2020) opines that most people associate *central vision* with focusing on particular object of interest, while *peripheral vision* is when something to the side attracts attention.[93] In a similar vein, Ho Vision Group (2020) argues that the *central vision* helps us identify "what," while our *peripheral vision* helps us identify "where." As a result, both central vision and peripheral vision are important to help us make sense and efficiently function in the visual world.[94]

THE CORE VISION

Coming back to the entrepreneurial world, we can rightly state that the core vision is critical to the entrepreneurial mindset – it is a picture of the future in your mind's eye. Why? Firstly, entrepreneurs have a vision for the future of their venture at the start, and it is important because such vision is an expression of the future of the venture, and can as a result, potentially motivate the entrepreneurial team. Secondly, because it is value driven, the vision can be the foundation for venture culture, practices and policies. Thirdly, a vision also engages stakeholders because it helps them to understand and see the future for the venture, and of course vision provides a direction for growth. However, we saw earlier that Organizations led by visionaries who are not properly supported by strong managerial leadership, may destroy wealth even more quickly than organizations led by managerial leaders. Supposedly as managerial leadership involves stability and order, and the preservation of the existing order.[95]

PERIPHERAL VISION

Peripheral vision is important because entrepreneurship is an iterative process. Although many ideas may be proposed, an entrepreneur must be able to weed out those opportunities that show little promise. They should examine the objectives of the venture, answering questions about its niche, ability to endure, and of course its profitability; by closely monitoring external change and market development, and accordingly, develop proprietary assets.[96] During the information gathering activity, for example, when understanding and insight are being sought, the analyst or entrepreneur is expected to think about possible *solutions* to existing *problems* – and to apply some practical screening at the same time, as a preliminary form of evaluation.[97]

In a resilient organization, finding possible solutions to problems, would entail not only finding solutions to existing problems, but going beyond that to figure out solutions to the likelihood of future problems that existing solutions would not be able to contain in the future. That said, when an insight about a problem is gained, it is often easier then to see solutions for it.[98]

While visioning has its benefits as a long-term planning tool, it fails to anticipate the breadth of possible forces that may come into play at any point in the future to assist or detract from a desired outcome. It is this sense of preparedness that strategic foresight aims to foster.[99] Table 3.1 provides some explanatory guidelines that establishes the causal link

Table 3.1 Strategic Management Model Elements

Strategic Elements	*Definition*
Mission	Why an organization exists. This implies that Mission is synonymous to Purpose in this context. Alternatively, mission is a means to approach a vision.
Vision	Where or what an organization wants to be in the Future.
Strategic Vision	A unique type of vision that is endowed or backed by the capacity to produce the needed results.
Core Values	Principles that people in an organization care about and believe in – and which influence their behavior.
Goals and Objectives	Goals are *broad* and *high-level* desired results. Objectives are specific, measurable outcomes necessary to make the vision a reality.
Strategy Formulation	The plan of how and when to achieve the goals and objectives.
Strategy Deployment	Deployment or execution of Strategic Plans.
Measurement & Control	The monitoring and feedback element that answers the questions: "How is the organization doing?" and "Are any modifications necessary?"
Critical Success Factors	What an organization has to do right to succeed.
Distinctive Competences	Unique capabilities that gives an organization an advantage over its competitors.

Sources: Adapted from Hitt, Ireland, and Hoskisson (2004); and Pryor, Anderson, Toombs, and Humphreys (2007).

between mission, vision, to the strategic management model elements that culminates into strategic foresight.

Goals are usually categorized into subsets known as objectives which are more specific in character – a series of objectives make up a goal. In a more technical term, objectives are usually intermittent, measurable specific outcomes of goals (i.e., broad based high-level desired results). Goals are usually associated with long term strategic plans. "*A goal is a dream with a deadline*" – *Napoleon Hill*. That said, at this juncture it seems we may have to draw a distinction between visioning and strategic visioning. In the sense that while *visioning* has its benefits as a long-term planning tool because it can clearly figure out where or what an organization wants to be in the future, *strategic visioning* on its part, is constantly hunted by the question on how to get to that vision without the loss of strategic control.

Recognizing Opportunities

While there is much ongoing debate among leading scholars about opportunity recognition, Piller (2018) defines opportunity recognition as a business or technological gap that a company or an individual realizes between the current situation and an envisioned future, in order to capture competitive advantage, respond to threat, or solve a problem.[100] In the same vein, Stroud (2018) argues that it is unlikely that customers will buy a product that does not does not solve a problem, and that customers are looking for solutions, not just "things."[101] For instance, if people have a need or want for a specific product that solves a particular problem, and you can identify that opportunity to create the product that will address that need or want - implies that recognizing a gap in the industry, is a rare and essential skill.[102] Consequently, opportunities are the focus of the entrepreneurial process.

However, once you have identified the opportunity, you must broaden your perspective as you holistically develop and execute your plan – being opportunity-obsessed means not being distracted by opportunities that do not serve the value creation imperative. But one should be cautious as to what we may erroneously refer to as *opportunities that do not serve the value creation imperative.* To this end, Trump (2008) subtly reveals that to effectively recognize opportunities, we should bear in mind that *opportunity* always hides behind problems, ugliness and failure – especially behind the failures of others.[103] This remains a potential daunting task, especially to smaller businesses. In a similar vein, Susman *et al.* (2006) found that small companies often have less control over key environmental elements than do their larger counterparts. Therefore small companies need to be especially vigilant in spotting potential problems and opportunities;[104] by watching their competition for new product introductions, new advertising campaigns, or new plant construction.[105]

Recently, research has revealed that there are three different ways to search for opportunities; *passive search, active search, and opportunity as creation. A passive search* (is a fortuitous discovery; here objective opportunities exist, but are discovered by accident), *Active search* (could be said to be objectively tailored, but with a streamlining of the search target), and finally *opportunity as creation* (in this case, imagination and the individual can create an opportunity from almost nothing). Opportunity can be identified through the following sources; a new resource, an underutilized resource, an external mandate (persons, stock markets, and shareholders), an internal mandate, and reaction on an identified trend.[106]

3.3.3 Market Segmentation to Business Plan: Tracing Sustainable Profit-Oriented Potentials

Step 1: Market Segmentation (Business Idea Generation)

Market Segmentation can alternatively be called Business Idea Generation or Developing a Business Vision. According to *Marketing-Insider* (2020a), market segmentation is the first step in designing a customer-driven marketing strategy. It is the initial stage of developing a marketing logic by which the firm can create customer value and build profitable customer relationships.[107] They define market segmentation as the process of dividing a market into distinct groups of customers who have different characteristics, needs and behaviors and therefore require different products or marketing programs. In this way, we can look at a market segment as a group of consumers responding in a similar way to a set of marketing efforts.[108] As you know, these distinct groups can be based on: *geographic, demographic, psychographic and behavioral factors.*

To that end, Gardner (2017) argues that most companies tend to *segment* their markets by customer *demographics* or product characteristics and *differentiate* their offerings by adding features and functions.[109] In this regard, not every segmented market that is variable is equally useful for each company. For instance, a car manufacturer would gain little by distinguishing between vegetarians and non-vegetarians. Meanwhile, for a meat company, this may be the most important variable factor in the marketing strategy.[110]

To that end, Gardner (2017) argues while most companies tend to focus on market segmentation and product differentiation, a consumer has a different view of the marketplace – that of hiring the best product or service to do it.[111] This is known as the Jobs to be Done (JTBD) driven research, which is about understanding what people are doing, and the role a product or offer could play for them – and that the learning from it is typically insight oriented.[112]

THE ROLE OF FEASIBILITY STUDY IN MARKET SEGMENTATION

Prior to most new product development, there is the need for a *feasibility study* to help *identify the different segments during market segmentation.*Toma (2015) holds the opinion that feasibility study is very useful to guide the decision whether to go or not to go on a new project idea. The feasibility study should assess market, technical and financial feasibility for the product or service idea. It should be robust enough to test the concept.[113] Becerril (2015) maintains that feasibility study focuses on the technical side, and preoccupies itself with the estimation of resources (technical, human, equipment, tools, buildings, et cetera) to carry out the project.[114]

Meanwhile, Mullins (2010) argues that feasibility study is focused on the customer. The purpose of any business is to win a customer. The customer-driven feasibility study asks the critical questions necessary to satisfy the entrepreneurial team's curiosity about the attractiveness of the opportunity.[115] Camacho (2015) opines that feasibility study describes mostly if an idea is realizable under the current circumstances of the market. As such, it is the "logic-proof," the initial state, and the core of the project idea.[116] According to Louangrath (2015), feasibility study answers the initial question whether your project is doable with reasonable probability of success?[117]

Finally, Novak (1996) found that most people lump market analysis and feasibility studies together, but argues they are two different entities and typically occur at different times in the development process.[118] In general, a feasibility analysis tests whether a certain product will meet certain *financial or social goals in the market*, before daring into a *market analysis* which searches for the intersection of demand and supply that will create a market for a product at a given price.[119] In a similar vein, Koh (2015) argues that it also depends if business owners or executives know exactly how the market works and what the market lacks in, they will skip feasibility studies. Of course, theoretically speaking, feasibility study is a must for businesses that do not have a clear vision in the market, and hence market research is needed.[120]

The types of market research questions to ask before starting your business are general questions, and can be grouped under feasibility studies. This would include the following:

- How big is our potential market?
- Is this market going to grow or shrink? How much?
- Are there other products/services similar to ours? What are they?
- Who are our primary competitors? What is their market share?
- Is there any significant market share available for us?[121]

So in a nutshell, *a feasibility study is* essentially the primary or first step of market segmentation to help *identify the different segments* during market segmentation. While the rest of the market segmentation process beyond feasibility study is to clearly *distinguish between the different segments*, notably; *geographic, demographic, psychographic and behavioral factors*. However, where business owners or executives know exactly how the market works and what the market lacks, they will skip feasibility study. Today, for example, carrying out a feasibility study to know whether there is an existing market to sell a low-cost antiviral treatment or vaccine for COVID-19, is not required, since it's obvious the market lacks the product.

MARKET RESEARCH

Apparently, market research is the second level of market segmentation. It comes after the feasibility study. According to Queensland Government (2020), Market research involves gathering information on the following:

- Researching industry and market environment – to understand factors external to your business
- Researching customers – to develop a customer profile
- Researching competitors – to develop a competitor profile.[122]

Researching the industry and market environment focuses on information about any political, legal, economic, social and cultural issues or trends that can affect your business. With the use of this external research, you can gather information about the composition of your target market, gaps in the market, new market trends and where new market opportunities might lie.[123] *Researching customers:* You can use customer research to gather information on who customers or potential customers are and what, when, where and how they buy. Customer research can also give insight into your customers' attitudes toward your business and your products and services.[124] You need to learn what makes them tick and how you can solve their problems with your offerings.[125] *Researching competitors:* Your competitor research will gather information about existing and potential competitors. Such as your competitor's current market advantages, weaknesses in their promotional strategies, and how their customers view their products and services. In this regard, competitor research might cover:

- Current turnover and market share
- pricing structures
- products and services
- marketing, advertising and branding.[126]

In concurrence, Kosaka (2019) argues that one of the best ways to learn about your market and customers is by asking the right market research questions, which can identify opportunities to improve in your marketing strategy, operations, and industry.[127] Some market research questions will require research to find the answers. For instance, "How do your competitors drive traffic?" For other questions, you can directly ask your customers. Here, you can survey or interview customers to find answers and insights.[128]

Step 2: The Market Targeting Process

After distinguishing between the separate segments in the market, the company can select one or more of these segments to enter, which are generally grouped under *geographic, demographic, psychographic and behavioral factors.* Targeting is concerned with evaluating each segment's attractiveness for the company, and selecting one or more of the segments to enter - which it can generate the greatest customer value over time. This is known as the market targeting process.

Marketing-Insider (2020b) identifies the process of market targeting in two steps. First, they *evaluate* (assess) the market segments. Second, they *select* target market segments. The latter step goes hand in hand with choosing the *targeting strategy.*[129]

STAGE ONE OF MARKET TARGETING – EVALUATING MARKET SEGMENTS

According to *Marketing-Insider (2020a)*, in evaluating market segments, a firm should consider three factors. These are:

- The segment size and growth
- The segment structural attractiveness
- The company objectives and resources.

They argue that in response to the question as to what is the right size and the right growth for a company, there is no answer that applies to every company. In essence, it depends on the company itself because the company objectives and resources are as important as the segment size, growth, or structural attractiveness. Put in another way, a favorable size, growth and structural attractiveness of a segment has to match the company's own objectives and resources – especially long-term objectives.[130]

In addition to the segment size and growth, its structural attractiveness plays a significant role in market targeting. The major structural forces are nothing else than *Porter's Five Forces model of industry attractiveness.*[131] According to Porter, the first fundamental determinant of a firm's profitability is industry attractiveness, and competitive strategy must grow out of a sophisticated understanding of the rules of competition that determine an industry's attractiveness. As you know, these rules of competition are embodied in five competitive forces:

- Industry competitors – rivalry among existing firms and the intensity of rivalry
- Threat of new and potential new entrants
- Threat of substitute products or services
- Bargaining power of buyers
- Bargaining power of suppliers, and industry competitors.[132]

However, Team FME (2013) argues that many things have changed from the time Porter wrote about these Five Forces of Industry

Attractiveness, and are constantly changing in an incredibly rapid pace. For instance, they content that while Porter's Five Forces has its advantages, there are certain considerations one has to bear in mind when using it – as these were developed in an environment that was quite different from the one that organizations find themselves operating today.[133] These considerations are:

- Pace of change is now more rapid
- Market structures were seen as relatively static
- The model provides you with only a snapshot of your environment
- It can be difficult to define the industry
- The model does not consider non-market forces
- The model is most applicable for analysis of simple market structures
- The model is based on the idea of competition.

The above, notwithstanding, they equally noted that despite these limitations, Porter's Five Forces model has a role to play in helping management to evaluate and assess their current market environment. As it provides an excellent foundation for further research and intelligence gathering needed to formulate an organization's future strategy.[134]

On the basis of this compelling necessity to further gather the needed research and intelligence to formulate an organization's future strategy that goes beyond the current market environment, we recourse to *exploring emerging industry analysis and other complementary developments.* That said, somewhat similar to Porter's Five Forces is the Blue Ocean strategy. However, the Blue Ocean Strategy primarily resides on what is known as the *value innovation.* The value innovation deals with the simultaneous pursuit of differentiation and low cost, by creating a leap in value for both buyers and the company. In this regard, the *value innovation* is achieved only when the whole system of *utility, price*, and *cost* is aligned.[135]

This value-cost trade-off is resolved by answering the following questions that spans across four actions framework: eliminate, reduce, raise and create; also known as the *ERRC Grid* that addresses the following:

- Which of the factors that the industry takes for granted should be *eliminated*?
- Which factors should be *reduced well below* the industry's standard?
- Which factors should be *raised well above* the industry's standard?
- Which factors should be *created* that the industry has never offered?[136]

STAGE TWO OF TARGET MARKETING – SELECTING TARGET MARKET SEGMENTS

Marketing-Insider (2020b) defines a target market as one set of buyers who share common needs or characteristics the firm decides to serve. So, the company has to decide which and how many segments it will target that will be most profitable for the company (selecting target market) segments). That being said, market targeting strategies can take different forms. These are referred to as levels of market targeting. A firm can *target very broadly*, which is called *undifferentiated marketing*. Market targeting can also be *very narrow*, which is called *micromarketing*. If it is somewhere in between, it might be *differentiated* or *concentrated* market targeting.[137]

The following are the four different market targeting strategies that go hand in hand with the segments we choose. *Undifferentiated (Mass) Marketing – Broad Market Targeting:* The firm decides to ignore differences between market segments and to focus on the whole market. *Differentiated (Segmented) Market Targeting:* The firm decides to target different segments and also design separate offers for each. *Concentrated (Niche) Market Strategy:* The firm concentrates on one or a few segments or niches in a market.[138] MyCBGenie (2020) defines a niche as relating to the category of topics or problems that the products you are promoting solve.[139] *Micromarketing – Narrow Market Targeting:* Means tailoring the marketing programs and products to the needs and wants of local customer segments (local marketing) and to individual customers. Under local marketing, firms tailor brands and promotions to the needs and wants of local groups of customers, maybe cities, neighborhoods, specific stores, etc. The most extreme is individual marketing, which is tailored to the needs and wants of individual customers – also called one-to-one marketing.[140]

Market-Insider (2020b) argues that the factors influencing the choice of market targeting depends on many factors, and that none of the strategies above works best in every situation. Rather, it depends on several characteristics of the company, such as:

- The company's resources
- The degree of product variability
- The product life cycle
- Market variability
- Competitors' marketing strategies.

Step 3: Business Model Design and Lean Start-up Approach

According to Teece (2010), essentially, the Business Model Design (BMD) aims at defining how the enterprise delivers value to customers, enticing them to pay and converting the payments to profit. Meanwhile, the Lean Start-up Approach (LSA) is a term coined by Eric Ries (Ries, 2011) which refers to a business approach that aims to change the way that companies are built and new products are launched.[141]

From the foregoing, Ghezzi *et al.* (2015) argue that these two practical approaches (BMD & LSA) show inherent relationships with the legacy of both Strategic Management and Entrepreneurship literature streams, and could be positioned at the crossroad of the two.[142]

BUSINESS MODEL DESIGN (BMD)

We saw earlier that Eisenmann *et al.* (2013) define a business model as an integrated array of distinctive choices; which specifies a new venture's unique customer value proposition, and how it will configure its activities to deliver that value and earn sustainable profits.[143] However, Teece (2010) argued that the construct has been only very poorly understood. In a similar vein, Ghezzi *et al.* (2015) opine that scholars are essentially; still concerned with the theoretical foundation and definition of Business Models, and that the literature is developing largely in silos, according to the phenomena of interest of the respective researchers.[144]

That notwithstanding, the framework of BMD proposed by Osterwalder and Pigneur (2010), known as the business model canvas – is now widely adopted and employed by practitioners, and identifies nine parameters to decompose a business model: (i) value proposition; (ii) customer segments; (iii) channels; (iv) customer interface; (v) key activities; (vi) key resources; (vii) key partners; (viii) revenue model; (ix) cost structure.[145]

BUSINESS MODEL HYPOTHESES: LEAN START-UP APPROACH (LSA)

A hypothesis-driven approach, also known as the Lean Start-up Approach (LSA) helps reduce the biggest risk facing entrepreneurs: that of offering a product that no one wants. *Many start-ups fail because their founders waste resources building and marketing products before they have resolved business model uncertainty.* By contrast, *early-stage entrepreneurs who follow a hypothesis-driven approach do not view growth as their primary objective. Instead, their goal is to learn how to build a sustainable business.*[146]

On the aforementioned keynote, Eisenmann *et al.* (2013) outline three key advantages. First, the lean start-up approach evaluates an early stage start-up's entire business model, whereas most of its intellectual antecedents focus more narrowly on a start-up's product. Second, the lean start-up approach introduces two new concepts: *minimum viable products* (MVP) that efficiently test business model hypotheses, and *pivots* that change certain business model elements in response to failed hypothesis tests. Finally, unlike other methods for managing an early-stage venture, *the lean start-up approach balances the strong direction that comes from a founder's vision with the need for redirection that follows from market feedback.*[147] According to Ciligot (2019), an MVP is essentially, the basic model of your product that will fulfill the primary goal you want. In this regard, the main goal of an MVP is to develop a working product that provides immediate value, quickly, while minimizing costs.[148] Starting with an MVP will allow you to learn more about your end-user and the market you wish to enter as you test your assumptions. An MVP will also set the stage for future iterations of development and clarify the sequential steps to take in the project – whether that's changing directions entirely, or continuing down your set development path.[149]

The simplest MVPs take the form of "smoke tests." A smoke test gauges demand for a product that does not yet exist, for example, a web landing page that describes a planned product/service and invites a page visitor to register to be notified when the product is launched.[150] By bounding uncertainty before scaling, the hypothesis-driven approach optimizes use of a start-up's scarce resources.[151] Viki (2018) believes that this is the magic we are searching for, and until we find it we should not launch our products at scale.[152] That said, Eisenmann *et al.* (2013) argue that entrepreneurs should continue to utilize hypothesis-testing methods even after confirming their business model assumptions. The purpose of these tests shifts from business model validation to business model optimization.[153]

However, there are some situations in which the lean start-up process yields fewer advantages, in particular: (1) when mistakes must be limited, especially as new ventures do not always operate in environments where mistakes are tolerable; (2) when uncertainty about customer demand is low, for example low-cost COVID-19 cure that produce no adverse side effects; and (3) when long product development cycles preclude launching early and often. In these situations, an entrepreneur should modify lean techniques or seek an alternate development path.[154]

Step 4: Business Plan – Key Attributes

BUSINESS PLAN AS A BROAD-BASED PLAN THAT DEFINES THE COMPANY BRAND

A sound business plan should contain crucial budgets and cash flow forecasts that will show how much profit you can expect your business to make, how much finance you will need and the risk involved. This helps to demonstrate your business idea, how you want to implement it and the long-term viability thereof. In this regard, the order of logical occurrence prior to setting up a business plan is as follows: 1) Step 1:

Market Segmentation (Business Idea Generation)· The Role of Feasibility Study in Market Segmentation· Market Research 2) Step 2: The Market Targeting Process· Stage one of market targeting - evaluating market segments· Stage two of target marketing – selecting target market segments 3) Step 3: Business Model Design (BMD) and Lean Start-up Approach (LSA) 4) Step 4: Business Plan.

That being said, Oyugi (2015) found that business plan is a broader plan as it encompasses all that is required to translate ideas into reality, usually by detailing in writing. It is the whole business but on paper, because it includes all the functional areas of a business. It is a communication to the investors and financial institution about the intentions and how it can realistically go into operation.[155] To concur, Camacho (2015) argues that business plan is the broadest picture. It contains not only feasibility and marketing but other elements about who is going to develop the plans, how, why, e.g., mission, vision, team members. In order to be sound, the conforming elements (feasibility, marketing, et cetera) must be sound.[156]

According to Toma (2015), the business plan is needed to state the management team, advisors, the capital needs, operating plan, human resources plan, IP, marketing approach and other matters. It does need to have the owner/proponent quite involved in this step.[157] Louangrath (2015) opines that business plan answers the questions: What do you want to do? How do you plan to achieve it? Or in nutshell, this plan answers the question of "*what is it?*"[158]

In a conclusive note, Mullins (2010) argues that the business plan organizes the answers delivered by the feasibility study and goes on to develop marketing, operating, and financing strategies in an effort to sell the opportunity, in a sharply focused way, to investors and other stakeholders.[159]

MARKETING PLAN AS A SUBSET OF BUSINESS PLAN THAT PROJECTS AND POSITIONS THE COMPANY BRAND

Louangrath (2015) is of the opinion that the marketing plan answers the question: how do you plan to move your idea or product to the consumers, or users?[160] According to Camacho (2015), marketing plan depicts how you will take your product or service to the target market, and that it should contain elements of the feasibility study to prove it is doable.[161] Baniya (2015) opines that marketing plan is a functional plan to run a marketing unit.[162]

In a different platform, Lee (2015) believes that the *marketing plan is linked to the business plan in terms of brand – with the business plan defining the brand and the marketing plan describing how to project brand and position the company.*[163] To concur, Oyugi (2015) reveals that marketing plan is sometimes incorporated as part of a business plan.

In the sense that, while the business plan embraces all functional areas of a business organization, marketing plan is specific – focusing on the customer and how the needs are to be satisfied.[164] In a similar vein, Becerril (2015) maintains that both the feasibility study and marketing plan are part of, among other studies, business plan.[165]

GENERAL REMARKS ON AND BUSINESS PLAN AND THEIR KEY ATTRIBUTES

According to Koh (2015), a small-sized business may not need any business plans – but if investors are involved in the business, a hardcopy plan may be needed. He also argues that for larger businesses, some entrepreneurs or owners do not want a business or marketing plans; as these plans undermine their ability to function as a domain expert in the company.[166] On the contrary, some owners do follow strictly to the process of business plan, and by extension, the marketing plan, with the support of feasibility study. But the velocity of their market demand may sometimes discourage them from taking months to plan and study. So it also depends on the type of market.[167] To concur, Brinckmann *et al.* (2010) maintain that there is still no agreement in literature about the usefulness of a business plan, and also that empirical findings have been fragmented and contradictory. In addition, some scholars such as Bhidé (2000) argue that business plan interferes with the efforts of a company's founders to undertake a more valuable venture.[168]

However, in spite of such aforementioned theoretical disagreements, Burke *et al.* (2010) observed that the *business plan* is the document typically used by investors to evaluate funding opportunities,[169] and typically includes a set of key documents, organized around the following sections:

- general description of the firm;
- general description of products/services;
- strategic plan;
- marketing plan;
- operating plan;
- human resources and organization plan;
- financial plan, and economic and financial projections.[170]

From the foregoing, you would need to consider four core questions before you begin writing your business plan:

- What service or product does your business provide and what need does it fill?
- Who are the potential customers for your product or service and why would they purchase it from you?
- How will you reach these potential customers?
- Where will you get the financial resources to start your business?

That being said, Kraus and Kauranen (2009) state that business plan (BP) plays an important *linking role between entrepreneurship and strategic management*.Honig and Karlsson (2004) maintain that the BP is the document which describes the enterprise's strategy, i.e., content and process, thereby presenting the vision of the enterprise and how the enterprise is going to attain its vision. In particular, Abrams (2003) argues that the BP can serve as the basis of the strategy itself and as its formalized documentation.[171]

3.4 The Science of Entrepreneurship and Strategic Foresight

3.4.1 Conceptual Thinking Patterns in the Science of Entrepreneurship

Entrepreneurial Thinking

Ideally, most, if not all entrepreneurial ventures begin with effectual/nonlinear reasoning, or entrepreneurial thinking, which is accompanied by a vision and some existing means at the entrepreneur's disposal. With persistence and insistence amid trials and errors, specific goals start emerging toward the direction of the vision. Here two things progressively begin to unfold, notably: (1) the vision combines with the existing means to generate, shape and reshape specific goals over time; (2) these clarity and further clarity of goals, in turn, transmute the entrepreneurial vision from the status quo of vision clarity to vision building over time. In other words, the entrepreneur typically adapts his/her ideas progressively to create a solution, and afterwards, integrates this solution into an appropriate business model – and this process takes time to evolve.

In a related sense, Sarasvathy (2001) reasoned that, entrepreneurial thinking begins with a given set of means and allows goals to emerge contingently over time; from the varied imagination and diverse aspirations of the founders and the people they interact with.[172] That said, entrepreneurial thinking may not necessarily increase the probability of success of new strategic options, but it reduces the *costs* of failure by enabling the failure to occur earlier and at lower levels of investment. The challenge then is really to pick your partners, and package yourself early on before you have to put a lot of capital out.[173]

Managerial Thinking

Managerial thinking, also known as causal reasoning or predictive reasoning,[174] begins with a pre-determined goal and a given set of means, and seeks to identify the optimal; fastest, cheapest, and most efficient alternatives to achieve the given goal – and this phenomenon is commonly identified in every functional areas of business.[175] For instance, the "make" versus "buy" decision in production, or choosing the target market with the highest potential return in marketing, or picking a portfolio with the lowest risk in finance, or even hiring the best person in the job in human resource management, are all examples of problems of predictive reasoning.[176] Causal or predictive observations can be confirmed quickly by checking performance measures, such as sustained earnings and market share growth at corporations, whereas, in the nonprofit world, the social impact is a measure of performance.[177] Consequently, managerial leaders are more comfortable handling day-to-day activities, and are short-term oriented.[178]

According to Lozano, Gomez, and Rositas (2011), predictive reasoning, when fitted within the framework of *comprehensive management system* may pose some difficulties, in the sense that typically, managerial thinking or predictive reasoning is reactive and retrospective, instead of managing for the future.[179] Thus, the lack of strategic leadership and the prevalence of managerial leadership is one of the most important issues facing organizations today.[180]

Strategic Thinking

A more interesting an upward shift from typical managerial thinking is strategic thinking, which is also known as "creative" causal reasoning – it involves the *creation of additional alternatives* to achieve a given goal.[181] This form of *"creative" causal reasoning* is often used in what is generally referred to as strategic thinking,[182] which requires understanding the complex relationship between the organization and its environment, and utilizing that understanding to make decisions that facilitate the organization's enduring success.[183]

For *strategic thinking* to be effective, it usually goes along with *strategic influencing*. Dellaert and Davydov (2017) perceive *strategic influencing* as the process of ensuring commitment to the organization's strategic direction, by inviting others into the strategic process, forging relationships inside and outside the organization, and utilizing organizational culture and systems of influence.[184] On this line of reasoning, Rowe (2001) brings out some distinctive characteristics of strategic leadership that emanates from *strategic thinking* as follows:

- That there is a synergistic combination of managerial and visionary leadership;
- that there is emphasis on ethical behavior and value-based decisions;
- that they oversee operating (day-to-day) and strategic (long-term) responsibilities;
- that they formulate and implement strategies for immediate impact

and preservation of long-term goals to enhance organizational survival, growth, and long-term viability;
- that they have strong, positive expectations of the performance they expect from their superiors, peers, subordinates, and themselves;
- that they use strategic controls and financial controls, with emphasis on strategic controls;
- that they use, and interchange, tacit and explicit knowledge on individual and organizational levels;
- that they use linear and nonlinear thinking patterns; and finally
- that they believe in strategic choice, that is, their choices make a difference in their organizations and environment.[185]

As we delve further into this chapter, we will discover that these distinctive characteristics of strategic leadership identified by Rowe (2011), also incorporate elements that emanate from *strategic foresight.* The latter incorporates all aspects of strategic thinking, but is designed to open up an expanded range expanded range of options of strategic options available beyond strategic thinking.

How the Critical Factors of Entrepreneurial Processes Relate

Firstly, let us examine the relationship between *strategic thinking vs. entrepreneurial thinking.* The thin line that distinguishes strategic thinking/creative causal reasoning from entrepreneurial/effectual thinking is that, the *strategic thinking* pattern is characterized by the requirement for generating new means to be used for pre-determined goals, while, *entrepreneurial thinking* is characterized by the use of existing means to generate imagined ends (i.e., goals that emerge contingently over time).

Secondly, let's look at the relationship between *managerial thinking vs. entrepreneurial thinking: Managerial thinking* uses existing means to accomplish pre-determined goals, which is pretty easy to achieve. While *entrepreneurial thinking* uses existing means, but the goals emerge contingently over time, which is quite complicated. At the level of *means*, there is a causal link between *managerial thinking* and *entrepreneurial thinking* as they both employ the use of existing means. But in terms of goals they depart from each other – in this sense, managerial thinking use pre-determined goals, while the goals of entrepreneurial thinking typically emerge contingently over time.

Thirdly, in the relationship between *strategic thinking and managerial thinking*, both have *predetermined goals*, but managerial thinking on its part makes use of *existing means at its disposal* to achieve the *predetermined goals*, whereas strategic thinking has the burden *to generate new or alternative* means to achieve the *predetermined goals.*

Transcending Entrepreneurial Mindset to Strategic Foresight

STRATEGIC FORESIGHT VS. STRATEGIC THINKING

Foresight refers to processes of anticipation,[186] and is a part of *strategic thinking* designed to open up an expanded range of perceptions of the strategic options available.[187]

At this juncture, it should be worth noting that "foresight" and "strategic foresight" are not synonymous. In this regard, there is a subtle distinction between "foresight" and "strategic foresight." Foresight refers to processes of anticipation, and is a part of strategic thinking designed to open up an expanded range of perceptions of the strategic options available. While strategic foresight incorporates all aspects of strategic thinking, but is equally designed to open up expanded range of perceptions of strategic options available beyond strategic thinking. In other words, this means that, while "Foresight" is a subset of strategic thinking, "Strategic foresight" on its part, not only incorporates all elements of strategic thinking, but equally provides a framework for incubating expanded range of perceptions of strategic options, not available in strategic thinking.

STRATEGIC FORESIGHT VS. TRADITIONAL PLANNING

Also of importance is to note that *strategic foresight differs* from *traditional planning* (i.e., a subset of managerial thinking). To this end, *traditional planning* tends toward robustness (i.e., trying to prevent failure) by the frequent use of predictive tools or linear thinking. While *strategic foresight* considers plausible, possible, probable and preferred futures equally. Put in another way, strategic foresight favors resilience, which is about early detection and fast recovery.[188]

According to Raford, as a speculative exercise bolstered with analysis, strategic foresight combines the characteristics of being agile, and being anticipatory about "doing things right versus doing the right things."[189]

3.4.2 The Critical Thinking Business Model (The CTB Model): A New Approach

This chapter has reached an understanding that in order to have a better grasp of entrepreneurship and its value creation imperatives; it suggests a new critical thinking approach known as The Critical Thinking Business Model (the CTB Model). Primarily, the model examines critical thinking aspects of the different components of business loops in ascending order of complexity. In this regard, this model seeks to approach new ventures and existing ventures value creation imperatives from two generational phases, sub-divided into four loops. The first two loops are: managerial thinking (1st loop), and entrepreneurial thinking (2nd loop) are classified under the 1st Generation CTB Model. The second two loops which are: strategic thinking (3rd loop), and strategic foresight and their complements (4th loop) are classified under the 2nd Generation CTB Model (*see* Fig. 3.2). In addition, the model also examines the challenges of critical thinking based on the logical step-by-step process inherent in a business – that is, from entrepreneurial thinking, to managerial thinking, to strategic thinking.

The first two loops are categorized under the 1st Generation Critical Thinking Business Model (1st Generation CTB Model) because they both use given means or available means to get to achieve their goals. But differs in the sense that the goals of *managerial thinking* is predetermined, thereby positioning itself as the 1st loop of the 1st Generation CTB Model, whereas, *entrepreneurial thinking* has its goals contingently emerging overtime, it therefore qualifies as the 2nd loop of the 1st Generation CTB Model.

As shown on Fig. 3.2, the first business loop of the 1st Generation CBT Model begins from "managerial thinking," and then transitions into the 2nd loop of the 1st Generation CBT Model, which involves "entrepreneurial thinking." However, when a business is already established, it is already categorized as first business loop since it is essentially preoccupied with challenges of "managerial thinking." At the macro-scale, as well as at the firm level, this argument clinches to the

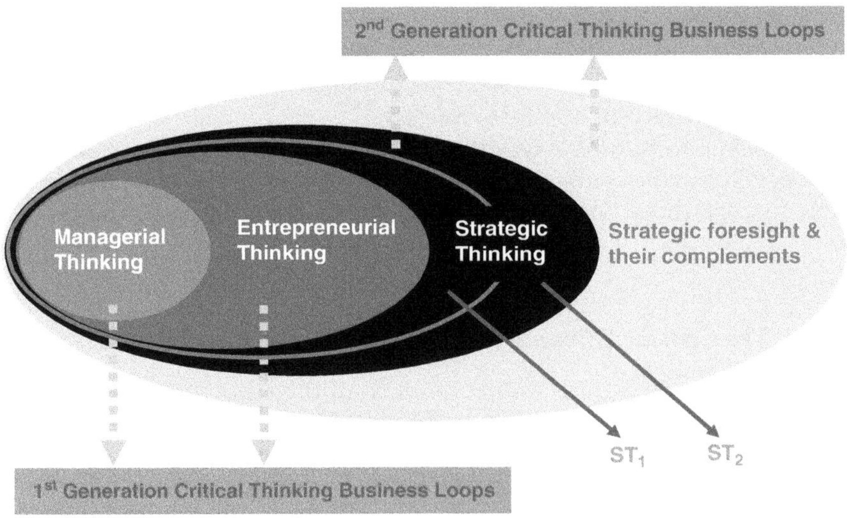

Figure 3.2 Four Loops of the 1st- and 2nd-Generations Critical Thinking Business Model

Source: Author created.

theory of rational expectation. According to the theory of rational expectation, expected events occur because all adjustments have already taken place beforehand. However, not all adjustments can take place in advance due to institutional constraints, and that unexpected events or surprises do occur.

As you move further to the right, you start confronting the initial challenges of strategic thinking (ST_1), and then to the more advanced stage of strategic thinking (ST_2) which both belong to the 3rd loop of the 2nd Generation Critical Thinking Business Model (2nd Generation CTB Model. At this latter stage (ST_2), we refer to it as the "invisible space" because it does not only require the need to create additional alternatives or means to meet predetermined goals as in ST_1, but in addition, ST_2 requires a good understanding of some vital elements of strategic foresight (the invisible space).

And finally, in the extreme right you find strategic foresight and their complements. Some refer to it as the "White Space" (Johnson, 2010) and others say it's the "blue Ocean" (Kim and Maubourgne, 2014).

Undeniably, "entrepreneurial thinking" is the major preoccupation for start-ups, and has its unique challenges. But as you transition from "entrepreneurial thinking" toward the extreme right of the second generation business loops, the challenges become increasingly complex.

Loops of the 1st-Generation CTB Model and Strategic Thinking

MISSING ALIGNMENTS BASED ON LOGICAL STEPS FROM START-UP VENTURES

As mentioned earlier, featuring among the 1st Generation *Critical Thinking Business* model are managerial thinking and entrepreneurial thinking. But for purposes of convenience, we are going to add *strategic thinking* which we classified under the 2nd Generation CTB Model. From here we can figure out from Fig. 3.3, some missing alignments responsible for wrong decision making; following the challenges inherent in the logical step-by-step process from entrepreneurial thinking, through managerial thinking, to strategic thinking.

As you can see in Fig. 3.3, entrepreneurial thinking and managerial thinking have one thing in common – they use *given means or available means at their disposal* as indicated in the green rectangles to the left. While they differ with regards to *how their goals emerge* as indicated on the blue and green rectangles to the right.

Furthermore, managerial thinking and strategic thinking have *predetermined goals* as their common characteristics as shown in the green colored rectangles to the right. While they differ as to *how their means are being generated* as indicated on the *green* and *blue* rectangles to the left.

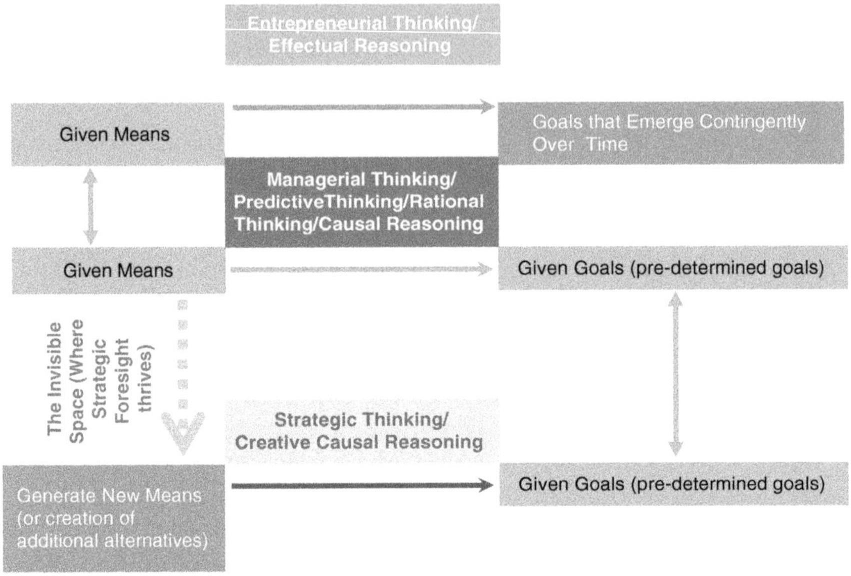

Figure 3.3 Logical Business Steps in the First Three Loops of the CTB Model and Alignment Needs
Source: Author created.

Strangely, *there is no clear causal relationship between entrepreneurial thinking and strategic thinking.* Their connectivity can only be realized via managerial thinking. The major risk here is that managerial thinking is preoccupied with short term profitability and by maintaining the existing order. Therefore, transcending entrepreneurial thinking into strategic thinking (in the case of entrepreneurial start-ups) or corporate entrepreneurial thinking (in the case of established organizations) becomes an uphill task. As accomplishing any of them would require that you break through the potentially myopic framework of managerial thinking and then thrust into a distant future. But conversant with the well-known limitations of managerial thinking, it is obvious that navigating through this trajectory, will too often inherently be seriously flawed and handicapped.

This already points out one of the reasons behind the complexities in business thinking, and why many organizations frequently run into the temptation of wrong decision making. Successful organizations would need to master *strategic foresight* so as to successfully connect entrepreneurial thinking to strategic thinking – via managerial thinking, both forward and backward – without necessarily being pinned down by the myopic limitations of managerial thinking.

ALIGNMENTS IN BUSINESS PROCESS AND DECISION-MAKING MODELS

Regular Sequence of Business Mapping Pattern Agreeably, business thinking exhibit varying degrees of complexities. But the question is, how do decision making complexities manifest themselves in different scenarios? As mentioned earlier, a new venture should normally begin from a given set of means where the goals emerge contingently over time as in entrepreneurial thinking, which then metamorphose to using the given set of means to align with pre-determined goals as in managerial thinking, and finally to generate new means or the creation of additional alternatives to meet up with the challenges of pre-determined goals as in strategic thinking. Put in another way, regular business process tend to follow the logical sequence of *business process* mapping of (1), (2), and (3), which normally evolves from:

1. Using existing means, and goals evolve contingently over time (entrepreneurial thinking)
2. Using existing means with predetermined goals (managerial thinking)
3. Generating new means or the creation of additional alternatives to match the evolving challenges, as well as retain significant strategic control over both foreseeable and unforeseeable repercussions on predetermined goals (strategic thinking).

Likelihood of Not Attaining the Desired Level Decision Making Outcome As opposed to the logical sequence of regular step-by-step *business process* mapping of (1), (2), and (3) as shown above, the magnitude of the likelihood of an organization not attaining the desired level decision making outcome, tends to follow a different sequence in descending order of complexity – from managerial thinking, strategic thinking, and entrepreneurial thinking, as follows:

1. Mapping out given means with predetermined goals – a unique characteristic of *managerial thinking*, is the simplest decision making mode and lowest risk propensity to undesirable outcomes.
2. Mapping out the creation of additional alternatives (i.e., generating new means) with predetermined goals – a unique characteristic of *strategic thinking*. This risk of undesirable outcomes is high. This especially applies to strategic leaders that embrace foresightedness in their decision making teams.
3. Employing existing or given means and aligning them with goals that would have to emerge contingently over time – a characteristic that

is unique to *entrepreneurial thinking* involve the highest risk of undesirable outcomes.

The Second-Generation CTB Model

Broadly speaking, Strategic Foresight and its complements, which is the ultimate end of the business Generational loops in the CBT Model, more precisely in the 2nd Generation CTB Model, tries to anticipate the breadth of possible forces that may come into play at any point in the future to assist or detract from a desired outcome. It is this sense of preparedness that strategic foresight aims to foster.

However, to be more specific, the 2nd Generation CTB Model perceives *Strategic Foresight* as a Second Phase of Strategic Thinking designed to open up expanded range of the strategic options available to an organization. The First Phase of Strategic Thinking is: (ST_1) and ST_2). *Secondly*, strategic foresight is also seen as the capacity to sense an emerging reality and to act in harmony. The capacity to sense an emerging reality and to act in harmony would require that foresighted thinkers involved in strategic planning, policy and decision making, should think differently so as to change the way things are usually done – which means changing the rules. By some measures, the second perspective sees strategic foresight as an *extension of entrepreneurial thinking* that embodies critical elements of business intelligence and predictive analytics.

Next, we saw earlier that there are some misalignments or even missing links in what was supposed to be the causal relationship between entrepreneurial thinking, managerial thinking, and strategic thinking (see Fig. 3.3). What would the scenario look like, if we attempt to create a causal link between the following missing links and alignments of business goals and means (Fig. 3.4)? This is how the scenario should look like in terms of complexity.

As illustrated in Fig. 3.4, there is the need to bridge the gap between the missing links and alignments as identified in descending order of complexity:

1st is Link A: Easy Alignment. Alignment between given set of means and pre-determined goals is the easiest to come by. This is typical of managerial leadership.

2nd is Link B: Missing Alignment. Alignment between existing means and generating new means is moderately complex. This involves Strategic Thinking Level 1 (ST_1), and requires strategic leaders as well as smart managerial leaders who work in synergy with visionary leaders.

3rd is Missing Link C: Reconciling predetermined goals with goals that emerge contingently over time is moderately highly complex. The

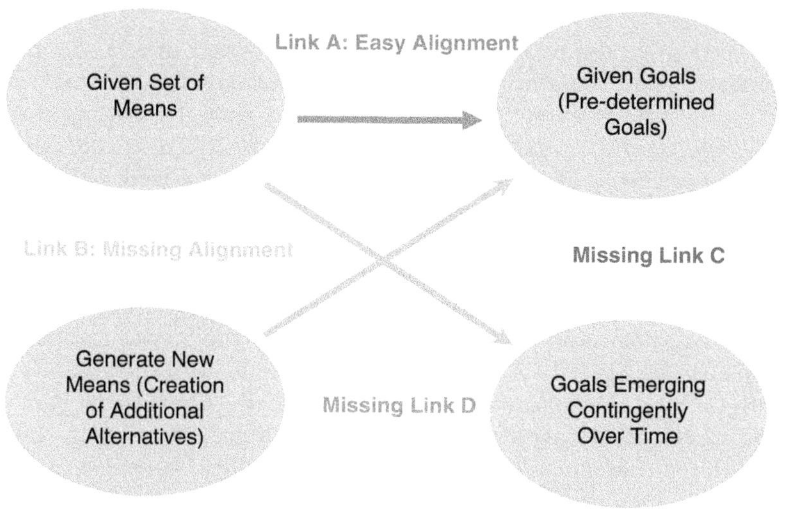

Figure 3.4 Complexities in the Missing Links and Alignments between Means and Goals
Source: Author created.

future looks bright in these kinds of endeavors; as smart fishermen can exploit and catch more fish in these fairly known areas of the vast red ocean, but the path might too often be rugged and misleading. This involves Strategic Thinking Level 2 (ST_2), and requires transformational leaders.

4th is Missing Link D: Reconciling the creation of additional alternatives (generation of new means) and aligning them with goals that emerge contingently over time. This is highly complex, and by far the most critical; and has often bedeviled even firms at the frontiers of competition. It is like fishermen strategizing to delve into unchartered areas of the vast blue ocean for fishing with little or no prior knowledge about its potentials and dangers. This involves strategic foresight and their complements, and requires sustainability leadership.

Conclusion

As a start-up entrepreneurial venture, while we emphasize two of the most important priories, which are: (1) there must be a significantly available market for the product; and (2) the entrepreneur must have a workable business model. Two issues become apparent here. *First*, the entrepreneur must address the sustainability challenges of the start-up venture as early as possible – preferably at the pre-seed stage of the venture. *Second*, there is the need for the start-up venture to make profit as soon as possible or windup.

How do we align the two issues? The *first issue* – that of ensuring the entrepreneur has *foothold of the sustainability challenges of the start-up venture* can best be answered, although not exclusively, by making sure there is a *significantly available market for the product*. The *second issue* – that of *making profit as soon as possible* can be best resolved, although not exclusively, by making sure *the venture has a workable or viable business model.*

In a nutshell, therefore, both profitability and sustainability have to be taken into consideration, right from the business idea generation stage (i.e., market segmentation stage), categorized under the pre-seed stage of a start-up entrepreneurial venture. As you can guess, both sustainability and profitability don't follow entirely the same path. On the one hand, while the *sustainability* aspect of the start-up venture starts being confronted with the conceptual framework of sustainability challenges at the beginning, and then gradually starts embracing execution challenges as the venture transitions from the pre-seed stage, to the seed stage, to the start-up stage, and beyond; the *profitability* aspect of the venture, on the other hand, starts facing immediate execution challenges to start generating income as soon as possible; so that the venture can break even and eventually starts making profit as soon as possible.

Typically, the challenges of productivity actually start surfacing when the start-up venture begins making profit. But the timeframe varies depending on the competitive environment, for instance, where the start-up venture is found in an industry that is quite competitive, the challenges of productivity surfaces much earlier. Even if the industry is not quite competitive, but where there are threats of rival products or substitutes from other industries in the market, it would tend to exert pressure on the performance and the profit margin of the new venture. As such, it would hasten up the need for the start up to begin scaling up with productivity so as to remain in business (see Fig. 3.5).

In another development, Kernodle (2020) argues that in order to move toward our goals, we need to have a clear vision of what those goals are, for example, aligning the goals of profitability with a workable business model.[190] Consequently, in addition to any other alignment factor, vision and goals must be perfectly aligned at all times – for any business venture to be profitable, and better still, such alignment is indispensible for sustaining such venture.

Without any exaggeration, it is the level of awareness and the ability to master the sequential levels of complexities – by exploring the use of strategic foresight that synergistically reconcile visionary, strategic, operational and tactical challenges of the various components of value creation – that marks the decisive point where winners emerge, runners up identify themselves, survivors thrive to exist, and losers wind-up.

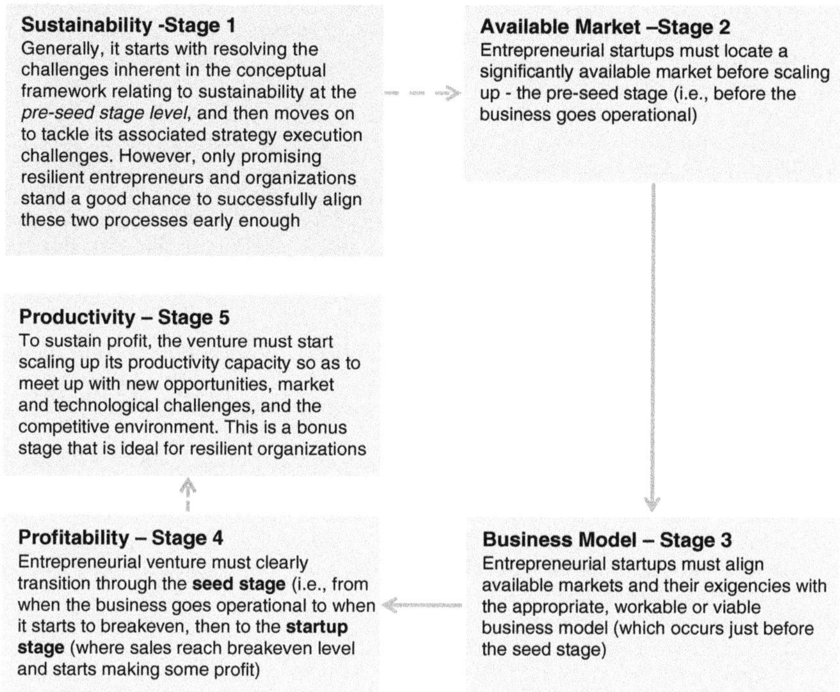

Figure 3.5 Magic Alignments in Entrepreneurial Start-Up Ventures
Source: Author created.

Notes

1 Slywotzky, Adrian. The Art of Profitability. *Grand Central Publishing*. Unknown Edition, 1 Sept. 2003, *Bookauthority.org*, https://bookauthority.org. Accessed 23 June 2020.
2 As cited by Stam, Erik and Elizabeth Garnsey. "Entrepreneurship in the Knowledge Economy." Center for Technology Management Working Paper Series, *University of Cambridge. No: 2007/04, April 2007, p. 5*, https://www.repository.cam.ac.uk/handle/1810/289919
3 Stam, Erik and Elizabeth Garnsey (2008), op. cit., p. 4.
4 Yunus, Muhammad. "Yunus Social Business Model: Module 1, Unit 3," in *Enabling* Entrepreneurs to Shape a Better World. Excerpts from MOOC course materials, Social Entrepreneurship Akademie, in partnership with edx.org, 2018, p. 3.
5 Yunus, Muhammad (2018), loc. cit.
6 As cited by Morris, M. H., et al. "A Portfolio Perspective on Entrepreneurship and Economic Development." *Springer*, 11 Sept. 2015, pp. 1–16, doi:10.1007/s11187-015-9678-5.
7 Morris et al. (2015); ibid.
8 Morris et al. (2015), op. cit., pp. 2-3.
9 Ibid; p. 3.
10 Ibid.

11 Cherry, Kendra. "What Is Cognitive Bias?" *Verywellmind.com*, reviewed by Amy Morin (psychotherapist), LCSW, 19 July 2020a, https://www.verywellmind.com/what-is-a-cognitive-bias-2794963. Accessed 11 June 2020.
12 Cherry, Kendra (2020a), loc. cit.
13 Cherry, Kendra (2020a), loc. cit.
14 Cherry, Kendra (2020a), loc. cit.
15 Cherry, Kendra (2020a), loc. cit.
16 Wilson, C. G., et al. "Age-Differences in Cognitive Flexibility When Overcoming a Preexisting Bias Through Feedback." *Journal of Clinical and Experimental Neuropsychology*, vol. 40, no. 6, 2018, pp. 586–94, doi:10.1080/13803395.2017.1398311. Accessed 2 Aug. 2020.
17 Cherry, Kendra (2020a), loc. cit.
18 As cited by Ghezzi et al. (2015), ibid.
19 Cherry, Kendra. "The Dunning-Kruger Effect." *Verywellwind.com*, medically reviewed by Steven Gans, MD, 14 June 2019, https://www.verywellmind.com/an-overview-of-the-dunning-kruger-effect-4160740. Accessed 2 Aug. 2020.
20 Sharot, Tali. "The Optimism Bias." *Primer*, vol. 21, no. 23, PR941–R945, 6 Dec. 2011, https://doi.org/10.1016/j.cub.2011.10.030. Accessed 2 Aug. 2020.
21 Ibid.
22 iResearchNet. "Planning Fallacy." *Psychology*, 2020, psychology.iresearchnet.com/social-psychology/decision-making/planning-fallacy. Accessed 2 Aug. 2020.
23 Ibid.
24 As cited by AchieveIt. "The Planning Fallacy: How to Avoid Becoming a Victim." *Achieveit.com*, 2020, https://www.achieveit.com/resources/blog/the-planning-fallacy-how-to-avoid-becoming -a-victim. Assessed 2 Aug. 2020.
25 iResearchNet (2020), loc. cit.
26 AchieveIt (2020), loc. cit.
27 Olivola, Y. Christopher. "The Interpersonal Sunk-Cost Effect." *Psychological Science*, vol. 27, July 2018, pp. 1072–83, https://doi.org/10.1177/0956797617752641. Accessed 3 Aug. 2020.
28 Davis, Z. M. "Sunk Cost Fallacy." *LessWrong*, 12 April 2009, https://www.lesswrong.com/posts/tyMdPwd8x2RygcheE/sunk-cost-fallacy. Accessed 3 Aug. 2020.
29 Toggl track. "What Is the Sunk Cost Fallacy? And How to Avoid It in 5 Steps." *Toggl track*, 5 April 2018, https://toggl.com/blog/sunk-cost-fallacy. Accessed 3 Aug. 2020.
30 Toggl track (2018), loc. cit.
31 Olivola, Y. Christopher (2018), loc. cit.
32 Ibid.
33 Sawruk, Coralie. "Leaders: avoid sunk fallacy [infographics]." *Coraliesawruk.com*, 2020, https://www.coraliesawruk.com/avoid-sunk-cost-fallacy. Accessed 3 Aug. 2020.
34 Riepe, W. Mark. "Don't Look Back: How to Avoid the Sunk Cost Fallacy." *Schwab.com*, 8 March 2018, https://www.schwab.com/resource-center/insights/content/dont-look-back-how-to-avoid-sunk-cost-fallacy. Accessed 3 Aug. 2020.
35 Cherry, Kendra. "Why the Halo Effect Influences How We Perceive Others." *Verywellmind.com*, reviewed by Amy Morin, LCSW (a psychotherapist), July 19, 2020b, https://www.verywellmind.com/what-is-the-halo-effect-2795906. Accessed 6 Nov. 2020.

36 Cherry, Kendra (2020b), loc. cit.
37 Cherry, Kendra (2020b), loc. cit.
38 Parrett, Matt. "Beauty and the Feast: Examining the Effect of Beauty on Earnings Using Restaurant Tipping Data." *Journal of Economic Psychology*, Vol. 49, Aug. 2015, pp. 34–46, https://doi.org/10.1016/j.joep.2015.04.002. Accessed 6 Nov. 2020.
39 Clifford, M. Margaret and Elaine Walster. "The Effect of Physical Attractiveness on Teacher Expectations."*Sociology of Education*, vol. 46, no. 2: American Sociological Association, Spring, 1973, p. 248, https://www.jstor.org/stable/2112099, doi: 10.2307/2112099.
40 Cherry, Kendra (2020b), loc. cit.
41 Cherry, Kendra (2020b), loc. cit.
42 Barry, C. and K. Halfmann (2016), op. cit., p. 53.
43 Eker, T. Harv (2005), op. cit., p. 5.
44 As cited by Eker, T. Harv (2005), op. cit., p. 10.
45 Leung, Millie. "The 8 Secrets of Becoming A Successful Entrepreneur." *Millieleung.com*, 2019, https://millieleung.com/secrets-of-entrepreneurs/.
46 Eker, T. Harv (2005), op. cit., p. 10.
47 Ibid; pp. 10-11.
48 Eker, T. Harv (2005), op. cit., p. 11.
49 Barry, C. and K. Halfmann (2016), op. cit., p. 51.
50 As cited by Barry, C. and K. Halfmann (2016), loc. cit.
51 MyCBGenie. "Clickbank Marketing Secrets: Learn the Secrets of The Gurus, Get More Traffic and Dominate Clickbank." *MyCBGenie.com*, 2020, pp. 7–8, https://mycbgenie.com/download.asp?fl=ClickbankMarketing Secrets.zip&name=Dennis&email=nyamecabiz@yahoo.com. Accessed 29 June 2020.
52 MyCBGenie (2020), op. cit., p. 8.
53 Barry, C. and K. Halfmann (2016), op. cit., p. 51.
54 Ibid.
55 As cited by Barry, C. and K. Halfmann (2016), ibid.
56 Ibid.
57 Ibid.
58 Trump, J. Donald. "Trump Never Give Up: How I Turned My Biggest Challenges into Success. Donald Trump with Meredith McIver." Hoboken: John Wiley & Sons, Inc., 2008, p. xvi.
59 Hill, Napoleon (2009), op. cit., p. 5.
60 Ibid; pp. 5-6.
61 Trump, J. Donald (2008), op. cit. p. xvii.
62 Goldstein, Andy. "Entrepreneurial Resilience:" in Entrepreneurial Mindset. *MOOC Learning Materials*, course excerpts from LMU Entrepreneurship Center, in partnership with edx.org, 2018.
63 Trump, J. Donald (2008), op. cit., p. xvi.
64 Goldstein, Andy (2018), loc. cit.
65 Trump, J. Donald (2008), op. cit., p. xvi.
66 Goldstein, Andy (2018), loc. cit.
67 Ibid.
68 Rowe, W. Glenn (2001), op. cit., p. 89.
69 Trump, J. Donald (2008), op. cit., p. 23.
70 Barrowclough D.V. and R. Kozul-Wright. "Institutional Geometry of Industrial Policy in Sustainable Development." In *Industrial Policy and Sustainable Growth. Sustainable Development*, edited by A. Murat Yulek, Springer, Singapore, 2018, https://doi.org/10.1007/978-981-10-5741-0_25. Accessed 1st July 2020.

71 Sondhe, S. Ratanjit (2010), op. cit., p. 7.
72 Newey, Lance. "Portfolio management: Getting the right mix of innovation projects:" in Innovation: From Plan to Product. *MOOC Learning Materials*, excerpts from University of Queensland, in partnership with edx.org, 2018.
73 Rowe, W. Glenn (2001), op. cit., p. 83.
74 Sondhe, S. Ratanjit (2010), op. cit., p. 10.
75 Yunus, Muhammad (2018), op. cit., p. 3.
76 Yunus, Muhammad (2018), op. cit., p. 1.
77 Stenn, L. Tamara. Social Entrepreneurship as Sustainable Development: Introducing the Sustainability Lens. *Palgrave Macmillan*, 1st Edition, 2017, https://bookauthority.org. Accessed 23 June 2020.
78 Yunus, Muhammad (2018), op. cit., p. 1.
79 Sondhe, S. Ratanjit (2010), op. cit., p. 12.
80 Bhalla et al. (2011), op. cit., p. 8.
81 Gronau, Norbert. "Future of Works and Skills for Workers in the Industry 4.0 Era:" in How to Revolutionize Your Business in Industry 4.0. *MOOC Learning Materials*, based on course excerpts from a data – University of Potsdam, in partnership with edx.org, 2018, pp. 2–10.
82 Ullrich, André. "Change of Work:" in How to Revolutionize Your Business in Industry 4.0. *MOOC Learning Materials*, course excerpts from University of Potsdam, in partnership with edx.org, 2018.
83 See Ullrich, André. "Attitude Acceptance:" in How to Revolutionize Your Business in Industry 4.0. *MOOC Learning Materials*, course excerpts from University of Potsdam, in partnership with edx.org, 2018.
84 Rowe, W. Glenn (2001), op. cit., p. 83.
85 Engel, C. and E. U. Weber (2007), op. cit., p. 336.
86 Ceru, J. Dennis (2018), loc. cit.
87 Sarasvathy, D. Saras. "What Makes Entrepreneurs Entrepreneurial?" *Harvard Business Review*. University of Washington School of Business, Seattle, 2001, p. 5; and Frans Berkhout and Julia Hertin. "Foresight Futures Scenarios: Developing and Applying a Participative Strategic Planning Tool." *Greener Management International* 37 (Spring), 2020.
88 Ceru, J. Dennis (2018), loc. cit.
89 Haycock, K., et al. "Strategic Thinking: Lessons for Leadership from the Literature." *Library Leadership & Management*, vol. 26, no. 3/4, 1 Oct. 2012, p. 1.
90 Ibid.
91 Sailer, Klaus. "Social Innovation:" in Enabling Entrepreneurs to Shape a Better World. *MOOC Learning Materials*, course excerpts from Social Entrepreneurship Akademie, Strascheg Center for Entrepreneurship, in partnership with edx.org, 2018.
92 Yun, Ethan. "Central Vision vs. Peripheral Vision." *Oxsight.co.uk*, 17 Jan. 2020, https://www.oxsight.co.uk/news/central-vision-vs-peripheral-vision. Accessed 6 Aug. 2020.
93 Yun, Ethan (2020), loc. cit.
94 Ho Vision Group. "Central vs. Peripheral Vision." *HoVisionGroup.com*, 2020, hovisiongroup.com/central-vs-peripheral-vision. Accessed 6 Aug. 2020.
95 Rowe, W. Glenn (2001), op. cit., p. 81.
96 Ceru, J. Dennis (2018), loc. cit.
97 Owen, L. Charles (2008), op. cit., p. 5.
98 Owen, L. Charles (2008), loc. cit.
99 Petrus van de Pol et al. (2014), op. cit., p. 6.

100 Piller, Frank. "Trend Analysis and Opportunity Recognition." *Customer-Centric Innovation. MOOC Learning Materials*, course excerpts from RWTH Aachen University, in partnership with edx.org, 2018.
101 Stroud, Samanda. "Business Tips for New Product Design and Development." *Cadcrowd.com*, 11 Sept. 2018, https://www.cadcrowd.com/blog/business-tips-for-new-product-design-development. Accessed 6 Aug. 2020.
102 Ibid.
103 Trump, J. Donald (2008), op. cit. p. 164.
104 Susman et al. (2006), op. cit., p. 10.
105 Susman et al. (2006), loc. cit.
106 Piller, Frank (2018), loc. cit.
107 Marketing-Insider. "Market Segmentation – Dividing Consumer Markets into Segments." *Marketing-insider.eu*, 2020a, https://marketing-insider.eu/marketing-explained/part-i-defining-marketing-and-the-marketing-process/market-segmentation/amp/. Accessed 17 March 2020.
108 Marketing-Insider (2020a), loc. cit.
109 Gardner, David. "Radical Vs. Incremental Innovation: The Right Approach for the Right Time," *Marumatchbox.com*, 14 Nov. 2017, https://marumatchbox.com/radical-vs-incremental-innovation-the-right-approach-for-the-right-time/. Accessed 2 March 2020.
110 Marketing-Insider (2020a), loc. cit.
111 As cited by Gardner, David (2017), loc. cit.
112 Gardner, David (2017), loc. cit.
113 Toma, Darrell. "What Is the Fine Difference between a Business Plan, Feasibility Studies and a Marketing Plan?" *ResearchGate.net*, Question Asked 2nd Feb. 2015, https://www.researchgate.net/post/What_is_the_fine_difference_between_a_business_plan_feasibility_studies_and_a_marketing_plan. Accessed 17 March 2020.
114 Becerril, A. Enrique. "What Is the Fine Difference between a Business Plan, Feasibility Studies and a Marketing Plan?." *ResearchGate.net*, Question Asked 2nd Feb. 2015, loc. cit. Accessed 19 March 2020.
115 Mullins, John. "What to Do Before You Write a Business Plan." *The European Business Review*, July–Aug. 2010, p. 31, www.europeanbusinessreview.com/.
116 Camacho, Salvador. "What Is the Fine Difference between a Business Plan, Feasibility Studies and a Marketing Plan?" *ResearchGate.net*, Question Asked 2nd Feb. 2015, loc. cit. Accessed 19 March 2020.
117 Louangrath, Paul. "What Is the Fine Difference between a Business Plan, Feasibility Studies and a Marketing Plan?" *ResearchGate.net*, Question Asked 2nd Feb. 2015, loc. cit. Accessed 19 March 2020.
118 Novak, R. Lee. "Market and Feasibility Studies: A How-To Guide." *University of Oregon*, May 1996, p. 4, https://pages.uoregon.edu/rgp/PPPM613/downloads/How%20to%20do%20a%20Market%20Analysis.pdf. Accessed 17 March 2020.
119 Ibid.
120 Koh, Daniel. "What Is the Fine Difference between a Business Plan, Feasibility Studies and a Marketing Plan?" *ResearchGate.net*, Question Asked 2nd Feb. 2015, loc. cit. Accessed 19 March 2020.
121 Womply. "Important Market Research Questions to Ask Before Starting a New Business." *Womply.com*, 2020, https://www.womply.com. Accessed 13 June 2020.
122 Queensland Government. The State of Queensland 1995-2020, https://www.business.qld.gov.au. Accessed 12 June 2020.
123 Ibid.

124 Queensland Government (1995-2020), loc. cit.
125 Womply (2020), loc. cit.
126 Queensland Government (1995-2020), loc. cit.
127 Kosaka, Kim. "29 Market Research Questions to Guide Your Marketing Strategy." *Alexa Internet, Inc.*, 2019, https://blog.alexa.com/market-research-questions. Accessed 22 May 2020.
128 Ibid.
129 Marketing-Insider. "Market Targeting – Target Segments efficiently and effectively." *Marketing-Insider.eu,* 2020b, https://marketing-insider.eu/marketing-explained/part-i-defining-marketing-and-the -marketing-process-/market-targeting/amp. Accessed 13 June 2020.
130 Marketing-Insider (2020b), loc. cit.
131 Marketing-Insider (2020b), loc. cit.
132 Porter, E. Michael. "Competitive Strategy: The Core Concepts." Chapter 1, *COMPETITIVE ADVANTAGE: Creating and Sustaining Superior Performance*, New York: The Free Press – Macmillan, 1985, p. 4.
133 Team FME. *Porter's Five Forces: Strategy Skills*, 2013, p. 28, www. free-management-ebooks.com.
134 Team FME (2013), op. cit., pp. 28-29.
135 Kim and Mauborgne (2014), op. cit., p. 5.
136 Kim and Mauborgne (2014), op. cit., p. 6.
137 Marketing-Insider (2020b), loc. cit.
138 Marketing-Insider (2020b), loc. cit.
139 MyCBGenie (2020), op. cit., p. 3.
140 Marketing-Insider (2020b), loc. cit.
141 As cited by Ghezzi et al. (2015), ibid.
142 Ghezzi et al. (2015), loc. cit.
143 Eisenmann et al. (2013), op. cit., p. 2.
144 As cited by Ghezzi et al. (2015), op. cit., p. 4.
145 Ibid.
146 Eisenmann et al. (2013), op. cit., p. 1.
147 Eisenmann et al. (2013), op. cit., p. 12.
148 Ciligot, Chris. "How to Plan a Minimum Viable Product: a Step-By-Step Guide," *Clearbridge mobile*, 5 April 2019, https://clearbridgemobile.com/planning-a-minimum-viable-product-a-step-by-step-guide. Accessed 22 May 2020.
149 Ibid.
150 Eisenmann et al. (2013), op. cit., pp. 17&23.
151 Ibid.
152 Viki, Tendayi (2018), loc. cit.
153 Eisenmann et al. (2013), op. cit., p. 11.
154 Eisenmann et al. (2013), op. cit., pp. 11-12.
155 Oyugi, L. Jacob. "What Is the Fine Difference between a Business Plan, Feasibility Studies and a Marketing Plan?" *ResearchGate.net*, Question Asked 2nd Feb. 2015. Accessed 19 March 2020, loc. cit.
156 Camacho, Salvador (2015), loc. cit.
157 Toma, Darrell (2015), loc. cit.
158 Louangrath, Paul (2015), loc. cit.
159 Mullins, John (2010), op. cit., p. 31.
160 Louangrath, Paul (2015), loc. cit.
161 Camacho, Salvador (2015), loc. cit.
162 Baniya, Rojan. "What Is the Fine Difference between a Business Plan,

Feasibility Studies and a Marketing Plan?" *ResearchGate.net*, Question Asked 2nd Feb. 2015, loc. cit. Accessed 19 March 2020.
163 Lee, K. Sylvia. "What Is the Fine Difference between a Business Plan, Feasibility Studies and a Marketing Plan?" *ResearchGate.net*, Question Asked 2nd Feb. 2015, loc. cit. Accessed 19 March 2020.
164 Oyugi, L. Jacob (2015), loc. cit.
165 Becerril, A. Enrique (2015), loc. cit.
166 Koh, Daniel (2015), loc. cit.
167 Ibid.
168 As cited by Ghezzi et al. (2015), op. cit., p. 5.
169 As cited by Ghezzi et al. (2015), ibid.
170 As cited by Ghezzi et al. (2015), ibid; pp. 4-5.
171 As cited by Ghezzi et al. (2015), op. cit., p. 4.
172 Sarasvathy, D. Saras (2001), op. cit., p. 2.
173 Sarasvathy, D. Saras (2001), op. cit. p. 8.
174 Please, note that in order to better acquaint the readers with diverse terminologies, and to avoid boredom; this book or better still, this chapter will be using "managerial thinking," "causal reasoning," "linear thinking," and "predictive reasoning" interchangeably to mean one and the same thing.
175 Sarasvathy, D. Saras (2001), op. cit., p. 1.
176 Ibid.
177 Bhalla et al. (2011), op. cit., p. 3.
178 Rowe, W. Glenn (2001), op. cit., p. 82.
179 Lozano et al. (2011), op. cit., p. 3.
180 Rowe, W. Glenn (2001), op. cit., p. 82.
181 Again, to better acquaint readers with a greater vocabulary and to avoid boredom, "creative causal reasoning" and "strategic thinking" will be used interchangeably to mean one and the same thing. Some scholars argue that strategic thinking is the main driving force behind strategic leadership.
182 Ibid.
183 Dellaert, M. and S. Davydov (2017), op. cit., p. 10.
184 Dellaert, M. and S. Davydov (2017), loc. cit.
185 Rowe, W. Glenn (2001), op. cit., p. 82.
186 Tuomo Kuosa. "Practising Strategic Foresight in Government." *RSIS Monograph*, no. 19, Singapore: S. Rajaratnam School of International Studies, 2011, p. 9. As cited by Petrus van de Pol et al. (2014), op. cit., p. 7.
187 Voros, Joseph. "A Primer on Futures Studies, Foresight and the Use of Scenarios," *prospect, the Foresight Bulletin*, no. 6, Dec. 2001, p. 4; as cited by Petrus van de Pol et al. (2014), ibid.
188 Dave Snowden. "Risk and Resilience," *YouTube video*, uploaded on 15 May 2011; as cited by Petrus van de Pol et al. (2014), ibid.
189 Raford, Noah. "Foresight and surprise." *The Lift Conference*, CICG, Geneva, Switzerland, 6-8 Feb. 2013; as cited by Petrus van de Pol et al. (2014), op. cit., pp. 5 & 7.
190 Kernodle, Melanie. "7 Characteristics of A Highly Productive Mindset." *Lifehack.org*, 2 Nov. 2020. Accessed 15 Nov. 2020.

Works Cited

Abrams, M. Rhonda. *The Successful Business Plan: Secrets & Strategies*. 7th Edition. Planning Shop, Palto Alto, Calif, 2003. Print.

Accounting Tools. "Lower of Cost or Market (LCM)." *Accounting Tools.com*,

20 Jan. 2019, https://www.accountingtools.com/articles/2017/5/13/lower-of-cost-or-market-lcm.

AchieveIt. "The Planning Fallacy: How to Avoid Becoming a Victim." *Achieveit.com*, 2020, https://www.achieveit.com/resources/blog/the-planning-fallacy-how-to-avoid-becoming -a-victim.

Alton, Larry. "5 Competitive Advantages Startups Have Over Big Businesses." *Entrepreneur.com*, 17 June 2015, https://www.entrepreneur.com/article/247412.

Baniya, Rojan. "What Is the Fine Difference between a Business Plan, Feasibility Studies and a Marketing Plan?" *ResearchGate.net*, Question Asked 2nd Feb. 2015.

Barrowclough, D.V. and R. Kozul-Wright. "Institutional Geometry of Industrial Policy in Sustainable Development." In *Industrial Policy and Sustainable Growth. Sustainable Development*, edited by A. Murat Yulek, Springer, 2018, https://doi.org/10.1007/978-981-10-5741-0_25.

Barry, Carly and Kameko Halfmann. "The Effect of Mindset on Decision-Making." *Journal of Integrated Social Sciences*, vol. 6, no. 1, 2016, pp. 49–74. www.JISS.org.

Becerril, A. Enrique. "What Is the Fine Difference between a Business Plan, Feasibility Studies and a Marketing Plan?" *ResearchGate.com*, Question Asked 2nd Feb. 2015.

Bhalla, Vikram, et al. *High-Performance Organizations: The Secrets of Their Success*. The Boston Consulting Group (BCG), 1 Sept. 2011, pp. 3–13, https://www.bcg.com/publications/2011/high-performance-organizations-secrets-of-success.

Bhidé, V. Amar. *The Origins and Evolution of New Businesses*. Oxford University Press, 1st Edition, 2010.

Bouchard, Véronique. "Exploring Corporate Entrepreneurship: A Corporate Strategy Perspective." *European Entrepreneurial Learning*, EM Lyon, Dec. 2001, pp. 1–30.

Boyd, Ken. "Lower Costs and Increase Revenue Using the Gross Profit Formula." *Quickbooks.intuit.com*, 24 July 2020, https://quickbooks.intuit.com/r/bookkeeping/gross-profit.

Boyte-White, Claire. "The Best Way to Calculate Profitability for Startups." *Investopedia.com*, 14 June 2020, https://www.investopedia.com/ask/answers/020415/what-best-way-calculate-profitability-startups.asp.

Brandau, Jean and Andrea Young. "Competitive Intelligence in Entrepreneurial and Start-Up Businesses." *Competitive Intelligence Review*, vol. 11, no. 1, John Wiley & Sons, Inc., 03 Jan. 2001, pp. 74-84, https://doi.org/10.1002/(SICI)1520-6386(200031)11:1<74::AID-CIR10>3.0.CO;2-X.

Brinckmann, Jan, et al. "Should Entrepreneurs Plan or Just Storm the Castle? A Meta-Analysis on Contextual Factors Impacting the Business Planning–Performance Relationship Small in Firms." *Journal of Business Venturing*, vol. 25, no. 1, 2010, pp. 24–40.

Burke, A., et al. "The Multiple Effects of Business Planning on New Venture Performance." *Journal of Management Studies*, vol. 47, no. 3, 2010, pp. 391–415.

Camacho, Salvador. "What Is the Fine Difference between a Business Plan, Feasibility Studies and a Marketing Plan?." *ResearchGate.net*, Question Asked 2nd Feb. 2015.

Ceru, J. Dennis. "Mindset of the Entrepreneur." MOOC Learning Materials, Course Excerpts from Babson College of Entrepreneurship, in partnership with edx.org, 2018.

Chen, James. "Operational Efficiency." *Investopedia.com*, 6 Dec. 2019, https://www.investopedia.com/terms/o/opertationalefficiency.asp.

Chen, James. "Income Statement." *Investopedia.com*, 13 May 2020, https://www.investopedia.com/terms/i/incomestatement.asp.

Cherry, Kendra. "The Dunning-Kruger Effect." *Verywellwind.com*, medically reviewed by Steven Gans, MD, 14 June 2019, https://www.verywellmind.com/an-overview-of-the-dunning-kruger-effect-4160740.

Cherry, Kendra. "What Is Cognitive Bias? *Verywellmind.com*, reviewed by Amy Morin (psychotherapist), LCSW, 19 July 2020a, https://www.verywellmind.com/what-is-a-cognitive-bias-2794963.

Cherry, Kendra. "Why the Halo Effect Influences How We Perceive Others." *Verywellmind.com*, reviewed by Amy Morin, LCSW (a psychotherapist), July 19, 2020b, https://www.verywellmind.com/what-is-the-halo-effect-2795906.

Ciligot, Chris. "How to Plan a Minimum Viable Product: a Step-By-Step Guide," *Clearbridge mobile*, 5 April 2019, https://clearbridgemobile.com/planning-a-minimum-viable-product-a-step-by-step-guide.

Clifford, M. Margaret and Elaine Walster. "The Effect of Physical Attractiveness on Teacher Expectations." *Sociology of Education*, vol. 46, no. 2: American Sociological Association, Spring, 1973, pp. 248–58, https://www.jstor.org/stable/2112099, doi: 10.2307/2112099.

Corporate Finance Institute (CFI). "What Is the Balance Sheet?" *Corporatefinanceinstitute.com*, 2020a, https://corporatefinanceinstitute.com/resources/knowledge/accounting/balance-sheet/.

Corporate Finance Institute (CFI). "Expenses." *Corporatefinanceinstitute.com*, 2020b, https://corporatefinanceinstitute.com/resources/knowledge/accounting/expenses.

Davidsson, Per. *Researching Entrepreneurship*, vol. 5. Springer, Berlin, 2005.

Davis, Z. M. "Sunk Cost Fallacy." *LessWrong*, 12 April 2009, https://www.lesswrong.com/posts/tyMdPwd8x2RygcheE/sunk-cost-fallacy.

Dellaert, Marc, and Sergey Davydov. "Influencing: The Skill of Persuasion - Building Commitment and Getting Results." White Paper, Center for Creative Leadership, 2017, pp. 1–12, https://www.ccl.org/wp-content/uploads/2017/01/Influencing-the-skill-of-persuasion.pdf/.

Eisenmann, Thomas, et al. *Hypothesis-Driven Entrepreneurship: The Lean Startup*, Harvard Business School Publishing, Boston, 10 July 2013, pp. 2–26. 9-812-095, Rev: www.hbsp.harvard.edu/educators.

Eker, T. Harv. *Secrets of the Millionaire Mind: Mastering the Inner Game of Wealth. Library of Congress Cataloging-in-Publication Data*. HarperCollins Publishers, Pymble, Toronto, Auckland, London, New York, Feb. 2005, pp. 1–47, Adobe Acrobat eBook Reader.

Engel, Christoph and U. Elke Weber. "The Impact of Institutions on the Decision How to Decide." *Journal of Institutional Economics*, vol. 3, no. 3, 2007, pp. 323–49, : The JOIE Foundation, doi:10.1017/S1744137407000744.

Fears, J. Rufus. "The Lessons of the Roman Empire for America Today." *Heritage.org*, 2005, http://www.heritage.org/research/lecture/the-lessons-of-the-roman-empire-for-america-today.

Fehr, Ernest. "The Economics of Impatience." *Nature*, vol. 17, 2020, pp. 269–72, doi: 10.1038/415269a

FreshBooks. "What Is Unearned Revenue? A Definition and Examples for Small Businesses." *FreshBooks.com*, 2020a.

FreshBooks. "How to Calculate Net Sales." *FreshBooks.com*, 2020b, https://www.freshbooks.com/hub/accounting /calculate-net-sales.

Gardner, David. "Radical Vs. Incremental Innovation: The Right Approach for the Right Time," *Marumatchbox.com*, 14 Nov. 2017, https://marumatchbox.com/radical-vs-incremental-innovation-the-right-approach-for-the-right-time/.

Ghezzi, A., et al. "A Comparative Study on the Impact of Business Model Design& Lean Startup Approach versus Traditional Business Plan on Mobile StartupsPerformance." ICEIS 2015: Proceedings of the 17th International Conference on Enterprise Information Systems, vol. 3, April 2015, pp. 196–203 (or pp. 2–9), https://doi.org/10.5220/0005337501960203.

Gibbons, M., et al. *The New Production of Knowledge: The Dynamics of Science and Research in Contemporary Societies*. Sage Publications, London, 1994.

Goldstein, Andy. "Entrepreneurial Resilience:" in Entrepreneurial Mindset. *MOOC Learning Materials*, course excerpts from LMU Entrepreneurship Center, in partnership with edx.org, 2018.

Green, Holly. "Phases of Innovation." *Forbes.com.*, 14 Dec. 2011, https://www.forbes.com/sites/work-in-progress/2011/12/14/phases-of-innovation/#7c59c8b14996.

Gronau, Norbert. "Future of Works and Skills for Workers in the Industry 4.0 Era:" in How to Revolutionize Your Business in Industry 4.0. *MOOC Learning Materials*, based on course excerpts from the University of Potsdam, in partnership with edx.org, 2018, pp. 2–10.

Haycock, K., et al. "Strategic Thinking: Lessons for Leadership from the Literature." *Library Leadership & Management*, vol. 26, no. 3/4, 1 Oct. 2012, pp. 1–14.

Hayes, Adam. "Cost of Goods Sold." *Investopedia.com*, 27 April 2020, https://www.investopedia.com/terms/c/cogs.asp.

Hechavarria, M. Diana and Ingram, Amy. "A Review of Entrepreneurial Ecosystem and the Entrepreneurial Society in the United States: An Exploration with the Global Entrepreneurship Monitor Dataset." *Journal of Business and Entrepreneurship*, Fall 2014 Special Issue, pp. 1–16.

Hill, Napoleon. *Think and Grow Rich*, 2005, first published in 1937. This is a summary of the original book, republished as Summary Think and Grow Rich. *Success Book Summary*. Published by SUCCESS Media, Lake Dallas, July 2009, pp. 1–6.

Hogan, Chris. "What is the Difference Between Income and Net Worth." *Daveramsey.com*, 2020, https://www.daveramsey.com/blog/income-vs-networth.

Honig, B., and T. Karlsson. "Institutional Forces and the Written Business Plan." *Journal of Management*, vol. 30, no. 1, 2004, pp. 29–48.

Hoskisson, E. Robert, et al. *Competing for Advantage*. 2nd Edition. Thomson South-Western, 1 Jan. 2004.

Ho Vision Group. "Central vs. Peripheral Vision." HoVisionGroup.com, 2020, hovisiongroup.com/central-vs-peripheral-vision.

Internal Revenue Service (IRS). "Accounting Periods and Methods." *Publication 538*, Cat. No. 15068G, Jan. 2019, pp. 1–21, IRS.gov/Pub538.

iResearchNet. "Planning Fallacy." *Psychology*, 2020, psychology.iresearchnet.com/social-psychology/decision-making/planning-fallacy.

Jacobe, Dennis. "*Lessons Learned About Starting a Small Business.*" *GALLUP NEWS SERVICE*, 18 Sept. 2006, https://news.gallup.com/poll/24574/Lessons-Learned-About-Starting-Small-Business.aspx.

Johnson, W. Mark. *Seizing the White Space: An interview with Mark Johnson.* Emerald Group Publishing Limited, April 2010, pp. 1–6, https://www.emeraldgrouppublishing.com/archived/learning/management_thinking/interviews/johnson_m.htm.

Kahneman, Daniel. *Thinking, Fast and Slow*. Farrar, Straus, and Giroux, New York, 2011.

Kernodle, Melanie. "7 Characteristics of A Highly Productive Mindset." *Lifehack.org*, 2 Nov. 2020.

Khairuzzaman, Akm. 3D Printing in Drug Development & Emerging Health Care." Center for Drug Evaluation and Research (CDER)/Food and Drugs Administration (FDA), 2020, pp. 1–49, www.fda.gov.

Kim, W. Chan and Renée Mauborgne. "Blue Ocean Strategy: From Theory to Practice." *California Management Review*, vol. 47, no. 3: Spring 2005, pp. 105–21.

Koh, Daniel. "What Is the Fine Difference between a Business Plan, Feasibility Studies and a Marketing Plan?" *ResearchGate.net*, Question Asked 2nd Feb. 2015.

Kosaka, Kim. "29 Market Research Questions to Guide Your Marketing Strategy." *Alexa Internet, Inc.*, 2019, https://blog.alexa.com/market-research-questions.

Kraus, Sascha, and Ilkka Kauranen. "Strategic Management and Entrepreneurship: Friends or Foes." *International Journal of Business Science and Applied Management*, vol. 4, no. 1, 2009, pp. 37–50.

Lance, Jack. "Understanding Cost of Goods Sold for Service Businesses." *Financialsoft.biz*, 22 June 2016, financialsoft.biz/understanding-cost-of-goods-sold-for-service-businesses.

Lee, K. Sylvia. "What Is the Fine Difference between a Business Plan, Feasibility Studies and a Marketing Plan?" *ResearchGate.net*, Question Asked 2nd Feb. 2015.

Leung, Millie. "The 8 Secrets of Becoming A Successful Entrepreneur." *Millieleung.com*, 2019, https://millieleung.com/secrets-of-entrepreneurs/.

Liberman, N., and Y. Trope. "Construal Level Theory of Intertemporal Judgment and Decision." *Time and Decision*, edited by G. Loewenstein, D. Read, and R. Baumeister, Russell Sage Foundation, New York, 2003. pp. 245–76.

Liberto, Daniel. "Pretax Profit Margin." *Investopedia.com*, 10 April 2019, https://www.investopedia.com/terms/p/pretax-margin.asp.

Liberto, Daniel. "Unearned Revenue." *Investopedia.com*, updated 27 Oct. 2020.

Louangrath, Paul. "What Is the Fine Difference between a Business Plan, Feasibility Studies and a Marketing Plan?" *ResearchGate.net*, Question Asked 2nd Feb. 2015.

Lozano, O., et al. "Organizational DNA: Customer & Operations Strategy." *Sintec*. Sistemas Interactivos de Consultoría, S.A. de C.V., Mexico City, Monterrey, Bogota, Sao Paulo, 2011, pp. 1–5.

Lumencandela. "Valuing Inventory." *Lumencandela*, 2020, https://courses.lumenlearning.com/boundless-accounting/chapter/valuing-inventory.

Mathews, A. John. "Design of Industrial and Supra-Firm Architectures: Growth and Sustainability." *Journal of Organization Design*, vol. 1, no. 2, Aug. 2012, pp. 42–63. doi: 10.7146/jod.6454.

Marketing-Insider. "Market Segmentation – Dividing Consumer Markets into Segments." *Marketing-insider.eu*, 2020a, https://marketing-insider.eu/marketing-explained/part-i-defining-marketing-and-the-marketing-process/market-segmentation/amp/.

Marketing-Insider. "Market Targeting – Target Segments Efficiently and Effectively." *Marketing-Insider.eu*, 2020b, https://marketing-insider.eu/marketing-explained/part-i-defining-marketing-and-the-marketing-process-/market-targeting/amp.

Money-Zine. "Pretax Margin." *Money-Zine.com copyright* 2020, https://www.money-zine.com/definitions/investing-dictionary/pretax-margin.

Morah, Chizoba. "Business Startup Costs: It's in the Details." *Investopedia.com*, 27 Nov. 2019, https://www.investopedia.com/articles/pf/09/business-startup-costs.asp.

Morris, M. H., et al. "A Portfolio Perspective on Entrepreneurship and Economic Development." Small BusEcon, vol. 45, 11 Sept. 2015, pp. 1–16, https://doi.org/10.1007/s11187-015-9678-5

Morris, M. H., et al. "A Portfolio Perspective on Entrepreneurship and Economic Development." *Springer*, 11 Sept. 2015, p. 2, doi: 10.1007/s11187-015-9678-5.

Mullins, John. "What to do before you write a business plan." *The European Business Review*, July–Aug. 2010, pp. 29-31, www.europeanbusinessreview.com/.

Murphy, B. Chris. "Financial Statements." *Investopedia.com*, 26 July 2020, https://www.investopedia.com/terms/f/financial-statements.asp.

Murphy, Chris. "Operating Costs." *Investopedia.com*, 27 July 2020, https://www.investopedia.com/terms/o/operating-cost.asp.

MyCBGenie. "Clickbank Marketing Secrets: Learn the Secrets of The Gurus, Get More Traffic and Dominate Clickbank." *MyCBGenie.com*, 2020, pp. 1–36.

Newey, Lance. "Portfolio Management: Getting the Right Mix of Innovation Projects:" in Innovation: From Plan to Product. *MOOC Learning Materials*, excerpts from University of Queensland, in partnership with edx.org, 2018.

Novak, R. Lee. "Market and Feasibility Studies: A How-To Guide." *University of Oregon*, May 1996, pp. 3-35, https://pages.uoregon.edu/rgp/PPPM613/downloads/How%20to%20do%20a%20Market%20Analysis.pdf.

Olivola, Y. Christopher. "The Interpersonal Sunk-Cost Effect." *Psychological Science*, vol. 27, July 2018, pp. 1072–83, https://doi.org/10.1177/0956797617752641.

Osterwalder, Alexander, and Pigneur Yves. *Business Model Generation: A Handbook for Visionaries, Game Changers, and Challengers*, 1st Edition. John Wiley & Sons, Hoboken, NJ, 2010.

Owen, L. Charles "Design, Advanced Planning and Product Development," 3o Congresso Brasileiro de Pesquisa e Desenvolvimento em Design, Rio de Janeiro, Brazil: Oct. 26, 1998. International Symposium: Nuevos Metodos & Tecnologias para el Diseño de Productos, Santiago, Chile: Nov. 12, 1998, pp. 1–13.

Owen, L. Charles. "Insight and Ideas." *Institute of Design – Illinois Institute of Technology*, a web article written for: The Business Process Management Institute. Web site: www.BPMInstitute.org, Feb. 2008, pp. 3–5.

Oyugi, L. Jacob. "What Is the Fine Difference between a Business Plan, Feasibility Studies and a Marketing Plan?" *ResearchGate.net*, Question Asked 2nd Feb. 2015.

Parrett, Matt. "Beauty and the Feast: Examining the Effect of Beauty on Earnings

Using Restaurant Tipping Data." *Journal of Economic Psychology*, vol. 49, Aug. 2015, pp. 34–46, https://doi.org/10.1016/j.joep.2015.04.002.

Petrus van de Pol, et al. "*Foresight as a Strategic Long-Term Planning Tool for Developing Countries.*" Global Center for Public Service Excellence (GCPSE), UNDP, Singapore, 2014, pp. 4–18.

Piller, Frank. "Trend Analysis and Opportunity Recognition." *Customer-Centric Innovation. MOOC Learning Materials*, course excerpts from RWTH Aachen University, in partnership with edx.org, 2018.

Porter, E. Michael. "Competitive Strategy: The Core Concepts." Chapter 1, *COMPETITIVE ADVANTAGE: Creating and Sustaining Superior Performance*. The Free Press – Macmillan, New York, 1985, pp. 1–30.

Pryor, G. Mildred, et al. "Strategic Implementation as a Core Competency: The 5Pís Model." *Journal of Management Research*, vol. 7, no. 1, April 2007.

Queensland Government. The State of Queensland 1995-2020, https://www.business.qld.gov.au.

Radeke, Frank (2011), "Toward Understanding Enterprise Architecture Management's Role in Strategic Change: Antecedents, Processes, Outcomes," *EBS Business School*, Institute of Research on Information Systems, Wiesbaden.

Riepe, W. Mark. "Don't Look Back: How to Avoid the Sunk Cost Fallacy." *Schwab.com*, 8 March 2018, https://www.schwab.com/resource-center/insights/content/dont-look-back-how-to-avoid-sunk-cost-fallacy.

Ries, Eric. *The Lean Startup: How Today's Entrepreneurs Use Continuous Innovation to Create Radically Successful Businesses*. Crown Business, New York, 2011.

Rowe, W. Glenn. "Creating Wealth in Organizations: The Role of Strategic Leadership." *Academy of Management Executive*, vol. 15, no 1, Feb. 2001, pp. 81–94.

Sailer, Klaus. "Social Innovation:" in Enabling Entrepreneurs to Shape a Better World. *MOOC Learning Materials*, course excerpts from Social Entrepreneurship Akademie, Strascheg Center for Entrepreneurship, in partnership with edx.org, 2018.

Sarasvathy, D. Saras (2001), op. cit., pp. 2–8.

Sawruk, Coralie. "Leaders: Avoid Sunk Fallacy [infographics]." *Coraliesawruk.com*, 2020, https://www.coraliesawruk.com/avoid-sunk-cost-fallacy.

Scott, Chris. "Four Ways to Measure Profitability and Grow Your Business." *Quickbooks.intuit.com*, 18 Sept. 2019, https://quickbooks.intuit.com/r/pricing-strategy/4-ways-to-measure-your-profitability.

Segal, Troy. "Profit Margin." *Investopedia.com*, 5 April 2020, https://www.investopedia.com/terms/p/profitmargin.asp.

Sharot, Tali. "The Optimism Bias." *Primer*, vol. 21, no. 23, 6 Dec. 2011, pp. PR941–R945, https://doi.org/10.1016/j.cub.2011.10.030.

Shpak, Scott. "How to Distinguish Between Operating and Non-operating Income in Relation to the Income Statement." *AZCentral.com*, 25 April 2018, https://yourbusiness.azcentral.com/distinguish-between-operating-nonoperating-income-relation-income-statement-17472.html.

Slywotzky, Adrian. *The Art of Profitability. Grand Central Publishing.* Unknown Edition,1 Sept. 2003, *Bookauthority.org*, https://bookauthority.org.

Sondhe, S. Ratanjit. "Wealth Creation vs. Job Creation: Why Creating Jobs Isn't the Real Answer to Our Economic Problems." *Probizwriters.com*, 2010, pp. 1–18.

Stam, Erik and Garnsey, Elizabeth. "Entrepreneurship in the Knowledge Economy." *University of Cambridge*, 2008, pp. 1–24, https://www.academia.edu.

Stenn, L. Tamara. *Social Entrepreneurship as Sustainable Development: Introducing the Sustainability Lens. Palgrave Macmillan*, 1st Edition 2017, https://bookauthority.org.

Stroud, Samanda. "Business Tips for New Product Design and Development." *Cadcrowd.com*, 11 Sept. 2018, https://www.cadcrowd.com/blog/business-tips-for-new-product-design-development.

Surbhi, S. "Difference Between Net Income and Net Profit." *Keydifferences.com*, 2 Feb. 2015, https://keydifferences.com/difference-between-net-income-and-net-profit.html.

Susman, G., et al. "Innovation and Change Management in Small and Medium-Sized Manufacturing Companies." Sponsored Research Prepared for: United States Department of Commerce, the National Institute of Standards and Technology Manufacturing Extension Partnership, Prepared by Smeal College of Business, The Pennsylvania State University. Final Report of Task 4 RFP 05-480-5823, Contract No. SB1341-03-Z-0015/65364, 30 June 2006, pp. 3–49.

Tardi, Carla. "Inventory Valuation – LIFO vs. FIFO." *Investopedia.com*, 5 April 2020, https://www.investopedia.com/articles/02/060502.asp.

Team FME. *Porter's Five Forces: Strategy Skills*, 2013, pp. 4–29, www. free-management-ebooks.com.

Teece, D.J. "Business Models, Business Strategy and Innovation." *Long Range Planning*, vol. 43, no. 2–3, 2010, pp. 172–94.

The Free Dictionary by Farlex. "Amortization." *Copyright ©2003-2020 Farlex, Inc.*, https://financial-dictionary.thefreedictionary.com/Amortization.

Toggl track. "What Is the Sunk Cost Fallacy? And How to Avoid It in 5 Steps." *Toggl track*, 5 April 2018, https://toggl.com/blog/sunk-cost-fallacy. Accessed 3 Aug. 2020.

Toma, Darrell. "What Is the Fine Difference between a Business Plan, Feasibility Studies and a Marketing Plan?." *ResearchGate.net*, Question Asked 2nd Feb. 2015.

Trope, Y., and N. Liberman. "Construal-level Theory of Psychological Distance." *Psychological Review*, vol. 117, no. 2, Apr 2010, pp. 440–63. doi:10.1037/a0018963

Trump, J. Donald. *Trump Never Give Up: How I Turned My Biggest Challenges into Success. Donald Trump with Meredith McIver*. John Wiley & Sons, Inc, Hoboken, 2008, pp. xvi to xvii, and from pp. 1–168.

Tuovila, Alicia. "Non-Operating Expense." *Investopedia.com*, 14 July 2019, https://www.investopedia.com/terms/n/non-operating-expense.asp.

Tversky, Amos, and Daniel Kahneman. "Availability: A Heuristic for Judging Frequency and Probability." *Cognitive Psychology*, vol. 5, no. 2, Sept. 1973, pp. 207–32.

Ullrich, André. "Attitude Acceptance:" in How to Revolutionize Your Business in Industry 4.0. *MOOC Learning Materials*, course excerpts from University of Potsdam, in partnership with edx.org, 2018.

Ullrich, André. "Change of Work:" in How to Revolutionize Your Business in

Industry 4.0. *MOOC Learning Materials*, course excerpts from University of Potsdam, in partnership with edx.org, 2018.

Viki, Tendayi. "Innovation Is Management." *Forbes.com*, 8 Jan. 2017, https://www.forbes.com/sites/tendayiviki/2017/01/08/innovation-is-management/#48a3ff8f3e65.

Viki, Tendayi. "*Six Principles For Creating A Good Corporate Innovation Process.*" *Forbes Media LLC*, 26 March 2018, https://www.forbes.com/sites/tendayiviki/2018/03/26/six-principles-corporate-innovation-process/#4ba5a45544f4.

Watson, Jessica. "Top 10 Reasons for Entrepreneurs Failure in 2018," *Mercy – CBNation*, 21 March 2018, https://rescue.ceoblognation.com/2018/03/21/top-10-reasons-for-entrepreneurs-failure-in-2018/.

Wilson, C. G., et al. "Age-Differences in Cognitive Flexibility When Overcoming a Preexisting Bias Through Feedback." *Journal of Clinical and Experimental Neuropsychology*, vol. 40, no. 6, 2018, pp. 586–94, doi: 10.1080/13803395.2017.1398311.

Womply. "Important Market Research Questions to Ask Before Starting a New Business." *Womply.com*, 2020, https://www.womply.com.

Yun, Ethan. "Central Vision vs. Peripheral Vision." *Oxsight.co.uk*, 17 Jan. 2020, https://www.oxsight.co.uk/news/central-vision-vs-peripheral-vision.

Yunus, Muhammad. "Yunus Social Business Model: Module 1, Unit 3," in *Enabling Entrepreneurs to Shape a Better World*. Excerpts from MOOC course materials, Social Entrepreneurship Akademie, in partnership with edx.org, 2018, pp. 1–5.

4 Organizational Dynamics of Global Manufacturing, Innovation, and the New Game of Product Design: Productivity Perspective

Introduction

This chapter examines innovative ways in which companies can significantly improve productivity. Primarily, it explores ways firms can mobilize resources with which they can use to revolutionize products' physical appeal, quality, and functionality at affordable costs, and then create more value. In this regard, it also examines how firms can simplify *their production structure and align their operating model with the true sources of value in their business.* This chapter looks beyond the traditional management's approach to growth, which for the past three decades has traditionally focused on labor efficiency (doing the same with less) as the main driver for growth – by trying to lower the cost of input to produce the same output. That being said, while this chapter upholds the contribution of labor efficiency as a major contributory factor to a firm's growth, it primarily emphasizes the need to step up productivity (doing more with the same) so as to meet up with today's fast-changing complexities in consumer tastes and demands. This means, going beyond the idea of *reducing input* (resources) to produce the same *output* (value) to *expanding output* (value) with the use of the same *input* (resources).

Having said that, this chapter tackles it by primarily exploring how the dynamics of *imitation, technology transfer, and innovation* among other factors can contribute to achieving this purpose. Essentially, Imitation is an effort to learn and improve the technology developed by other firms. Technology transfer can be due to technology spillover through firm-to-firm or person-to-person contacts (the contagion effect). Innovation is the effort to develop a new technology to improve factor productivity, to invent a new product, or to improve the quality of some existing products.

From the foregoing, the analysis of McKinsey Global Institute (2015) estimated that roughly *three-quarters* of the total global potential for productivity growth comes from the broader adoption of existing best practices – which we can characterize as "catch-up" productivity improvements. The remaining *one-quarter* comes from the spheres of technological, operational, and business innovations that go beyond today's best practices, which have the effects of *pushing the frontiers* of the world's GDP potential.[1]

Furthermore, in *developed economies,* McKinsey Global Institute analysis reveals that more than half (55%) of what they find as *feasible productivity gains could come from closing the gap between low-productivity companies and plants and those that have high productivity.* They also observed that there are opportunities to continue to incorporate leaner supply-chain operations throughout retail. Meanwhile, across countries, they noted that large differences in average productivity within the same industry indicate industry-wide opportunities for improvement. For instance, low productivity in retail and other service sectors in Japan and South Korea reflects a large share of traditional small-scale retailers that could still be improved on. High costs in the US health-care system partly reflect the excessive use of clinically ineffective procedures. Even agriculture, automotive manufacturing, and other sectors that have historically made strong contributions to productivity growth have ample room to continue to diffuse innovations and become more efficient.[2]

4.1 Legacy of the First Industrial Revolution – Its Aftermath and Critical Caveats

4.1.1 Defining the Contextual Meaning of Industrial Revolution

Much is being said about radical economic change, the new machine age, the industrial revolution, and a new age of automation, just to name a few. While the landmark terminology here is the industrial revolution, it is itself a complex combination of many issues that requires thorough understanding.

This chapter defines an Industrial Revolution as a period of rapid economic takeoff, that is closely followed by sustained higher levels of economic growth; orchestrated by either radical innovations in technology, breakthrough innovations in technology, and or technology diffusion, and which leads to a further developmental stage in the organization and management of the entire value chain process involved in the manufacturing industry, the economy, and its requisite social transformation.

As history would remind us, countries that have witnessed industrial revolutions did so in sequential stages – especially pertaining to the iron logic of the industrial revolution. Even for later developed or developing countries, industrialization must always go through several major and distinctive stages *sequentially*, with each stage facing its own problem of missing markets and market creators. Hence, successful economic development requires many rounds of step-by-step *sequential* "big pushes" from the bottom up by both the local and central governments.[3] Karimov (2013) defines industrialization as the sustained structural transformation of a traditional economy into a modern economy, driven by high productivity activities in manufacturing.[4]

In recent times, new trends of industrialization are emerging and dominating the advanced economies in the form of *knowledge-intensive industrialization,* alternatively referred to as the *soft power of industrialization.* To that end, previous McKinsey Global Institute (MGI) research has shown that profits have migrated toward idea-intensive industries such as pharmaceuticals and technology, while margins have been squeezed in *capital-intensive* and *labor-intensive* industries including automobiles, machinery, and retail.[5]

4.1.2 Stages of Industrial Revolutions and Their Key Characteristics

The first characteristic of the industrial revolution has been the metamorphosis from a backward agrarian economy toward proto-industrialization. Enabling a shift from a traditional industrial policy with a focus on infant industry protection, to a new development policy with focuses on competition and improving the market institution.[6] From there it moves to first industrial revolution, then to the second industrial revolution, to the welfare state, and finally to the fourth industrial revolution.

Since the first industrial revolution, manufacturing has statistically accounted for the fastest GDP growth rate in the history of economic development when compared to other industries. To concur, Industry Canada (2012) found that in terms of new product commercialization, the Canadian manufacturing sector is at the forefront. For example, between 2007 and 2009, 43% of Canadian manufacturers introduced new product innovations, compared to 13% in all other industries.[7]

Agrarian Economy

Agrarian economy is one of the oldest forms of economies still in existence. It comes from the word "agrarian" which means agriculture. An agrarian economy is a type of economy that relies primarily on the agricultural industry, including livestock farming or crop production. It is a form of the economy whose major factor of production is agricultural land. The prosperity of the agrarian economy is also influenced by other factors such as adequate rainfall, suitable climate, and inputs like fertilizers.[8]

Proto-Industrialization

Economic historians have noted that certain areas of Europe, such as *Flanders* in *Belgium* and *Lancashire* in *England,* were "industrialized" in the 17th and 18th centuries even before the Industrial Revolution took off in the United Kingdom. This industrialization was characterized by rural, family-based production of textiles and garments without modern machinery, and was often brokered by urban merchants.[9]

Proto-industrialization begins *as a side job in villages where agricultural productivity is low.* They can sell cloth and garments to nearby rich villages where agricultural productivity is high. It is a sort of specialization (a division of labor) within a relatively small geographical area: villages with fertile soil produce farm products and villages with poor soil produce manufactured goods, and they exchange output with each other. They sometimes also sell their products to larger markets.[10] In the United Kingdom, for example, production was coordinated and financed by a class of wealthy merchants under the "putting out" system. While Japan benefited from the political stability of the Edo period (1603–1868) and continued its proto-industrialization in the early Meiji period (1868–1890). In China, this and other stages made use of collectively (not privately) owned enterprises.[11]

First Industrial Revolution

The First Industrial Revolution occurred sometime in 1760 *through the introduction of mechanical production facilities with the help of water and steam power.*[12]

This stage involves light industries – and such light industries have been dominated by the mass production of textiles, through the use of rudimentary systems such as wood-framed and water-powered machinery in Great Britain, while in Japan it took the form of imported technologies. In the United States, mass production of textiles was driven by water power, especially along New England's fast-moving rivers, such as the first cotton-spinning mill (Blackstone River, Pawtucket, RI) founded by Samuel Slater. China made progress in this stage in much the same way as the previous three nations did, by becoming the largest producer and exporter of textiles, cotton, furniture, and toys[13] among other global products ranking.

Second Industrial Revolution

Meanwhile, the Second Industrial Revolution began again in Great Britain sometime in 1830 through *the introduction of mass production with the help of electrical energy.*[14] At this stage, *light industries* (which dominated the First Industrial Revolution – 1st IR) usually precede *heavy industries* (which dominated the Second Industrial Revolution – 2nd IR). For example, by the end of the Meiji era (1912), which was shortly before the outbreak of WW1, Japan was successfully industrialized in *light industries,* especially textiles. But heavy machinery industries were still embryonic. The vigorous development of these industries started later, during and after WW1 (Ohno, 2005).

That said, the second IR is divided into two components: (1) a boom in the industrial trinity of *energy, transportation, and locomotive power;* and (2) the *mass production of the means of mass production.*

The Welfare State (WS)

According to Donati (2015), the traditional welfare state (WS henceforth) has embodied the political and ethical principles of Western society throughout the last century, both in Europe and, in a different form, in North America – in as much as it has represented the dream of the modern state.[15]

The traditional welfare state is based on the logic of the *lib/lab* order of societal systems. The term '*lib-lab*' is used to express the dual structure inherent to post World War II Western democratic society, which involves the continuous negotiation and compromise between, on the one hand, the freedom of market (*lib*) and, on the other hand, the state in its function of control exercised for the sake of social equality (*lab*). *Lib-lab* therefore represents a system for the management of the whole society, which combines the rival ideologies of *liberalism* on the one side and *socialism* on the other side.[16]

Donati (2015) equally noted that in reality, this *social sphere,* situated between *the state* and *civil society,* is also the object of attention and exchange on the part of the market economy. In *Europe* for instance, *the "non-political" sphere is primarily conditioned by the state,* while in the *US it is primarily linked to the market.* In either case, however, the state and the market tend to absorb that "non-political" sphere, at least in the sense of imposing ethical criteria dictated by politics or by the economy. In other words, it means there is the colonization of the "non-political" sphere by politics or by the economy.[17] Fig. 4.1 tries to depict the *social sphere* within the traditional welfare state (WS).

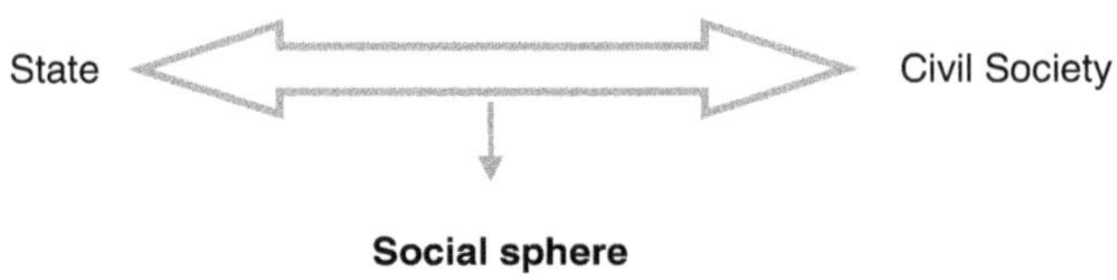

Figure 4.1 Situates the Social Sphere in the Traditional Welfare State
Source: Author created.

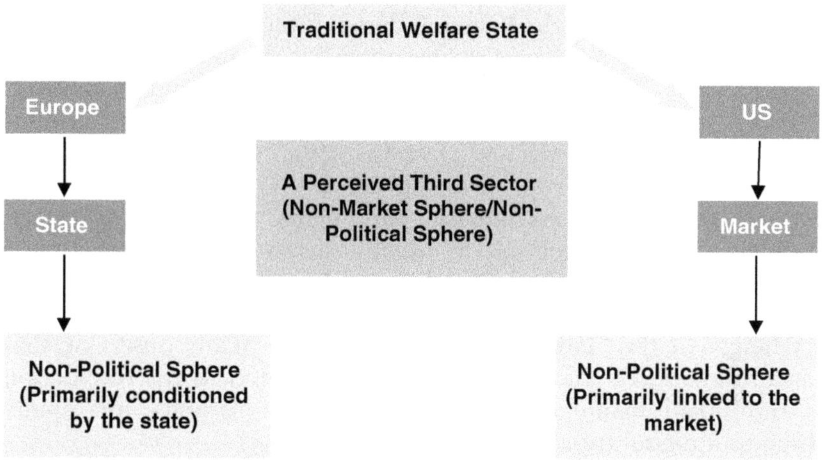

Figure 4.2 How the Social Sphere is Perceived in Europe and the United States in the Traditional WS
Source: Author created.

Again, Fig. 4.2 shows how the social sphere, which is situated between the state and civil society – as an object of attention and exchange on the part of the market economy, is being perceived in Europe and the USA.

The Third Industrial Revolution

The Third Industrial Revolution, according to Schlaepfer *et al.* (2015), began in 1965 through *the application of electronics and IT to further automate production*[18] with *the help of a sustainable post-carbon future (i.e., environmental renewable energy)*. According to Rifkin (2012), it brought two major forces to the limelight: (1) On the one hand, he saw it as a new vision that requires a clear understanding of the technological forces that impact the environmental or ecological system - that precipitates related profound transformations in our society.[19] On the other hand, he saw it as creating a new economic paradigm that will transform the world, represented by five major features, notably: a shift to lateral power; distributed capitalism; democratizing manufacturing; near-zero cost marketing and logistics; and new business models and jobs in the 21st century. Among which, the most pervasive features of the third industrial revolution have been: a shift to lateral power, distributed capitalism or shared economy, and democratizing manufacturing.[20]

The Fourth Industrial Revolution

Stadler (2015) describes the Fourth Industrial Revolution as referring to a further developmental stage in the organization and management of the entire value chain process involved in the manufacturing industry, and which functions on the basis of *cyber-physical production systems (CPPS) that merges the real and virtual worlds.*[21]

Another term for this process is industry 4.0. The concept of industry 4.0 is widely used across Europe, particularly in Germany's manufacturing sector.[22] Stadler (2015) equally observed that in the United States and more generally in English-speaking countries, some commentators us the appellations the "internet of things," the "internet of everything," or the "industrial internet." While equally observing that what all these terms and concepts have in common, is the recognition that traditional manufacturing and production methods are rapidly shifting to a digital transformation process.[23]

4.2 Global Manufacturing and Critical Trends in Design Perspectives

4.2.1 *Organizational Dynamics in the Product Design Perspective*

Value Proposition and Landmark Evolutions on Product Design

VALUE PROPOSITION

In today's world, *it is as important to know what to make as it is to know how to make it.* Again, as technological know-how proliferates, knowing what to make becomes more important every year.[24] This is referred to as a value proposition. MaRS (2020a) defines a product's value proposition as a statement of the functional, emotional, and self-expressive benefits; delivered by the brand that provides value to the target customer. It consists of several key components:

- What you offer and how you offer it to target customers
- What type of value or benefit is associated with your offering (for example, cost savings, time savings, revenue increase, customer/employee satisfaction), and how much of it the customer can expect
- How the value is generated
- Why it differs from anything else on the market.[25]

A product's *functional benefits* are based on a product's attribute that provides the customer with functional utility. Examples of functional benefits include the phone's capability of an iPhone, and the warmth of a wool sweater. *Self-expressive benefits* provide an opportunity for someone to communicate his or her self-image. For instance, a *self-expressive benefit* can include the elegance and the feeling of being cool projected by the Apple iPhone, the raw masculinity projected by the Harley-Davidson motorcycle brand, or the luxury displayed by carrying a Louis Vuitton bag. And finally, *emotional benefits* provide customers with a positive feeling when they purchase or use a particular brand. They add richness and depth to the experience of owning and using the brand.[26]

Additionally, MaRS (2020a) contends that value must always be considered from the buyer's perspective. Any functional, emotional, or self-expressive value will vary depending on the customer's specific situation. Therefore, understanding the customer's role (that is, economic buyer, technical buyer, and end-user) is critical when developing a value proposition.[27]

LANDMARK EVOLUTIONS ON PRODUCT DESIGN

From the foregoing, it's obvious that the connection between *form andfunction* has been one of the most controversial issues in the history of design. When products were first mass-produced in *Victorian* times, they were highly decorated to look like hand-made products – whether their decoration was appropriate or not.[28] Later on the development of "reform" groups such as the *Arts and Crafts* movement gradually brought about change in the *concept of design*. The *form* of products was to be *simplified* and the products well made from *suitable materials*.[29]

The above, notwithstanding, *product design* as we understand today is often traced to the birth of *mechanized production* during the Industrial Revolution. Before this, objects were made through *craft production*, where *conception* and *realization* were usually undertaken by an *individual creator*. But the *advent of industrial processes and the division of labor separated design from making*. Yet, design enjoyed no special status among the many interrelated aspects of *mechanized manufacture*. It was only through design reformers, such as William Morris, that it acquired theoretical and philosophical dimensions.[30] Interestingly, at the turn of the 20th century, *developments in materials and technology* enabled the production of innovative new products such as the telephone. Many of these products were so innovative that there was no benchmark on which to base their designs.[31]

Meanwhile, it is largely agreed that the widespread adoption of manufacturing and traditional production operations of information and communications technology (ICT) is increasingly blurring the boundaries between the real world and the virtual world in what is known as the Cyber-Physical Production Systems (CPPSs).[32] Stadler (2015) defines *CPPSs as online networks and social machines that are organized in a similar way to social networks*. As such, they link IT with mechanical and electronic components which then communicate with each other through a network. For example, the *radio frequency identification* (RFID) technology was a very early form of this technology that has been in use since 1999.[33]

Today, it is no news that manufacturers of all sizes compete in a global economy, and many no longer rely on local markets as the primary source of growth.[34] Ideally, to grow and thrive in today's competitive global markets, manufacturers need to see a fair and open marketplace, where competitors play by the same rules so that manufacturers can succeed both at home and increasingly reach new customers and seize new opportunities overseas.[35] More especially as the 21st-century manufacturing competitiveness is witnessing a rapid convergence of the digital and physical worlds – where advanced hardware, combined with advanced software, sensors, big data, and analytics results in smarter products, processes, and more closely connected customers, suppliers, and manufacturers.[36]

Customer Centricity and Its Product Design Alignments

Early involvement of all critical functions that are required for any given product is essential, meanwhile, aligning customer centricity with product design, technology, and manufacturing needs is critical. From the foregoing, Stroud (2018) argues that market competitiveness may not have as much influence on the success of a product as people may think. For instance, *where a new product design can be differentiated from other products that have a similar purpose, then it is just as likely to be successful.* Thus, often, when a product fails, it is not just an issue with the product itself, but with the way it is presented to the market. The following points are more often to blame for the poor presentation of the product to the market:

- Poor alignment with the market (i.e., customers don't want it)
- Technical issues (it is difficult or expensive to produce)
- Insufficient marketing efforts (the relevant audience don't know about it)
- Bad timing (the product took too long to get to the market, or was beaten there by a competitor).[37]

Consequently, Harrington (2013)[38] and Stroud (2018) suggest that by answering the following questions, you can start to determine whether your product design has the important features it needs for market success.

1. Is your product unique or innovative? – *First,* consider the aspects of your product that make it unique from similar products that might

already be in the market. *Second,* could the unique aspects of your product be considered innovative to the industry?

2. Does your product have a function? – It's one thing to be unique, but if it does not serve a practical purpose, customers would not be interested in choosing it over a competing product.
3. Does the product solve a problem?
4. Does the product provide value to your customers? – Adding value that customers want is critical to designing a successful product.
5. Will your product appeal to a broad market and will it be easily accessible?
6. Is your product easy to use? – Can you easily explain how it works? Or better still, if your customers can easily see how a product works without needing it explained, then they will be more inclined to buy it.
7. Is it multifunctional? – Customers may be more interested in products that have multiple uses or functions, rather than a product that only serves a single purpose.
8. Is it credible; are there testimonials? – Getting promotion by actual customers so that the results have to be proven and believable is ideal or producing demos to show how the product works can be instrumental in the product's success.
9. Does the price of your product match its perceived value?
10. Is your product inexpensive to buy, but has good quality?
11. Does your product look good? – It is essential to strike a balance between having a product that is useful and having a product that looks good.
12. Can you answer questions about your product?

MODEL MAKING AND PROTOTYPING

According to Hallgrimsson (2012), *model making* and *prototyping* are different activities, even though they are in principle associated. Within this framework, he defines *prototyping* as a design method that uses *physical prototypes* to study and test how a new product will be used, and how it will look in a "manufactured state." Alternatively, he defines *model making as* a step-by-step method for producing the prototype.[39]

In a further development, Isa and Liem (2014) identified the following classifications as being perceived by designers to be most familiar with their designing activities. These classifications are; soft model, hard model, presentation model, and prototype.[40] They manifest the following characteristics:

Soft Model – It is rough modeling; it is used to assess the overall size, proportion, and shape of many proposed concepts; it is used for fast evaluation of basic sizes and proportions; and finally, it can be reshaped and refined by hand to explore and improve its tactile quality.

Hard Model – It is technically non-functional, yet they are close replicas of the final design; it's made from wood, dense foam, plastic, or metal; and has some "working" features such as buttons that push or sliders that move.

Presentation Model – They are models that are constructed and matched from computer-aided design (CAD) data; it's a complete model and fully detailed composition of the product; and typically, some components of this model will be simplified or neglected due to cost or time shortages.

Prototype – It's a high-quality model or functioning product that is produced to realize a design solution; and typically, would be tested and evaluated before the product is considered for production.[41]

Marti (2019) argues that no matter the goal, the reason why we use prototypes is to get an early representation of our product idea that can be fabricated quickly and cheaper than using complex production processes. But he however argues that often, there is a misconception of what a physical prototype really is, and what are its limitations compared to a final product. These limitations vary across different prototype categories such as soft goods, consumer goods, and electronic products. That said, there is always a way to fabricate your ideas, but knowing these limitations will help you make informed decisions about your final product.[42] In a similar vein, Ullman (2003) argues that physical models might be classified differently in different fields of design development, but noted there seem to be very limited classifications that clearly explains the actual characteristics and functions of each physical models in the design process.[43] That said, Isa and Liem (2014) argue that lack of classifications will make it harder for the designer to understand the true potential of physical models in various fields.

IMPORTANCE OF CREATING PRODUCT DESIGN GOALS TO GIVE FOCUS AND DRIVE

Before starting the design process, it is important to set clear product design goals. If you do not have clear goals, the whole process may become unorganized, unfocused, and inefficient. In the same vein, Deep Nishar contends that a great product manager has the brain of an engineer, the heart of a designer, and the speech of a diplomat.[44] Thus, defining goals for your product and reviewing them regularly to ensure they are being achieved, will help in every stage of the process. In addition, you could even create a checklist containing your product design goals. Typical goals could include:

- Approximate production cost
- Approximate development timeframe

- Size and appearance of the product
- Approximate production time of the product
- Primary product purpose
- How the product will be used.[45]

Furthermore, Skidmore (2018) suggests that you could create a checklist for ergonomic viability goals such as:

- Is the design easy to handle?
- Could the design cause potential harm or stress?
- Is the design easy to use/operate?
- Is the design easy to understand?

Moreover, these goals can be used to analyze your product during the prototype and testing stage.[46]

UNDERSTANDING THE CUSTOMER-CENTRIC PERSPECTIVE

It is widely accepted that the competition today, both in the product and services space is tougher than ever. Superior UX (superior user experience) and CX (customer experience) are the two key battlefields with the most at stake. In addition, CX often integrates the user-centered design model. For instance, the user-centered design improves the customer experience (CX) when associated with a website, a product, or service.[47] Furthermore, user-centered design is based on the concept that the best-designed products or services come from understanding the needs of the people who will use them. However, Nibusinessinfo (2020b) found that most products or services undergo market testing and user research, but this often comes too late in the new product development process when significant changes might not be possible.[48] They argue that ideally, you should actively engage with potential end-users in the early stages of developing a product or service.[49]

In addition, user-centered design techniques are themselves an essential part of inclusive design. The latter involves developing products, services, or environments so that as many people as possible can use them.[50] These aspects of customer-centricity largely relies on the argument that customers are no longer enticed by-products alone – they also crave "an experience" for the price they pay, such as fast shipping, added training, attractive user interfaces, et cetera. Added to this list, are two other components that relate to online company reputation, notably: personalization, and emotional connectivity.[51]

It is worth mentioning here that there are some subtle differences between UX and CX. According to Tim Lowden (Lowden, 2014) of the Office of Citizen Services and Innovative Technologies, User Experience (UX) deals with *people interacting with your product and the experience they receive from that interaction.* UX is measured with metrics like: success rate, error rate, abandonment rate, time to complete task and clicks to completion (the latter applies to digital products).[52] Customer Experience (CX), in contrast, *encompasses all the interactions a person has with your brand.* It might be measured in: overall experience, likelihood to continue use and likelihood to recommend to others. In a nutshell, UX is part of a broader CX, but CX contains some aspects outside of a product UX does not have.[53]

Arguably, UX has come to confirm the birthplace of product-led growth (PLG) in today's highly competitive product design platform. *PLG relies on the idea that if a product is good, it will infiltrate the market and grow on its own.*[54] That being said, prior to the present era of product-led growth (PLG), the dominant business model has for long been sales-or marketing-led growth models, which *create a need for the product by primarily focusing on the dynamics of the sales force or marketing teams to convert potential customers into future buyers.*[55] SlideModel (2020b) argues that as the landscape is shifting toward customer-centricity (i.e., from sales-or marketing-led growth to product-led growth), most buyers are no longer interested in the product itself. To that end, Steve Jobs argued that people don't buy from you for your own betterment; they buy from you for a better version of themselves.[56] In this light, Econsultancy (2018) argues that organizations committed to CX are shown to outperform their peer's companies as they continue to focus on the customer experience (CX), and in contents required to facilitate this.[57]

That being said, product-led companies – which are a natural outgrowth of customer experience (UX), take a bottom-up approach to customer acquisition. According to Bartlett (2020), the "Product-led growth" (PLG) is an end user-focused growth model that "*relies on the product itself as the primary driver of customer acquisition, conversion, and expansion.*"[58] In other words, PLG is a business methodology in which user acquisition, expansion, conversion, and retention are all driven primarily by the product itself.[59] It creates company-wide alignment across teams – from engineering to sales and marketing – around the product as the largest source of sustainable, scalable business growth.[60] Bartlett (2020) argues that *software distribution* today is best described as "product-led growth," and it looks a lot like *consumer growth models.* For example, when you need to attract tons of individual end-users to a free product, human-dependent growth doesn't scale. The only choice is to de-labor the distribution engine behind your product by empowering end-users to find, evaluate, and adopt your product on their own.[61]

TRANSCRIBING PROTOTYPING TO MODEL MAKING

In the reasoning of Isa and Liem (2014), when it comes to the task of mapping out design ideas to the realities of manufacturing the design, prototyping is important in the following ways: Firstly, to anticipate how products can be produced and assembled as efficiently as possible. Secondly, within the materialization and pre-production stages, prototypes will mostly be used to test and measure the final design requirements and to make sure that it functions, *technically* as well as from a *use* perspective.[62] In a similar direction, Professor Jeff Hoffman of the Massachusetts Institute of Technology (MIT) maintains that *a basic principle of systems engineering* is that you should fully understand the requirements that a system needs to satisfy before you design it, and that faulty requirements usually lead to engineering disasters.[63] In the reasoning of Owen (1998), to see the multiple values of design most clearly, one has to take into account quality, design details, and design concepts.

Skidmore (2018) argues that you do not have to compromise on quality to save on expense. Take for example, when faced with the question: Do you save money just to create an inferior product? Or do you use high-quality material and create a superb end product that customers can comfortably use? To him, the second option is always preferable, even if the cheaper option is only slightly inferior.[64] In this regard, quality assurance and customer satisfaction are inextricably linked.[65] To concur, Stroud (2018) argues that *it is possible to reduce costs without reducing quality; as this will give you competitive edge against competitors with similar but more expensive products.*[66] In the same line of reasoning; Owen (1998) contends that *design* should first and foremost be viewed through the *lens of quality,* which is now a universally-recognized requisite for success in business. So *quality* is the first layer of product design. For instance, *Quality for products* (and artifacts generally), is almost always associated with *craftsmanship*(that is, how well the product is made). However, there are more dimensions to *quality,* and they can be best appreciated through a consideration of not only how things are designed (craftsmanship), but also includes what benefits are accrued[67] (the ergonomic value). In this regard, well-designed products are easier to make where *quality as craftsmanship* is achieved through paying attention to issues of *engineering design* and *design for manufacturing.*[68]

Detail design is at the second layer of the *design core.* Here the role of design is to contribute to performance, human factors and appearance. Design specialists (engineering designers, product designers, industrial designers, communication designers and others) invent and refine features or details at this level to make the product work better functionally, work better for people physiologically and psychologically, and work better symbolically within social and cultural niches.[69]

At the third layer, *design concept* contributes most to *competitiveness* (for all products – including systems, institutions and services). This is true, *as concepts that are holistic and thoroughly thought out present themselves to buyers and users as qualitatively better (and worth more).* As such, well-conceived product designs, typically distribute innovations among their features so systemically that they are exceedingly difficult to copy by competitors.[70]

4.2.2 *Comparative Products Design vs. Architectural Geopolitics*

The Bases of Comparative Product Architecture

PRODUCT-PROCESS ARCHITECTURE

It is well established that Product Architecture (PA) is one of the key activities for any industrial action in product development. As such, it becomes imperative for this activity to ensure simultaneity in productivity and time, so as to ensure that the products meet the expectations of customers in terms of technical performance, innovation and delivery time.[71] There are generally two basic types of *product-process* architecture: (1) *"integral architecture,"* with complex interdependence between *product functions* and *product structures* (such as automobiles), and (2) *"modular architecture,"* in which the relationship between a product's *functional* and *structural* elements has a simple and clear one-to-one correspondence – such as personal computers.[72]

However, beyond the basic types of *product-process* architecture, there are also variations in between them. For example, in *modular architecture* we can have *close modular architecture, open modular architecture,* and *quasi-modular architecture;* and for *integral architecture* we can figure out *open integral architecture,* and *closed integral architecture.*[73] According to Mathews (2012), all these variations tend to have a strong bearing on the organizational architecture of the industries producing such products. For instance, he argues that industries generally start by producing products in closed-integral form – with a large company supplying the integral product, and serviced by a supply chain in which there may be extensive vertical integration.[74]

PRODUCT DESIGN INFORMATION

The relationship between *functions* and *structure* elements suggest that besides *product-process* architecture, there is also *product design information,* which has at least two aspects: the *product structure information* and the *product function information. The* product structure information represents what a product is, or the shape (form) and materials of a product.[75] In other words, product structure information explains the *design features uniquely identical to a particular product* or to *a set of identical products.* While the product function information represents *what a product does for its customers* or the *product's distinctive characteristics in terms of performance when used.*

In a similar vein, Fujimoto (2007) argues that the *product design information* is normally created prior to the commercial production of physical products. Put in another way, the product's *functional design information* is usually created first and then translated into its *structural design information.*[76] For example, Mathews (2012) points out a one-to-one correspondence between functional and structural elements in the *modular product architecture* as follows: in the personal computer the function of *processing* is handled by the *CPU,* the function of *input* by the *keyboard,* the function of *display* by a *flat panel display,* and so on. While in the *integral architecture,* the existence of many-to-many correspondence can be seen in the automotive vehicle; for instance, *fuel efficiency* is linked to the *engine* as well as to the *design of the body and suspension,* while the *suspension effects* is linked not just to *fuel efficiency* but also the *quality of the ride and the handling of the vehicle.*[77]

THE RELATIONSHIP BETWEEN MODULARITY AND PRODUCT SYSTEMS INTEGRATION

According to Mathews (2012), while *modular systems* have been with us for a long time, *design platforms* emerged first in the military. Interestingly, design platforms have driven the pace of technological change in multiple sectors, and then spread to the automotive sector, where *modular platforms* have enabled companies to offer wide consumer choice based on a few core modules such as chassis, transmission, and car engines.[78] The phenomenal emergence of *modularity* and *platforms* together, with each driving the other in the process is now described in the business literature as *co-evolution.*[79]

In a related development, Baldwin and Clark (2000) suggest that design rules for modularity essentially encompass three categories, modular architecture, interface design rules, and standards:[80]

1. *modular architecture* – specifies what the modules *do* and how they *fit* together.
2. *interface design rules* – specify the *rules* of modular interconnection[81] between functions and structural elements. Here we can distinguish between "open" design rules, which are standardized at the industry level (i.e., beyond a particular firm), and "closed" design rules, where the design rule is limited to a particular firm.[82]

3. *standards* – they *test* and *prove* a module's *ability* to *fit* within the overall system and also *enable* one module to be *compared* with another within the system.[83]

Owen (1991) argues that this approach to organize information is unique and deals directly with the design problem inherent in the Product Integrity goal of holism,[84] which requires that components need to have "organic" associations with each other, and working in tandem to achieve the purposes of the system. In other words, design team has to see to it that the *right functions* go together in the *design process.*[85] Mathews (2012), argues that the more an industry moves toward modularity, the greater is the likelihood that one firm will be able to initiate a new level of integration to bring components together into a platform. And as platforms emerge, the more pressure they place on the industry to modularize.[86] To concur, Powell *et al.* (1996); Rothaermel and Deeds (2004); and Hobday *et al.* (2005) maintain that there is an increasing trend for new products to be developed in networks of specialized firms because the pace of technology development is so fast that no single firm can have the resources to handle all the necessary development in-house.[87]

Again, on the perspective of modular system and technology diffusion, many authors have expressed the view as captured by Kamuriwo and Baden-Fuller (2016) that the *product system integrator* needs a diverse scientific and technological knowledge base, sufficient to support the necessary *knowledge flows* and *cross-domain linkages,* but not so great as to know everything that is undertaken by partners.[88] To concur, Rothaermel and Deeds (2006) argue that what is less-understood and less researched are the considerable challenges that product system integrators face in outsourcing development work for non-modular high technology products, which are underpinned by knowledge which is complex, ambiguous and highly tacit – such as biotechnology drug development.[89]

The Bases of Architectural Geopolitics

In the reasoning of Fujimoto (2006), each country or region has its own historical path, which gives rise to some identical emergent capability-building process that weaves a concentration of region/country-specific capability, which then metamorphose into a certain type of organizational capability – that is uniquely concentrated in that region or country. In a related vein, products with a certain type of product-process architecture tend to match better with a certain type of organizational capability, which results in relatively high productive performance.[90]

But this widely accepted view of Fujimoto does not appear to be consistent with the research findings of Tsuru and Morishima (2011).

The latter's research findings was of the view that, in China, as well as in Japan and Korea, even in the same industry and among firms of the same size, there is considerable variation in the use of modular and integral architectures. As a result, it cannot be said that a particular product architecture is dominant – they argued. That is to say, product architecture is not something that is exogenously determined by, for example, industry characteristics, but instead it is strategically chosen by firms depending on a number of factors at a particular time.[91]

Fundamental Logic of Architectural-Based Comparative Advantage

According to the hypothesis of Fujimoto (2007), *architecture-based comparative advantage* is said to exist where a certain dynamic fit between *organizational capabilities in manufacturing* and *product-process architecture* tends to create comparative advantage for a given industry in a given country or a region.[92]

However, Mathews (2012) goes a step further and tries to point out a clear distinction between *architecture-based comparative advantage* and *architecture-based competitive advantage* by advancing the arguments of Wang (2008). In this regard, Wang (2008)[93] posited that while *comparative advantages* in terms of low labor costs (which includes natural resource endowments) plays an important role, at least in the early stages, it is the *competitive advantages* created by the approach to industry design, involving clusters and modular networks that really drive the industries forward. Little wonder why Rocha (2011) believes that modular product architecture is not suitable for customization strategies, *once it requires a product designed from scratch for each order,* especially as it may jeopardize costs and delivery times when compared to the advantages inherent in mass customization.[94] Consequently, *the underlying purpose of product modularity is to have different products, with minimal differentiation.*[95]

In addition to low costs, comprising of: labor costs in terms of average wages for skilled workers and managers; infrastructure costs; corporate taxes (i.e., tax breaks and regulations, and other incentives for local investment); and natural resource endowments – firms are now also looking at value-added dimensions on how they might benefit over time. To this end, Mathews (2012) goes further to explain the views of Wang (2008) who argues that local firms opt for a *low-cost, low-price strategy* as a means of gaining entry. As such, depending on first-tier and second-tier components suppliers is an optimal way to achieve this. In addition, local firms also pursue an *imitation strategy*, by engaging in *mass production of copied components* which come to be standardized at the industry level.[96]

Nonetheless, the reasoning of Owen (1998) appears to be at variance with the aforementioned approach. He argues that as today's business environment is very volatile, we must fundamentally rethink the process of new product development. In this direction, he emphasized that in the present dispensation, revolutionary changes may be more frequently appropriate than evolutionary changes – more so, as conventional development process is ill-prepared, especially if competition is the provocateur.[97]

In a nutshell, besides low-cost, low-price strategy, and imitation strategy, other factors that could be created to enhance comparative advantage include: *Skill pool* (the size of the labor pool with required skills), *the scalability of labor resources* in the long term (i.e., the ability to supply sufficient labor resources to meet growing demand); *vendor landscape* (the size of the local sector providing IT services and other business functions); *business and living environment* (governance support, business environment, living environment, accessibility); *quality of infrastructure* (telecommunication and IT, real estate, transportation, power); *risk profile* (*security issues, disruptive events,* regulatory risks, macroeconomic risks, intellectual property risk); and *market potential* (market potential can be assessed based on the attractiveness of the local market such as current GDP and GDP growth rate, as well as access to nearby markets in the host country and adjacent regions).

4.2.3 The Circular Economy Product Design

General Orientation

According to Hannon *et al.* (2016), over the past 150 years companies have steadily refined their ability to invent products and produce them efficiently, delivering a wide range of goods to consumers and improving financial returns to shareholders.[98] They however contend that this system is far from optimal; especially as companies have hardly begun to reckon with the waste that occurs after products are purchased.[99] To this end, they argue that when a consumer uses a product infrequently or discards it because it has worn out, at least some of the energy and material that went into making the product has been wasted.[100]

This has given rise to both business and environmental challenges, consequently paving the way for ongoing research gearing toward engineering design for a circular economy, which tends to address three key issues; *the availability of resources, reduce waste, and the increasing pressure on the environment.* The aforementioned is characterized by four manufacturing features that are classified under four manufacturing "Rs," these are: *Design for reuse, design for repair, design for remanufacturing, and design of recycling* – alternatively referred to as engineering design for a circular economy as opposed to the traditional linear economy use-waste-model.

The question is; to what extent do these strategies for circularity actually help us achieve what we want? Peck (2018), reasons that a circular economy is not a goal in itself. It is a means toward an end – and the end is to provide a more sustainable resource base for our global society.[101] In the same vein, Ester van der Voet (2018b) argues that the extraction and use of resources has been the basis for the development and creation of wealth for societies.[102]

Ester van der Voet (2018b) further argues that every nation; as it strives to improve its development and welfare, it climbs the materials ladder. The world population is growing, which means that more resources are needed to support all these people. Welfare around the world is also steadily growing, and as welfare grows, the amount of resources per person also increases. Additionally, increasing economic development also leads to technological development, which implies that products are becoming more complicated. For instance, by now, a product like a laptop or a mobile phone contains almost the complete periodic table of elements.[103] On this keynote, Stahel (2010) introduced the following guiding principles for circular design:

- Do not repair what is not broken.
- Do not remanufacture something that can be repaired.
- Do not recycle a product that can be remanufactured.
- Replace or treat only the smallest possible part in order to maintain the existing economic value of the technical system."[104]

Den Hollander, Bakker, Hultink (2017) argue that the Circular Economy (CE) revolves around prolonging and extending useful product lifetime, by preserving embedded economic value in the most effective way so as to preserve resources.[105]

Design for Reuse/Redistribute

Part of the cyclic factor of sustainable design is the *reuse* of products, which minimizes the extraction and processing of raw materials and the energy resources required for recycling.[106] Therefore, reuse is the action or practice of using something again, whether for its original purpose (conventional reuse) or to fulfill a different function (creative reuse or repurposing). It should be distinguished from recycling, which is the breaking down of used items to make raw materials for the manufacture of new products.

The design of products for a Circular Economy is also the design of products for new forms of business value creation. Azcarate (2018) found that innovative companies are increasingly coming to the understanding that designing products for *service-life extension and service-life intensification* can increase the value of their brand, attract new customers, and increase the loyalty of their existing customer-base. In this sense, the Circular Economy attempts to balance the need of individuals, companies, and nations to create more value and income, with a more sustainable approach to the use of resources. As a result, the service and the sharing economy are two models which can facilitate this. The service economy*is driven by the business interests of the manufacturing and/or service providing company,* while the sharing economy*often happens between users, without providing any incentives to the product manufacturer.*[107]

Design for Repair/Maintain/Prolong

We may all agree that any technical product is in danger of breaking. So to pick up the principle of reuse and to keep products as long as possible in use, we need to repair them. Prumbohm (2018) identified three main ways a company can profit from their design for repair, and four factors that need to be considered when designing products for repair,[108] highlighted as follows:

Three main ways a company can profit from their design for repair;

1. Providing a repair service to the customers
2. Sale of spare parts
3. Provide market distinctions by the products being easy to repair by the customers

Factors to be considered when designing a product for repair;

1. Easy access: less tools, no glue, and ideally without any tool
2. Simple, modular structure of the product
3. No critical security conditions should appear during the maintenance
4. Documentation or user guides for repair.[109]

In addition, he identified two characteristics prominent in repairs. The *first* is "Industrial repair," or rather "Repair by companies." In this regard, as the business model of companies differs, so does their way of designing products. The *second* is the growing sector of "domestic repair." For many companies, the repair and maintenance activities are a core part of their revenue streams. This may lead to products which are intentionally made difficult for consumers to repair themselves, and this can, in turn, have negative effects on a Circular Economy. But some companies welcome users interacting with their products, and repairing them as needed. Obviously, there is tension between these two ways of thinking, and have their own effect on Design for Repair.[110]

Design for Remanufacturing/Refurbishing

In the opinion of Jönbrink (2018) the main objective of remanufacturing is to create products in a condition "as new." That is done by collecting used products and then sort them, clean them, repair them, and finally combine them with new parts and sell them as new.[111]

DRIVERS AND BARRIERS

The main drivers for remanufacturing have been profitability, sustainability, and legal aspects or requirements. Today, productivity is increasingly becoming one of the main drivers of remanufacturing. However, the following have been identified as barriers for remanufacturing:

The fear of market cannibalization – arises out of the fear that sales of the company's new products will decrease, and that the loss of these sales will be bigger than the profit from the selling of remanufactured products. This is known as *market cannibalization*. However, there are plenty of examples where new customer groups are reached by the introduction of remanufactured products, thus leading to an expanded market share.

Keeping track of delivered products – as it might be difficult in getting them back for the remanufacturing process. This can be even more difficult if the products are sold globally, and have a long or varying service lifetime. Yet another barrier can be insecurity about the quality of the products or components that are coming back for remanufacturing. For instance you may have the questions, are they damaged, or are they good enough to be used again?

The ambiguous role of legal aspects, regulations and standards – might not only be a driver, they might also be a barrier if you have problems adjusting your products and offerings to meet the new demands. One example can be that the old product you are taking back contains chemicals which are forbidden today, even if they were of standard use at the time the product was originally made.

HOW TO DESIGN FOR REMANUFACTURING

1. *Take a holistic view!* Most importantly, you have to keep in mind to optimize not only the remanufacturing, but the whole life cycle: from raw material, through production, use, and finally the end of service, when the remanufacturing will take place, and create a new life for the product.
2. *The choice of materials is important.* Use quality materials which can be reused for many product lives or loops. That is, even if a product will be remanufactured, it is also important to use materials,

which in the very end, after many life cycles, can be effectively recycled. Here, the chemical content of a product is a tricky thing. Chemicals can, for example, improve the service lifespan for plastics. However, they can also become a risk, since some chemicals might turn out to be hazardous or even forbidden in the future, thus making reuse of those products or components impossible. One way to handle this is to try to choose materials which are less harmful already from the start.

3. *Make it easy to disassemble the product with as few, and ordinary tools as possible.* Make disassembly points accessible, preferably from one side. Use fastening devises which can be easily opened and closed multiple times. If you are using screws, design the fastening element so that it's easy to open. For example, use few types and sizes of screw, as well as screw types which are easy to open by hand.
4. *Properly align the interface between similar working modules.* One opportunity to improve the product for remanufacturing is to divide it into different modules, and to put all the parts that need to be exchanged or upgraded into one single module, thus lowering the effort needed to upgrade the product.
5. *Avoid cross-dependences between modules,* otherwise we might be forced to update a working module simply as a consequence of updating another, outdated one. Make it easy to upgrade the product, for example by exchanging whole components or by updating software.
6. *Make it easy to clean.* Avoid small holes or grooves which collect dirt and are hard to clean properly. Make sure that all parts are able to withstand the same detergents and temperatures. Make heavily stained surfaces able to withstand mechanical cleaning.
7. *Leverage best information management practices.* As companies turn toward remanufacturing, information management is becoming increasingly important. As a product maker, getting information back regarding the quality of your products, the ways in which your customers are using them, and the reasons why they break or otherwise stop working as intended, can be extremely valuable. To make the best use of this opportunity:

   - Create a system for identification of the individual product, or even components within the product. You can use different means, such as Radio Frequency Identification (RFID), Bar-Code or QR-code.
   - Create a system to save important data regarding the product, as this information will be crucial during the remanufacturing process.

- Create a system to keep track of your products, to know where they are at the end of their service life.

Design for Recycling

Essentially, recycling takes waste materials and products and reprocesses them to manufacture something new. Some materials, such as paper and boards, can be made into the same products and others can be made into something completely different, such as plastic cups into pencils. Recycling is an important aspect of a modern consumer society with millions of tons of waste being disposed of in landfill sites or incinerated, causing environmental concerns.[112]

Obviously, design for reuse, repair, or remanufacturing are generally better alternatives, as they retain much, if not all of the materials, embedded energy, and value of the existing product. With this in mind, we can design our products in such a way that, when the time comes to disassemble and recycle them, we can do so in the most effective and economical way possible. Interestingly, California's Department of Resources Recycling and Recovery (CalRecycle), through landmark initiatives such the *Integrated Waste Management Act,* and the *Beverage Container Recycling and Litter Reduction Act,* California works toward a society that uses less, recycles more, and takes resource conservation to higher and higher levels.[113] According to CalRecycle (2018), as at 12 December 2018, the state of California became the nation's leader with an approximate 65 percent diversion rate for all materials, and today recycling supports more than 140,000 green jobs in California.[114]

According to Lohrengel (2018), when we recycle a product we must break it down into its basic raw materials, not only do we destroy the energy and value that we put into the product; we also need to invest new energy and resources into the recycling process, and then invest some more energy if we want to transform these recycled materials back into a new product.[115] That notwithstanding, recycling is definitely better than disposing of our products as waste in incineration or a landfill, so we should try to use recycling as a last option – although it has its own drawbacks.

CalRecycle (2018) believes that through innovation and creativity, sound advancements in science and technology, and efficient programs that improve economic vitality and environmental sustainability, it will inspire and challenge Californians to achieve the highest waste reduction, recycling and reuse goals in the nation.[116]

4.2.4 How Materials Science and Engineering Helps in Shaping Business Thinking

The developments in materials and manufacturing technologies, together with changes in lifestyle have revolutionised product design in the 20th century.[117] For instance, materials such as metal alloys, polymers and composites enabled new ways of designing and manufacturing. These developments are largely being set in motion by fast evolutions or revolutions in Materials Science and Engineering (MSE) among other competing factors. That said, MSE comprises of the synegistic combination of the *science of processing* (methods of design), *science of structures* (methods of manufacturing), *science of properties* (type of materials) – to reach the desired outcome, or to produce optimal results.

Thus, among the numerous advantages of materials within the framework of Materials Science and Engineering (MSE), is its unique ability to *imbue products with personality*.For instance, product aesthetics are also expressed through materials, which is one of the roles that appearance plays toward influencing consumers. As consumers expect perfection, what we hold and touch, is more crucial than ever – especially when we want to position products as unique, when compared with competitors.[118] For example, Apple's designers invested untold hours massaging the materials, finishes, and intricate details to produce the jewel-like surfaces of iPods and iPhones. Also of interest, Google's new digital design guidelines, called Material Design – uses physical materials as a metaphor for its design aesthetic, so users can relate digital graphics to physical space and motion.[119]

Generally, materials for products and structures can be divided in four main groups: metals, polymers, ceramics and composites (Table 4.1).

The knowledge of materials and their properties is of great significance for a design engineer. For instance, a design engineer must be

Table 4.1 Four Main Groups of Materials for Products and Structures

Metals	*Ceramics*	*Polymers*	*Composites*
Aluminum	Clay	Polyvinyl chloride (PVC)	Wood
Copper	Silica glass	Teflon	Carbon fiber resins
Steel (iron alloy)	Alumina	Various plastics	Concrete
Nickel	Quartz	Glue (adhesives)	
Titanium		Kevlar	

Source: Adapted from TeachEngineering. Introduction to Material Science and Engineering. *TeachEngineering.org,* Engineering University of Colorado, *TeachEngineering.org,* 2020, p. 3, https://www.teachengineering.org/content/uoh_/lessons/uoh_matlsci/uoh_matlsci_lesson01_intropresentation_v4_tedl_dwc.pdf. Accessed 7 January 2020.

familiar with the effects which the manufacturing processes and heat treatment have on the properties of the materials.[120] As a result, the selection of a proper material for engineering purposes is one of the most difficult problems for the designer. The best material or combination of materials is the one which serves the desired objective at the minimum cost. The following factors should be considered while selecting the material:[121]

1. Availability of the materials,
2. Suitability of the materials for the working conditions in service, and
3. The cost of the materials.

The important properties, which determine the utility of materials are; physical, chemical and mechanical properties.[122]

Undeniably, *we survive based on the materials we control.* As you can see on Table 4.2, the ages of mankind have names, and all these names are related to some specific materials, notably; the Stone Age, the Copper Age, the Bronze Age, the Iron Age, the Steel Age, the Non-ferrous and Polymeric Materials Age, the Silicon Age, the Nano-or Bio-materials Age.[123] Miltenović *et al.* (2014) anticipated that the 21st century will be dominated by the intensive production and use of polymeric materials, and in the middle of the 21st century the increasing application of composite and ceramic materials should logically dominate production.[124] In concurrence, Kaspar and Vielhaber (2017) found that the trend in modern lightweight systems is increasingly turning away from the singular steel and aluminum designs toward far more innovative composite constructions.[125] In a related sense, but on a different platform, Ester van der Voet (2018a) argues that *the extraction and use of resources has been the basis for the development and creation of wealth for societies.*[126]

4.3 The Iron Logic of Product/Service Innovation and Their Commercialize Implications

4.3.1 Concept, Definitions, Purpose, Scope, and Levels of Innovation

Concepts and Definitions

CONCEPTS

In the reasoning of Penker, Junermark, and Jacobson (2018), innovation concepts are like living organisms as they require energy and resources to survive. By implication, *innovation can only thrive when it emerges from an organization committed to growth and sustainability of enterprise.*[127] Furthermore, they argue that instead of thinking of cultivating an

Table 4.2 Names of the Ages of Mankind and How They Are Related to Some Specific Materials

Age	*Materials We Control*
THE STONE AGE (>10,000 BC) – Naturally Occurring Materials	• Special rocks, skins, wood, ceramics and glasses, natural polymers and composites
THE COPPER AGE (5000 BC)	• Good to excellent corrosion resistance • High thermal conductivity • Very high electrical conductivity
THE BRONZE AGE (4,000 BC–1000 BC)	• Bronze is an alloy that consists primarily of copper with the addition of other ingredients. • All the additional ingredients produce an alloy much harder than copper alone
THE IRON AGE (1,000 BC–1,620 AD)	• High temperature furnaces • Cast iron technology (1620s) established the dominance of metals in engineering
STEEL AGE (1859 and Up)	• High Strength Alloys
NON-FERROUS AND POLYMER AGE (light (1940s) and special alloys)	• Aluminum, Titanium and Nickel (super alloys) – aerospace • Silicon – Information • Plastics and Composites – food preservation, housing, aerospace and high speeds
EXOTIC MATERIALS AGE?	• Nano-Material and bio-Materials • It is anticipated that the 21st century will be dominated by the intensive production and use of polymeric materials, and in the middle of the 21st century the increasing application of composite and ceramic materials should logically dominate production

Very Important Note: Materials “Drive” our Society!
Ages of “Man:” we survive based on the materials we control (Mukasyan, 2019).

Sources: Adapted from Mukasyan, Alexander (2019); and Metal Supermarkets. “The Difference between Ferrous and Non-Ferrous Metal.” *MetalSupermarkets.com,* 23 September 2015, https://www.metalsupermarkets.com/how-steel-is-made/ (accessed 14 August 2019); and Miltenović, A., Banić and Miltenović, V. (2014), op. cit., p. 531.

innovation in isolation, organizations are more successful when they generate a cluster of innovations, manage them side-by-side, and evaluate how they interact as a portfolio of strategic initiatives.[128]

DEFINITIONS

Bordia *et al.* (2005) defines innovation as the ability to define and develop *new products and services* and deliver them to the market. As such, it is the fundamental source of value creation in companies and an important enabler of competitive advantage.[129] But innovation does not limit itself to new products and services; it extends to the *improvement of existing products and services* – that is, those having an incremental character. In fact, overall, a significant portion of innovations usually manifests an incremental character.

From the forgoing, Gkanas, Magkou-Kriticou, Makridis, Stubos, and Bakouros (2013) identified the following key characteristics as uniquely belonging to innovation (see Fig. 4.3): *Firstly,*innovation is a commercial concept not simply a technological, or even an intellectual property one. They further argue that, however novel an innovation is, unless firms are able to successfully exploit their innovation in commercial terms, it is not relevant for the purposes for which it serves.*Secondly,* there are degrees of innovation. *The innovative process can involve the creation of completely new products or services or, more commonly, simply the*

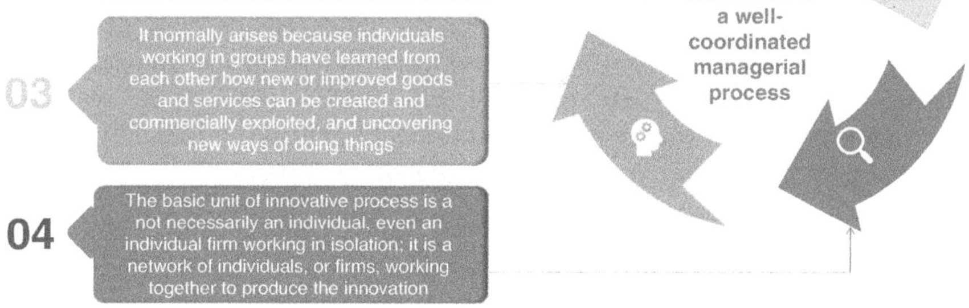

Figure 4.3 Innovation as a Well-Coordinated Managerial Process
Source: Author created. But useful data was extracted from Gkanas *et al.* (2013), pp. 5–6; Kim and Mauborgne (2014), p. 15; University of Queensland Business School (2018); and free template adapted from slidemodel.com.

improvement of existing products and services. In these cases, innovation can be radical or incremental in character, respectively.[130] It might also be disruptive. *Thirdly,* they believe that whatever the degree of innovation, it normally arises because individuals working in groups have learned from each other how new or improved goods and services can be created and commercially exploited.[131] *Fourthly,* the basic unit of innovative process is not necessarily an individual, or even an individual firm working in isolation, *it is a network of individuals, or firms, working together to produce the innovation.*[132]

The University of Queensland, Australia sums it up in a simple way – that *innovation is a managerial process* (*see* Fig. 4.3). And those organizations that can master the conversion of ideas to new products, services and processes are consistently more innovative than organizations that try to manage innovation as a random process of discovery.[133] In a similar vein, Viki (2018) maintains that innovation is management, and that understanding this principle is vital to success for those that want to create a lasting innovation culture in their companies. He argues that innovation is not just about working on random ideas to see what sticks.[134] In the same direction, Henderson (2017) posited that being innovative means you harness your creative ability. But doesn't end there, it requires creativity plus work to result to innovation.[135] In a similar vein, Green (2011) defines innovation as the act of applying knowledge to the creation of new processes, products, and services that have value for at least one of your stakeholder groups.[136]

From the foregoing, innovation can be defined *as a well-coordinated managerial process of ideas generation and conversion into viable business models, dedicated to the improvement of existing values or to the creation of completely new values.* In this regard, Kim and Mauborgne (2014) suggest that a useful exercise for a corporate management team pursuing profitable growth is to plot the company's current and planned portfolios on a Pioneer-Migrator-Settler (PMS) map.[137]

They define "Settlers" as "me-too businesses," while "Migrators" are business offerings better than most in the marketplace, and finally an industry's "pioneers" are the businesses that offer unprecedented value. These are companies that leverage blue ocean strategists, and are the most powerful sources of profitable growth. And logically, these businesses tend to have a mass following of customers.[138]

Purpose and Scope

According to Gustafsson *et al.* (2012), innovation is often manifested as a change in the competences of the company, the competences of the customer, the prerequisite of the offering, or what the customer co-creates.[139] Henderson (2017) maintains that innovation is not solely represented by new devices, ideas or methods, but also by the process of uncovering new ways to do things. It can also pertain to modifying business models and adapting to changes to achieve better products and services.[140] But *companies need to develop a clear point of view about where the world is going and the key trends that could impact their business.* Additionally, they then need to develop a clear innovation strategy that informs the types of new ideas they will invest in for the future.[141] In this regard, Satell (2013) found that innovation is often conflated with strategy. He defines strategy as a coherent and substantiated logic for making choices. In other words, strategy creates a clear path to a goal. Put in another way, strategy is about achieving objectives.[142] Strategy is a high level function, which concerns the overall direction of the company and therefore necessitates considerable involvement of senior management, as well as, at times, high-priced consultants. *The outcome is a plan that puts relative strength against relative weakness or opportunity.*[143]

Viki (2018) suggests that in *addition to a clear innovation strategy, companies also need a clear process for managing new ideas once they have them.* He found that surprisingly a good number of companies do not have a clear process for managing innovation. Across these companies, teams working on different innovation projects all work in different ways. As such, there is no consistency around innovation best practice, which makes it difficult for leadership to track and measure progress.[144] Consequently, *it is not only our products that need continuous improvement. We also need to continuously improve the processes we use to create them.*[145] In this regard, Llopis (2014) argues that *innovation* and *workplace transformation* represent two-sides of the same coin. Especially as workplace transformation enable employees to adopt an "entrepreneurial mindset" to showcase their ideas and ideals, which in turn makes them become the foundation for organizational growth and sustainability.[146]

In the same strand of reasoning, Newman (2017) observed that *innovation* and *transformation* are often used synonymously, but argues they are different especially in the digital world. In some instances, transformation can lead to innovation. In others, innovation can lead to transformation, but this mutually causal relationship is often overlooked since they are thought to mean the same thing. While indeed related, it is crucial for modern business leaders to know the difference between the two terms.[147] That being said, one of the major differentiating factors between *transformation* and *innovation* is *speed* – or the lack of it. Transformations take time – moving from one state to another is a process. Innovation, on the other hand, usually refers to a sudden spark or creativity, and the incipient actions that lead to implementing that spark into a company's strategy.[148]

Newman (2017) contends that innovation requires encouragement, collaboration, and communication, but it typically implies clear steps that must be taken – it's the start of something great. What happens after is transformation – which is the implementation process following that first spark of innovation. It also suggests an eventual end once the transformation has been completed.[149] However, the different modes of innovation tend to impose varied and diverse consequences on product design and manufacturing, including services. It is this onward challenge to do and make things happen that is propelling new paradigm shifts in innovation. Dunn III (1992) opined that as technological change permeates the whole of human existence, one day's marvel becomes a necessity of ordinary life the next day.[150] As a result, *the scientific community has a difficult but highly productive time when people begin to doubt the old "truth" and a "new truth" is proposed to challenge it.*[151] This is the conflating "sweet spot" between innovation and transformation.

Modes of Innovation

As a starting point, Gardner (2017) suggests that is important to be clear about the kind of innovation you are seeking before selecting the kind of research you do.[152] Innovations can be grouped into about seven broad categories/levels: (1) Ad hoc innovation, (2) sustainable innovation (improvement innovation/ ameliorative innovation), (3) incremental innovation, (4) recombinative innovation (recombinant innovation), (5) breakthrough innovation, (6) disruptive innovation, and (7) radical innovation.

AD HOC INNOVATION

According to Gallouj (2002), ad hoc innovation can be defined in general terms as the interactive (social) construction of a solution to a particular problem posed by a given client. It is an important form of innovation in consultancy services, where the available knowledge and experience accumulated over time are harnessed and put to work synergistically, in order to create fresh solutions and new knowledge that changes the client's situation in a positive and original way.[153]

In addition, ad hoc innovations are often produced jointly by the service provider and the client.[154] They usually appear during the normal process of delivering the service and are frequently not recognized as innovations until after the service has been provided.[155] *Ad hoc innovation represents a definite change of state when compared with the routine provision of consultancy services, and finds concrete expressions in attempts to formalize the experience acquired.*[156] Thus, the difference between ad hoc innovation and the change inherent in the provision of all consultancy services is that *it marks a non-random, permanent change of state* that is mediated through the codification of the experience acquired and, in many cases, through an expansion of a firm's organizational memory.[157] Finally, Gallouj (2002) argues that this *non-random, permanent change of state* clearly sets it apart from the *random changes* that take place in the configurations of consultancy service provision.[158]

SUSTAINABILITY INNOVATION

According to Satell (2012a), sustaining innovation is the type of innovation where *there is a clearly defined problem and a reasonably good understanding of how to solve it.*[159] He argues that sustaining innovation is probably the most common in the corporate world and is often referred to as *engineering* rather than *science.* Much of sustainability innovation is done by internal R&D labs, but many firms outsource it as well. For instance, Satell (2012a) recounts that when Steve Jobs wanted a mouse for the Macintosh computer; he went to IDEO with clear technical specifications knowing that they had the right skills to produce what he wanted.[160]

Similar to sustainability innovation, Satell (2012a) argues that *basic research* is the type of work done at universities and some R&D labs, where there isn't a clearly defined outcome, but the point is to discover more about how things work. But while basic research rarely leads directly to new products or services, many corporations invest serious money into it. For instance, some companies, like IBM, have internal labs doing primary research, while others invest by way of research grants to outside scientists and academic affiliations.[161]

INCREMENTAL INNOVATION

In the reasoning of Imber (2013), incremental innovation involves improvements to an existing product, service, or process.[162] In a similar vein, Gardner (2017) defines incremental innovation as referring to innovation processes that seek to improve existing systems and products to make them better, cheaper or faster.[163] A hybrid car is an example of incremental innovation. It does not change the nature or capability of a car; it just adds a second source of power. That's the kind of idea that could come from asking people for ideas to make cars more environmentally friendly.[164]

According to Montague (2017), these pleasant surprises along the product journey delight participants and instill loyalty. For instance, mobile app and game designers know that variable rewards keep users coming back. Like a slot machine, if we receive rewards that vary over time, but we don't know exactly when the reward will happen, we come back again and again.[165]

RECOMBINATIVE INNOVATION

This mode of innovation is based on the systemic re-use or "recycling" of existing "components" or characteristics. But does not preclude the creation, in some cases, of radically new "products" requiring specific competences, design work and a certain degree of creativity.[166]

Interestingly, incremental innovation, which is innovation based on the addition of product characteristics can be regarded as a form of recombinative (recombinant) innovation, particularly when the characteristics added have their origins from pre-existing products.[167]

In addition, Bressand and Nicholaïdis (1988) highlighted two other possible forms, particularly in the domain of services. The *first* involves the creation of a new product by *combining the characteristics of two or more existing products.* The *second* involves the creation of new products by *splitting up an existing product,* separating out various characteristics and turning certain elements into autonomous products.[168]

In his latest book, *Research Universities,* the University of Michigan's Jason Owen-Smith argues that many of the most interesting innovations today are the result of existing knowledge and technologies that have probably not been combined before. He argues that *atypical (not typical or not usual) combinations that are rarer to come by are often the source of higher-impact discoveries.* In addition, he found that *many of those bits of atypical combinations come from outside a given organization, or must traverse boundaries among separate units within it.*[169] In concurrence with the subject matter of this chapter, the rise to prominence of the recombinative innovation model can be interpreted in two ways:

1. It is easy to put into practice because it draws on what exists. Faced with a new problem, the first response will be to mobilize the most accessible knowledge, methods and technologies: those that have already been mastered or that can be easily acquired.
2. Cognitive leaps are unlikely and costly. As a result, firm's cognitive advances tend to be based on current knowledge (see available bias).[170]

From the foregoing, Engel and Weber (2007) found that while we can agree that the problem-solving mode used in a given situation may be designed on the spot;[171] but too often, when individuals decide how to decide, the default option is to select the most appropriate preconfigured problem-solving mode that directly relates to the given characteristics of the task.[172]

In addition, Gallouj (2002) argues that the recombinative innovative model tends to have certain fundamental implications, particularly for services:

1. The capacity of this model of innovation depends on the ability to explore and mobilize an extended set of knowledge and techniques.[173]
2. It favors the need to design a modular architecture for products and services. Firstly, in terms of products, this mode of implementation requires that the "product" be broken down into clearly identified and defined elements. Secondly, for services, the characteristics of

the service and of the way in which it is obtained have to be rigorously specified.[174]

3. The recombinative model is located at the industry level, where clusters of innovations emerging from different services industries are combined to constitute systems. Examples of this process would include the systems that tend to develop around supermarkets, insurance, banking, consultancy services, et cetera.[175]
4. More generally, as soon as the question of (re)combination is raised, questions should also be asked about – what is it that is being combined? For instance, is it knowledge or characteristics (if so, which ones?), it is goods and services (if so, which ones?), is it human resources or institutions (if so, which ones and how?). Gallouj (2002) argues that this amounts to a shift away from analysis of cognitive processes toward notions of networks and local innovation systems.[176]

BREAKTHROUGH INNOVATION

Imber (2013) defines breakthrough innovation as changes to an existing product, service, or process *that has a significant impact on the business.* For example, it could open up a new consumer category for the business, or change the way existing customers interact or perceive the organization. This innovation results in a company leapfrogging ahead of its competitors – *but the innovation originates from core organizational offerings.*[177] To that end, Satell (2012a) opines that transistors and the discovery of the structure of DNA are both good examples of breakthrough innovation.[178] But the latter also involves characteristics of recombinant innovation.

DISRUPTIVE INNOVATION

According to Grace (2019), disruptive innovation occurs when new entrants challenge incumbent firms, often despite inferior resources. And that disruptive innovation occurs not by the use of innovative technology alone, but rather in combination with business model innovations.[179] In a similar vein, disruptive innovation (as coined by Clayton Christensen) are new products or services that enter at the bottom of the market and overtime move up and displace established market leaders.[180] The following four important qualities of disruptive innovation have been identified:

1. The new product or service enters at the bottom of an established market.
2. It begins as a substandard product that is not seen as a threat by established market leaders.

3. Adopters are "non-consumers," who couldn't access product or service previously because of cost or accessibility.[181]
4. Topically, disruptive innovation is correlated with new business units and new business models.[182]

In addition, Imber (2013) argues that the innovation becomes truly disruptive when the product or service fulfills or attains the following status: Adoption becomes more widespread; it improves in quality; and finally reaches tipping point with established market leaders waking up one day to realize that their market share has slipped away, and there is no way to get it back. Examples of disruptive innovation include: the digital camera, and personal computers.[183]

RADICAL INNOVATION

Grace (2019) defines radical innovation as innovation that occurs internally within organizations, and involves the creation of new knowledge or successful commercialization of completely novel products and ideas.[184] Gardner (2017) maintains that radical innovations are focused on developing revolutionary new technologies, markets, and business models that change the world.[185] Radical innovation may involve displacing current products, modifying relationships between customers or suppliers, or creating completely new product categories.[186] In a similar vein, Spanjer (2018) found that radical innovation has unique characteristics that involve combinations of technologies that were never linked before, or innovation partnerships between unlikely partners. These connections lead to radical innovations, for example, cars powering homes, and buildings becoming computers.[187]

Additionally, Gardner (2017) holds the view that the iPhone is a famous example of radical innovation. He argues that it reimagined the scope of what a "phone" could do and rewrote the rules for many markets including photography, e-commerce, maps/navigation systems, television, movies, and music.[188] But noted however that, although Steve Jobs was right to suggest the idea for an iPhone, it would never have come out of a focus group, but anyone who suggests that consumers can't provide valuable input to fuel radical innovation would be wrong.[189]

4.3.2 Phases of Innovation, Principles, Management, and Systems Integration

Principles of Innovation

In the reasoned arguments of Llopis (2014), innovation begins with those people who touch the business across all functional and departmental areas, and involves any employee that is a student of the business, knows their customers and their specific needs.[190] They take the time to analyze their competitors and the evolution of industries, brands and the emerging role of technology. *Innovators are those who can see, sow, grow and share opportunities.*[191]

UNDERSTANDING FACTORS THAT LEAD TO THE FAILURE OF MOST INNOVATION PROJECTS

Before delving further into examining the principles of innovation and beyond, it is worthwhile we understand why innovations fail.

It is largely agreed that a successful innovation should consider the end-to-end of the spectrum. As such, the technology needs to be time and needs sensitive, and how it fits in the existing system (its economic viability). There is the need for an appropriate business model to be developed so as to incubate the innovation. Your idea or innovation needs to be embraced by the society. And fitting it into the laws and regulations of the area where your innovation will have to thrive.

To this end, Spanger (2018) opines that there are four different aspects or challenges you can face if you are innovating. *First,* it begins with the viability of the technology, for example, how the innovation fits into the system. *Second,* there should be an appropriate business model. *Third,* society's acceptance, for instance, we also as society should want to embrace your innovation or your idea. *Last* but not the least, there should be laws and regulations related to the innovation. As such, the innovation should fit into the laws and regulations applied to the area where you want to put it in.[192] In a related development, Kim and Mauborgne (2014) argue that companies need to build their blue ocean strategy in the sequence of buyer utility, price, cost, and adoption.[193]

The following factors – although not an exhaustive list – are crucial in understanding factors that lead to failure of most innovations, and how to go about with them. Step 1: Understand what failure looks like in innovation. Step 2: Understand why innovations fail. Step 3: Lessons to learn for future success.

STEP 1: UNDERSTAND WHAT FAILURE LOOKS LIKE IN INNOVATION

While failure is uncomfortable, it is something that is likely to happen during the creation of new value. How you deal with it determines whether the failure is limited to a single short-term initiative or on a longer-term learning opportunity that could lead to a number of future success within your organization.[194]

Steen (2018a) found that when organizations work on innovation, they are testing new ideas about the organization and its environment. To understand innovation, you must understand what failure looks like – here he talks of a good and a bad failure. And that failure in innovation is not just about something not working, but takes on other forms; it happens when we fail to give innovation projects the best possible chance of success, which would be proportionate to the investments required to enable the project.[195] That being said, the following are a reflection of questions surrounding failed innovations:

- Was it unaligned or aligned with the needs of the business?
- Was there not sufficient market needs for the product?
- Was it badly managed?
- Was it as a result of failure to learn or there was nothing to learn from it?
- Was it a risk worth taking that didn't pay off?
- Was it that the innovation did not offer significant advantages over competing products?
- Was it that the manufactured product did not meet the standard anticipated by the product designers?

Until we know what failure looks like, it's hard to talk about success, for example, Johnson (2010) remarked that Kodak Company invented digital photography in 1975 but did not bring a digital camera successfully to market for another 30 years. Xerox famously devised the mouse, the laser printer, and the graphical user interface but failed to commercialize any of them. Finally, the Digital Equipment Corporation spends billions of dollars developing a personal computer, but never sells a single one.[196]

STEP 2: UNDERSTAND WHY INNOVATIONS FAIL

Innovation is a project, but essentially with a specific orientation of spurring up business growth; by adapting or shaping their offerings to suit consumer taste, as well as create or stimulate a new demand.

That being said, with regards to project management cycle in general, Meg Gawler (2005) identified the following primary causes of poor performance in projects:

1. Poor project design, planning and preparation, where one or more of the essential factors for success are overlooked;
2. projects not relevant to the beneficiaries;
3. risks and assumptions insufficiently taken into account;
4. factors affecting long-term sustainability ignored;
5. inability to make the right decisions at the right time over the lifetime of the project (which is related to inadequate monitoring and feedback); and

6. lessons from past experience not incorporated into new projects and practice (that is, lack of evaluations, or inadequate use of them).[197]

Coincidentally, if Gawler's six arguments are regrouped, they align with the three reasons advanced by Steen (2018a) why innovations fail, notably: *(1) Failure to align innovation with the needs of the business; (2) failure to learn from innovations that don't meet expected targets; and (3) failure to manage the end-to-end innovation process.* Mehta (2019) refers to the latter as the inability to develop the product or offering in the way you desire – of critical importance to the failure of innovation projects is *the inability to get customer traction.*[198] So let's throw some more light on the following points, which are critical understanding why innovations fail.

Failure to Align Innovation with the Needs of the Business In this case, innovation must be aligned with the current or future strategy of the organization in the following ways:

- It must be partnered with strategy for long-term success
- It must be aligned with the long-term needs of the business
- It can take advantage of emerging opportunities and navigate around strategic threats that affect the organization.[199]

Inability to Get Customer Traction According to Saario (2020), for an innovation to be turned into business, it must obviously be related to customers' needs. But maintains that customers do not always know what they need – or do not know what to request. To this end, he opines that the key to seeing the right opportunities can be found in monitoring the market, basic research and customer behavior.[200] In a similar vein, Mehta (2019) suggests that if your innovation was developed but failed in the marketplace because customers did not embrace it, then take a hard look to *see if the customer experience you offered truly provided a marked improvement over the current way of doing things?* In other words, *did it have a significantly positive experience over current market offerings?*[201] One of the most common reasons innovations fail in the marketplace is that *the advantage they provide over current alternatives is not perceived as high enough.* Or there were likely other blockers, such as a lack of awareness, high cost or other disadvantages that were simply too high to overcome?[202]

Failure to Manage the End-to-End Innovation Process In an innovation project, it is important to hear different opinions. In this regard, Saario (2020) contends that the different opinions and skills can best be assembled when the *whole value chain is involved in the project.* In technology projects, for example, the network should include the participation of applied research, technology developers, experts on the raw material chain, customers, investors, suppliers, start-up companies, and end users, et cetera.[203] In a similar development, Steen (2018a) argues that the following aspects need to be taken into consideration:

- Managing the innovation process well, means doing the best possible outcome relative to the level of investment and risk
- Overall, innovation requires capability, patience, and the corporate memory to learn about what went wrong and what can be done to improve the chances of success in the future.

In this regard, Mehta (2019) suggests that if your failure is not being able to build a product as desired, the first step is to keep trying, and you also discuss your roadblocks with people from different teams and with different backgrounds, or even different industries.[204] Or if it doesn't go well, sometimes it may be best to put the development effort on hold and let a different set of individuals take the initiative forward. He found that throughout the history of innovation, ideas that did not work at one point in time found success at a later time with a different set of people.[205]

Failure to Learn from Innovations that Don't Meet Expected Targets According to Steen (2018), the failure to learn from innovations that don't meet expected targets stems from two causes:

- That organizations surprisingly have a short memory
- That organizations fail to learn from underperforming innovations

In this regard, he argues that these are learning opportunities that produce valuable knowledge.[206] To concur, Mehta (2019) contends that you can only learn from failure through a meticulous analysis of why an initiative failed. As such, *failures are likely to result in future successes when organizations have an approach to evaluate why initiatives fail, and then disseminate that information so the knowledge becomes institutional.*[207] He also stressed the importance to identify individuals who were responsible for innovation failure. On the basis that if the efforts to succeed were genuine, then these individual have become much wiser through their flops, so that they can put their valuable learning and experience into other important initiatives.[208]

He further argues that individuals who have tried and failed, and have learned valuable lessons in the process are often not in the same roles the second time around, or even at the same company. In the latter case, their newfound knowledge from earlier failures lets them create new value in other organizations, while the company that suffered the initial failure is no better off as they have lost the people who have gained the most of valuable lessons from innovation failure.[209]

STEP 3: LESSONS TO LEARN FOR FUTURE SUCCESS

In relation to innovation, Gawler (2005) identified five key ingredients for project success,[210] which by certain measures can be valuable as learnable lessons for future success in innovation. These are:

- proper and participatory planning;
- addressing real problems that are priorities for the stakeholders;
- a competent and motivated project team;
- sufficient management and organizational support; and
- the different parties involved in the project should stick to their commitments.

He argues further that a successful project is the result not only of the accuracy of the technical solution, but also of the acceptance by all the parties involved of the need for, and the approach to implementing the project.[211] As a result, in conjunction with those of Steen (2018), the following observations could be further identified:

- Innovation is a Manageable Process that Includes
  - Idea generation/ concept
  - Idea selection (for incremental innovations)
  - Idea development

- Reliability and Scalability
  - There is the need to develop management capabilities across all stages that are reliable and scalable

- Innovation and Strategy are Two Sides of the Same Coin
  - The business strategy directs the innovation strategy, and then the innovation allows companies to explore new strategies in relation to the relevant innovation portfolio management – that is, the right mixes of projects, and business models.

Interestingly, the Canadian Government has come out with a powerful and incredibly dynamic initiative, called the "Innovative Solutions Canada" with the ultimate goal to Accelerate Canada's innovators and entrepreneurs' journey to market – *by having the federal government act as a first customer*. Under this platform – and from a financial perspective, participating federal departments and agencies set aside a portion of funding to support the creation of innovative solutions by Canadian small businesses. Furthermore, but from a technical standpoint, participating federal departments and agencies regularly (as need arises) issue public innovation challenges designed around a desired outcome rather than a known product or process specification, and is based on each department's mission and mandate.[212] Such moves have the advantages of connecting and submerging some of the inherent barriers responsible for the failure of innovators to transform their innovative ideas into commercial reality.

Therefore Canada's Government's dedication to support innovation at the early-stage of innovation development and at the pre-commercial stage of the innovation, through its "Innovations and Skills Plan"[213] is a new subtle way of advancing collective capitalism among innovators.

Innovation Management

FRONT-END ACTIVITIES, BACK-END ACTIVITIES, AND COMMERCIALIZATION

In the reasoning of Green (2011), to produce true innovation, you have to actually do something different that has value. Put in another way, you have to follow through on the good ideas. This requires a very different set of skills and resources than idea generation.[214] To concur, Llopis (2014) argues that the best leaders know that innovation must come from multiple sources, both internally and externally.[215] When people and their different points of view and experiences converge, they create the types of innovations that individuals could not have done or found alone.[216]

From the foregoing, Koen, Bertels, and Kleinschmidt (2014) maintain that the innovation process (or innovation management) in large companies may be divided into three parts: *(1) the front end, (2) new product development process (back end activities), and (3) commercialization (see* Fig. 4.4*). They argue that* the front end of innovation*forms the foundation for future product development activities,* since the decisions made in this early stage determine the innovation options available for later development and commercialization.[217] Similarly, within the framework of innovation management, Chaochotechuang, Daneshgar, and Sindakis (2015) provide a simplistic view of the New Product Development (NPD) process by classifying the NPD activities/stages into two major groups of activities called "front end" activities and "back end" activities. The *front end activities* (or front end of innovation) comprises of ideation, and concept development, while the *back end activities* (or back end of innovation) comprise of product design, and product testing.[218] However, ideation goes along with opportunity identification. As shown on Fig. 4.4, under opportunity identification and ideation we have *basic research* which identify opportunities, and *refinement* which involves fundamental research to refine the ideas of basic research prior to *technology development.*

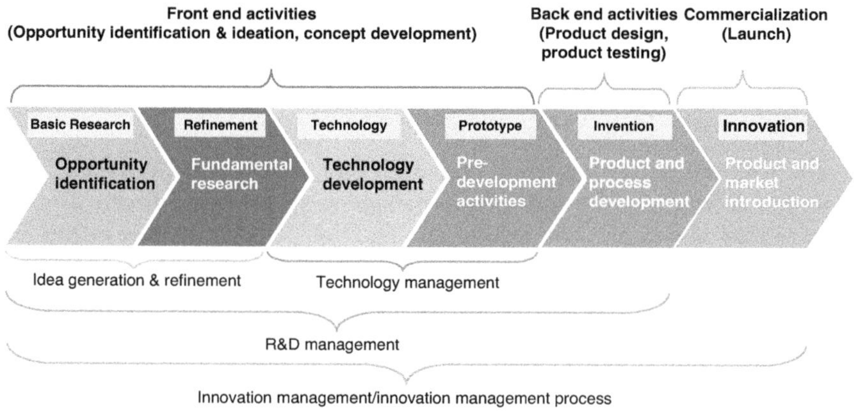

Figure 4.4 Innovation Management: Front End, Back End, and Commercialization

Sources: Adapted from multiple sources: Specht *et al.* (2002), as cited by Brem, Alexander and Voigt (2009), p. 352; Chaochotechuang, Daneshgar, and Sindakis (2015), p. 143; Dahan and Hauser (2001), as cited by Chaochotechuang *et al.* (2015), p. 142; and others.

Brem and Voigt (2009) argues that in dealing with technology aspects of innovation (which is part of the front end activities), it means handling different stages of research, and by extension, special management duties and responsibilities.[219] In this direction, Saario (2020) found that when developing new technologies, moving from a laboratory-scale innovation to the full-scale plant often includes too many uncertainties. And that managing these risks is facilitated by pilot tests at a sufficiently large scale before full-scale implementation.[220] Furthermore, in R&D management, which covers both the "front end" and the "back end" activities of innovation management, there can be pitfalls at every step – whenever things are done for the first time on an industrial scale, surprises are difficult to avoid. To this end, he suggests that the most important things are to *recognize opportunities* on the one hand, and recognize the *division of responsibility in shared projects* on the other.[221]

Finally, the third part of innovation management is *commercialization.* When the front end activities (first of part innovation management – i.e., ideation and concept development), and the back end of activities (second part of innovation management – i.e., the new product development process) have been executed properly, commercialization should be easy. But Saario (2020) argues that in practice, successful commercialization is not only dependent on our own actions – *the timing and the market situation must also be right.*[222] In addition, the whole company must work together. This means *commercialization* requires seamless cooperation between sales, marketing, production, procurement and finance.[223]

That being said, Industry Canada (2012) found that at each stage of the innovation process, manufacturers, for instance, assess progress and realign their strategies to maximize the probability of success.[224]

CRITICAL PHASES OF INNOVATION/PILLARS OF INNOVATION

As a follow-up to the front end activities, back end activities, and commercialization of innovation management process, Green (2011) argues that if you are not getting any traction with your innovation efforts, it may be that your organization lacks the skills and competences to complete one or more of the following phases, notably: Phase I (discovery), phase II (evaluation), and phase III (execution).

Phase I – Discovery: Phase I has two basic objectives: developing core innovation competences and generating new and creative ideas, which often includes gathering customer insights and translating them into workable ideas. *Key players during this phase are individual contributors and managers who encourage and support them.*[225] With regards to developing core innovation *competency,* Satell (2013) argues that every organization has its own history and set of capabilities which determine its innovation competency. For instance, an old-line industrial firm cannot just wake up one day and decide to operate like a hot Silicon Valley tech startup overnight, nor should they try. But however holds that every enterprise can improve.[226]

Phase II – Evaluation: This phase separates the wheat from the chaff, as potential ideas and opportunities undergo a rigorous screening process. New ideas are discussed, tested, evaluated, and compared for their potential to add value to customers, generate new revenue streams, or accomplish a specific innovation goal. The primary objective is to identify the highest-value opportunities and determine the feasibility of turning them into reality. *Key players during this phase are managers and leaders who have set clear strategic direction and guidance.*[227] In concurrence, Satell (2013) contends that resource allocation is critical to *strategy* and therefore needs to be an integral part of aligning innovation to strategic objectives.[228]

Phase III – Execution: This phase involves making sure that the high-value opportunities identified during the evaluation phase align with your organizational capabilities. Then *senior management* has to commit the time, money, and resources to make the innovation happen. This is followed by close tracking of the business performance of the new product or service, as well as measuring the process used to develop the innovation and looking for ways to improve it. Key players during this phase are *senior management/leaders.* To concur, Satell (2013) equally argues that even the most competent firm which deploys resources wisely, still needs to manage innovation effectively.[229]

Innovation Management and Systems Integration

THE DESIGN INNOVATION PROCESS

For any meaningful innovation management process to take place, the innovation management process and its required systems integration needs to be aligned in order to optimize productivity performance. Successful innovation is the combination of *creative ideas and sustainably profitable business models.*

As we saw earlier, it is widely accepted that the competition today, both in the product and services space is tougher than ever. Again, as discussed earlier, Superior UX (or superior user experience) and CX (customer experience), are the two key battlefields with the most at stake. In addition, CX often integrates the user-centered design model. For instance, user-centered design improves the customer experience (CX) when associated with a website, a product or service. In addition, user-centered design techniques are themselves an essential part of inclusive design. That said, inclusive design involves developing products, services or environment so as many people as possible can use them. Inclusive designs make it possible to:

- understand the reality of people's lives
- evaluate products and services you develop
- ensure products or services are genuinely inclusive.[230]

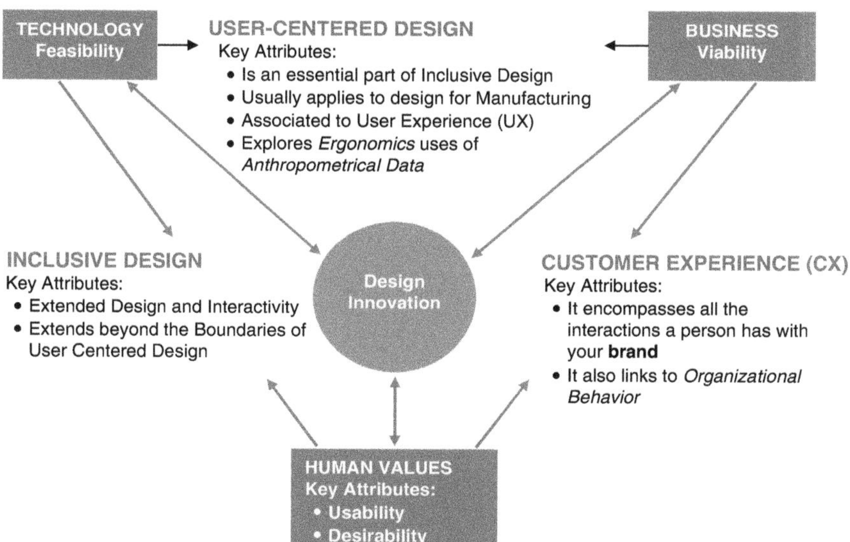

Figure 4.5 What Lies Behind Design Innovation Process? The Customer-Centric Perspective

Source: Author created, but some data was extracted from SlideModel.com (2020a).

Again, one aspect of a customer-centric culture is the *customer experience.* The role of the latter involves creating the best possible *customer experience (CX)* you can, by placing the customer in the heart of the company's marketing, product development, and operations. That said, while CX "summarizes" all customer perceptions created during interactions with your brand across various channels, customer-centricity stands for a wider commitment to ensuring the absolute success of every customer heading your way.[231]

Undeniably, these aspects of customer-centricity is now the key to winning more businesses, and as we saw earlier, it largely relies on the argument that customers are no longer enticed by products alone – they also crave "an experience" for the price they pay; such as fast shipping, added training, attractive user interfaces, et cetera (*see* Fig. 4.5). Finally, as we saw earlier, this list also include: personalization, and emotional connectivity – these two other components enhance online company reputation.[232]

As shown on Fig. 4.5, we can observe the following relationships. *First,* TECHNOLOGY Feasibility – BUSINESS Viability primarily works in tandem with USER-CENTERED DESIGN which is an essential part of *inclusive design.* That being said, User-centered design is based on the concept that the best-designed products or services come from understanding the needs of the people who will use them. This usually applies to design for *Manufacturing.* It also goes along with *User Experience (UX),* which deals with people interacting with your product and the experience they receive from that interaction. This also extends to the *Ergonomics* uses of *anthropometrical data* to determine the optimum size, shape and form of a product, and make it easier for people to use. *Second,* TECHNOLOGY Feasibility – HUMAN VALUES ((Usability, Desirability) commonly applies to INCLUSIVE DESIGN, which involves developing products, services or environment so as many people as possible can use them. It is genuinely inclusive in the sense that it addresses issues of *Design and Interactivity*far beyond what is envisaged in User Centered Design. Finally, BUSINESS Viability – HUMAN VALUES (Usability, Desirability) usually applies to CUSTOMER EXPERIENCE (CX), which encompasses all the interactions a person has with your *brand.* It might be measured in: overall experience, likelihood to continue use, and likelihood to recommend to others. It also works in synergy with *Organizational Behavior. Again, while CX is one aspect of the customer-centric culture or customer-centricity – the latter stands for a wider commitment to ensuring the absolute success of every customer heading your way.*

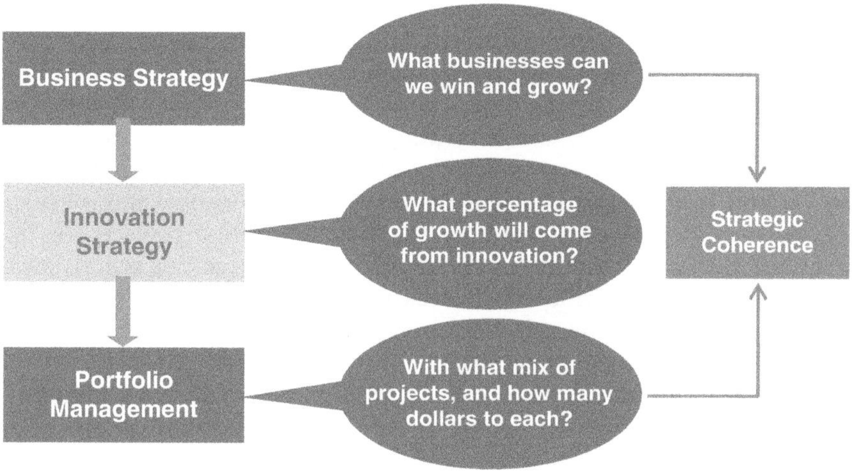

Figure 4.6 Organization's Decision Process Strategy for Innovation
Source: Adapted from Newey (2018).

BUSINESS STRATEGY AND INNOVATION VS. PORTFOLIO MANAGEMENT

The process of investing in innovation within organizations is called portfolio management. Building a successful portfolio involves learning how to design and organize a whole set of innovation projects with a clear set of risk/return and time horizon criteria in mind. In the organization's decision processes, *portfolio management works to implement both the overall business strategy and the innovation strategy*. It could be a strategic or tactical portfolio management (*see* Fig. 4.6).

Newey (2018) maintains that where there is risk, there is the need to diversify. As such, managers are entrusted with the resources given to them by shareholders and must use their expertise to invest those resources wisely, often for short, medium and long-term returns. One way that managers will seek to do this is through innovation. Investing in innovation is like investing in shares – it has certain risk and return profiles.[233] And managers invest in innovation to create extended value for the organization. Generating short, medium and long-term returns from innovation then requires diversifying our 'shares' in innovation across different project types. This spreads our risk and return. Organizations utilize portfolios to balance their innovation investments, spreading the risk and return across short, medium and long-term horizons.[234]

As shown on Fig. 4.6, the business strategy identifies what businesses the company will win and grow. The innovation strategy identifies how much of business growth will come through innovation. Portfolio management identifies the right mix of projects to invest in and how much to spend on each to achieve growth. A proper alignment of these three processes can be referred to as *strategic coherence.* But in reality we often see organizations that do not have formal portfolio management processes. Organizations without portfolio management tend to say yes to too many new projects on an ad hoc basis. Money gets wasted as different parts of the organization are innovating without any strategic coherence.

Also, they may all be using different criteria for project selection leading to variable project quality across the organization. Another trap of poor performing companies is that they list their innovation projects for the year and then rank them based on some financial forecasting criteria such as *net present value,* which is a forecast of how much money the project will make for the business. In such a scenario, the business keeps selecting the highest net present value projects until the available budget is spent. Companies using this method end up with portfolios that are biased to projects that are short-term, low cost, low risk and strategically misaligned. This concept can be illustrated using a 3 horizons model.

Horizon 3 is the businesses of the future. At Horizon 3, exploratory innovations are refined, they move through *horizon 2* (mid-term prospects) to *horizon 1,* which is closely aligned with the core business, the "now." That said, low risk, low cost projects tend to score best on indicators like *net present value.* So the business has a big focus on *Horizon 1* (short-term) which is usually sustaining and incremental innovation type projects. But end up having virtually little to nothing in Horizon 2 and Horizon 3 in a project score test.

Essentially, in effective portfolio management, what good organizations do is aiming to achieve 5 goals:

1. Create strategic alignment between project selection, business strategy, and innovation strategy
2. Maximize the financial value and/or social impact of the portfolio across short, medium, and long-term horizons
3. Balance innovations against risk/reward, time horizon, and stage of development
4. Promote sufficiency – ensuring there are enough projects to achieve the innovation strategy goals
5. And finally, matching the right number of projects to available resources

In this regard, Jönbrink (2018) argues that a good way to identify possible futures for your product is to use different possible future scenarios, which give important ideas about how they should be designed.[235]

For strategic consistency, products designed today must fit future systems. Some examples of changes which can have an impact on how your products should be designed are: new legislation, infrastructure and transport, production technology, and new recycling processes.[236] Steen

(2018b) suggests the *use of scenarios to test organizational innovation strategy*.[237] In this regard, he argues that organizations require a clear strategy that follows through, to translate the innovation strategy into operational plans.[238]

Conclusion

It takes innovation to increase productivity. But different modes of innovation would yield different outcomes. Essentially, the higher the complexity of the innovation, the greater risk involved and the greater potential it can bring to productivity. But organizations must weigh their organizational competency, and align them with their overall business strategy. This would help determine if their existing business model or a new business model would be required to pursue an investment in innovation. Additionally, it would give a clear direction as to what mix of projects would work productively well with their innovation strategy.

That being said, this chapter tends to adopt a comprehensive approach to the definition of innovation. It defines innovation *as a well-coordinated managerial process of ideas generation and conversion into viable business models, dedicated to the improvement of existing values or to the creation of completely new values*. Additionally, innovation is essentially a project, but with a specific orientation of spurring up business growth; by adapting or shaping their offerings to suit consumer taste, as well as create or stimulate a new demand. Consequently, this chapter supports the view of Llopis (2014) who argues that innovators are those who can see, sow, grow and share opportunities.

It is largely agreed that a successful innovation should consider the end-to-end of the spectrum. As such the Rules of Thumb in innovation would include the following: The technology needs to be time and needs sensitive, and fits in the existing system (its economic viability). There is the need for an appropriate business model to be developed so as to incubate the innovation. Your idea or innovation needs to be embraced by the society, and you should fit it into the laws and regulations of the area where your innovation will have to thrive.

Notes

1 Manyika et al. "Global Growth: Can Productivity Save the Day in an Aging World?" *The McKinsey Global Institute (MGI)*, San Francisco, Jan. 2015, p. 8, www.mckinsey.com/mgi/.
2 Manyika et al. (2015), op. cit., p. 8.
3 Wen, Yi. "The Making of an Economic Superpower – Unlocking China's Secret of Rapid Industrialization." *FEDERAL RESERVE BANK OF ST. LOUIS Research Division*, Working Paper 2015-006B, St. Louis, 2015, p. 158, http://research.stlouisfed.org/wp/2015/2015-006.pdf.
4 Karimov, Aziz. "Industrialization and Industrial Policy in South Korea: Some

Development Lessons For Transiting Estonia," *United Nations University – World Institute for Development Economics Research,* Tartu, 2013, p. 3.
5 Barton, D., et al. "Measuring the Economic Impact of Short-Termism." *McKinsey Global Institute,* McKinsey & Company, Discussion Paper, Feb. 2017, p. 4, www.mckinsey.com/mgi.
6 Fang, Cai and Xiaojing Zhang. "Reform Dividends to Sustain China's Economic Growth." *China's New Sources of Economic Growth: Human Capital, Innovation and Technological Change,* vol. 2, The Australian National University: ANU Press, 2017, pp. 23–43.
7 Industry Canada (2011), op. cit., p. 4.
8 https://www.reference.com/world-view/agrarian-economy-f98768cc0542e81.
9 Ohno, Kenichi. "The Economic Development of Japan: The Path Travelled by Japan as a Developing Country." *GRIPS Development Forum,* National Graduate Institute for Policy Studies, Tokyo, 2005, p. 36.
10 Ohno, Kenichi (2005), loc. cit.
11 Fortier, George and Yi Wen. "The Visible Hand: The Role of Government in China's Long-Awaited Industrial Revolution." *Research Division, Federal Bank of St. Louis,* Working Series Paper, 2016-016A, p. 7, https://dx.do1.org/10.20955/wp.2016.016.
12 Stadler, Antonia. "Challenges and Solutions for the Digital Transformation and Use of Exponential Technologies." Deloitte AG, Zurich: The Creative Studio, 27 May, 2015, p. 3.
13 Fortier, George and Wen, Yi (2016), op. cit., p. 7.
14 Stadler, Antonia (2015), op. cit., p. 3.
15 Donati, Pierpaolo. "Beyond the Traditional Welfare State: 'Relational Inclusion' and the New Welfare Society." *Associazione Italiana di Sociologia (AIS), Sezione Politica Sociale,* Roma: AIS-PS-SP Working Paper (WP No. 1), 2015, p. 2.
16 Donati, Pierpaolo (2015), op. cit., p. 3.
17 Donati, Pierpaolo (2015), op. cit., p. 5.
18 Stadler, Antonia (2015), op. cit., p. 3.
19 Rifkin, Jeremy. "The Third Industrial Revolution: How the Internet, Green Electricity, and 3-D Printing are Ushering in a Sustainable Era of Distributed Capitalism." World Economy, New York City: The World Financial Review, 2012, p. 12, www.worldfinancialreview.com.
20 Rifkin, Jeremy (2012), op. cit., p. 9.
21 Stadler, Antonia (2015), op. cit., p. 3.
22 Ibid.
23 Ibid.
24 Owen, L. Charles (1998), op. cit., p. 2.
25 MaRS. "Value Proposition: A Reflection of the Relationship between Your Customer and Brand." *Learn.marsdd.com,* 2020a, https://learn.marsdd.com/article/value-proposition-a-reflection-of-the-relationship-between-your-customer-and-brand/. Accessed 209 Nov. 2020.
26 MaRS. "Elements of Product's Value Proposition: Functional, Self-expressive and Emotional Benefits." *Learn.marsdd.com,* 2020b, https://learn.marsdd.com/article/elements-of-a-products-value-proposition-functional-self-expressive-and-emotional-benefits/. Accessed 29 Nov. 2020.
27 MaRS (2020b), loc. cit.
28 Course Hero (2011), op. cit., p. 2.
29 Ibid.
30 Course Hero (2011), op. cit., p. 1.
31 Course Hero (2011), op. cit., p. 2.

32 Stadler, Antonia (2015), op. cit., p. 2.
33 Ibid.
34 Timmons, Jay and David Farr. "Competing to Win: Manufacturers' Agenda For Economic Growth And American Exceptionalism." Washington, DC: National Association of Manufacturers, Feb. 2017, p. 6, www.nam.org/competingtowin.
35 Ibid.
36 Giffi et al. Advanced Technologies Initiative: Manufacturing & Innovation, *Deloitte and Council on Competitiveness,* Deloitte Touche Tohmatsu Limited, 2015, p. 4.
37 Stroud, Samanda. "Business Tips for New Product Design and Development." *Cadcrowd.com,* 11 Sep. 2018, https://www.cadcrowd.com/blog/business-tips-for-new-product-design-development.
38 Harrington, Kevin. "10 Qualities of A Successful Product." *Forbes.com,* 8 Oct., 2013, https://www.forbes.com/sites/kevinharrington/2013/10/08/10-qualities-of-a-successful-product/#556cf9f1126b. Accessed 27 Jan. 2020.
39 As cited by Isa, S. S. and A. Liem. "Classifying Physical Models and Prototypes in the Design Process: A Study on the Economical and Usability Impact of Adopting Models and Prototypes in the Design Process." *International Design Conference – Design 2014,* Dubrovnik Croatia, 19–22 May 2014, p. 1.
40 Isa, S. S. and A. Liem (2014), op. cit., p. 4.
41 Isa, S. S. and A. Liem (2014), loc. cit.
42 Marti, Jesus. "What Can You Expect From Physical Prototypes." *Medium.com,* 6 Sep. 2019, https://medium.com/abilista/limitations-physical-prototype-c2981aca084a. Accessed 26 Jul. 2019.
43 Isa, S. S. and A. Liem (2014), op. cit., pp. 2–4.
44 As cited by Gilley, Cliff. "The Product Manager's Influence Map: A Practical Guide to Organizational Alignment and Relationship-Building for Product Teams." *Go.pendo.io,* 2020, p. 4, http://go.pendo.io/rs/185-LQW-370/images/TheProductManagersInfluenceMap.pdf. Accessed 29 Nov. 2020.
45 Skidmore, Paul (2018), loc. cit.
46 Skidmore, Paul (2018), loc. cit.
47 Nibusinessinfo. "User-centered Design: Advantages of User-centered Design." Invest Northern Ireland in partnership with indirect government services, 2020b, https://www.nibusinessinfo.co.uk/content/advantages-user-centred-design. Accessed 25 Jul. 2020.
48 Nibusinessinfo. "User-centered Design: User-centered Design Process." Invest Northern Ireland in partnership with indirect government services, 2020c, https://www.nibusinessinfo.co.uk/content/user-centred-design-process. Accessed 25 Jul. 2020.
49 Ibid.
50 Nibusinessinfo. "User-centered Design: Advantages of Inclusive Design." Invest Northern Ireland in partnership with indirect government services, 2020d, https://www.nibusinessinfo.co.uk/content/advantages-inclusive-design. Accessed 25 Jul. 2020.
51 SlideModel. "Product-Led Growth (PLG): The Ultimate SaaS Business Growth Strategy to Pursue." *SlideModel.com,* 20 May 2020b, https://slidemodel.com/product-led-growth-plg. Accessed 20 Jul. 2020.
52 Lowden, Tim. "User Experience (UX) vs. Customer Experience (CX): What's the Dif?" *Dogital.gov* – General Services Administration's (GSA) Technology Transformation Services, 7 Jul. 2014, https://digital.gov/2014/07/07/user-experience-ux-vs-customer-experience-cx-what's-the-dif. Accessed 23 Jul. 2020.
53 Ibid.

54 Productboard. "Product-Led Growth." *Productboard.com,* 2020, https://www.productboard.com/glossary/product-led-growth. Accessed 25 Jul. 2020.
55 Productboard (2020), loc. cit.
56 As cited by SlideModel (2020b), loc. cit.
57 Econsultancy. "Digital Intelligence Briefing – 2018 Digital Trends." Econsultancy in partnership with Adobe, Feb. 2018, https://econsultancy.com/reports/digital-intelligence-briefing-2018-digital-trends. Accessed 21 Jul. 2020.
58 Bartlett, Blake. "What Is Product Led Growth? How to Build a Software Company in the End User Era." *OpenViewpartners.com,* 1 Jul. 2020, https://openviewpartners.com/blog/what-is-product-led-growth/#.XxbYSTMo9Tc. Accessed 1 Jul. 2020.
59 Productled. "What Is Product-led Growth." *Productled.org,* 2020, https://www.productled.org/foundations/what-is-product-led-growth#Chap1. Accessed 23 Jul. 2020.
60 Ibid.
61 Bartlett, Blake (2020), loc. cit.
62 Isa, S. S. and A. Liem. (2014), op. cit., p. 2.
63 Hoffman, Jeff. "Engineering the Space Shuttle." *MOOC Learning Materials,* course excerpts from MIT's Department of Aeronautics and Astronautics, in partnership with edx.org, 2018.
64 Skidmore, Paul (2018), loc. cit.
65 OptiProERP. "5 Quality Assurance Best Practices for Manufacturers." *OptiProERP,com,* 2020, https://www.optiproerp.com/blog/5-quality-assurance-best-practices-for-manufacturers/amp. Accessed 12 Aug. 2020.
66 Stroud, Samanda (2018), loc. cit.
67 Owen, L. Charles "Design, Advanced Planning and Product Development," 3° Congresso Brasileiro de Pesquisa e Desenvolvimento em Design, Rio de Janeiro, Brazil: Oct. 26, 1998. International Symposium: Nuevos Metodos & Tecnologias para el Diseño de Productos, Santiago, Chile: November 12, 1998, p. 1, https://id.iit.edu/wp-content/uploads/2015/03/Design-advanced-planning-product-development-Owen_santiago98.pdf.
68 Owen, L. Charles (1998), loc. cit.
69 Ibid.
70 Ibid.
71 Marinho, J. P., et al. "The Relationship between Product Architecture and Mass Customization in [the] Housing Sector." Industrialization, prefabrication, assembly and open building, *Proceedings IGLC-22,* Oslo, Jun. 2014, p. 1011.
72 See Ulrich, K. "The Role of Product Architecture in the Manufacturing Firm." *Research Policy*, *24*, 1995, pp. 419–440; as cited by Fujimoto, Takahiro. "Architecture-Based Comparative Advantage: A Design Information View of Manufacturing." *Evolutionary and Institutional Economics Review*, vol. 4, no. 1, pp. 55–112, Faculty of Economics, University of Tokyo, Tokyo, 2007, p. 2.
73 Ibid.
74 Mathews, A. John (2012), op. cit., pp. 47–48.
75 Alexander, C. *Notes on the Synthesis of Form.* Harvard University Press, Cambridge, MA, 1964; as cited by Fujimoto (2007), op. cit., p. 60.
76 Fujomoto, Takahiro (2007), op. cit., p. 62.
77 Mathews, A. John (2012), op. cit., p. 47.
78 Mathews, A. John (2012), op. cit., p. 46.
79 Ibid.

80 Baldwin, C. Y. and K. B. Clark (2000). *Design Rules, Volume 1: The Power of Modularity.* MIT Press, Cambridge, MA; as cited by Mathews, A. John (2012), op. cit., p. 46.
81 As cited by Mathews, A. John (2012), ibid.
82 Tsuru, Tsuyoshi and Motohiro Morishima. "Product Architecture, Organizational Design, and HRM Practices: Comparing Japanese, Korean, and Chinese Firms." *Hitotsubashi University Research Project of Policies for East Asia,* Hitotsubashi University, Fukino Project Discussion Paper Series, No. 027, Tokyo, Apr. 2011, p. 15.
83 Baldwin, C.Y. and K. B. Clark (2000); as cited by Mathews, A. John (2012), op. cit., p. 46.
84 Owen, L. Charles (1991), op. cit., p. 4.
85 Ibid.
86 Mathews, A. John (2012), op. cit., p. 46.
87 As cited by Kamuriwo, Dzidziso S., and Charles Baden-Fuller. "Knowledge integration using product R&D outsourcing in biotechnology." *Research Policy* vol. 45 (2016), 1031-1045, London: Elsevier B.V., 2016, p. 1031, http://dx.doi.org/10.1016/j.respol.2016.02.009.
88 Kamuriwo, D. Samuel and Charles Baden-Fuller (2016), op. cit., p. 1031.
89 Kamuriwo, D. Samuel. and Charles Baden-Fuller (2016), op. cit., p. 1031.
90 Fujimoto, Takahiro. "Architecture-Based Comparative Advantage: Architecture-based Comparative Advantage in Japan and Asia." Manufacturing Management Research Center Graduate School of Economics, University of Tokyo, 21COE, University of Tokyo, *MMRC Discussion Paper* No. 94, Aug. 2006, p. 4, http://merc.e.u-tokyo.ac.jp/mmrc/dp/pdf/MMRC94_2006.pdf.
91 Tsuru, Tsuyoshi and Motohiro Morishima (2011), op. cit., p. 17.
92 Fujimoto, Takahiro (2007), op. cit., p. 55.
93 Wang, H. "Innovation in Product Architecture: A Study of the Chinese Automobile Industry."*Asia Pacific Journal of Management,* 2008, *p. 516.* As cited Mathews, A. John (2012), op. cit., p. 52.
94 As cited by Marinho et al. (2014), op. cit., p. 1012.
95 Marinho et al. (2014), loc. cit.
96 Mathews, A. John (2012), op. cit., p. 47.
97 Owen, C. L. Charles (1998), op. cit., p. 2.
98 Hannon et al. (2016), op. cit., p. 23.
99 Ibid.
100 Ibid.
101 Peck, David. Engineering Design for a Circular Economy. *MOOC Learning Materials,* course excerpts from Delft University of Technology, in partnership with edx.org, 2018.
102 Ester van der Voet. Engineering Design for a Circular Economy. *MOOC Learning Materials,* course excerpts from Delft University of Technology, in partnership with edx.org, 2018b.
103 Ibid.
104 Stahel, W. R. *The Performance Economy*, 2nd Edition. London: Palgrave Macmillan, 2010, p. 195; as cited by Den Hollander, M., et al. "Product Design in a Circular Economy: Development of a Typology of Key Concepts and Terms: Key Concepts and Terms for Circular Product Design." *Journal of Industrial Ecology*, vol. 21, no. 3, 2017, p. 519.
105 Den Hollander et al. (2017), op. cit., p. 523.
106 Course Hero (2011), op. cit., p. 5.
107 Azcarate, J. Engineering Design for a CirculaEngineering Design for ar

Economy. *MOOC Learning Materials,* course excerpts from Delft University of Technology, in partnership with edx.org, 2018.
108 Prumbohm, Max. "Design for Repair:" in Engineering Design for a Circular Economy. *MOOC Learning Materials,* course excerpts from Delft University of Technology, in partnership with edx.org, 2018.
109 Prumbohm, Max (2018), loc. cit.
110 Prumbohm, Max (2018), loc. cit.
111 Jönbrink, Anna-Karim. Engineering Design for a Circular Economy. *MOOC Learning Materials,* course excerpts from Delft University of Technology, in partnership with edx.org, 2018.
112 Course Hero (2011), op. cit., p. 6.
113 CalRecycle. "About CalRecycle." *Calrecycle.ca.gov,* Last updated: Dec. 12 2018, https://www.calrecycle.ca.gov/AboutUs/. Accessed 12 Aug. 2019.
114 Ibid.
115 Lohrengel, Armin. Engineering Design for a Circular Economy. *MOOC Learning Materials,* course excerpts from Delft University of Technology, in partnership with edx.org, 2018.
116 CalRecycle (2018), loc. cit.
117 Course Hero (2011), op. cit., p. 4.
118 Montague, Monty. "The Amazing Role of Aesthetics in Product Design." *Boltgroup.com,* 21 Jun. 2017, p. 3, https://boltgroup.com/aesthetics-in-product-design.
119 Montague, Monty (2017), op. cit., pp. 3–4.
120 Unknown Author. "Chapter 2: Engineering Materials and Properties," A Textbook of Machine Design. *Sedyono.wordpress.com,* 2019, p. 16, https://sedyono.files.wordpress.com/2015/10/ch-02.pdf. Accessed 11 Dec. 2019.
121 Unknown Author (2019), op. cit., p. 17.
122 Ibid.
123 Mukasyan, Alexander (2019), loc. cit.; & Metal Supermarkets. "The Difference between Ferrous and Non-Ferrous Metal" Metal Supermarkets." *Metalsupermarkets,com,* 23 Sept. 2015, https://www.metalsupermarkets.com/the-difference-between-ferrous-and-non-ferrous-metal/. Accessed 9 Jan. 2020.
124 Miltenović et al. (2014), op. cit., p. 531.
125 Kaspar, Jerome and Michael Vielhaber. "Fiber-Reinforced Composite Design Within A Lightweight and Material-Oriented Development Process." *21st International Conference On Engineering Design,* Iced17, 21–25 Aug. 2017, The University of British Columbia, Vancouver, Canada, p. 330.
126 Ester van der Voet. "Resource Challenge: Why Design for R?" in Engineering Design for a Circular Economy. *MOOC Learning Materials,* course excerpts from Delft University of Technology, in partnership with edx.org, 2018a.
127 Penker, Magnus, et al. Sustainable Growth and Profits: Making Your Innovation Strategy, Organization, and Initiatives. *Innovation 360°,* Volume 5: The Complete Guide to Business Innovation, CreateSpace Indepedent Publishing Patform, 1st Edition, 14 Feb. 2018, https://bookauthority.org. Accessed 23 Jun. 2020.
128 Ibid.
129 Bordia et al. (2005), op. cit., p. 1.
130 Gkanas, E. I., et al. "Nanotechnology and Innovation: Recent Status and the Strategic Implication for the Formation of High Tech Clusters in Greece, in between a Global Economic Crisis." *HCTL Open International. Journal of*

Technology Innovations and Research – HCTL Open IJTIR, vol. 2, Mar. 2013, pp. 5–6, https://www.researchgate.net/publication/236119607.
131 Ibid; p. 6.
132 Ibid.
133 University of Queensland Business School. Innovation: From Plan to Product. *MOOC Learning Materials,* excerpts of course description from University of Queensland Business School, Australia, in partnership with edx.org, 2018.
134 Viki, Tendayi. "Innovation Is Management." *Forbes.com,* 8 Jan. 2017, https://www.forbes.com/sites/tendayiviki/2017/01/08/innovation-is-management/#48a3ff8f3e65. Accessed 22 Feb. 2020.
135 Henderson, Theodore. "Why Innovation Is Crucial To Your Organization's Long-Term Success." *Forbes.com,* 8 May 2017, https://www.forbes.com/sites/forbescoachescouncil/2017/05/08/why-innovation-is-crucial-to-your-organizations-long-term-success/#4731c4383098. Accessed 22 Feb. 2020.
136 Green, Holly (2020), loc. cit.
137 Kim and Maubourgne (2014), op. cit., p. 15.
138 Ibid.
139 Gustafsson et al. (2012), op. cit., p. 7.
140 Henderson, Theodore (2017), loc. cit.
141 Viki, Tendayi (2018), loc. cit.
142 Satell, Greg (2013), loc. cit.
143 Satell, Greg. "The Truth About Innovation." *DigitalTonto.com,* 3 Jun. 2012b, https://www.digitaltonto.com/2012/the-truth-about-innovation/. Accessed 30 Mar. 2020.
144 Viki, Tendayi (2018), loc. cit.
145 Viki, Tendayi (2018), loc. cit.
146 Llopis, Glenn (2014), loc. cit.
147 Newman, Daniel. "Innovation vs. Transformation: The Difference In A Digital World." *Forbes.com,* 16 Feb. 2017, https://www.forbes.com/sites/danielnewman/2017/02/16/innovation-vs-transformation-the-difference-in-a-digital-world/#5e5a0ec065e8. Accessed 28 Mar. 2020.
148 Ibid.
149 Ibid.
150 Dunn III, J. Richard (1992), op. cit., p. 1.
151 Dunn III, J. Richard (1992), op. cit., p. 8.
152 Gardner, David (2017), loc. cit.
153 Gallouj, Faïz. Innovation in the Service Economy: The New Wealth of Nations. Cheltenham, Northampton: Edward Elgar Publishing, 2002, p. 77.
154 Gallouj, Faïz (2002), op. cit., pp. 77–78.
155 Ibid; p. 78.
156 Gallouj, Faïz (2002), loc. cit.
157 Ibid; pp. 78–79.
158 Ibid; p. 79.
159 Satell, Greg. "4 Types of Innovation (And How to Approach Them)." *DigitalTonto,* 16 May 2012a, https://www.digitaltonto.com/2012/4-types-of-innovation-and-how-to-approach-them/. Accessed 30 Mar. 2020.
160 Satell, Greg (2012a), loc. cit.
161 Satell, Greg (2012a), loc. cit.
162 Imber, Amantha. "Breakthrough Innovation vs. Disruptive Innovation." *Inventium.com,* 19 Jun., 2013, https://www.inventium.com.au/breakthrough-innovation-vs-disruptive-innovation/. Accessed 2 Mar. 2020.

163 Gardner, David (2002), loc. cit.
164 Gardner, David (2002), loc. cit.
165 Montague, Monty (2017), op. cit., p. 3.
166 Gallouj, Faïz (2002), op. cit., p. 79.
167 Ibid.
168 As cited by Gallouj, Faïz (2002), ibid.
169 Gaskell, Adi. "How Universities Support Recombinative Innovation." *Disruptor League,* 12 Nov. 2018, https://disruptorleague.com/2018/11/12/how-universities-support-recombinative-innovation. Accessed 1 May 2010.
170 Gallouj, Faïz (2002), op. cit., p. 84.
171 Engel, C. and E. U. Weber (2007), op. cit., pp. 329–330.
172 Engel, C. and E. U. Weber (2007), op. cit., p. 335.
173 Gallouj, Faïz (2002), loc. cit.
174 Gallouj, Faïz (2002), op. cit., p. 85.
175 Gallouj, Faïz (2002), op. cit., pp. 85–86.
176 Gallouj, Faïz (2002), op. cit., p. 86.
177 Imber, Amantha (2013), loc. cit.
178 Satell, Greg (2012a), loc. cit.
179 Grace, Allie. "What 40 Years of Research Reveals About the Differences Between Disruptive and Radical Innovation." *FileMaker Developer Experts – Neo Code,* 21 May 2019, https://www.neocode.com/blog/what-40-years-of-research-reveals-about-the-differences-between-disruptive-and-radical-innovation/. Accessed 2 Apr. 2020.
180 Imber, Amantha (2013), loc. cit.
181 Ibid.
182 Grace, Allie (2019), loc. cit.
183 Imber, Amantha (2013), loc. cit.
184 Grace, Allie (2019), loc. cit.
185 Gardner, David (2017), loc. cit.
186 Grace, Allie (2019), loc. cit.
187 Spanjer, Willy. Engineering Design for a Circular Economy. *MOOC Learning Materials,* course excerpts from Delft University of Technology, in partnership with edx.org, 2018.
188 Gardner, David (2017), loc. cit.
189 Ibid.
190 Llopis, Glenn (2014), loc. cit.
191 Ibid.
192 Spanjer, W. (2018), loc. cit.
193 Kim and Mauborgne (2014), op. cit., p. 19.
194 Mehta, Kumar (2019), loc. cit.
195 Steen, John. "Corporate Innovation: What is 'failure' in managing innovation," in Innovation: From Plan to Product. *MOOC Learning Materials,* course excerpts from University of Queensland Business School, Australia in partnership with edx.org, 2018a.
196 Johnson, W. Mark (2010), op. cit., p. 1.
197 Gawler, Meg (2005), op. cit., p. 1.
198 Mehta, Kumar (2019), loc. cit.
199 Steen, John (2018a), loc. cit.
200 Saario, Ari. "Five Steps to Successful Commercialization of an Innovation – Can the Pitfalls be Avoided?" *Valmet.com,*https://www.valmet.com/media/articles/experts-voice/five-steps-to-successful-commercialization-of-an-innovation/. Accessed 25 Nov. 2020.
201 Mehta, Kumar (2019), loc. cit.

202 Ibid.
203 Saario, Ari (2020), loc. cit.
204 Mehta, Kumar (2019), loc. cit.
205 Mehta, Kumar (2019), loc. cit.
206 Steen, John (2018a), loc. cit.
207 Mehta, Kumar (2019), loc. cit.
208 Ibid.
209 Mehta, Kumar (2019), loc. cit.
210 Gawler, Meg (2005), op. cit., p. 1.
211 Ibid.
212 Innovative Solutions Canada. From Innovation, Science and Economic Development Canada. *Government of Canada,* 11 Jul. 2019, http://www.ic.gc.ca/eic/site/101.nsf/eng/home/.
213 Innovative Solutions Canada (2019), loc. cit.
214 Green, Holly. "Phases of Innovation." *Forbes.com.,* 14 Dec. 2011, https://www.forbes.com/sites/work-in-progress/2011/12/14/phases-of-innovation/#7c59c8b14996.
215 Llopis, Glenn (2014), loc. cit.
216 Ibid.
217 Koen, P. A., et al. "Managing the Front End of Innovation—Part II: Results from a Three-Year Study." RESEARCH-ON-RESEARCH, *Research-Technology Management*, May/Jun. 2014, p. 25.
218 Chaochotechuang, P., et al. "Innovation Strategies of New Product Development (NPD)." *International Journal of Knowledge and Systems Science*, vol. 6, 1 Apr. 2015, p. 143. DOI: 10.4018/IJKSS.2015040104. Accessed 25 Nov. 2020.
219 Brem, Alexander and Kai-Ingo Voigt. "Integration of Market Pull and Technology Push in the Corporate Front End and Innovation Management – Insights from the German Software Industry." *ScienceDirect:* Elsevier – Technovation, vol. 29, no. 5, 2009, p. 352, www.sciencedirect.com.
220 Saario, Ari (2020), loc. cit.
221 Saario, Ari (2020), loc. cit.
222 Saario, Ari (2020), loc. cit.
223 Ibid.
224 Industry Canada (2012), op. cit., p. 1.
225 Green, Holly (2011), loc. cit.
226 Satell, Greg (2013), loc. cit.
227 Green, Holly (2011), loc. cit.
228 Satell, Greg (2013), loc. cit.
229 Satell, Greg (2013), loc. cit.
230 Nibusinessinfo (2020d), loc. cit.
231 SlideModel (2020a), loc. cit.
232 SlideModel (2020b), loc. cit.
233 Newey, Lance (2018), loc. cit.
234 Ibid.
235 Jönbrink, Anna-Karin (2018), loc. cit.
236 Ibid.
237 Steen, John. "Using scenarios to test your innovation strategy," in Innovation: From Plan to Product. *MOOC Learning Materials,* course excerpts from University of Queensland Business School, Australia in partnership with edx.org, 2018b.
238 Ibid.

Works Cited

Ashby, Michael F. "Chapter 2: Engineering Materials and Properties." Materials Selection in Mechanical Design, 5th Edition. Butterworth-Heinemann, an imprint of Elsevier: Oxford, United Kingdom; Cambridge, MA, 2nd Nov. 2016, pp. 1–660. Michael F. Ashby is a Royal Society Research Professor Emeritus, University of Cambridge, winner of a 2018 Textbook Excellence Award (Texty) from the Textbook and Academic Authors Association.

Azcarate, J. "Design for Reuse." In Engineering Design for a Circular Economy: DelfX PDCE01x. *MOOC Learning Materials*, course excerpts from Delft University of Technology, in partnership with edx.org, 2018. Juan is PhD researcher at TU Delft, Faculty of Architecture and the Built Environment.

Baldwin, C. Y. and K. B. Clark, *Design Rules, Volume 1: The Power of Modularity*. MIT Press, Cambridge, MA, 2000.

Barton, D., et al. "Measuring the Economic Impact of Short-Termism." *McKinsey Global Institute*, McKinsey & Company, Discussion Paper, Feb. 2017, pp. 1–9.

Bartlett, Blake. "What is Product Led Growth? How to Build a Software Company in the End User Era." *OpenViewpartners.com*, 1 Jul. 2020, https://openviewpartners.com/blog/what-is-product-led-growth/#.XxbYSTMo9Tc.

Bordia, R., et al. "Innovation's OrgDNA," *Booz & Company Inc.*, 2005, pp. 1–10, www.booz.com/.

Brantley, Bill. "How Organizational Drag is Wasting the Time, Talent, and Energy of Your Agency's Workforce." *GovLoop.com*, 13 Mar. 2017.

Brem, Alexander and Kai-Ingo Voigt. "Integration of Market Pull and Technology Push in the Corporate Front End and Innovation Management – Insights from the German Software Industry." *ScienceDirect: Elsevier – Technovation*, vol. 29, no. 5, 2009, pp. 351–367, www.sciencedirect.com.

CalRecycle. "About CalRecycle." *Calrecycle.ca.*gov, Last updated: Dec. 12 2018, https://www.calrecycle.ca.gov/AboutUs/.

Chaochotechuang, P., et al. "Innovation Strategies of New Product Development (NPD)." *International Journal of Knowledge and Systems Science*, vol. 6, no 2, 1 Apr. 2015, pp. 139–147. doi: 10.4018/IJKSS.2015040104.

CNCCOM. "The Benefits of Computer Numerical Control (CNC)." *CNC.com*, 26 Nov. 2015, https://www.cnc.com/the-benefits-of-computer-numerical-control-cnc/.

Coex. "About PETG Filament." *Coexllc.com*, https://coexllc.com/about-petg-filament/, https://www.compoundchem.com/wp-content/uploads/2015/03/The-Chemical-Structures-of-DNA-RNA-Aug-2018.pdf.

Course Hero. "Technology & Design: Influences on Product Design." AS LEVEL Section A FACT FILES. *Coursehero.com*, 2011, pp. 1–7, https://www.coursehero.com/file/40838121/A2AS-TECH-Support-10370pdf/.

Cousineau, Marc. "How to make condition-based maintenance more effective." *Fiixsoftware.com*, 21 Feb. 2019, https://resources.fiixsoftware.com.

Cousineau, Marc. "Implementing predictive maintenance with the help of preventive maintenance." *Fiixsoftware.com*, 25 Sep. 2018, https://www.fiixsoftware.com.

Dahan, Ely and John R. Hauser. *Product Development - Managing a Dispersed Process.* Handbook of Marketing. Editors: Barton Weitz and Robin

Wensley, Center for Innovation in Product Development at M.I.T., Nov. 2001.

Den Hollander, M., et al. "Product Design in a Circular Economy: Development of a Typology of Key Concepts and Terms: Key Concepts and Terms for Circular Product Design." *Journal of Industrial Ecology*, vol. 21, no. 3, 2017, pp. 517–24.

Donati, Pierpaolo. "Beyond the Traditional Welfare State: 'Relational Inclusion' and the New Welfare Society." *Associazione Italiana di Sociologia (AIS), Sezione Politica Sociale*. Roma: AIS-PS-SP Working Paper (WP No. 1), 2015, pp. 2–20.

Dunn III, J. Richard. "From Gettysburg to the Gulf and Beyond: Coping with Revolutionary Technological change in Land Warfare." *The Institute for National Strategic Studies*, Mc Nair Papers, Number 13, Mar., 1992, pp. 1–98.

Econsultancy. "Digital Intelligence Briefing – 2018 Digital Trends." *Econsultancy in partnership with Adobe*, Feb. 2018, https://econsultancy.com/reports/digital-intelligence-briefing-2018-digital-trends.

Engel, C. and E. U. Weber. "The Impact of Institutions on the Decision How to Decide." *Journal of Institutional Economics: The JOIE Foundation*, vol. 3, no. 3, 2007, pp. 323–49. doi: 10.1017/S1744137407000744.

Ester van der Voet. "Resource Challenge: Why Design for R?" in "Design for Reuse." Engineering Design for a Circular Economy: DelfX PDCE01x. *MOOC Learning Materials*, course excerpts from Delft University of Technology, in partnership with edx.org, 2018a. Ester van der Voet is an Associate Professor at the Institute of Environmental Sciences (CML) at Leiden University

Ester van der Voet. "Reuse: How to Ensure Sustainability," in "Design for Reuse." Engineering Design for a Circular Economy: DelfX PDCE01x. *MOOC Learning Materials*, course excerpts from Delft University of Technology, in partnership with edx.org, 2018b. Ester van der Voet is an Associate Professor at the Institute of Environmental Sciences (CML) at Leiden University.

Fang, Cai and Xiaojing Zhang. "Reform Dividends to Sustain China's Economic Growth." *China's New Sources of Economic Growth: Human Capital, Innovation and Technological Change*, vol. 2, The Australian National University: ANU Press, 2017, p. 28.

Faris, Stephanie. "Four Primary Types of Manufacturing Processes." *Bizfluent.com*, 21 Nov. 2018, https://bizfluent.com/info-8622375-four-primary-types-manufacturing-processes.html.

Fiix. The Short Guide to Preventive Maintenance. *Fiix software.com – Ebook, Toronto*, 2020c, p. 7, www.fiixsoftware.com.

Fiix. "Planned Maintenance." *Fiixsoftware.com*, 2020d, https://www.fiixsoftware.com/planned-mainteance.

Fiix. "Reactive maintenance." *Fiixsoftware.com*, 2020e, https://www.fiixsoftware.com/maintenance-strategies/reactive-maintenance/.

Fiix. "Predictive maintenance." *Fiixsoftware.com*, 2020f, https://www.fiixsoftware.com/maintenance-strategies/predictive-maintenance.

Fortier, George and Yi Wen. "The Visible Hand: The Role of Government in

China's Long-Awaited Industrial Revolution." *Research Division, Federal Bank of St. Louis*, Working Series Paper, 2016-016A, https://dx.do1.org/10.20955/wp.2016.016.

Fujimoto, Takahiro. "Architecture-Based Comparative Advantage: A Design Information View of Manufacturing." *Evol. Inst. Econ. Rev*, vol. 4, no. 1: *55–112*, Faculty of Economics, University of Tokyo, Tokyo, 2007, pp. 56–106.

Fujimoto, Takahiro. "Architecture-Based Comparative Advantage: Architecture-based Comparative Advantage in Japan and Asia." *Manufacturing Management Research Center Graduate School of Economics*. University of Tokyo, 21COE, University of Tokyo, *MMRC Discussion Paper* No. 94, Aug. 2006, pp. 1–8.

Gallouj, Faïz. *Innovation in the Service Economy: The New Wealth of Nations*. Cheltenham, Northampton: Edward Elgar Publishing, 2002, pp. 77–87.

Gardner, David. "Radical Vs. Incremental Innovation: The Right Approach for the Right Time," *Marumatchbox.com*, 14 Nov. 2017, https://marumatchbox.com/radical-vs-incremental-innovation-the-right-approach-for-the-right-time/.

Gawler, Meg. "Project Design in the Context of Project Cycle Management – Sourcebook." *WWF Introductory Course*, Prévessin-Moëns: ARTEMIS Services for Nature Conservation and Development, Feb. 2005, pp. 1–56.

Gaskell, Adi. "How Universities Support Recombinative Innovation." *Disruptor League*, 12 Nov. 2018, https://disruptorleague.com/2018/11/12/how-universities-support-recombinative-innovation.

Giang, Ken. "PLA vs. ABS: What's the difference?" *3Dhubs.com*, 2020, https://www.3dhubs.com/knowledge-base/pla-vs-abs-whats-difference/.

Giffi et al. "Advanced Technologies Initiative: Manufacturing & Innovation." *Deloitte and Council on Competitiveness*. Deloitte Touche Tohmatsu Limited, 2015, pp. 2–70.

Gilley, Cliff. "The Product Manager's Influence Map: A Practical Guide to Organizational Alignment and Relationship-Building for Product Teams." *Go.pendo.io*, 2020, pp. 3–44.

Gkanas, E. I., et al. "Nanotechnology and Innovation: Recent Status and the Strategic Implication for the Formation of High Tech Clusters in Greece, in between a Global Economic Crisis." *HCTL Open International. Journal of Technology Innovations and Research – HCTL Open IJTIR*, Volume 2, Mar. 2013, pp. 2–12.

Grace, Allie. "What 40 Years of Research Reveals About the Differences Between Disruptive and Radical Innovation." *FileMaker Developer Experts – Neo Code*, 21 May 2019, https://www.neocode.com/blog/what-40-years-of-research-reveals-about-the-differences-between-disruptive-and-radical-innovation/.

Green, Holly. "Phases of Innovation." *Forbes.com.*, 14 Dec. 2011, https://www.forbes.com/sites/work-in-progress/2011/12/14/phases-of-innovation/#7c59c8b14996.

Gustafsson, A., et al. "Customer co-creation in service innovation: A matter of communication?" *Journal of Service Management*, vol. 23, no. 3, Jun. 2012, pp. 4–32.

Hallgrimsson, Bjarki. *Prototyping and Model Making for Product Design. Part of Series: Portfolio Skills & Product Design*. Laurence King Publishing, London, 2012, https://testlibrary.tcdc.or.th/record/view/b00027525.

Hannon, E., et al. "The circular economy: Moving from theory to practice." McKinsey Center for Business and Environment, Special edition, Oct. 2016, pp. 23–25.

Harrington, Kevin. "10 Qualities of A Successful Product." *Forbes.com*, 8 Oct. 2013, https://www.forbes.com/sites/kevinharrington/2013/10/08/10-qualities-of-a-successful-product/#556cf9f1126b.

Henderson, Theodore. "Why Innovation Is Crucial To Your Organization's Long-Term Success." *Forbes.com*, 8 May 2017, https://www.forbes.com/sites/forbescoachescouncil/2017/05/08/why-innovation-is-crucial-to-your-organizations-long-term-success/#4731c4383098.

Hobday, Michael, et al. "Systems Integration: A Core Capability of the Modern Corporation." *Industrial & Corporate Change,* vol. 14, no. 6, 2005, pp. 1109–1143.

Hoffman, Jeff. "Engineering the Space Shuttle." *MOOC Learning Materials*, course excerpts from MIT's Department of Aeronautics and Astronautics, in partnership with edx.org, 2018.

Imber, Amantha. "Breakthrough Innovation vs. Disruptive Innovation." *Inventium.com*, 19 Jun., 2013, https://www.inventium.com.au/breakthrough-innovation-vs-disruptive-innovation/.

Indeed. "How to Measure Productivity and Increase Efficiency in the Workplace." *Indeed.com*, 2 Oct. 2020, https://www.indeed.com/career-advice/career-development/how-to-measure-productivity.

Industry Canada. Product Design, Research and Development: A Canadian Manufacturing Perspective. *Publishing and Depository Services*, Public Works and Government Services Canada, Ottawa, 2012, pp. 1–30.

Innovative Solutions Canada. From Innovation, Science and Economic Development Canada. *Government of Canada*, 11 Jul. 2019, http://www.ic.gc.ca/eic/site/101.nsf/eng/home/.

Isa, S. S. and Liem, A. "Classifying Physical Models and Prototypes in the Design Process: A Study on the Economical and Usability Impact of Adopting Models and Prototypes in the Design Process." *International Design Conference – Design 2014*, Dubrovnik Croatia, 19–22 May 2014, pp. 1–12.

Johnson, W. Mark, *"Seizing the White Space." Featured Interview*. Emerald Group Publishing Limited, Apr. 2010, pp. 1–6.

Jönbrink, Anna-Karim. Engineering Design for a Circular Economy. *MOOC Learning Materials*, course excerpts from Delft University of Technology, in partnership with edx.org, 2018.

Kamuriwo, Dzidziso S., & Baden-Fuller, Charles. "Knowledge integration using product R&D outsourcing in biotechnology." *Research Policy*, vol. 45, 2016, pp. 1031–1045, London: Elsevier B.V., 2016, pp. 1031–1045, http://dx.doi.org/10.1016/j.respol.2016.02.009.

Karimov, Aziz. "Industrialization and Industrial Policy in South Korea: Some Development Lessons For Transiting Estonia," *United Nations University – World Institute for Development Economics Research, Tartu*, 2013, pp. 3–21, http://www.mtk.ut.ee/sites/default/files/mtk/dokumendid/karimov_industrialization_and_industrial_policy_in_south_korea.pdf.

Kaspar, Jerome and Michael Vielhaber. "Fiber-Reinforced Composite Design Within A Lightweight and Material-Oriented Development Process." *21stInternational Conference On Engineering Design*, Iced17, 21-25 Aug. 2017, The University of British Columbia, Vancouver, Canada, pp. 329–338.

Khairuzzaman, Akm. *3D Printing in Drug Development & Emerging Health Care.*" Center for Drug Evaluation and Research (CDER)/ Food and Drugs Administration (FDA), (2020), pp. 1–49, www.fda.gov.

Kernodle, Melanie. "7 Characteristics of A Highly Productive Mindset." *Lifehack.org*, 2 Nov. 2020.

Kim, Chan W. and Mauborgne Renée. "Blue Ocean Strategy: Blue Ocean Strategy Tools and Frameworks." *Blueoceanstrategy.com*, 2014, pp. 4–28, https://www.scribd.com/document/371155007/Blue-Ocean-Strategy-Tools-Frameworks.

Koen, P. A., et al. "Managing the Front End of Innovation—Part I: Results from a Three-Year Study." *Research-Technology Management*, vol. 57, no. 2, May/Jun. 2014, pp. 34–43, DOI: 10.5437/08956308X5702145.

Levinson, Chelsea. "Definition of the Manufacturing Industry." *Bizfluent.com*, 11 Jun. 2018, https://bizfluent.com/facts-6853113-definition-manufacturing-industry.html.

Llopis, Glenn. "5 Ways Leaders Enable Innovation In their Teams." *Forbes.com*, 7 Apr. 2014, https://www.forbes.com/sites/glennllopis/2014/04/07/5-ways-leaders-enable-innovation-in-their-teams/#4843aad88c4c.

Lohrengel, Armin. Engineering Design for a Circular Economy. *MOOC Learning Materials*, course excerpts from Delft University of Technology, in partnership with edx.org, 2018.

Lowden, Tim. "User Experience (UX) vs. Customer Experience (CX): What's the Dif?" *Dogital.gov – General Services Administration's (GSA) Technology Transformation Services*, 7 Jul. 2014, https://digital.gov/2014/07/07/user-experience-ux-vs-customer-experience-cx-what's-the-dif.

Mankins, Michael. "Great Companies Obsess Over Productivity, Not Efficiency." *Harvard Business Review*, 1 Mar. 2017, https://hbr.org/2017/03/great-companies-obsess-over-productivity-not-efficiency?referral=03758&cm_vc=rr_item_page.top_right.

Manyika et al. *Global growth: Can Productivity Save the Day in an Aging World? The McKinsey Global Institute (MGI)*, San Francisco, Jan. 2015, pp. vi–vii & 1-122.

MaRS. "Value Proposition: A Reflection of the Relationship between Your Customer and Brand." *Learn.marsdd.com*, 2020a, https://learn.marsdd.com/article/value-proposition-a-reflection-of-the-relationship-between-your-customer-and-brand/.

MaRS. "Elements of Product's Value Proposition: Functional, Self-expressive and Emotional Benefits." *Learn.marsdd.com*, 2020b, https://learn.marsdd.com/article/elements-of-a-products-value-proposition-functional-self-expressive-and-emotional-benefits/.

Mathews, John A. "Design of Industrial and Supra-Firm Architectures: Growth and Sustainability." *Journal of Organization Design*, vol. 1, no. 2, Aug. 2012, pp. 42–69, doi:10.7146/jod.6454.

Marti, Jesus. "What Can You Expect From Physical Prototypes." *Medium.com*,

6 Sep. 2019, https://medium.com/abilista/limitations-physical-prototype-c2981aca084a.

Marinho, J. P., et al. "The Relationship between Product Architecture and Mass Customization in [the] Housing Sector." Industrialization, prefabrication, assembly and open building, *Proceedings IGLC-22*, Oslo, Jun. 2014, pp. 1007–15.

McMillan, Stewart. "6 reasons you should be using CNC machines." *Softtech.com*, 14 Jan. 2020, https://softtech.com/resources/6-reasons-using-cnc-machines/.

Mehta, Kumar. "How To Turn An Innovation Failure Into Success." *Forbes Media LLC*, 11 Mar. 2019, https://www.forbes.com/sites/kmehta/2019/03/11/how-to-turn-an-innovation-failure-into-success/#7becbe523fc7.

Metal Supermarkets. "The Difference between Ferrous and Non-Ferrous Metal." *Metalsupermarkets,com*, 23 Sep. 2015.

Miltenović, Aleksandar, et al. "Role and Importance of Lightweight Design in the Product Development." COMET a 2014: 2nd International Scientific Conference; University of East Sarajevo, Faculty of Mechanical Engineering, Conference on Mechanical Engineering Technologies and Applications. 2nd-5th Dec. 2014; Jahorina B&H, Republic of Srpska, 2014, pp. 529–38.

Montague, Monty. "The Amazing Role of Aesthetics in Product Design." *Boltgroup.com*, 21 Jun., 2017, pp. 1–4, https://boltgroup.com/aesthetics-in-product-design.

Mukasyan, Alexander. Materials Science and Engineering. *MOOC Learning Materials* – course excerpts, University of Notre dame, IndianaBrem, and Moscow Institute of Steel and Alloy, in partnership with edx.org, 2019.

MultiCam Canada. "6 Advantages of CNC Machining Over Conventional Machining." *Multicam.ca*, 14 Feb. 2017, https://multicam.ca/6-advantages-cnc-machining/.

Newey, Lance. "Portfolio management: Getting the right mix of innovation projects:" in Innovation: From Plan to Product. MOOC Learning Materials, excerpts from University of Queensland, in partnership with edx.org, 2018.

Newman, Daniel. "Innovation vs. Transformation: The Difference In A Digital World." *Forbes.com*, 16 Feb. 2017, https://www.forbes.com/sites/danielnewman/2017/02/16/innovation-vs-transformation-the-difference-in-a-digital-world/#5e5a0ec065e8.

Nibusinessinfo. "User-Centered Design: Advantages of User-centered Design." *Invest Northern Ireland in partnership with indirect government services*, 2020b, https://www.nibusinessinfo.co.uk/content/advantages-user-centred-design.

Nibusinessinfo. "User-centered design: User-centered design process." *Invest Northern Ireland in partnership with indirect government services*, 2020c, https://www.nibusinessinfo.co.uk/content/user-centred-design-process.

Nibusinessinfo. "User-Centered Design: Advantages of Inclusive Design." *Invest Northern Ireland in partnership with indirect government services*, 2020d, https://www.nibusinessinfo.co.uk/content/advantages-inclusive-design.

Ohno, Kenichi. "The Economic Development of Japan: The Path Travelled by Japan as a Developing Country." *GRIPS Development Forum*, National Graduate Institute for Policy Studies, Tokyo, 2005, pp. 2–215.

OptiProERP. "5 Quality Assurance Best Practices for Manufacturers."

OptiProERP,com, 2020, https://www.optiproerp.com/blog/5-quality-assurance-best-practices-for-manufacturers/amp.

Owen, Charles L."Design, Advanced Planning and Product Development," 3o Congresso Brasileiro de Pesquisa e Desenvolvimento em Design, Rio de Janeiro, Brazil: 26 Oct. 1998. International Symposium: Nuevos Metodos & Tecnologias para el Diseño de Productos, Santiago, Chile: Nov. 12, 1998, pp. 1–13.

Owen, Charles L. "Product Integrity by Design." *Institute of Design*, Illinois Institute of Technology Chicago, 1991, pp. 1–5.

Peck, David. Engineering Design for a Circular Economy. *MOOC Learning Materials*, course excerpts from Delft University of Technology, in partnership with edx.org, 2018.

Penker, Magnus, et al. Sustainable Growth and Profits: Making Your Innovation Strategy, Organization, and Initiatives. *Innovation 360°*, Volume 5: The Complete Guide to Business Innovation, CreateSpace Indepedent Publishing Patform, 1st Edition, 14 Feb. 2018, pp. 1–158.

Polyplastics. "What Is Injection Molding?" *Polyplastics.com*, 2020, https://www.polyplastics.com/en/support/mold/outline/.

Productboard. "Product-Led Growth." *Productboard.com*, 2020, https://www.productboard.com/glossary/product-led-growth.

Productled. "What Is Product-Led Growth." *Productled.org*, 2020, https://www.productled.org/foundations/what-is-product-led-growth#Chap1.

Powell, W. W., et al. "Interorganizational Collaboration and the Locus of Innovation: Networks of Learning in Biotechnology." *Administrative Science Quarterly,* vol. 41, 1996, pp. 287–306.

Prumbohm, Max. "Design for Repair." Engineering Design for a Circular Economy. *MOOC Learning Materials*, course excerpts from Delft University of Technology, in partnership with edx.org, 2018.

Rifkin, Jeremy. *"The Third Industrial Revolution: How the Internet, Green Electricity, and 3-D Printing are Ushering in a Sustainable Era of Distributed Capitalism."* World Economy, New York City, 2012, pp. 8–12. www.worldfinancialreview.com.

Rocha, Cecília Gravina Da. A Conceptual Framework for Defining Customization Strategies in the House – Building Sector. Thesis Presented to the Postgraduate Program in Civil Engineering of the Federal University of Rio Grande do Sul as part of the requirements for the Degree of Doctor in Engineering,Porto Alegre: PPGEC/UFRGS, 6 Dec. 2011, https://lume.ufrgs.br/handle/10183/38795.

Rogers, Tony. "Everything You Need To Know About Injection Molding." *Creativemechanisms.com*, 21 Dec. 2015, https://www.creativemechanisms.com/blog/everything-you-need-to-know-about-injection-molding.

Rothaermel, Frank T. and David L. Deeds. "Exploration and Exploitation Alliances in Biotechnology: A System of New Product Development." *Strategic Management Journal,* vol. 25, 2004, pp. 201–221. doi: https://doi.org/10.1002/smj.376.

Russell, Sean. "Types of Plastic Manufacturing." *Bizfluent.com*, 26 Sep. 2017, https://bizfluent.com/list-6361007-types-plastic-manufacturing.html.

Saario, Ari. "Five Steps to Successful Commercialization of an Innovation – Can the Pitfalls Be Avoided?" *Valmet.com*, 2020, https://www.valmet.com/media/articles/experts-voice/five-steps-to-successful-commercialization-of-an-innovation/.

Sadasivam, Magesh. "What Is the Difference between 2D Printing and 3D

Printing?" *Quora.com*, 1 Aug. 2019, https://www.quora.com/What-is-the-difference-between-2D-printing-and-3D-printing.

Satell, Greg. "How To Manage Innovation." *Forbes Media LLC*, 7 Mar. 2013, https://www.forbes.com/sites/gregsatell/2013/03/07/how-to-manage-innovation-2/#7e6b34784785.

Satell, Greg. "4 Types of Innovation (And How to Approach Them)." *DigitalTonto*, 16 May 2012a, https://www.digitaltonto.com/2012/4-types-of-innovation-and-how-to-approach-them/.

Satell, Greg. "The Truth About Innovation." *DigitalTonto.com*, 3 Jun. 2012b, https://www.digitaltonto.com/2012/the-truth-about-innovation/. Accessed 30Mar.2020.

Schlaepfer, Ralf C., et al."Industry 4.0: Challenges and solutions for the digital transformation and use of exponential technologies." Deloitte AG, Zurich: The Creative Studio, 27 May 2015, pp. 1–26.

Skidmore, Paul. "11 Tips for Good Ergonomic Product Design and Development." *Cadcrowd.com*, 12 Dec. 2018, https://www.cadcrowd.com/blog/11-tips-for-good-ergonomic-product-design-and-development.

SlideModel. "Product-Led Growth (PLG): The Ultimate SaaS Business Growth Strategy To Pursue." *SlideModel.com*, 20 May 2020b, https://slidemodel.com/product-led-growth-plg.

Spanjer, Willy. Engineering Design for a Circular Economy. *MOOC Learning Materials*, course excerpts from Delft University of Technology, in partnership with edx.org, 2018.

Sparkonix. "Types of EDM Machines? Its Applications and Benefits." *Sparkonix (India) – Sparknix.com*, 30 Aug. 2019, https://www.sparkonix.com/types-of-edm-machines-its-application-and-benefits/.

Specht, Günter, et al. *F&E-Management: Kompetenz im Innovations management.* UTB für Wissenschaft, Stuttgart Schaffer-Poeschel, 2002.

Stadler, Antonia. "*Challenges and Solutions for the Digital Transformation and Use of Exponential Technologies.*" Deloitte AG, Zurich: The Creative Studio, 27 May 2015, pp. 1–25.

Stahel, Walter R. *The Performance Economy.* 2nd Edition. Palgrave Macmillan, London, 2010.

Steen, John. "Corporate Innovation: What Is 'Failure' in Managing Innovation." Innovation: From Plan to Product. *MOOC Learning Materials*, course excerpts from University of Queensland Business School, Australia in partnership with edx.org, 2018a.

Steen, John. "Using Scenarios to Test Your Innovation Strategy." Innovation: From Plan to Product. *MOOC Learning Materials*, course excerpts from University of Queensland Business School, Australia in partnership with edx.org, 2018b.

Stroud, Samanda. "Business Tips for New Product Design and Development." *Cadcrowd.com*, 11 Sept. 2018, https://www.cadcrowd.com/blog/business-tips-for-new-product-design-development.

Studer, Jesse. "Elastomer and Plastic Materials." *Valve Magazine*, 02 Jul. 2019, https://www.valvemagazine.com/magazine/sections/materials-q-a/10034-elastomer-and-plastic-materials.html.

TeachEngineering. *Introduction to Material Science and Engineering. TeachEngineering.org*, Engineering University of Colorado, 2020, pp. 1.28.

Tcagley. "Metrics: Four Types of Productivity." *Software Process and Management*, 5 Apr. 2016, https://tcagley.wordpress.com/2016/04/05/metrics-four-types-of-productivity/.

The Productivity Commission (PC). "What is Productivity and How Is It Measured?" *PC News – Australian Government*, May 2015, pp. 17–19, https://www.pc.gov.au/.

Timmons, Jay and David Farr. *"Competing to Win: Manufacturers' Agenda For Economic Growth And American Exceptionalism."* Washington, DC: National Association of Manufacturers, Feb. 2017, pp. 1–25.

Tsuru, Tsuyoshi and Motohiro Morishima. "Product Architecture, Organizational Design, and HRM Practices: Comparing Japanese, Korean, and Chinese Firms." *Hitotsubashi University Research Project of Policies for East Asia*, Hitotsubashi University, Fukino Project Discussion Paper Series, No. 027, Tokyo, Apr. 2011, pp. 1–26.

Ullman, David G. *The Mechanical Design Process.* Mcgraw-Hill Series in Mechanical Engineering, 3th Edition. McGraw-Hill Higher Education, New York, 2003.

University of Queensland Business School. Innovation: From Plan to Product. *MOOC Learning Materials*, excerpts of the course description from University of Queensland Business School, Australia, in partnership with edx.org, 2018.

U.S. Bureau of Labor Statistics. "Productivity 101." *BLS.gov*, 2020. Accessed 15 Nov. 2020.

Varotsis, Alkaois B. "Introduction to FDM 3D Printing." *3Dhubs.com*, 2020, https://www.3dhubs.com/knowledge-base/pla-vs-abs-whats-difference/.

Viki, Tendayi. "Six Principles for Creating a Good Corporate Innovation Process," *Forbes Media LLC*, 26 Mar. 2018, https://www.forbes.com.

Wagner, Nancy. "What Is a Manufacturing Process?" *Bizfluent.com*, 26 Sept. 2017, https://bizfluent.com/facts-7417479-manufacturing-process-.html.

Wang, Hua. "Innovation in Product Architecture: A Study of the Chinese Automobile Industry." *Asia Pacific Journal of Management,* Springer, vol. 25, no. 3, Sep. 2008, pp. 509–35.

Wen, Yi. The Making of an Economic Superpower: Unlocking China's Secret of Rapid Industrialization. World Scientific Publishing Company, Singapore, 2016, pp. 1–337.

3D Engineer. "2D vs. 3D Printing." *3DEngr.com*, 15 Jun. 2018. Accessed 11 Nov. 2020.

5 Organizing Beyond the Frontiers of Competition and Disruptive Change: Profitability, Productivity, and Sustainability Perspectives

Introduction

This chapter explores THE ART OF COMPETITIVENESS by bonding the causal links between the factors of profitability, productivity, and sustainability. The chapter also found that the relationship between profitability, productivity, and sustainability tends to follow a cycle, especially in resilient organizations. In addition, this relation also has a contagious effect, that is, poor performance in one of these factors will either directly or indirectly contaminate the others. But a competitive edge in one of the factors will not necessarily guarantee that it will spill over to the other factors. That said, every company has responsibilities to multiple groups of people inside and outside the firm, and those various groups often have competing interests. For instance, employees generally want higher wages and more benefits, but investors who have risked their money in the company want management to keep costs low so profits are strong enough to drive up the stock price. Both sides have a valid position; neither one is "right" nor "wrong."

In creating a competitive edge over other companies in the market, firms generally tend to adopt one or more of three major sequential orientations:

1. Creating excellent ways of attracting new customers
2. Strategizing on retaining existing customers
3. Winning customers from competitors.

The Chinese military genius and writer Sun Tzu had long noticed the trick on how to outperform and outclass a more powerful adversary or competitor since the 5th century. As contained in his iconic military treatise "The Art of War," this states that: *If you know the enemy and know yourself, you need not fear the result of a hundred battles. If you know yourself but not the enemy, for every victory gained you will also suffer a defeat. If you know neither the enemy nor yourself, you will succumb in every battle.* Interestingly, this landmark ingenuity has equally continued to win the admiration of business executives especially in Asia and other emerging markets – who use this reasoning to aid strategic, operational, and sometimes tactical decision making.

This takes us to the concept of *catching existing waves vs. creating new waves*. Entrepreneurs and established businesses who catch existing waves can prosper at the outset just because the trend is on their side, as market imbalances disappear, those who had never developed distinctive capabilities or established defensible competitive positions tend to crash. Thus, wave riders must anticipate market saturation, intensifying competition, and the next wave. They have to abandon the me-too approach in favor of a new, more durable business model. For those creating new waves, they are radical in their approach as they are usually the industry pioneers who do and make things happen.

5.1 Preparing as a Learning Organization for Radical Innovation and Disruptive Change

5.1.1 Why It Will Become an Increasingly Urgent Priority

Preparing as a learning organization for radical innovation and disruptive change is arguably an urgent priority for industry leaders, runners-up, and early adaptors. Today's business environment requires a different worldview – as the benefits from improving efficiency (i.e., by doing the same with less input) appear to have petered out. Put in another way, efficiency (bottom-line growth) is no longer the secret to superior performance. So what about productivity? In affirmation, Mankins (2017) opines that in the coming decades, it will be critical for business leaders to adopt a productivity mindset (i.e., by doing more with the same input). Having said that, instead of focusing on continuously managing the denominator (input), by cutting headcount or labor hours, executives should identify ways to boost the numerator, and increase output.[1] He suggests that by systematically removing obstacles to productivity, deploying talent strategically, and inspiring a larger percentage of their workforce, leaders can dramatically improve productivity and reignite top-line growth.[2]

As a rule of thumb, any business must, first of all, understand what factors that current competitors work on and compete on. Stroud (2018) argues that customers are interested in *value, ease of use, and ingenuity*. In a related development, Grace (2019) argues that common to every industry, city, and society, there are unresolved issues for which conventional methods and wisdom have not yet been able to overcome. It is within this framework that THE ART OF COMPETITIVENESS resides. For instance, Stam and Garnsey (2008) argue that radical changes in ICT and biotechnology have created market opportunities that are more effectively developed by new firms than by established companies.[3] However, Grace (2019) argues that incumbent firms that are very effective at radical innovation are more likely to succeed in warding off credible threats posed by disruptive innovation.[4]

In a related development, Gustafsson and Johnson (2012) argue that from a managerial perspective, it is beneficial when working with *incremental innovation* to spend time with customers, or become immersed in the customer's context as much as possible. According to Victorino *et al.* (2005), examples of this can be found within the hospitality industry, where understanding of customer choice has been found to significantly facilitate service innovation. To concur, Olson and Bakke (2001) suggest that treating customers as more equal partners in the process increases the chances of product and market success.[5]

However, the communication process of co-creation for radical innovation seems to behave quite differently from what applies to incremental innovation. Gustafsson *et al.* (2012) found that there are two dimensions that are significant in radical innovation – these are *frequency* and *content.* With respect to *frequency,* they argue that companies should learn from customers through *frequent contact,* which is the same as in the case of incremental innovations.[6] But, with regards to *content,* they argue that companies should not be overly concerned with suggestions of the *content* of a potential new offering. Especially as radical solutions can often be considered unthinkable in advance or hard to imagine, but customers know a good idea when they see and use it. The reason why it is difficult to suggest solutions to customers that are truly radical (i.e., often considered unthinkable or hard to imagine) is that customers create solutions based on their previous experiences of usage of different products or services.[7] To concur, Steve Jobs, the late CEO of Apple strongly argued that a lot of times people don't know what they want until you show it to them."[8] This is true because contents or solutions that are radically new people, people too often find it hard to mentally process the information - until you show them a workable product model. This is so because they are unable to find appropriate previous experiences of usage to do a comparison with the radically new idea.

This argument is also shared by Dunn III (1992), who observed that *Technology, Economics, and Politics – all do change, but human nature does not.* And that human nature is such that people will only change their old way of doing things when it is absolutely clear that a new way offers something much better, or it is absolutely clear that the old way is not working at all. Consequently, organizations that see themselves as successful are usually highly resistant to change – past success is often the enemy of necessary change.[9] On this keynote, Dunn III (1992) believes that this trend owes much to the fact that *each generation looks at history* through the tinted lenses of its own time and experience.[10] Little wonder why he further emphasized that *human resistance to change is particularly strong in organizations that see themselves as successful and dominant,* whereas *organizations seeking leverage against a more powerful adversary are most willing to assume the risks inherent in adopting a new framework for change.*[11]

5.1.2 What It Takes to Preparing for Radical Innovation and Disruptive Change

Creating the Culture of Value Creation

As the world is always changing, we should not make the mistake to think that customers' tastes will stay the same for long. To this end, Charles (2019) argues that your brand needs to be able to change with the times and keep up with the evolution of the surrounding culture.[12] And that regardless of what size your business is, make sure that all of the leadership from top to bottom is on board with being flexible. The more your company can able to move quickly and easily, the better.[13]

In a similar vein, Ceru (2018) found that the critical issue about the business ecosystem is getting out of your comfort zone and continuously reflect not only how you can ensure that your business will survive, but how it thrives over time. In addition, he posits that all businesses and all initiatives face constant competitive pressure from ever-changing business factors. As a result, the business ecosystem is never static and you cannot afford to be static either – any business that does not adapt and change over time is doomed to extinction.[14]

Consequently, preparing your company as a learning organization for radical innovation and disruptive change will become an increasingly urgent priority.[15] As we saw earlier, the Chinese military genius and writer Sun Tzu, had long noticed this trick since the 5th century, as contained in his iconic military treatise "The Art of War," which states that: *If you know the enemy and know yourself, you need not fear the result of a hundred battles. If you know yourself but not the enemy, for every victory gained you will also suffer a defeat. If you know neither the enemy nor yourself, you will succumb in every battle.* Interestingly, this landmark ingenuity has equally continued to win the admiration of business executives especially in Asia and other emerging markets – who use this reasoning to aid strategic, operational, and sometimes tactical decision making.

Again, as we saw earlier, this takes us to the concept of *catching existing waves versus creating new waves.* In this regard, entrepreneurs and established businesses who catch existing waves can prosper at the outset just because the trend is on their side, as market imbalances disappear, those who had never developed distinctive capabilities or established defensible competitive positions tend to crash. Thus, wave riders must anticipate market saturation, intensifying competition, and the next wave. They have to abandon the me-too approach in favor of a new, more durable business model. For those creating new waves, they are radical in their approach as they are usually the industry pioneers who do and make things happen.

It is worth mentioning that whether *catching existing waves or creating new waves*, firms generally invest in two types of global R&D: adaptive and asset-seeking.[16] *Adaptive R&D* aims to adjust product offerings to local market conditions; it tends to be closely related to production activities and is required to ensure that products meet customers' needs, and that time to market is minimized.[17] *Asset-seeking R&D* investment aims to acquire strategic assets such as new technologies and to gain access to expertise. Thus, with this type of investment, manufacturers generally consider supply-related factors in locating R&D facilities.[18] On the logic of the resource-based view (RBV) of the firm, as we saw earlier, Jay Barney argues that firms possess valuable resources and rare resources, and the appropriate use of such resources *will lead to competitive advantage*. In addition, we saw that if a firm can protect against resource imitation, substitution or transfer, the competitive advantage can even be sustained over a long period.[19]

Competing on price has traditionally been a viable option for businesses throughout history. But besides competing on price as a conventionally viable competitive tool, this chapter focuses on organizing beyond the frontiers of competition, and it identifies six critical strategic options businesses can explore. These are:

- Competing on Superior Product Appearance and Branding in Consumer Choice
- Competing on a Mix of Product Extension and New Product Development Strategies
- Competing on Customer-Centricity and Customer Success Management
- Exploring Product-Life Options in the Circular Economy Design
- Tapping into the Rationale of Big Data and Predictive Analytics
- Leveraging Best Strategies for Robotics Technology and AI.

But for some technical reasons, this chapter will provide detailed discussions on the first two strategic competitive options, which are: (1) Competing on superior product appearance and branding in consumer choice; (2) and competing on a mix of product extension and new product development strategies. While some key highlights relating to *competing on price* and the four other strategic options we will be briefly discussed. These are:

- Competing on Price
- Exploring Product-Life Options in the Circular Economy Design
- Tapping into the Rationale of Big Data and Predictive Analytics
- Leveraging Best Strategies for Robotics Technology and AI
- Competing on Customer-Centricity and Customer Success Management

COMPETING ON PRICE: THE BIG PICTURE

We mentioned earlier that if a company does not have much *pricing power,* an increase in their prices would lessen the demand for their products. A company that has substantial pricing power is one that provides a rare or unique product with few rivals in the market. In this case, if the company raises its prices, the increase may not affect demand because there are no alternative products on the market that consumers can choose instead.[20]

COMPETING ON CIRCULAR PRODUCT DESIGN: THE BIG PICTURE

It is the case with any design decision and solution that an optimum is looked for, and a balance drawn between cost and benefit. Within the framework of circular economy product design, balancing the needs against the impact on the environment is becoming increasingly more difficult for manufacturers; as they strive to develop new products and processes. This calls for the use of product life-cycle assessment.[21] Product life-cycle assessment (PLCA) is a technique now widely used to assess and evaluate the impact of the product or packaging through the extraction and processing of raw materials, the production phase, and life-cycle processes including distribution, use, and final disposal of the product.[22]

Research suggests that each year, some 80% of the material value worth $2.6 trillion of material in fast-moving consumer goods is thrown away, and never recovered. But in a circular economy, more of this material would be used again in some form.[23] To concur, Rossé, Stuchtey, and Vanthournout (2016) found that the circular economy, enabled by new technology, could help Europe to improve its resource productivity by up to 3%. In addition, they estimate that by 2030, this surge would not only generate cost savings as high as €600 billion a year (and an additional €1.2 trillion in other benefits), but could also translate into a GDP increase of up to seven percentage points over the current development scenario. This makes the promise of the circular economy quite significant.[24] That said, companies that successfully design products for a circular economy stand to capture considerable value and create lasting, rewarding relationships with customers.[25]

TAPPING INTO THE RATIONALE OF BIG DATA AND PREDICTIVE ANALYTICS: WHY IT MATTERS?

Predictive analytics uses the data you already hold in your business to look forward and tell you what's going to happen in the future. Equipped with such tools that can automate this process for your business decision making – renders it fact-based and truly data-driven rather than based on subjective judgments and hunches.[26] Meanwhile, there is evidence that the combination of big data and predictive analytics in all domains has the great potential to positively affect decision support and operations, such as cost management systems and resource allocation.[27]

As advancement in technology is making it economically feasible to store and analyze huge amounts of data, Big Data includes a mix of structured, semi-structured, and unstructured real-time data originating from a variety of sources. Predictive analytics on its part encompasses a variety of statistical techniques from modeling, machine learning, and data mining that analyze current and historical facts to make predictions about the future, or otherwise unknown events. Further, predictive analytics provides a methodology for tapping intelligence from large data sets.[28] In the reasoning of Basılgan (2011), it is possible to guess that Joseph Schumpeter (1934) had already predicted the transition from Data-Centric process to Predictive Analytics.[29]

That being said, many visionary companies such as Google, Amazon, etc. have realized the potential of big data and predictive analytics in gaining a competitive advantage. These techniques provide several opportunities like discovering patterns or better optimization algorithms. Managing and analyzing big data also constitutes few challenges – notably; size, quality, reliability, and completeness of data.[30] Consequently, this signals some kind of a paradigm shift in terms of analytical focus - that is, a shift from descriptive analytics to predictive analytics.

LEVERAGING BEST STRATEGIES FOR ROBOTICS TECHNOLOGY AND AI

According to Ciocarlie (2018), robotics is the science of building devices that physically interact with their environment, and that the most useful robots do it precisely, powerfully, repeatedly, tirelessly, fast, or some combinations of these. Meanwhile, the most interesting robots may even do it intelligently.[31] In the reasoning of Keisner, Raffo, and Wunsch-Vincent (2015), artificial intelligence (AI) is generally defined as its own area of computer science; that is focused on computer-based devices being capable of making intelligent human-like decisions.[32]

What is Robotics? According to Keisner, Raffo, and Wunsch-Vincent (2015), robots are evolving from programmed automation, over semi-autonomous to more autonomous complex systems. Meanwhile, as far as automation is concerned, a robot has the ability to interpret its environment and adjust its actions to achieve a goal. Fully autonomous systems are able to operate and make "decisions" to complete tasks without human interaction.[33] Owen-Hill (2017) defines robotics as a branch of technology that deals with robots. Robots are programmable machines that are usually able to carry out a series of actions autonomously, or semi-autonomously. He identifies three important factors which he argues, constitute a robot:

1. Robots interact with the physical world via sensors and actuators.
2. Robots are programmable.
3. Robots are usually autonomous or semi-autonomous.[34]

As an interesting development in the robotics industry, "cobots" are a new generation of robots that don't need to be walled off from humans – they work alongside employees.

Getting It Right with Artificial Intelligence (AI) Technology Scope and Development of Artificial Intelligence Artificial intelligence (AI) is a branch of computer science. It involves developing computer programs to complete tasks that would otherwise require human intelligence. AI algorithms can tackle learning, perception, problem-solving, language-understanding, and/or logical reasoning. In other words, the definition of artificial intelligence (AI) would need to fulfill two requirements:

1. An area of computer science that deals with giving machines the ability to seem like they have human intelligence
2. the capability of a machine to imitate intelligent human behavior

Owen-Hill (2017) found that AI is used in many ways within the modern world, for example, AI algorithms are used in Google searches, Amazon's recommendation engine, and SatNav route finders. He argues that the key aspect that differentiates AI from more conventional programming is the word "intelligence." Non-AI programs simply carry out a defined sequence of instructions, while AI programs mimic some level of human intelligence.[35] In this regard, *artificially intelligent robots* are the bridge between *robotics* and *AI*. These are robots that are controlled by AI programs. But many robots are not artificially intelligent. For instance, until quite recently, all industrial robots could only be programmed to carry out a repetitive series of movements. As you can guess, repetitive movements do not require artificial intelligence. Consequently, non-intelligent robots are quite limited in their functionality. This is because AI algorithms are often necessary to allow the robot to perform more complex tasks.[36]

Artificial Intelligence (AI) As a Unique Technology Wave Taddeo and Luciano (2018); and Yang *et al.* (2018) found that AI applications are becoming pervasive as users rely on them to deal with a variety of tasks, from delivering goods to ensuring national defense. Assigning these tasks to AI brings huge benefits to societies. It lowers costs, reduces risks, increases consistency and reliability of the information, and enables new solutions to complex problems. To this end, there are indications that AI applications can lower diagnostic errors by 85% in breast cancer patients, and AI cybersecurity systems can reduce the average time to identify and neutralize cyberattacks from 101 days to a few hours.[37]

However, Asaro (2012); and Yang *et al.* (2018) argue that delegating tasks to AI applications may also lead to harmful, unintended consequences, especially when it involves sensitive decisions or tasks and excludes or even precludes human supervision.[38]

The European Commission in its *Draft Ethics Guidelines for Trustworthy AI* reasoned that having the capability to generate tremendous benefits for individuals and society, AI also gives rise to certain risks that should be properly managed. Given that, on the whole, AI's benefits outweigh its risks, we must ensure to follow the road that maximizes the benefits of AI while minimizing its risks.[39] To ensure that we stay on the right track, they suggested that a human-centric approach to AI is needed; forcing us to keep in mind that the development and use of AI should not be seen as a means in itself, but as having the goal to increase human well-being. Trustworthy AI should be the focus since human beings will only be able to confidently and fully reap the benefits of AI if they can trust the technology.[40]

Therefore, Artificial intelligence (AI) is not just a new technology that requires a regulation. It is a powerful force that is reshaping daily practices, personal and professional interactions, and environments. Thus, for the well-being of humanity, it is crucial that this power is used as a force of good. *Ethics* plays a key role in this process by ensuring that regulations of AI will harness its potential while mitigating its risks.[41] Finally, the key that makes AI different than most other technologies is its strong research background.

COMPETING ON CUSTOMER-CENTRICITY AND CUSTOMER SUCCESS MANAGEMENT

A Recap of Customer-Centricity Again, we said earlier that while *customer experience* (CX) summarizes all customer perceptions created during interactions with your brand across various channels, customer-centricity stands for a wider commitment to ensuring the absolute success of every customer heading your way.[42] In addition, customer-centricity appears as a stark contrast to previously dominant product-centricity – an approach where a company tries to sell as many products as possible; by every means necessary with the hope that more people will buy from them, instead of cultivating long-term profitable relationships with the existing customers. That said, according to an American proverb,

"To keep a customer demands as much skill as to win one."[43] However, while product-centricity has been around for much longer than customer-centricity, the former practice is gradually losing its viability.[44]

We saw again that Customer Experience (CX) is the new battlefield for brands, as it has overtaken price as a key factor impacting purchase decisions both among B2B and B2C buyers. This makes customer-centricity now the key to winning more business.[45]

The Rationale of Customer Success Management The essence of customer success management (CSM) is to create real-time visibility into common customer issues and allocate sufficient resources in advance for guiding the customers through bottlenecks.[46] This takes us to the question: what's the difference between Customer Success and Customer or Client Services? Customer/Client success is a continuous effort in ensuring that your customers are on the right track – it's a proactive approach. Customer service is a more reactive approach that assumes post-factum help to experienced problems.[47] As such, companies with an established customer success life-cycle, constantly analyze and brainstorm where a customer may get a potential hitch and try to mitigate those inefficiencies in advance. A simple example would be a digital bank that reduces the number of required forms for opening a new checking account and introducing auto-fill options, rather than waiting until some customer complaints that they couldn't open a new account.[48]

The Customer Success Association – CSA (2019) argues that for any business that depends upon continuing income streams from its customers, the choice is becoming clear: (1) that you either actively manage your customer relationships as strategic portfolio assets; or (2) you effectively cede control over them and your company's future to chance and/or the competition.[49] That being said, the emerging role of Customer Success Management (CSM) is about finding solutions to the core issues of *customer portfolio development, retention and expansion.* According to CSA (2019), to be successful, your program needs to be based on the following three pillars:

- In-depth knowledge of the customers
- Deep or effective expertise in the product being sold
- Extensive domain expertise – that is, industry expertise and business domain knowledge.

Of which, customer acquisition is only the very first step in an extended journey for both customer and company.[50]

Consequently, the pivotal role of the Customer Success Team (CST) is to increase sustainable proven profitability for both the Customers and your Business. Therefore, being able to prove your worth in both directions is the most crucial aspect. In this regard, CSA (2019) argues that virtually all

Customer Success Management initiatives start out as *"churnfighters,"* that is, reactive tactical teams charged with saving an at-risk customer relationship. But as a Customer Success Team, you can't stop there. Of course, the obvious challenge is to gather and use the data from every interaction; to move your team out of *reactive mode* into far more *effective proactive* stances.[51] To accomplish that, most Customer Success (CS) plans embody the integration of functions and activities of Marketing, Sales, Professional Services, Training, and Support into a new profession.[52]

Nurturing the Culture of Value Creation

We said earlier that for businesses to thrive and continuously maintain a competitive edge, it needs to be adaptable to new models, or better still, it should be innovative enough to create new models in its own right, if and when needs arise. To stay ahead of the competition, or beat the competition, it is imperative a business should adapt itself to create new models through radical innovation, and possibly, disruptive innovation for entrepreneurial startup ventures.

But then, for an established firm to actually create these kinds of innovation, it would somehow need to mimic the traditional entrepreneurial start-off process, to a certain controllable extent. To this end, it can make use of the organizational fundamental building blocks also known as the *"genetic" material of the company (see* Fig. 5.1). In effect, it can create a *task force unit* that will give priority of place to the informal OrgDNA building blocks, which by coincidence, is also closely associated with the informalities and flexibilities of the entrepreneurial start-up's conceptual design process. Essentially, it is after this *task force unit* has succeeded to achieve the set target of its radical or innovation process - that it can make real sense to begin the process of integrating this newly created business model, gradually into the mainstream of the formal OrgDNA building blocks.

As shown in Fig. 5.1, once an innovation venture has been integrated into the formal OrgDNA building blocks or common bases, it then produces its synthesized templates in the form of informal OrgDNA building blocks. But much caution needs to be applied when integrating such innovation management process from a *task force unit* into the mainstream of corporate activities – as the former carries the genome or genetic aspects of informality, greater flexibility and tolerance to ideas that are identical to entrepreneurial start-up ventures, and equally those of the task force units engaged in an innovation process.

5.2 Competing on Superior Product Appearance and Branding in Consumer Choice

For many consumers nowadays, product design has become an important means of self-expression. Consumers choose products not just

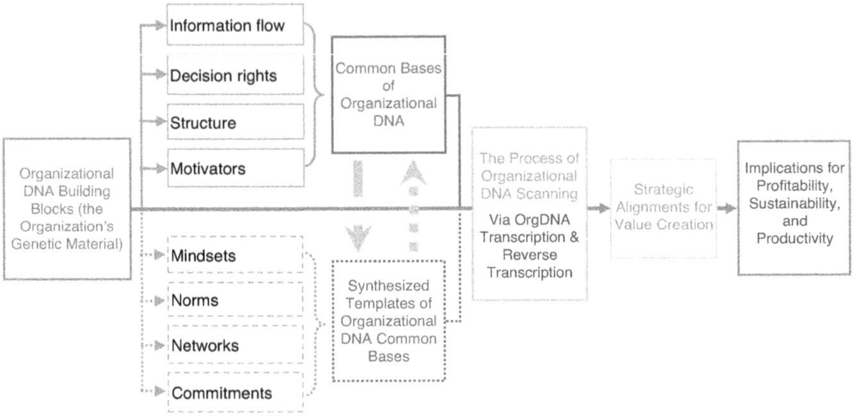

Figure 5.1 How OrgDNA Bases Pair and Their Synthesized Templates Work
Source: Author created.

for what they do, but for what they tell the world about their lifestyle choices. In a similar vein, Montague (2017) opines that people select products in part because of the image they want to project about themselves. People yearn for products with a form that communicates the character, personality, and values they want to be known for – and having this gives them pride in ownership.[53] For example, the purchase of a pair of trainers takes into account many factors such as how comfortable they are, but the overriding reason for buying them may be their appearance and branding. As such, one of the main reasons for choosing one product from another with similar functions is its aesthetic qualities.[54]

Essentially, one of the roles of the designer is to provide the product with the right style or image for a particular target market group. Get this wrong and the product will not sell; get it right then it will become an object of desire for aspiring consumers.[55] In addition, where so many products are mass-produced and sold in their millions, the designer may have to inject a sense of individuality or personality into an object. For instance, the Italian design company *Alessi* is famous for its playful design of affordable objects and appliances for the kitchen, using bright and colorful polymers and stainless steel to create contemporary and humorous products.[56]

5.2.1 The Different Roles of Product Appearance in Consumer Choice

It is critical to strike a balance between having a product that is useful and also looks good. In this regard, Stroud (2018) argues that if your product does not look appealing, then it won't sell, regardless of how useful it might be. Thus, the product should be designed with *function* in mind first, but *aesthetics* should still be considered in the design process.[57]

Furthermore, the appearance of a product can influence consumer choice in different ways. Distinguishing these different appearance roles will help managers to make better use of product appearance as a marketing tool. That being said, based on a literature review, six different roles of product appearance for consumers have been identified: communication of aesthetic, symbolic, functional and ergonomic information, attention drawing, and categorization.[58] In a similar vein, based on a recent study, Muddana (2019) found that the appearance of products influenced consumers' evaluations of them in six different ways: conveying aesthetic appeal, symbolic, function, ergonomics, drawing attention, and categorization.[59]

Furthermore, a study carried out by Creusen and Schoormans (2004) identified six different roles that influenced consumers' evaluation of product choices, which are: (1) aesthetic value, (2) symbolic value, (3) functional value, (4) ease of use or ergonomic value, (5) attention drawing, and (5) ease of categorization of the product.[60] They also found that among the six different roles that influenced consumers' evaluation of product choices, *aesthetic and symbolic roles* were mentioned most often.[61] To this end, Montague (2017) argues that innovation is by definition, new and unfamiliar – and people are not immediately drawn to the unfamiliar, and that's where aesthetics come in. Aesthetics compels people to look, touch, and engage with something new, and it fosters adoption of innovation by providing delight and sparkling emotional connections.[62]

Interestingly, the study of Creusen and Schoormans (2004) also revealed that aesthetic and symbolic values were often intertwined. For example, many of the survey respondents liked a rounded appearance because it looks modern and friendly. Again, someone might like a certain *aesthetic appearance* (e.g., color) but not purchase it because the *symbolic associations* are not suited to his or her person (e.g., a childlike appearance for an adult).[63]

Product Appearance in Aesthetic Product Value

According to Montague (2017)*aesthetics* is one of the ways we judge, feel, and "know" the world.[64] In this regard, aesthetics inspires us to try a product, and influences our adoption of new, unfamiliar products. It reveals content, usage, and function. It provides delight, instills pride, and inspires loyalty.[65] Put in another way, Holbrook (1980) posited that the aesthetic value of a product pertains to the pleasure derived from seeing the product, without consideration of utility.[66] For instance, a consumer can value the "look" of a product purely for its own sake.[67] Aesthetics entails all the visual aspects of a product including font, text size, color, and images.[68] According Bamossy *et al.* (1983) aesthetic responses are primarily emotional or feeling responses, as such, they are very personal.[69] Consequently, it is very likely that when product alternatives are similar in functioning and price, consumers will prefer the one that appeals the most to them aesthetically.[70]

According to Murdoch and Flurscheim (1983), *appearance* of a product communicates messages, as it may look "cheerful," "boring," "friendly," "expensive," "rude," or "childish."[71] Appearance is crucial online. For instance, a critical factor in clinching sales online is the appearance of the product in the photo images.[72] The best brand imaging campaigns have a clear message about what their company stands for. They know how to create a compelling presentation that incorporates all the core offerings, service, and all the values in a way that is pleasing to the eye and easy to understand. This is especially important online because a few seconds is a long time for someone surfing the web. For example, if your message doesn't make an impact within ten seconds, you may likely lose your opportunity to promote your business.[73]

Product Appearance in Symbolic Product Value

Symbolic product value is synonymous to self-expressive benefits as it provides an opportunity for someone to communicate his or her self-image.[74] In the same vein, McCracken (1986) contends that consumer goods carry and communicate symbolic meaning. Hirschman and Holbrook (1982) argue that symbolic value can even be the key determinant for product selection. And according to Levy (1959), symbolic value can even account for the selection of products that are clearly inferior in their tangible characteristics.[75]

LINKING OF BRAND MEANING TO ELEMENTS OF THE SYMBOLIC PRODUCT VALUE

According to Belk (1988), Landon (1974), Sirgy (1982) and Solomon (1983), the choice for a specific product or brand may convey the kind of person you are or want to be; consumers use products to express their (ideal) self-image to themselves and to others. Symbolic product value heightens the connection between the brand and the customer by focusing on something linked to his or her personality. In this way, symbolic product value focuses on the *act of using the product,* as opposed to the *emotional benefits* associated with the result of using the product.[76] In addition, McCracken (1986) and Sirgy (1982) found that symbolic meaning can be coupled to a product or brand on the basis of, amongst other things, advertising, country of origin, or the kind of people using it.[77]

According to Murdoch and Flurscheim (1983), the linking of brand meaning to elements of the symbolic product value will be easier when the associations that these elements engender by themselves correspond to the desired brand image. For example, the use of bright colors and a large size, which is associated with aggression, will make it easier to position a car brand as aggressive. Also, Schmitt and Simonson (1997) found that angular forms are associated with dynamism and masculinity, while roundness evokes softness and femininity.[78] However, the product itself can also communicate symbolic value in a more direct way, namely by its appearance.[79]

CULTURE – SYMBOLIC INTERPRETATION VS. THE AESTHETIC EXPERIENCE

Culture is an important determinant of the interpretations that consumers give and the associations that they have with certain factors of a product's appearance.[80] For instance, Whitfield and Wiltshire (1983) argue that color associations vary from culture to culture. To concur, Muller (2001) found that in America and Europe, white stands for purity and brides traditionally are dressed in white, while in Japan it is a color of mourning. Furthermore, meaning is context dependent. The impression that colors give may change completely by combining certain colors.[81]

Also, the meaning of forms and colors may change in time, as meanings are continuously transformed by movements in art, and fashion, et cetera.[82] The same style can be considered "good taste" at one point in time, while being considered "bad taste" ten years later, because the connotations associated with it or the interpretations given to it have changed. For example, orange was a modern color for clothes, furniture and (plastic) products in the seventies, and later on was generally perceived as old-fashioned and ugly in the eighties, and became used in products and clothing again in the nineties.[83] But Creusen and Schoormans (2004) suggest that *aesthetic and symbolic value should be distinguished,* as they may tend to have opposite influences on preference. For instance, someone who likes a colorful design may not buy it because it looks "too childish."[84]

Product Appearance and Functional Product Value

We saw earlier that a product's functional benefits are based on a product's attribute that provides the customer with functional *utility*. The goal is to select functional benefits that have the greatest impact with customers and support a strong position relative to competitors.[85] Consequently, in order for a product to be successful, it needs to be functional.[86] Löbach (1976) and Veryzer (1995) maintain that the functional value of a product pertains to the utilitarian functions that a product can perform. In other words, it answers the question pertaining to *what* you can use it for.[87]

The utilitarian functions of a product can be directly obvious from its appearance. For example, when you see a handle, you know the product is portable. So product appearance can be proactively used in order to give consumers a certain impression about the functional product value.[88] But, MaRS (2020b) cautions that it is important to keep in mind that functional benefits often fail to differentiate, it can be easy to copy and may even reduce strategic flexibility.[89]

Product Appearance and Ergonomic Product Design

Skidmore (2018) defines ergonomic design as the process of developing a product/service that is easy to use and provides a favorable, enjoyable experience for the end user. It involves creating and designing a product in its most effective and useful form.[90] In a similar vein, Löbach (1976), and Veryzer (1995) contend that the ergonomic value of a product entails the adjustment of a product to human qualities.[91] To that end, product ergonomics or "human factors" concerns the *comprehensibility* and *usability* of a product, the *suitability to perform* and *correctly communicate* its utilitarian functions.[92] According to March (1994), usability entails cognitive aspects of use, such as how logical a product is to operate, as well as emotional aspects – in the sense that it is not frustrating in operation and gives an enjoyable usage experience. So it answers the question pertaining to *how* the end user can use it.

According to Acevedo (2020), ergonomic products are most often; computer products, office equipment, production equipment, travel, and videos.[93] Skidmore 2018) argues that as ergonomic design customizes a product to meet specific user needs, the approach is hugely beneficial for hands-on products such as tools, office equipment, and furniture. He identifies the following as some of the main benefits of ergonomic product design: safety, comfort, ease of use, and enjoyment.[94] That being said, the following tips for ergonomic design can be of great benefit.

1. Create product design goals to give focus and drive. We saw earlier that before starting the design process, it is important to set clear product design goals. And that you could create a checklist for ergonomic viability goals such as:
    - Is the design easy to handle?
    - Could the design cause potential harm or stress?
    - Is the design easy to use/operate?
    - Is the design easy to understand?
2. Find your target customer before considering ergonomics.
3. Ensure your team understands the basics of ergonomics (Skidmore, 2018).
4. Consider ergonomics early in the design process. Ignoring ergonomics

can lead to designs that are likely to fail commercially – as they don't fit the needs of the user.[95]

5. Gather statistical data from customers relating to previous product version (Skidmore, 2018).
6. Look at competitors' designs for inspiration and ergonomic analysis. This is common practice in the world of business – to analyze what your competitors are creating. But, Skidmore (2018) argues that conventional designs are not always ergonomic.
7. Consider which types of ergonomics applies to your product design.
8. Find out what common problems customers have encountered when using this type of product (Skidmore, 2018).
9. Create product prototypes to test ergonomic viability. Prototypes are an integral part of the ergonomic design process, as it enables you to see if what you have researched and designed is applicable to a real-world product. Good prototypes not only communicate with people, but also possess the leverage to persuade people.[96] In this regard, Bo Bennett argues that selling your product idea is the ability to gracefully persuade, and not manipulate a person or persons into a win-win solution.[97]

Attention Drawing Ability of Product Appearance: Psychological Eye-Catching Packaging Design

Things that are visually different from their counterparts tend to stand out and capture our attention. You can use this principle to your advantage, especially as packaging design affects our subconscious mind. For example, if all of your competitors are using blue packaging, consider using yellow or orange to isolate your package and steal the focus.[98] Creusen and Schoormans (2004) argue that gaining attention is an important first step in enabling consumer product purchase.[99] Engel, Blackwell, and Miniard (1995) define attention as the allocation of information processing capacity to a stimulus. As such, people attend to stimuli that contrast with their background and are novel.[100]

People subconsciously respond to visual stimuli. In fact, this is one of the core principles of marketing psychology,[101] sometimes called "Neuromarketing," it applies neuropsychology to content, marketing, and sales as a way to influence purchasing decisions.[102] Packaging design influences our behavior even when we have no intention of buying anything.[103] As such, knowing how to get people to respond favorably to your packaging design will help you sell more products. In a similar vein, Garber (1995) and Garber, Burke, and Jones (2000) found that when a product "stands out" visually from competitive products, chances are higher that consumers will pay attention to the product in a purchase situation, as it "catches their eye." For food products, most especially, the attention-drawing ability of a package has been found to heighten the probability of purchase.[104]

In this regard, (Lundin, 2017) suggests that smart choices in color, structure and shape, texture and touch, and typography can make all the difference, as briefly explained below. Size is also another smart choice to consider.

1. *Color* evokes emotion in packaging design. Color should capture the shopper's attention; color should create appropriate emotional associations; and color should reinforce brand identity.
2. *Structure and shape* influence emotions in packaging design. Shape has the potential to be the single most unique identifier for your product packaging.[105]
3. *Texture and touch* impact reactions in packaging design. Choosing a texture for your packaging that is *pleasant to touch* will encourage customers to hang on to it a bit longer. As such, it will in turn, extend that feeling of psychological ownership and motivate the customer to purchase the item. In addition, packaging textures can influence how people perceive your product – that is, *the way a package feels* can make implications about the product itself. In addition, choosing a packaging texture that reflects what the consumer will find inside, works to your advantage. For instance, if your product is luxurious, then choose packaging material that feels luxurious. Still, if your product is earthy and natural, then a raw, earthy texture may be the right choice.[106]
4. *Typography* evokes emotional reactions in packaging design. Knowing what a font is communicating, independently of the words themselves is vital to making the right font choice. For typography, the following considerations are paramount:

   - Choose fonts for the meaning they convey, not just because they look cool.
   - Select fonts that are easy to read and that convey the essence of your product and brand.[107]

5. *Size* is also an important factor. Creusen and Schoormans (2004) argue that in general, the attention-drawing ability of a product can be enhanced by increasing its size and by using bright colors.[108] However, a larger size might have its own sales drawbacks, especially when it applies to products whose end users are females.

Product Appearance and Categorization

Creusen and Schoormans (2004) argue that when a product is difficult to categorize based on its appearance, consumers may not regard the product as a purchase alternative. So in general, product appearance that differs slightly from the prototype, are evaluated more positively than products that are very typical or very atypical. In some cases, however, strong differentiation from or strong similarity to the prototype of another product alternative will be a beneficial strategy.[109]

Strong differentiation for the prototype: For products for which prestige, exclusiveness or novelty are important, an atypical appearance is advisable. An atypical appearance is also advisable when a product has to be differentiated from other products in the category, for example when there are many competing alternatives. Also, new functional attributes are better communicated by an atypical appearance. Differentiation from the category decreases comparison with other products from the category.[110]

Exemplar based categorization – or strong similarity to the prototype or another product alternative: Cohen and Basu (1987) argue that one can also design the appearance of a product to resemble another well-known and positively valued product alternative. This heightens the probability that people will evaluate the product based on knowledge about, or affections towards the product it resembles, which is called exemplar based categorization. They contend that this strategy may be beneficial when there is one dominant brand in the category with which it is difficult to compete.[111]

5.2.2 Underpinnings of Branding

Branding is defined by Kimbarovsky (2020) as an iterative process of researching, developing, and implementing a unique set of features for your business, and to help consumers and the public associate those features with your products or services,[112] whereas a brand is a set of features that differentiate one organization from another. That being said, a company's brand is defined by the business name, logo or symbol, design, brand voice, and everything visual about the company. In addition, the brand also includes the sum total of the experiences that customers, social media followers, fans, and prospects have with your company.[113] In the same vein, Lumen (2020) defines a brand as consisting of any name, term, design, style, words, symbols or any other feature that distinguishes the goods and services of one seller from another. A brand also distinguishes one product from another in the eyes of the customer.[114] That said, all of its elements (i.e., logo, color, shape, letters, and images) work as a psychological trigger or stimulus that causes an association to all other thoughts we have about this brand. Tunes, celebrities, and catchphrases are also oftentimes considered brands.[115]

According to Gregory (2020), your brand is defined by a customer's overall perception of your business, while branding is the activity of creating that perception. In this direction, she maintains that the definition of brand building is to generate awareness about your business strategies and campaigns, with the goal of creating a unique and lasting image in the marketplace. Put in another way, positive image + standing out = brand success.[116] Consequently, branding can be broken down into three phases:

1. Brand Strategy – you can think of brand strategy as the blueprint for how you want the world to see your business.
2. Brand Identity – brand identity is the visible elements of a brand, which includes; logo, typography, colors, packaging, messaging, experience and it complements. It reinforces the existing reputation of a brand and distinguishes the brand in consumers' minds. As such, brand identity should ideally correspond to the intent behind the branding.
3. Brand Marketing – you can think of it as the way that businesses or organizations highlight and bring awareness to products or services by connecting values and voice to the right audience through strategic communication.[117]

Finally, Charles (2016) opines that if you want more engagement with those you wish to do business with, you have to build the strongest brand in your space.[118] In the brand world, it's all becoming focused on the entire brand experience – every touch-point, or all the senses.[119] The following sub-headings explain some of the brand characteristics that make your brand stand out, or some of the general traits that successful brands consistently have.

A Successful Brand Has Purpose

Branding isn't about the company; it's about making a connection with the audience. Through branding, you can convey truths, universal ideas, observations, and trends visually. When this is done effectively, people will agree with the message and understand it.[120] In other words, what people look for when they want to connect with a company's story is the purpose. They may not be aware of it, but prospects are that they are looking for some motivating factor that they have in common with you – so that they can connect with.[121] In concurrence, Damon Richards argues that your customers don't care how much you know, until they know how much you care.[122]

Nowadays, people have a lot of choice in most fields about where they want to spend their money, and often the only thing that may differentiate you from competitors is your sense of mission. This means that your purpose should be clear and easy to understand.[123] Your brand's purpose needs to be expressed whenever and wherever you can express it. For example, if you are a coffee shop that focuses on using only sustainable ingredients, you might print facts about the rainforest on your cups. This way, potential customers can connect with you and become more passionate about buying from you.[124]

Effective Branding Stimulates Emotions

We saw earlier that emotional benefits provide customers with a *positive feeling* when thy purchase or use a particular *brand* (MaRS, 2020b). Consequently, choosing one product over another is ultimately powered by the consumer's *emotional relationship with the brand.* In this regard, Buchanan (2020) found that companies with strong brands outperform weaker brands in the same industry by 3:1 in terms of customer acquisition costs (CAC).[125] He argues that many businesses underinvest in brand because they feel that the outcomes are not easily measured.[126] Too often, this is the challenge when the approach is focused on short-term performance metrics at the expense of long-term shifts in brand strength.[127] In a further development, Howell (2020) found that consumers who are emotionally connected to a brand are less price sensitive, and that this explains why Apple can charge so much more for its products.[128]

As an addition to emotional appeal to brands, Muddana (2019) argues that the most significant factor that affects emotion is color. Each color is associated with specific feelings, and research has shown that it accounts for 90% of quick judgments about the product. This means that color has a significant impact on people's buying behaviors. The choice of color for a brand can affect its recognition by up to 80%. Many consumers say that they decide not to revisit a website if it has an unappealing aesthetic.[129] To concur, according to Montague (2017), studies show that consumers rank product appearance as one of the most important traits in purchase. In his estimate, 85% say that color is one of the primary reasons for selecting a new product.[130]

In a further development, Muddana (2019) found that people are more likely to buy if their first impression in the packaging appearance is positive. Packaging is also essential nowadays due to the growing prominence of online purchasing.[131] But appearance is not just about physical packaging. It's also relevant in realms such as social media, customer service, and web content. So for companies to create better branding for their products, they need to understand the importance of appearance throughout all areas of business and marketing operations.[132]

A Successful Brand Is Agile

We saw earlier that as the world is always changing, we should not think that customers' tastes will stay the same for long. This means that your brand needs to be able to change with the times. Your brand needs to be able to keep up with the evolution of the surrounding culture. In this direction, Lloyd (2017) suggests that high-growth companies need new ways to adapt their business, product, culture, and brand with an agile approach to brand strategy.[133] To this end, Charles (2016) argues that old brands like Coca Cola have struggled dealing with a changing landscape in the past. So it's worth the efforts to avoid repeating such mistakes.[134] This means regardless of what size your business is, *all of the leadership from top to bottom needs to be on board with being flexible.* The more able your brand can move quickly and easily, the better.[135]

According to Maayan (2020), *incorporating agile marketing values early in leadership* can significantly improve brand agility. This is especially pivotal to startup ventures; since startups do not come with an extensive history of "how things are done" leaders may be less likely to oppose agile strategies. Furthermore, early startup hires that begin with agile workflows are more likely to carry that understanding and mindset into leadership roles in the future.[136] This early indoctrination enables startups to create a business culture that supports and promotes brand agility. When implemented well, this can grant teams greater flexibility to do what they know and can drive marketing innovation for the company.[137]

In the reasoning of Nelly (2020), one of the ways to make a brand more agile is to *gain strategic insight from trusted community ambassadors.* A brand advocate can be one of your most powerful tools. That said, such an influencer has an army of fans who pay such close attention to everything they do, the products they use, where they shop, even the food they eat.[138] In this respect, brands can work with various influencers of all sizes to gain strategic insight into their specific communities.[139] Finally, *Smart Insights (2016)* argues that the best chance for your brand to hit the target *lies on small content and quick ads produced in short bursts, or cycles.* To this end, they found that regular online marketing brands for example, usually spend too much time and resources on a single strategy, whereas with agile marketing, the strategy is to produce as much content as possible and hope one takes off.[140] And the advantage in this strategy is that you don't spend much resource on an ad that might fail. Also, when you produce a lot of content or ads, chances of at least one going viral are high.[141]

A Successful Brand Is Unique

A strong brand communicates what your company does, how it does it, and at the same time, establishes trust and credibility with your prospects and customers.[142] What this means is that you can't always be everything to everyone; sometimes you will have to carve out a micro-niche and serve a very specific sector of the customer-base.[143]

Your brand is one of the most unique and valuable assets you own. Once it holds a position of distinction and value in your customers' and users' minds, and it is reflected in a meaningful way in your products, it gives you a unique advantage. It distances you further from competitors.[144] Kimbarovsky (2020) identified a few reasons why branding is important and why strong branding must be part of your branding strategy:

- 91% of consumers say they are more likely to buy from an authentic brand than a dishonest brand.
- 77% of consumers make purchases based on a brand name.
- 82% of investors believe that brand strength and name recognition are important factors in guiding them in their investment decisions.[145]

From the forgoing, Gregory (2020) identified 12 useful guides to building a successfully unique brand.[146] Commentaries to this guide are spread out in the following 12 steps:

1. Step 1 – Discover the purpose behind your brand (by asking these questions clearly);
    - Why do you exist? Why should people care?
    - How are you different?
    - What problem do you solve?
2. Step 2 – Research brands within your industry (by asking the following questions);
    - Is the competitor consistent with their message and visual identity across channels?
    - What is the quality of the competitor's products or services?
    - Does the competitor have customer reviews you can read, or social mentions about them?
    - In what ways does the competitor market their business, both online and offline?
3. Step 3 – Define your brand's target audience (*the key is to get specific,* by figuring out detailed behaviors and lifestyle of your consumers. Also, you can gain a competitive advantage when branding your business by *narrowing down your audience to a niche or niches*).
4. Step 4 – Define your brand mission statement (craft a clear and concise expression of what your company is most passionate about. The mission statement should define a purpose for existing).
5. Step 5 – Outline qualities and benefits for your brand (by asking the question, what are you offering that no one else is offering? This means you have to focus on the *key qualities and benefits* that make your company branding unique. For example, we offer a better way to support profitability, productivity, and sustainability.
6. Step 6 – Form your brand voice (is *how you communicate with your customers* and how they respond to you. Also, you may want to choose a brand voice that makes sense and resonates with your target audience).
7. Step 7 – Let your brand personality shine (your clients and customers are looking for an *experience tailored to their needs,* and backed by *genuine personal interaction*).

8. Step 8 – Build a brand story and messaging (this part of the brand development process goes *beyond your business logo or tagline* to define key aspects of who you are, what you offer, and why people should care.
9. Step 9 – Create a brand logo and tagline.
10. Step 10 – Integrate your brand everywhere.
11. Step 11 – Stay true to your brand (*consistency is key,* unless you decide to change your brand into something that is more effective based on measured consumer response).
12. Step 12 – Be your brand's biggest advocate.

A Successful Brand Is Consistent – Cohesiveness Builds Loyalty

People feel uncomfortable when other people are inconsistent and unpredictable, when they say one thing, then change their minds and say another. It causes them to lose trust. The same is true with your brand. If you don't stick to one main idea, people will lose the feeling of trust and consistency that they associate with your brand very quickly. In addition, be sure that your company "walks the talk" and that your actions are in line with your goals.[147]

That being said, in order to keep customers loyal to your brand, it's essential to employ cohesive branding in all phases of media both online and in physical store locations. Every place that people see your products, they need to recognize them.[148] This is accomplished by consistently using the same color schemes, fonts, images and messaging. Business cards and signage should match the design and aesthetics of the website. This also comes into play with invoice designs and employee apparel aesthetics.[149]

Every time you repeat the message on a different media channel or platform, you are reinforcing the brand image and creating more customer loyalty. If the first impression about your brand is about convenience and cost savings, then this message needs to be repeated each time the customer encounters the company in various scenarios and locations.[150]

A Successful Brand Tells Stories

Storytelling is what will breed a feeling of true familiarity, and it is remarkably effective at generating trust. Simply put, having stories to associate with your brand makes it stick in the mind of your customer more permanently.[151] Two of the most prominent modes of brand storytelling are the *visual brand language* and the *intra-sensory perception.*

VISUAL BRAND LANGUAGE

It is imperative that a Visual Brand Language be created from the foundation of your Brand – specifically the brand pillars, brand attributes, brand values, and brand personality. Think about some of the brands listed below: The feel and balance of a DeWalt drill, the sound of a BMW engine and the quiet "dumph" of the driver door as it secures you in place, the intuitive and enjoyable use of an Apple iPhone, or the signature growl of a Harley engine.[152] Think also about Caterpillar, Harley-Davidson and John Deere, et cetera. They are all leveraging their brand and its value through their Visual Brand Language.[153]

INTRA-SENSORY PERCEPTION

Montague (2016) found that the intra-sensory perception of Sound, Smell and Feel – all matters in design. Thus, to build your brand story, it is worth the effort to remember and consider your customer's intra-sensory perception as you create product experiences.[154] In this regard, he maintains that retailers have known about intra-sensory perception for years. For example, from Disney to Apple, as well as many retail stores create environments that entertain and inform customers through the entire experience of sounds and smells, the interplay of visual media and lighting, and the kinesthetic sensation of space – which are all designed to communicate the product or brand message.[155] He argues that while *sight* dominates our sense of design, other senses like *sound, touch,* and *smell* contribute to the *emotional connection* a user has with a product and brand. Consequently, to build a brand story and communicate the meaning of a product, we consider all sensibilities across all touchpoints.[156]

Sound Product sounds can be divided into two types: consequential sound and intentional sound. *Consequential sounds* are generated by operating the product. *Intentional sounds* are added to the product. Both types have meaning to the user.[157]

Consequential sound – Through *consequential sounds* we know when the battery runs low on our power drill, when our vacuum cleaner gets clogged, or when a plastic lid didn't quite click into place. Designers consider the material, shape, stiffness, load, energy, and lubricity of product parts to design the best sound. For instance, car door sounds have long been associated with quality (or lack thereof). Car manufacturers have *acoustical engineers* dedicated to creating just the right sound – and just the right emotion – through the design of a door.[158]

Intentional sounds help us operate microwave ovens and smartphones et cetera. The style, tone, intensity, and frequency of sound allow the designer to communicate with consumers in appropriate ways. Product sounds that mimic other sounds in our lives create memories and emotions useful in guiding the overall product/brand experience (such as your mobile phone alarm sounds).[159]

Smell Smell is most closely connected with our limbic system – the part of the brain concerned with instinct and mood. Some smells help us relax, some invigorate us.[160] Product designers can leverage smells in design to make connections with users. For instance, they can figure out what works best for their customers between the sensations for synthetics vs. naturals, metals vs. plastics, painted and printed finishes – all can be selected based on the attributes they communicate through smell. For example, the smell of a new book, a new car, or a soft comfy chair – all connotes memories and messages.[161]

Touch Montague (2016) found that in a family of door pulls which they recently designed, the visual aesthetics were key attractive features. However, the feel of the product was just as important in the overall sensory experience. He observed that the sensations most mentioned by users during testing were the finish on the metal – brushed, polished, or textured – and the shape of the handle.[162]

A Successful Brand Is Simple

Keep the message that your brand is trying to convey as simple as possible. If a brand is too hard to figure out, your potential customers would ignore you.[163] For example, think about *Nike!* The entire meaning of their brand – the idea of pushing beyond one's limits and breaking through in spite of trying odds – is summarized easily in three words: *JUST DO IT.* You can create a shoot of simplicity similar to this in order to help your customers remember you better.[164]

The question is what should you brand first – your business or yourself? The fundamental difference between a personal and a business brand is that; in one case, the customer falls in love with a person, and in the other case, with an idea. Iuliano (2016) found that statistically, you have about three seconds to make a first impression. In three seconds people will either love or hate your brand. That's the power of a personal brand – wherein you use the natural tendencies of snap judgment to your advantage. Conversely, if your target audiences like an idea but not the delivery, they won't buy the products.[165]

So before you start trying to brand yourself or your company, ask yourself: what will the customer fall in love with first? Is it me or the idea that I am representing – or both? But building a personal brand is easier than building a business brand; it's easier to become known for something than it is to build a huge business.[166] That notwithstanding, Iuliano (2016) argues that branding both yourself and your business is the ideal scenario. *Branding yourself* allows you to build relationships faster, and give you flexibility to pivot as you grow and adopt. It gives you the speed to create a community you can leverage, whereas *branding a business* gives you the organizational or team power to brand an idea.[167]

A Successful Brand Is Excitingly Engaging

According to Orr and Patel (2018), *excitement* is an emotion that fosters *engagement.* Positive experiences lead to increasing connections. Sports fans, for example, are so engaged that they frequently describe their beloved team as part of their personality.[168] They suggest some innovative ways business leaders can excite their customers, such as: using personalization, packaging products in unique ways, and building a contest (but noted that while contests do not necessarily build brand loyalty in the long term, they can be an exciting way to start a relationship), et cetera.[169]

In a related development, Gallup (2020) argues that nothing predicts organic growth like *customer engagement.* In this regard, while aggressive advertising campaigns, mega sales promotions, promises of low prices, and reward programs may get customers through the door, but they don't create the types of *emotional connections* that drive long-term profits and loyalty. For example, if your customers aren't "true believers," your company risks surviving based on a price relationship alone and would rarely ever prosper.[170] Gallup (2020) defines customer engagement as the emotional connection between your customers and your company. But cautions that "satisfying" customers doesn't have the same effect as "engaging" them.[171]

That said, according to their research, customers who are fully engaged bring in significant benefits when we look at engagement in specific industries. For example:

- Retail banking customers who are fully engaged bring 37% more annual revenue to their primary bank than actively disengaged customers.
- Consumer electronics shoppers who are fully engaged spend 29% more per shopping trip than actively disengaged customers.
- Hotel guests who are fully engaged spend 46% more per year than actively disengaged guests.
- Companies that successfully engage their B2B customers realize 63% lower customer attrition, 55% higher share of wallet, and 50% higher productivity.[172]

According to Forbes Coaches Council (2017), branding is not about your logo; it is about your message – what you are broadcasting to the world.[173] In concurrence, Muddana (2019) contends that when a person identifies with a message, they feel more of familiarity toward it, and they will naturally gravitate toward it on the store shelf.[174] People want to connect and influence the evolution of your brand.[175]

5.3 Competing on a Mix of Product Extension and New Product Development Strategies

Restructuring of production for achieving production-based competitive advantages, and integrated production concepts are a topic of major concern.[176] Industry Canada (2012) argues that reliance on new product development and product extensions varies by manufacturing industry.[177] For example, the Product Design, Research and Development Industry and Academic Research Committee (2011) found that *industrial electronics manufacturers* focus more on new product development and speed to market to meet narrow market windows and short product lifecycles, whereas the *aerospace industry* concentrates its efforts on product extension (new features, higher quality, and lower cost) due to the high risk and complexity of new product development and long product life cycles.[178]

So essentially, competing on a mix of product extension, and new product development favors two strategic-oriented competitive options, these are: *leveraging lightweight structural design materials*, and *competing on simultaneity of cost reduction, size reduction and superior performance*. In any of these cases, Taulien (2019) emphasizes the need to be a balance between designing the product from the firm's unilateral perception of things versus designing the product with user experience in mind,[179] but favors the idea of designing with user experience in mind. However, the ideal situation will be for firms to align these goals by achieving both goals simultaneously.[180]

5.3.1 Leverage Lightweight Structural Design Materials

Rationale for Lightweight Structural Design Materials

Lightweight design is often associated with the application of lightweight materials.[181] According to Dörr and Stark (2018), lightweight construction can be defined as the effort to change a design in such a way that the quotient of *useful weight* to *dead weight* improves, without having a negative impact on the functionality resulting from this change.[182] The Cambridge Dictionary defines *deadweight* (also known as dead load) as the weight of a structure, container, or vehicle when it is empty.[183] Meanwhile, *useful load* has been defined as the excess *load* which includes the crew and passengers, oil and fuel, auxiliary power system, and communication, navigation, and other equipment over the *dead weight* of the structure itself – an aircraft is a good example.[184]

In this regard, Kaspar and Vielhaber, (2017) found that lightweight materials and design have long been of central significance for product development across several industries such as the highly sensitive sector of aerospace.[185] Lighter and stronger materials will be of immense use to aircraft manufactures, leading to increased performance, spacecraft will also benefit where weight is a major factor. Nanotechnology would help to reduce the size of equipment, and consequently, a decrease of fuel consumption required to get in airplane.[186]

In addition, Heuss *et al.* (2012) found that today, the growing demand for technical capabilities in terms of more safety and comfort while simultaneously increasing the resource efficiency, is constantly leading to further requirements for lightweight engineering as one of the key elements within the automotive industry.[187] For example, because of the lightweight but incredibly strong properties of carbon fiber, this material has the potential to break into countless fields. As such, carbon fiber designs can greatly improve the safety and accuracy of many objects for everyday application.[188]

In the same vein, Miltenović *et al.* (2014) found that the concept of lightweight design is often considered as a system of lightweight construction, which represents a method for reducing the weight of technical systems or subsystems that take into account all the variable activity in the system, as well as the general technical and economic constraints.[189] Consequently, when considering the price of lightweight design, it is more appropriate to ask how much kilograms weight reduction should cost? The answer to this question depends on the area of application of lightweight design and variations in product manufacturing prices associated with weight reduction.[190]

Characteristics of Materials Used in Lightweight Design

Requirements related to the structure of lightweight construction should preferably be fulfilled by using lightweight materials of high stiffness and strength. Weight reduction can be achieved by using lower density materials. Table 5.1 provides an overview of the most commonly used material for lightweight construction.

Please note the following:

(a) 1 is lowest cost; 10 is highest cost.
(b) Nylon with 30% glass.
(c) Unidirectional carbon/epoxy.
(d) Die-cast silicon carbide (SiC) particles/aluminum.
(e) Titanium alloy metal matrix composites reinforced with silicon carbide fiber
(f) Alumina reinforced with 25% SiC whiskers.
(h) Woven SiC/SiC
(n.a)) Not Available

Table 5.1 Overview of Materials Used for Lightweight Constructions

1. Metal Materials	*Relative Costs (a)*	*2. Non-Metal Materials*	*Relative Costs (a)*
• Aluminum alloys	3	• Engineering plastics	1–4
• Magnesium alloys	4	• Ceramics	n.a
• Beryllium alloys	8		
• Titanium alloys	6		
• Titanium aluminide alloys	9		
• Steel (conventional lightweight design)	n.a		
3. Composite materials			
• Polymer-matrix composites			
• Discontinuous fibers (b)	2		
• Continuous fibers (c)	6		
• Metal-matrix composites			
• Discontinuous fibers (d)	5		
• Continuous fibers (e)	8		
• Structural ceramics	5		
• Ceramic-matrix composites			
• Discontinuous fibers (f)	7		
• Continuous fibers (h)	10		

Source: Adapted from Campbell, F. C. (editor). "Chapter 1: Introduction and Uses of Lightweight Materials." in Lightweight Materials – Understanding the Basics. *Asminternational.org*, 2012, p. 5, https://www.asminternational.org/documents/10192/1849770/05355G_Sample.pdf. Accessed 11 October 2020; Miltenović *et al.* (2014), op. cit., p. 532; Haghshenas, Meysam. "Metal–Matrix Composites." Reference Module in Materials Science and Materials Engineering, 28 October 2015. DOI: 10.1016/B978-0-12-803581-8.03950-3; Ward-Close, C. M. and Robertson, J. G. "Advances in the fabrication of titanium based composites." *Advanced Performance Materials*, Vol. 3 (3), pp. 251–262, 1 July 1996. DOI: 10.1007/BF00136790; and other sources.

When selecting materials we should bear in mind the advantages and disadvantages for use in lightweight design. That said; one of the most commonly used methods of weight reduction is achieved by a combination of different materials, where the dominant role is played by the application of composite materials. Also, as material properties largely depend on the operating temperature, the area of the operating temperature of the product is a very important factor for the choice of materials. For instance, at operating temperatures above 1000°C, ceramics and fire-resistant alloys should primarily be used, meanwhile for the area of low operating temperature, metal alloys is recommended for use.[191]

Thus, the forms of lightweight structures are derived by considering the definition of both form and design structure. In this regard, a survey carried out by Miltenović *et al.* (2014) found that composite materials have the advantage of long-term future viability because of the malleability of their properties for use in lightweight design.[192] In a similar vein, Sinke (2019a) maintains that the concept of specific mechanical properties is important if we need to create lightweight structures.[193]

Finally, Miltenović *et al.* (2014) arrive at a conclusion that the best features in the construction of lightweight structures with composite materials are primarily composite materials with carbon fiber.[194] As a result, carbon fiber is in demand by scientists, engineers, and innovators across the globe due to its light weight and strength.[195] In terms of stiffness, its tightly bonded structure makes carbon fiber a stiff material. This makes it difficult to misshape so it can be used in a variety of applications. As such, whether carbon fiber design is used in simple electronics or is built to strengthen an airplane, carbon fiber project will retain the rigidity necessary in the lightweight structure.[196] In addition, one of the primary benefits of choosing carbon fiber for your project is its resistance to heat. Carbon fiber product won't bend or melt under exceedingly high temperatures, making it an ideal alternative to metals and steels. For example, if your fiber is treated with temperatures exceeding 3,000 degrees Celsius, your final carbon fiber design will be able to withstand heats up to 1,000 W/mK.[197] Heat resistance is an important feature to consider when you craft a carbon fiber prototype.[198]

Another development is an initial investigation by Khedari, Suttisonk, Pratinthong, and Hirunlabh (2001) on the use of a new lightweight construction material, composed of cement, sand and fiber of waste from young coconut (Cocos nucifera) and durian (Durio zibethinus). Thermal conductivity, compressive strength and bulk density were investigated. The experimental investigation reveals that the addition of these fibers reduces the thermal conductivity of the composite specimen and yields a lightweight. Khedari *et al.* (2001) maintain that the composite satisfies the basic requirement of construction materials, and they could be used for walls and roofs. Furthermore, apart from saving energy consumption for the building, the proposed materials offer an alternative option to dispose waste of fruit industry.

However, in some types of products or industries, lightweight design might be disadvantageous as it may give the impression that the product can be fragile. So understanding how this plays on the functional value of the product is critical.

5.3.2 Simultaneity in Cost and Size Reduction, and Superior Performance

The dynamics of *product cost reduction, and product size reduction* is playing increasingly decisive roles in modern day firm competitive strategies. But the ultimate challenge will be to simultaneously execute these two competitive strategies, by incorporating the third element, which is *superior performance* – into the firms" value creation stream; without compromising any of the elements of profitability, productivity, and sustainability. That being said, with respect to superior performance, *OptiProERP (2020)* argues that if a manufacturer takes all the steps necessary to produce a *first-rate product* and *delivers to its customers on time*, the odds are very good that not only will they repeat customers, but they will recommend their products to others. In other words, the benefits (and the profits) will accrue over time.[199] One additional way to earn customers' trust is to provide cutomers with up-to-date quality assurance testing information on products purchased. This reinforces the perception that the company is totally committed to quality and transparency.[200] With regards to size reduction, Muddana (2019) contends that the fact that homes are becoming smaller due to urbanization also makes smaller package size a desirable quality for people who have limited space.[201]

For all designers, one of the first priorities for *sustainability* should be to reduce the quantities of any material chosen whenever possible. Therefore, packaging designers must optimize the amount of materials needed to package a product in order to minimize the consumption of resources, which will in turn achieve significant cost savings and improve profit margins.[202] Cost reduction is not about arbitrarily cutting any and all expenses. You need to understand the nature of your business costs and how these inter-relate with sales, inventories, cost of goods sold, gross profits and net profits.

In analyzing your expenses, use percentages rather than actual dollar amounts. For example, *if you increase sales and the dollar amount of an expense does not change, you have decreased that expense as a percentage of sales. When you decrease your cost percentage, you increase your percentage of profit.* On the other hand, if your sales volume remains the same, you can increase the percentage of profit by reducing a specific item of expense.

Your goal, of course, is to do both: to decrease specific expenses and increase their productive worth at the same time. Having said that, before you can determine whether cutting expenses will increase profits, you need information about your business – and that means having a good record-keeping system.

The most important technological development in recent years has been in the field of *microelectronics*. Not only have products reduced in size through technological advances but multi-functional products have become possible. For example, the mobile phone has reduced in size considerably from models first introduced in the 1980s, when most were too large to be carried along in jacket pockets. As a result, they were typically installed in vehicles as car phones. The miniaturization of mobile phones has been possible due to three key developments.

- Advanced integrated circuits (ICs) or microprocessors that allow more circuitry to be included on each microchip, thereby increasing functionality and power.
- Advanced liquid crystal displays (LCDs) enabling color screens that are brighter and require much smaller current, meaning greater energy efficiency and slimmer housings.
- Advanced battery technology including Lithium-Ion rechargeable batteries, providing a lightweight means of storing a lot of energy resulting in smaller and thinner fuel cells.[203]

But, Cross (2020) found that engineers at the University of Illinois have developed a new *polymer-based electrolyte* that enables *batteries* to be *self-healing* and *recyclable*. The researchers have been investigating the use of *solid, ion-conducting polymers* in order to overcome the limitations currently faced with *liquid electrolytes*. That being said, *Lithium-ion* batteries are typically made with *liquid electrolytes* which are prone to defects that have been known to cause the batteries to ignite during a short-circuit. The defects known as *dendrites* – are tiny treelike structures that can grow inside a lithium battery and pierce the protective shell which accelerates battery failure.[204] These flaws can provoke electrical problems in devices and even cause a potentially dangerous explosion or fire. This new study by *Christopher Evans,* lead author and University of Illinois materials science and engineering professor, and *Brian Jing,* a materials science and engineering graduate student and study coauthor; which was published in the *Journal of the American Chemical Society,* could help battery manufacturers produce commercial batteries that are more environmentally friendly due to their self-healing properties.[205]

Another example is *product convergence* that has enabled Bluetooth connectivity, Internet access, built-in cameras, camcorders, games and MP3 players to be included on a single device.[206] Still, the continued development of *smart materials* has seen them being applied to a whole range of innovative products and systems where their ability to respond to changes and return to their original state is a real advantage.[207] Some smart materials include:

- Smart glass – used to change light transmission properties of windows or skylights when a voltage is applied, i.e., changes opacity from transparent to translucent.
- Shape memory alloys (SMAs) – used in spectacle frames, and once deformed, it can regain or remember its original shape.

But, as some product roles can be interrelated, changes in one role may influence other roles. For instance, a small size is valued from an aesthetic point of view, but a larger size is chosen by some consumers because it looks more solid and reliable (i.e., functional value). So when something is changed in the product appearance in order to improve its performance on one role, this has implications for the performance on other roles.[208] Thus, in situation where product designers want to effect a size reduction so as to capture the aesthetic point of view of those that consider small size to be a modern design, it would be competitively advantageous for the ergonomic to equally clearly indicate how solid the product is, in spite of its new small size. This would be a smart move to win over the confidence of many of those who hold the perception that large size looks more solid and reliable when compared to small size in terms of functional value. Creusen and Schoormans (2004) also found that a small number of buttons on an answering machine made customers to believe this makes it simpler to operate. While more buttons was seen to be simply confusing.[209]

5.4 The Contagious Effects of Profitability, Productivity, and Sustainability

This section has identified two critical issues inherent in the strategic relationship between profitability, productivity, and sustainability. These are: (1) the success of any of the factors does not necessarily lead to the successful alignment of the other factors – the success chain reaction. (2) Timely intervention to address early signs of failure in any of the strategic alignment components is critical to save the others.

5.4.1 The Success Chain Reaction

The success of one any of the factors does not necessarily lead to the success of the others. For instance, the success in one alignment component, say *profitability,* does not necessarily lead to the success of the other strategic alignment components – that is, productivity and or sustainability. But it potentially levels the playing-field to improve the success rate of the other factors. Put in another way, the success of one or two of the factors would likely produce an accelerator effect, and not a multiplier effect. For there to be a multiplier effect so that the other factors could benefit from the spillover, management would need to do something productively new. Much said than done, the road to achieve this is often misguided largely due to the lethal effects of biases, and the lack of strategic foresight, et cetera.

This means that organizations would have to examine each of the factors as semi-autonomous structures, deal with their specific challenges, and then align them with each other in a synergy.

5.4.2 Addressing Early Signs of Alignment Failure

Timely intervention to address early signs of failure in any of the alignment factors is critical. The failure of any of the factors, if not addressed promptly and appropriately, will inevitably contaminate the others: usually in piecemeal – that is, one at a time; and sometimes in whole – that is, the other two are simultaneously engulfed in a dragnet. That said, the capacity for one factor to contaminate the others would largely depend among other things; on the strength of the OrgDNA base coefficient of the contagious element. The higher the coefficient of the contagious factor, the more deadly the contamination effect on the other elements, and vice versa.

Usually, the last factor to be contaminated is the OrgDNA base that is core or most successful to the organization. Meanwhile, the contamination effect of any of the failing alignment elements begins by puncturing the DNA base that is most vulnerable. The situation becomes even more complicated when the contamination from say, lack of clarity in Decision rights which is coefficient 2 (coef. 2) in our OrgDNA base index; creeps into its base pair, which is Motivators (coef. 1) in our index. For example, if lack of *profitability* in an organization is brought about by the inability of the organization to clarify decision rights (coef. 2); it will quickly contaminate its base pair, which is motivators (coef. 1). The situation would be further aggravated on *profitability* if such organization is already suffering or is showing some signs of inability to properly *motivate* its employees (failure in aligning motivators).

5.4.3 General Remarks

In a nutshell, we can conclude that the success of any of the alignment factors of profitability, productivity, and sustainability would only create a significant impact on the others if appropriate innovative steps are taken to ensure the spillover into the other factors. On the contrary, where failure hits any of the alignment factors, and nothing measurably appropriate is done to contain it; it will inevitably contaminate the other elements. And that the extent of the impact is largely determined by the OrgDNA coefficient that is associated with the contagious factor, in relation to the OrgDNA coefficient of the factor being contaminated.

That said, every other thing being equal, the higher the OrgDNA coefficient that is associated with the contagious factor, and the lower the OrgDNA coefficient of the factor being contaminated, the greater the NEGATIVE impact on the alignment factor. On the contrary, the lower the OrgDNA coefficient that is associated with the contagious element, and the higher the OrgDNA coefficient of the element being contaminated, the lesser the NEGATIVE impact.

Chapter Conclusion

As a conclusion of this chapter, it can be observed that from a startup stage, a new product or company follows an embryonic cycle that runs initially from *sustainability*, to *profitability*, and then to *productivity*. At growth stage, it follows another cycle by upgrading its scaling; beginning from *profitability*, to *productivity*, and then to *sustainability*. At a maturity, it begins a new cycle usually by reorganizing its stakes through a sequential priority from *sustainability*, to *profitability*, and then *productivity*.

The Recurrent Cycles from Startup to Maturity:

1. Embryonic stage = sustainability, profitability, productivity
2. Growth stage = profitability, productivity, sustainability
3. Maturity stage = sustainability, profitability, productivity

At a declining stage, in order for a company or product to bounce back into the competition; it would need to recycle its game-changer, by following a new cycle that goes from *productivity*, to *profitability*, and then to *sustainability*. In other words, this time around by laying first and paramount consideration on improving *productivity*, then secondly, to how this *productivity* could ensure *profitability*, and finally, to how this *profitability* could ensure *sustainability*.

The Cycle from Declining Stage back to Growth Stage

- Productivity, profitability, sustainability

But, this new cycle needs to be aligned and realigned over and over again to get rid of obsolescence and counterproductive repetitions - by taking into consideration the changing business landscape and competitive behavior.

Additionally, this chapter concludes that in creating a competitive edge over other companies in the market, firms generally tend to adopt one or more of three major sequential orientations:

4. Creating excellent ways of attracting new customers
5. Strategizing on retaining existing customers
6. Winning customers from competitors.

In order to succeed in these endeavors, innovative companies generally tailor their customer-centric activities around *superior value, ease of use, and ingenuity in the products and services* they offer. But the order of approach differs between startup entrepreneurial ventures and established firms.

Startup entrepreneurial ventures – generally adopt the following sequential logic:

1. They start by creating excellent ways of attracting new customers.
2. They begin strategizing on retaining existing customers
3. Winning customers from competitors (this is where disruptive innovation thrives).

Existing companies on the contrary, follow a sequential logic of:

1. Strategizing on retaining existing customers;
2. Creating excellent ways of attracting new customers; and
3. Winning customers from competitors (this is where radical innovation thrives).

Notes

1 Mankins, Michael (2017), loc. cit.
2 Ibid.
3 Stam, Erik and Garnsey, Elizabeth (2008), op. cit., p. 1.
4 Grace, Allie (2019), loc. cit.
5 As cited by Gustafsson et al. (2012), op. cit., p. 20.
6 Gustafsson et al. (2012), op. cit., p. 21.
7 Ibid.
8 As cited by Gardner, David (2017), loc. cit.
9 Dunn III, J. Richard (1992), op. cit., p. 21.
10 Dunn III, J. Richard (1992), op. cit., p. 10.
11 Dunn III, J. Richard (1992), op. cit., p. 19.
12 Charles, Jeff. "7 Important Traits of a Successful Brand." Published: 14 Jun. 2016, Last Updated: 12 De. 2019, https://smallbiztrends.com/2016/06/7-important-brand-characteristics.html.
13 Ibid.
14 Ceru, J. Dennis (2018), loc. cit.
15 See the Introduction and Executive summary of Ralf C. Schlaepfer (Head of Manufacturing Industry-Deloitte AG) and Markus Koch (Head of Manufacturing Consulting-Deloitte Consulting AG); as cited by Stadler, Antonia (2015), op. cit., p. 2.
16 As cited by Industry Canada (2012), op. cit., p. 9.
17 As cited by Industry Canada (2012), ibid.
18 As cited by Industry Canada (2012), ibid.
19 As cited by Tsui, Eric (2018a), op. cit., p. 2.
20 See Banton, Caroline. "Pricing Power." *Investopedia.com,* 25 Jun. 2019, https://www.investopedia.com/terms/p/pricingpower.asp. Accessed 19 Aug. 2020.
21 Course Hero (2011), op. cit., p. 5.
22 Ibid.
23 Towards the circular economy Vol. 2: Opportunities for the consumer goods sector, Ellen MacArthur Foundation, Jan. 2013, ellenmacarthurfoundation.org. As cited by Hannon, E., Magnin-Mallez, C., and Vanthournout, H. "Introduction." The circular economy: Moving from theory to practice. *McKinsey Center for Business and Environment,* Special edition, Oct. 2016, p. 25.
24 Rossé, M., Stuchtey, M., & Vanthournout, H. "Finding growth within: A new framework for Europe," The circular economy: Moving from theory to practice. *McKinsey Center for Business and Environment,* Special edition, 2016, Oct., p. 5.
25 Hannon, E., Magnin-Mallez, C., and Vanthournout, H. (2016), op. cit., p. 25.

26 EDUCBA. "7 Most Useful Comparison between Business Analytics vs. Predictive Analytics." *EDUCBA.com,* 2019b, https://www.educba.com/business-analytics-vs-predictive-analytics/. Accessed 15 Feb. 2019.
27 EDUCBA. "Learn 6 Useful Differences between Big Data vs. Predictive Analytics." *EDUCBA.com,* 2019a, https://www.educba.com/big-data-vs-predictive-analytics/. Accessed 12 Feb. 2019.
28 EDUCBA (2019a), loc. cit.
29 See Schumpeter, A. Joseph. The Theory of Economics Development. Oxford UK: Oxford University Press, 1934, pp. 62–63; as cited by Basılgan, Müslüm (2011), op. cit., p. 52.
30 EDUCBA (2019a), loc. cit.
31 Ciocarlie, Matei. Robotics. *MOOC Learning Materials,* course excerpt from Colombia University, in Partnership with edx.org, 2018.
32 Keisner, A., Raffo, J., & Wunsch-Vincent, S. "Breakthrough Technologies – Robotics, Innovation and Intellectual Property." *Economic Research Working Paper No. 30,* Economics & Statistics Series, Geneva: (WIPO), Nov., 2015, p. 5.
33 Keisner, A., Raffo, J., & Wunsch-Vincent, S. "Breakthrough Technologies – Robotics, Innovation and Intellectual Property." *Economic Research Working Paper No. 30,* Economics & Statistics Series, Geneva: (WIPO), Nov., 2015, p. 5.
34 Owen-Hill, Alex. "What's the difference between robotics and artificial intelligence?" *Blog.robotiq.com,* 19 Jul. 2017, https://blog.robotiq.com/whats-the-difference-between-robotics-and-artificial-intelligence/. Accessed 6 Feb. 2018.
35 Owen-Hill, Alex (2017), loc. cit.
36 Owen-Hill, Alex (2017), loc. cit.
37 As cited by Taddeo, Mariarosaria & Floridi, Luciano (2018), op. cit., p. 752.
38 As cited by Taddeo, Mariarosaria & Floridi, Luciano (2018), ibid.
39 The European Commission. "Draft Ethics Guidelines for Trustworthy AI: Working Document for stakeholders." *Consultation,* The European Commission's *High-Level Expert Group on Artificial Intelligence (AI):* Brussels, 18 Dec. 2018, p.i.
40 Ibid.
41 Taddeo, Mariarosaria & Floridi, Luciano (2018), op. cit., p. 751.
42 SlideModel (2020a), loc. cit.
43 As cited by Gilley, Cliff (2020), op. cit., p. 21.
44 Ibid.
45 SlideModel (2020a), loc. cit.
46 SlideModel (2020a), loc. cit.
47 SlideModel (2020a), loc. cit.
48 Ibid.
49 Customer Success Association (CSA). "Success." Mikael Blaisdell & Associates, Inc., 2019, https://www.customersuccessassociation.com/library/the-definition-of-customer-success/. Accessed 6 Oct. 2020.
50 Customer Success Association – CSA (2019), loc. cit.
51 Customer Success Association – CSA (2019), loc. cit.
52 Customer Success Association – CSA (2019), loc. cit.
53 Montague, Monty (2017), op. cit., p. 3.
54 Course Hero (2011), op. cit., p. 2.
55 Ibid.

56 Ibid.
57 Stroud, Samanda (2018), loc. cit.
58 Creusen, E. H. Mariëlle and Schoormans, P. L. Jan. "The Different Roles of Product Appearance in Consumer Choice." *Journal of Product Innovation Management,* Dec. 2004, pp. 2&18. DOI: 10.1111/j.0737-6782.2005.00103.x.
59 Muddana, Varshita. "The Importance of Your Product's Design and Appearance." *Soft Script Solutions,* 22 Mar. 2019, https://www.softscripts.net/blog/2019/03/products-design-appearance/. Accessed 26 Jan. 2020.
60 Creusen, E. H. Mariëlle & Schoormans, P. L. Jan (2004), op. cit., p. 2.
61 Creusen, E. H. Mariëlle & Schoormans, P. L. Jan (2004), op. cit., p. 15.
62 Montague, Monty (2017), op. cit., p. 3.
63 Creusen, E. H. Mariëlle & Schoormans, P. L. Jan (2004), op. cit., p. 17.
64 Montague, Monty (2017), op. cit., p. 1.
65 Montague, Monty (2017), op. cit., p. 2.
66 As cited by Creusen, E. H. Mariëlle & Schoormans, P. L. Jan (2004), op. cit., p. 4.
67 Creusen, E. H. Mariëlle & Schoormans, P. L. Jan (2004), ibid.
68 Muddana, Varshita (2019), loc. cit.
69 As cited by Creusen, E. H. Mariëlle & Schoormans, P. L. Jan (2004), op. cit., p. 4.
70 Creusen, E. H. Mariëlle & Schoormans, P. L. Jan (2004), loc. cit.
71 As cited by Creusen, E. H. Mariëlle & Schoormans, P. L. Jan (2004), op. cit., p. 5.
72 Creusen, E. H. Mariëlle & Schoormans, P. L. Jan (2004), op. cit., p. 5.
73 Muddana, Varshita (2019), loc. cit.
74 MaRS (2020b), loc. cit.
75 As cited by Creusen, E. H. Mariëlle & Schoormans, P. L. Jan (2004), op. cit., p. 5.
76 MaRS (2020b), loc. cit.
77 As cited by Creusen, E. H. Mariëlle & Schoormans, P. L. Jan (2004), ibid.
78 As cited by Creusen, E. H. Mariëlle & Schoormans, P. L. Jan (2004), op. cit., p. 5.
79 Ibid.
80 Creusen, E. H. Mariëlle & Schoormans, P. L. Jan (2004), op. cit., p. 5.
81 As cited by Creusen, E. H. Mariëlle & Schoormans, P. L. Jan (2004), ibid.
82 As cited by Creusen, E. H. Mariëlle & Schoormans, P. L. Jan (2004), ibid; pp. 5-6.
83 Creusen, E. H. Mariëlle & Schoormans, P. L. Jan (2004), op. cit., p. 6.
84 Ibid.
85 MaRS (2020b), loc. cit.
86 Stroud, Samanda (2018), loc. cit.
87 As cited by Creusen, E. H. Mariëlle & Schoormans, P. L. Jan (2004), op. cit., p. 6.
88 Creusen, E. H. Mariëlle & Schoormans, P. L. Jan (2004), loc. cit.
89 MaRS (2020b), loc. cit.
90 Skidmore, Paul (2018), loc. cit.
91 As cited by Creusen, E. H. Mariëlle & Schoormans, P. L. Jan (2004), op. cit., p. 6.
92 Ibid; pp. 6–7.
93 Acevedo, Laura (2020), loc. cit.
94 Skidmore, Paul (2018), loc. cit.

95 Nibusinessinfo (2020a), loc. cit.
96 Isa, S. S. and Liem, A. (2014), op. cit., p. 2.
97 Gilley, Cliff (2020), op. cit., p. 29.
98 Lundin, Katie. "4 Psychology-Based Design Tips For Eye-Catching Packaging Design." *Crowspring.com,* 9 Nov. 2017, https://www.crowdspring.com/blog/packaging-design-tips-psychology/. Accessed 12 Oct. 2020.
99 Creusen, E. H. Mariëlle & Schoormans, P. L. Jan (2004), op. cit., p. 7.
100 As cited by Creusen, E. H. Mariëlle & Schoormans, P. L. Jan (2004), op. cit., p. 7.
101 Lundin, Katie (2017), loc. cit.
102 Crowdspring. "Marketing Psychology." *Crowdspring.com,* 2020, https://www.crowdspring.com/marketing-psychology/. Accessed 13 Oct. 2020.
103 Lundin, Katie (2017), loc. cit.
104 As cited by Creusen, E. H. Mariëlle & Schoormans, P. L. Jan (2004), op. cit., p. 7.
105 Lundin, Katie (2017), loc. cit.
106 Lundin, Katie (2017), loc. cit.
107 Lundin, Katie (2017), loc. cit.
108 Creusen, E. H. Mariëlle & Schoormans, P. L. Jan (2004), op. cit., p. 7.
109 Creusen, E. H. Mariëlle & Schoormans, P. L. Jan (2004), op. cit., p. 8.
110 Creusen, E. H. Mariëlle & Schoormans, P. L. Jan (2004), loc. cit.
111 As cited by Creusen, E. H. Mariëlle & Schoormans, P. L. Jan (2004), op. cit., p. 9.
112 Kimbarovsky, Ross. "Branding: The Definitive Guide for 2020." *Crowdspring.com,* 9 Oct. 2020, https://www.crowdspring.com/blog/branding/. Accessed 13 Oct. 2020.
113 Kimbarovsky, Ross (2020), loc. cit.
114 Lumen. "Product Packaging and Branding." *Lumenlearning.com, 2020,*https://courses.lumenlearning.com/boundless-business/chapter/product-packaging-and-branding/. Accessed 29 Nov. 2020.
115 Ibid.
116 Gregory, Sonia. "11 Simple Steps for a Successful Brand Building Process." *Freshsparks.com,* 17 Nov. 2020, https://freshsparks.com/successful-brand-building-process/. Accessed 30 Nov. 2020.
117 Gregory, Sonia (2020), loc. cit.
118 Charles, Jeff (2016), loc. cit.
119 Holme, Ed. "Why Create A Visual Brand Language?" *Boltgroup.com,* 14 Jun. 2016, https://boltgroup.com/create-a-visual-brand-language. Accessed 27 Jan. 2020.
120 Muddana, Varshita (2019), loc. cit.
121 Charles, Jeff (2016), loc. cit.
122 Gilley, Cliff (2020), op. cit., p. 18.
123 Charles, Jeff (2016), loc. cit.
124 Ibid.
125 Buchanan, Bruce. "4 Factors Separating the Top Marketers from the Rest of the Pack." *Harvard Business Review,* 15 Jul.2020, https://hbr.org/sponsored/2020/07/4-factors-separating-the-top-marketers-from-the-rest-of-the-pack (sponsored context from rokt.com). Accessed 28 Sep. 2020.
126 Ibid.
127 Buchanan, Bruce (2020), loc. cit.
128 Howell, David. "7 Steps to Attracting Customers Away From Your Competitors." Fleximize.com, https://fleximize.com/articles/001027/7-steps-to-attracting-customers-away-from-your-competitors. Accessed 13 Oct. 2020.

129 Muddana, Varshita (2019), loc. cit.
130 Montague, Monty (2017), op. cit., p. 3.
131 Muddana, Varshita (2019), loc. cit.
132 Muddana, Varshita (2019), loc. cit.
133 Lloyd, Tracy. "Is an Agile Strategy the Right Approach for Brand Strategy?" *Emotivebrand.com,* 27 Oct. 2017, https://www.emotivebrand.com/agile-strategy/. Accessed 30 Nov. 2020.
134 Charles, Jeff (2016), loc. cit.
135 Charles, Jeff (2016), loc. cit.
136 Maayan, D. Gilad. "Agile Marketing Tips to Grow your Startup Even Faster." *Thenextweb.com,* 27 Oct. 2020, https://thenextweb.com/podium/2020/10/27/agile-marketing-tips-to-grow-your-startup-even-faster/. Accessed 30 Nov. 2020.
137 Ibid.
138 Nelly, M. "3 Ways UGC and Influencer Marketing Can Make Your Brand More Agile." *Pixlee.com,* 2020, https://www.pixlee.com/blog/3-ways-ugc-and-influencer-marketing-can-make-your-brand-more-agile/. Accessed 30 Nov. 2020.
139 Ibid.
140 Smart Insights. "7 Agile Marketing Tips To Help You Adapt To The Times." *Smartinsights.com,* 14 Oct. 2016, https://www.smartinsights.com/content-management/content-marketing-creative-and-formats/7-agile-marketing-tips-help-adapt-times/. Accessed 30 Nov. 2020.
141 Ibid.
142 Kimbarovsky, Ross (2020), loc. cit.
143 Charles, Jeff (2016), loc. cit.
144 Holme, Ed (2016), loc. cit.
145 Kimbarovsky, Ross (2020), loc. cit.
146 Gregory, Sonia. The Ultimate Guide to Building Your Brand: A Workbook with Templates, Tips & More. *FreshSparks,* 2020, pp. 2–15, https://freshsparks.com/successful-brand-building-process/. Accessed 30 Nov. 2020.
147 Charles, Jeff (2016), loc. cit.
148 Muddana, Varshita (2019), loc. cit.
149 Ibid.
150 Muddana, Varshita (2019), loc. cit.
151 Charles, Jeff (2016), loc. cit.
152 Holme, Ed (2016), loc. cit.
153 Holme, Ed (2016), loc. cit.
154 Montague, Monty. "Sound, Smell & Feel—It All Matters in Design," *Boltgroup.com,* 16 August 2016, https://boltgroup.com/sound-smell-feel-in-design. Accessed 27 Jan. 2020.
155 Montague, Monty (2016), loc. cit.
156 Ibid.
157 Montague, Monty (2016), loc. cit.
158 Ibid.
159 Ibid.
160 Montague, Monty (2016), loc. cit.
161 Ibid.
162 Montague, Monty (2016), loc. cit.
163 Charles, Jeff (2016), loc. cit.
164 Ibid.
165 Iuliano, Austin. "How to Build an Attractive Business and Personal Brand."

Smallbiztrends.com, 14 Feb. 2016, https://smallbiztrends.com/2016/02/build-a-business-brand.html. Accessed 1 Dec. 2020.

166 Iuliano, Austin (2016), loc. cit.

167 Iuliano, Austin (2016), loc. cit.

168 Orr, M. Linda, and Patel, Deep. "10 Innovative Ways to Excite Your Customers." *Entrepreneur.com,* 21 Mar. 2018, https://www.entrepreneur.com/article/310656. Accessed 1 Dec. 2020.

169 Orr, M. Linda, and Patel, Deep (2016), loc. cit.

170 Gallup. "Customer Engagement," *Gallup.com,* 2020, https://www.gallup.com/services/169331/customer-engagement.aspx. Accessed 1 Dec. 2020.

171 Gallup (2020), loc. cit.

172 Gallup (2020), loc. cit.

173 Forbes Coaches Council. "16 Unique Strategies To Improve Your Brand." *Forbes.com,* 20 Apr. 2017. Accessed 1 Dec. 2020.

174 Muddana, Varshita (2019), loc. cit.

175 Charles, Jeff (2016), loc. cit.

176 Corsten, Hans & Will, Thomas. "Integrated Production Concepts: Structural Reasons for Superior Competitive Performance." *MIR: Management International Review,* vol. 35, no. 1, 1995, pp. 69–88. JSTOR, www.jstor.org/stable/40228259. Accessed 11 Oct. 2020.

177 Industry Canada (2010), op. cit., p. 3.

178 As cited by Industry Canada (2010); ibid.

179 Taulien, Kalob. "JavaScript Essentials." *Udemy.com,* 2019. Accessed 8 Nov. 2019.

180 Ibid.

181 Tempelman, Erik. Materials Experience: Fundamentals of Materials and Design. Elsevier 2014. DOI: https://doi.org/10.1016/C2012-0-02198-9. Accessed 11 Oct. 2020.

182 Dörr, Jochen and Stark, Alexander. "Possibilities of Lightweight Material Construction." *Spotlightmetal.com,* 20 Jun. 2018, https://www.spotlightmetal.com/possibilities-of-lightweight-material-construction-a-721959/. Accessed 11 Oct. 2020.

183 Cambridge Dictionary. "Deadweight." *Cambridge University Press,* 2020, https://dictionary.cambridge.org/dictionary/english/deadweight. Accessed 11 Oct. 2020.

184 Merriam-Webster. "Useful load." *Merriam-Webster.com Dictionary,*https://www.merriam-webster.com/dictionary/useful%20load. Accessed 11 Oct. 2020.

185 Kaspar, Jerome & Vielhaber, Michael (2017), op. cit., p. 329.

186 Kumarasmy, Y. & Kanesan, K. "The Applications of Nanotechnology in Mechanical Engineering." *International Conference on Modeling & Simulation (ICMS'15),* at ASTRA University, Thanjavur-613401, Tamilnadu, India, 2015, p. 5.

187 As cited by Kaspar, Jerome & Vielhaber, Michael (2017), op. cit., p. 329.

188 Thuline, John. "What Everyday Materials Can Benefit From Carbon Fiber Designs?" Element6composites.com, 9 Aug., 2018b, https://element6composites.com/what-everyday-materials-can-benefit-from-carbon-fiber-designs/.

189 Miltenović et al. (2014), op. cit., p. 531.

190 Miltenović et al. (2014), op. cit., p. 535.

191 Miltenović et al. (2014), op. cit., pp. 532&533.

192 Miltenović et al. (2014), op. cit., p. 534.

193 Sinke, Jos. "Text Lecture 8b – Aerospace Materials:" in Introduction to Aeronautical Engineering. *MOOC Learning Materials,* course excerpt from Delft University of Technology, in partnership with edx.org, 2019a, p. 4.
194 Miltenović et al. (2014), op. cit., p. 538.
195 Thuline, John. "What Makes Carbon Fiber So Strong?" Element6composites.com, 8 Jul. 2018a, https://element6composites.com/what-makes-carbon-fiber-so-strong/.
196 Thuline, John (2018a), loc. cit.
197 Thermal conductivity of materials is measured in W/mK. See *Universal Science.com.* See http://www.universal-science.com/wp-content/uploads/2012/08/Thermal-conductivity-table.pdf/. Accessed 29 Nov. 2019. According to McGrath, Michael, W/mK stands for Watts per meter-Kelvin. See https://forum.digikey.com/u/michael_mcgrath/summary. Accessed 29 Nov. 2019.
198 Thuline, John (2018a), loc. cit.
199 OptiProERP (2020), loc. cit.
200 Ibid.
201 Muddana, Varshita (2019), loc. cit.
202 Course Hero (2011), op. cit., p. 4.
203 Ibid.
204 Cross, J. David. "New Polymer Enables Batteries to be Self-Healing and Recyclable." *Azom.com,* p. 1, 21 Jan. 2020, https://www.azom.com/news.aspx?newsID=52849. Accessed 6 Sep. 2020.
205 As cited by Cross, J. David (2020), ibid; pp. 1–2.
206 Course Hero (2011), op. cit., p. 4.
207 Ibid.
208 Creusen, E. H. Mariëlle & Schoormans, P. L. Jan (2004), op. cit., pp. 17, 18 & 20.
209 Creusen, E. H. Mariëlle & Schoormans, P. L. Jan (2004), op. cit., p. 16.

Works Cited

Acevedo, Laura. "What Are Ergonomic Products?" *Hearst,* https://smallbusiness.chron.com/ergonomic-products-16880.html.

Asaro, Peter. "On Banning Autonomous Weapon Systems: Human Rights, Automation, and the Dehumanization of Lethal Decision-Making." *International Review of the Red Cross,* vol. 94, no. 886, Summer 2012, pp. 687–86. doi: 10.1017/S1816383112000768

Bamossy, Gary, et al. "A Preliminary Investigation of the Reliability and Validity of an Aesthetic Judgment Test." Eds. Richard P. Bagozzi and Alice M. Tybout, *NA – Advances in Consumer Research,* vol. 10, Ann Arbor, MI: Association for Consumer Research, 1983, pp. 685–90.

Banton, Caroline. "Pricing Power." *Investopedia.com,* 25 Jun. 2019, https://www.investopedia.com/terms/p/pricingpower.asp.

Bartlett, Blake. "What is Product Led Growth? How to Build a Software Company in the End User Era." *OpenViewpartners.com,* 1 Jul. 2020, https://openviewpartners.com/blog/what-is-product-led-growth/#.XxbYSTMo9Tc.

Basılgan, Müslüm. "The Creative Destruction of Economic Development: The Schumpeterian Entrepreneur." *TODAİE's Review of Public Administration,* Volume 5, no. 3, Sep. 2011, pp. 35–76.

Bawden-Davis, Julie. "7 Excellent Ways to Get New Customers." *American express.com*, 25 Jun. 2019, https://www.americanexpress.com/en-us/business/trends-and-insights/articles/7-excellent-ways-to-attract-new-customers/.

Buchanan, Bruce. "4 Factors Separating the Top Marketers from the Rest of the Pack." *Harvard Business Review*, 15 Jul. 2020, https://hbr.org/sponsored/2020/07/4-factors-separating-the-top-marketers-from-the-rest-of-the-pack (sponsored context from rokt.com).

Campbell, F. C. Ed. "Chapter 1: Introduction and Uses of Lightweight Materials." *Lightweight Materials: Understanding the Basics*. eBook, Published by Materials Park, Ohio: ASM International, 2012, pp. 1–709. Available at https://www.asminternational.org/home/-/journal_content/56/10192/05355G/PUBLICATION

Course Hero. "Technology & Design: Influences on Product Design." AS LEVEL Section A FACT FILES. *Coursehero.com*, 2011, pp. 1–7, https://www.coursehero.com/file/40838121/A2AS-TECH-Support-10370pdf/.

Crowdspring. "Marketing Psychology." *Crowdspring.com*, 2020, https://www.crowdspring.com/marketing-psychology/.

Cambridge Dictionary. "Deadweight." *Cambridge University Press*, 2020, https://dictionary.cambridge.org/dictionary/english/deadweight.

Campbell, F. C. (editor). "Chapter 1: Introduction and Uses of Lightweight Materials." in Lightweight Materials—Understanding the Basics. *Asminternational.org*, 2012. eBook, Published by Materials Park, Ohio: ASM International, pp. 1–709. Available at https://www.asminternational.org/home/-/journal_content/56/1019 2/05355G/PUBLICATION

Ceru, J. Dennis. Mindset of the Entrepreneur. *MOOC Learning Materials*, course excerpts from Babson College of Entrepreneurship, in partnership with edx.org, 2018. Dennis J. Ceru is an Adjunct Professor of Entrepreneurship.

Charles, Jeff. "7 Important Traits of a Successful Brand." Published: 14 Jun. 2016, Last Updated: 12 Dec. 2019, https://smallbiztrends.com/2016/06/7-important-brand-characteristics.html.

Charles, Jeff. "7 Important Traits of a Successful Brand." Published: 14 Jun. 2016, Last Updated: 12 Dec. 2019, https://smallbiztrends.com/2016/06/7-important-brand-characteristics.html.

Ciocarlie, Matei. Robotics. *MOOC Learning Materials*, course excerpt from Colombia University, in Partnership with edx.org, 2018.

Cohen, Joel B. and Kunal Basu. "Alternative Models of Categorization: Toward a Contingent Processing Framework." *Journal of Consumer Research*, vol. 13, no. 4, 1987, pp. 455–72.

Corsten, Hans and Will, Thomas. "Integrated Production Concepts: Structural Reasons for Superior Competitive Performance." *MIR: Management International Review*, vol. 35, no. 1, 1995, pp. 69–88. JSTOR, www.jstor.org/stable/40228259.

Creusen, E. H. Mariëlle and Schoormans, P. L. Jan. "The Different Roles of Product Appearance in Consumer Choice." *Journal of Product Innovation Management*, Dec. 2004, pp. 2–20. doi: 10.1111/j.0737-6782.2005.00103.x.

Cross, J. David. "New Polymer Enables Batteries to be Self-Healing and Recyclable." *Azom.com*, p. 1, 21 Jan. 2020, https://www.azom.com/news.aspx?newsID=52849.

Customer Success Association (CSA). "Success." Mikael Blaisdell & Associates,

Inc., 2019, https://www.customersuccessassociation.com/library/the-definition-of-customer-success/.

Customer Success Association (CSA). "Success." Mikael Blaisdell & Associates, Inc., 2019, https://www.customersuccessassociation.com/library/the-definition-of-customer-success/. Accessed 6 Oct. 2020.

Dörr, Jochen and Stark, Alexander. "Possibilities of Lightweight Material Construction." *Spotlightmetal.com*, 20 Jun. 2018, https://www.spotlightmetal.com/possibilities-of-lightweight-material-construction-a-721959/.

Dunn III, Richard J. From Gettysburg to the Gulf and Beyond: Coping with Revolutionary Technological Change in Land Warfare. National Defense University Institute for National Strategic Studies Fort McNair Washington, DC 20319. Accession Number: ADA422085, McNair Papers Number 13. Report Date: 1 Jan. 1993, pp. 1–99, https://apps.dtic.mil/sti/citations/ADA422085

Dunn III, J. Richard. From Gettysburg to the Gulf and Beyond: Coping with Revolutionary Technological change in Land Warfare. *The Institute for National Strategic Studies,* National Defense University Institute for National Strategic Studies Fort McNair Washington, DC 20319. Accession Number: ADA422085, McNair Papers Number 13. Re port Date: 1 Jan 1993, pp. 1–99, Mc Nair Papers, Number 13, https://apps.dtic.mil/sti/citations/ADA422085.

EDUCBA. "Learn 6 Useful Differences between Big Data vs. Predictive Analytics." *EDUCBA.com*, 2019a, https://www.educba.com/big-data-vs-predictive-analytics/.

EDUCBA. "7 Most Useful Comparison between Business Analytics vs. Predictive Analytics." *EDUCBA.com*, 2019b, https://www.educba.com/business-analytics-vs-predictive-analytics/.

Engel, James F., et al. *Consumer Behavior*. 8th Edition, Fort Worth: Dryden Press, 1995, pp. 1–951, http://lib.ugent.be/catalog/rug01:000726736

Forbes Coaches Council. "16 Unique Strategies To Improve Your Brand." *Forbes.com*, 20 Apr. 2017.

Gallup. "Customer Engagement," *Gallup.com*, 2020, https://www.gallup.com/services/169331/customer-engagement.aspx.

Garber, Lawrence L. Jr. "The Package Appearance in Choice." Eds. Frank R. Kardes and Mita Sujan. *NA – Advances in Consumer Research*, vol. 22, Provo, UT: Association for Consumer Research, 1995, pp. 653–60.

Garber, Lawrence L. Jr., et al. *The Role of Package Color in Consumer Purchase Consideration and Choice*. Cambridge, MA: Marketing Science Institute (Working Paper Series, Report. No. 00-104), 2000, pp. 3–46.

Gardner, David. "Radical Vs. Incremental Innovation: The Right Approach for the Right Time," *Marumatchbox.com*, 14 Nov. 2017, https://marumatchbox.com/radical-vs-incremental-innovation-the-right-approach-for-the-right-time/.

Gilley, Cliff. "The Product Manager's Influence Map: A Practical Guide to Organizational Alignment and Relationship-Building for Product Teams." *Go.pendo.io*, 2020, pp. 3–44. Cliff Gilley and is an active board member with the Pacific Northwest Product Management Community.

Grace, Allie. "What 40 Years of Research Reveals About the Differences Between

Disruptive and Radical Innovation." *FileMaker Developer Experts – Neo Code*, 21 May 2019, https://www.neocode.com/blog/what-40-years-of-research-reveals-about-the-differences-between-disruptive-and-radical-innovation/.

Gregory, Sonia. The Ultimate Guide to Building Your Brand: A Workbook with Templates, Tips & More. *FreshSparks*, 2020, pp. 2–15, https://freshsparks.com/successful-brand-building-process/.

Gregory, Sonia. "11 Simple Steps for a Successful Brand Building Process." *Freshsparks.com*, 17 Nov. 2020, https://freshsparks.com/successful-brand-building-process/.

Gustafsson, A., et al. "Customer co-creation in service innovation: A matter of communication?" *Journal of Service Management*, vol. 23, no. 3, Jun. 2012, pp. 4–32.

Haghshenas, Meysam. "Metal–Matrix Composites." Reference Module in Materials Science and Materials Engineering, 28 Oct. 2015. 10.1016/B978-0-12-803581-8.03950-3.

Hannon, E., et al. "Introduction." The circular economy: Moving from theory to practice. *McKinsey Center for Business and Environment*, Special edition, Oct. 2016, pp. 3–38.

Heuss, Ruth, et al. Lightweight, Heavy Impact: How Carbon Fiber and Other Lightweight Materials Will Develop Across Industries and Specifically in Automotive. *Advanced Industries*. McKinsey&Company, Feb. 2012, pp. 1–24.

Hirschman, Elizabeth C., and Morris B. Holbrook. "Hedonic Consumption: Emerging Concepts, Methods and Propositions." *Journal of Marketing*, vol. 46, no. 3, 1982, pp. 92–101. JSTOR, www.jstor.org/stable/1251707.

Holbrook, Morris B. "Some Preliminary Notes on Research in Consumer Esthetics." Ed. Jerry C. Olson, *NA – Advances in Consumer Research*, vol. 07. Ann Arbor, MI: Association for Consumer Research, 1980, pp. 104–08.

Holme, Ed. "Why Create A Visual Brand Language?" *Boltgroup.com*, 14 Jun. 2016, https://boltgroup.com/create-a-visual-brand-language.

Howell, David. "7 Steps to Attracting Customers Away From Your Competitors." *Fleximize.com*, https://fleximize.com/articles/001027/7-steps-to-attracting-customers-away-from-your-competitors.

Industry Canada. Product Design, Research and Development: A Canadian Manufacturing Perspective. *Publishing and Depository Services*, Public Works and Government Services Canada, Ottawa, 2012, pp. 1–30.

Isa, S. S. and Liem, A. "Classifying Physical Models and Prototypes in the Design Process: A Study on the Economical and Usability Impact of Adopting Models and Prototypes in the Design Process." *International Design Conference – Design 2014*, Dubrovnik Croatia, 19–22 May 2014, pp. 1–12.

Iuliano, Austin. "How to Build an Attractive Business and Personal Brand." *Smallbiztrends.com*, 14 Feb. 2016, https://smallbiztrends.com/2016/02/build-a-business-brand.html.

Kaspar, Jerome and Vielhaber, Michael. "Fiber-Reinforced Composite Design Within A Lightweight and Material-Oriented Development Process." *21st International Conference On Engineering Design*, Iced17, 21–25 Aug. 2017, The University of British Columbia, Vancouver, Canada, pp. 329–38.

Keisner, A., et al. "Breakthrough Technologies – Robotics, Innovation and Intellectual Property." *Economic Research Working Paper No. 30*, Economics & Statistics Series, Geneva: (WIPO), Nov., 2015, pp. 3–38.

Khedari, J., et al. New Lightweight Composite Construction Materials with Low Thermal Conductivity. *Cement and Concrete Composites*, vol. 23, no. 1, pp. 65–70, 1 Feb. 2001. doi: 10.1016/S0958-9465(00)00072-X.

Kimbarovsky, Ross. "Branding: The Definitive Guide for 2020." *Crowdspring.com*, 9 Oct. 2020, https://www.crowdspring.com/blog/branding/.

Kumarasmy, Y. and Kanesan, K. "The Applications of Nanotechnology in Mechanical Engineering." *International Conference on Modeling & Simulation (ICMS'15)*, at ASTRA University, Thanjavur-613401, Tamilnadu, India, 2015, pp. 1–7.

Levy, Sidney J. "Symbols for Sale." *Harvard Business Review*, vol. 37, no. 4, Jul./Aug. 1959, pp. 117–19.

Lloyd, Tracy. "Is an Agile Strategy the Right Approach for Brand Strategy?" *Emotivebrand.com*, 27 Oct. 2017, https://www.emotivebrand.com/agile-strategy/.

Löbach, Bernd. *Industrial Design: Grundlagen der Industrieproduktgestaltung*. Muenchen: Verlag Karl Thiemig, 1976, pp. 1–206.

Lumen. "Product Packaging and Branding." *Lumenlearning.com*, 2020, https://courses.lumenlearning.com/boundless-business/chapter/product-packaging-and-branding/.

Lundin, Katie. "4 Psychology-Based Design Tips For Eye-Catching Packaging Design." *Crowspring.com*, 9 Nov. 2017, https://www.crowdspring.com/blog/packaging-design-tips-psychology/.

Maayan, D. Gilad. "Agile Marketing Tips to Grow your Startup Even Faster." *Thenextweb.com*, 27 Oct. 2020, https://thenextweb.com/podium/2020/10/27/agile-marketing-tips-to-grow-your-startup-even-faster/.

Mankins, Michael. "Great Companies Obsess Over Productivity, Not Efficiency." *Harvard Business Review*, 1 Mar. 2017, https://hbr.org/2017/03/great-companies-obsess-over-productivity-not-efficiency?referral=03758&cm_vc=rr_item_page.top_right.

MaRS. "Value Proposition: A Reflection of the Relationship between Your Customer and Brand." Learn.marsdd.com, 2020a, https://learn.marsdd.com/article/value-proposition-a-reflection-of-the-relationship-between-your-
customer-and-brand/.

MaRS. "Elements of Product's Value Proposition: Functional, Self-expressive and Emotional Benefits." Learn.marsdd.com, 2020b, https://learn.marsdd.com/article/elements-of-a-products-value-proposition-functional-self-expressive-and-emotional-benefits/.

McCracken, Grant. "Culture and Consumption: A Theoretical Account of the Structure and Movement of the Cultural Meaning of Consumer Goods." *Journal of Consumer Research*, vol. 13, no. 1, 1986, pp. 71–84.

Merriam-Webster. "Useful load." *Merriam-Webster.com Dictionary*, https://www.merriam-webster.com/dictionary/useful%20load. Accessed 11Oct.2020.

Miltenović, A., et al. "Role and Importance of Lightweight Design in the Product Development." *COMET a 2014: 2nd International Scientific Conference*; University of East Sarajevo, 2–5 Dec. 2014, pp. 529–38.

Montague, Monty. "Sound, Smell & Feel—It All Matters in Design,"

Boltgroup.com, 16 Aug. 2016, https://boltgroup.com/sound-smell-feel-in-design.

Montague, Monty. "The Amazing Role of Aesthetics in Product Design." *Boltgroup.com*, 21 Jun., 2017, pp. 1–4, https://boltgroup.com/aesthetics-in-product-design.

Muddana, Varshita. "The Importance of Your Product's Design and Appearance." *Soft Script Solutions*, 22 Mar. 2019, https://www.softscripts.net/blog/2019/03/products-design-appearance/.

Muller, Wim. Order and Meaning in Design. Series in Industrial Design. Utrecht: Lemma Publishers, 2001, pp. 1–354.

Murdoch, Peter and Charles H. Flurscheim. "Form." Ed. Charles H. Flurscheim. *Industrial Design in Engineering: A Marriage of Techniques*, 1st Edition. Worcester, UK: The Design Council, 1983, pp. 105–31.

Nelly, M. "3 Ways UGC and Influencer Marketing Can Make Your Brand More Agile." *Pixlee.com*, 2020, https://www.pixlee.com/blog/3-ways-ugc-and-influencer-marketing-can-make-your-brand-more-agile/.

Nibusinessinfo. "User-centered design: The importance of ergonomics." *Invest Northern Ireland* in partnership with *Nidirect government services*, 2020a, https://www.nibusinessinfo.co.uk/content/importance-ergonomics.

Olson, E.L. and G. Bakke. "Implementing the Lead User Method in a High Technology Firm: A Longitudinal Study of Intentions Versus Actions", *Journal of Product Innovation Management*, vol. 18 no. 2, 2001, pp. 388–95.

Orr, M. Linda, and Patel, Deep. "10 Innovative Ways to Excite Your Customers." *Entrepreneur.com*, 21 Mar. 2018, https://www.entrepreneur.com/article/310656.

Owen-Hill, Alex. "What's the difference between robotics and artificial intelligence?" *Blog.robotiq.com*, 19 Jul. 2017, https://blog.robotiq.com/whats-the-difference-between-robotics-and-artificial-intelligence/.

Productled. "What is product-led growth," *productled.org*, 2020, https://www.productled.org/foundations/what-is-product-led-growth#Chap1.

Rossé, M., et al. "Finding growth within: A new framework for Europe." The circular economy: Moving from theory to practice. *McKinsey Center for Business and Environment*, Special edition, Oct. 2016, pp. 5–10.

Schmitt, Bernd H., and Alex Simonson. *Marketing Aesthetics: The Strategic Management of Brands, Identity, and Image*. New York: The Free Press, 1997, pp. 1–345.

Schumpeter, Joseph A. *The Theory of Economics Development: An Inquiry into Profits, Capital, Credit, Interest, and the Business Cycle*. Oxford University Press, Oxford, UK, 1 Jan. 1934, pp. 1–255. Available at https://www.hup.harvard.edu/catalog.php?isbn=9780674879904&content=toc.

Sinke, Jos. "Text Lecture 8b – Aerospace Materials:" in Introduction to Aeronautical Engineering: DelftX AE1110x. *MOOC Learning Materials*, course excerpt from Delft University of Technology, in partnership with edx.org, 2019a, pp. 1–4.

Skidmore, Paul. "11 Tips for Good Ergonomic Product Design and Development." *Cadcrowd.com*, 12 Dec. 2018, https://www.cadcrowd.com/blog/11-tips-for-good-ergonomic-product-design-and-development.

SlideModel. "Why Customer Centricity Will Win You More Business (in 2020)." *SlideModel.com*, 14 May 2020a, https://slidemodel.com.

SlideModel. "Product-Led Growth (PLG): The Ultimate SaaS Business Growth Strategy To Pursue." *SlideModel.com*, 20 May 2020b, https://slidemodel.com/product-led-growth-plg.

Smart Insights. "7 Agile Marketing Tips To Help You Adapt To The Times." *Smartinsights.com*, 14 Oct. 2016, https://www.smartinsights.com/content-management/content-marketing-creative-and-formats/7-agile-marketing-tips-help-adapt-times/.

Stadler, Antonia. "Challenges and solutions for the digital transformation and use of exponential technologies." Deloitte AG, Zurich: The Creative Studio, 27 May, pp. 1–25.

Stam, Erik and Garnsey, Elizabeth. "Entrepreneurship in the Knowledge Economy." *University of Cambridge*, 2008, pp. 1–24, https://www.academia.edu.

Stroud, Samanda. "Business Tips for New Product Design and Development." *Cadcrowd.com*, 11 Sep. 2018, https://www.cadcrowd.com/blog/business-tips-for-new-product-design-development.

Taddeo, Mariarosaria and Luciano Floridi. "How AI Can Be a Force for Good." *Science*, vol. 361, no. 6404, 24 Aug. 2018, pp. 751–52. American Association for the Advancement of Science (AAAS): New York, DOI: 10.1126/science.aat5991

Taulien, Kalob. "JavaScript Essentials." *Udemy.com*, 2019. Accessed 8Nov.2019.

Tempelman, Erik. Materials Experience: Fundamentals of Materials and Design. Elsevier, 2014. https://doi.org/10.1016/C2012-0-02198-9.

The European Commission. "Draft Ethics Guidelines for Trustworthy AI: Working Document for stakeholders." *Consultation*. The European Commission's *High-Level Expert Group on Artificial Intelligence (AI)*, Brussels, 18 Dec. 2018.

Thuline, John. "What Everyday Materials Can Benefit From Carbon Fiber Designs?" Element6composites.com, 9 Aug., 2018b, https://element6composites.com/what-everyday-materials-can-benefit-from-carbon-fiber-designs/.

Thuline, John. "What Makes Carbon Fiber So Strong?" Element6composites.com, 8 Jul. 2018a, https://element6composites.com/what-makes-carbon-fiber-so-strong/.

Totango. 2018 – Customer Success Salary Survey & State of the Profession Report. *Totango.com*, 2018, pp. 2–18, https://www.totango.com/whitepapers/2018-customer-success-salary-survey-state-of-the-profession-report.

Tsui, Eric. "Resource-based view (RBV) of a firm: What is RBV?" MOOC Learning Materials, course excerpts from The Hong Kong Polytechnic University, in partnership with edx.org, 2018a, pp. 1–10.

Veryzer, Robert W. Jr. "The Place of Product Design and Aesthetics in Consumer Research." Eds. Frank R. Kardes and Mita Sujan, *NA – Advances in Consumer Research*, vol. 22, Provo, UT: Association for Consumer Research, 1995, pp. 641–45.

Veryzer, Robert W. Jr., and J. Wesley Hutchinson. "The Influence of Unity and Prototypicality on Aesthetic Responses to New Product Designs." *Journal of Consumer Research*, vol. 24, no. 4, 1998, pp. 374–94.

Victorino, L., et al. "Service Innovation and Customer Choices in the Hospitality Industry." *Managing Service Quality*, vol. 15, no. 6, 2005, pp. 555–76.

Ward-Close, C. M. and Robertson, J. G. "Advances in the fabrication of titanium based composites." *Advanced Performance Materials*, vol. 3, no. 3, 1 Jul. 1996, pp. 251–62. doi: 10.1007/BF00136790.

Whitfield, Allan and Tom Wiltshire. "Colour." Ed. Charles H. Flurscheim. *Industrial Design in Engineering: A Marriage of Techniques*, 1st Edition Worcester, UK: The Design Council, 1983, pp. 133–57.

Yang, Guang-Zhong, et al. "The Grand Challenges of Science Robotics." *Science Robotics*, vol. 3, no. 14, eaar7650, 31 Jan. 2018, pp. 1–14. American Association for the Advancement of Science (AAAS): New York. DOI: 10.1126/scirobotics.aar7650

6 Conclusions and Suggestions

Introduction

This chapter begins by explaining the path toward *strategic visionary planning*. It concludes that the best planning approach would require the assembling of the best organizational context-specific combinations of *incremental planning* and align them with those that match with *visionary planning* (e.g., zero-based planning) – which would lead to *strategic visionary planning*. This then creates a much clearer picture of the organization's strategic value creation imperatives because *strategic visionary planning* naturally provides a fertile ground for *strategic foresight* to flourish.

It also argues that in order *to properly carve out the path toward sustainability leadership*, a managerial thinker needs strategic thinking to make him or her a strategic manager, while a visionary thinker needs strategic thinking to make him or her a strategic visionary. Furthermore, a strategic manager and a strategic visionary would need some schooling in strategic foresight so as to become a sustainability leader. That is, a strategic manager + a strategic visionary = transformational leadership. While transformational leadership + servant leadership qualities = sustainability leadership.

This chapter also noticed some differences between *value creation imperatives* and *strategic value creation imperatives*. But this book favors *strategic value creation imperatives* because it perfectly aligns with profitability, productivity, and sustainability. Strategic value creation imperatives take the short-term, medium-term, and long-term considerations as constituting alignments in both their individual horizons and as a synergistic collection of indispensable parameters for a healthy and resilient organization.

It also argues that there are two kinds of leadership problems that constrain value creation: *(1) That most managers in organizations have leaders without a strategic vision,* so at best they can only guarantee low to moderate profits in the short-term and probably in the medium-term.

(2) That there is the existence of many visionary leaders with no appropriate management skills to link their vision to commercial reality.

It also found that strangely, the *job of the manager* clearly appears to work somewhat in an *opposite direction* with what obtains in the OrgDNA formal building blocks, when it comes to successful strategy execution.

It also observed that formal OrgDNA elements are attractive to companies because they are tangible – as they can be easily defined and measured. But they are only half the story as the *intangible* elements also matter in the life of an organization. And finally, this chapter also advances some new and useful suggestions to make a business venture clearly standout in the competition.

6.1 Conclusions

6.1.1 General Conclusions

In explaining the path toward *strategic visionary planning,* this chapter arrives at the understanding that incremental planning has been closely associated with managerial thinking (leadership) or role, but usually lacks the foresight to adequately secure the future long-term viability of the organization. Zero-based planning has been closely associated with visionary thinking. In most cases, visionary thinking is primarily handicapped by the missing causal link between short-term and medium-term attainment of objectives in terms of survivability and profit maximization of the organization. Whereas, managerial thinking is, too often, handicapped by myopia (short-sightedness), which is associated with the inability to properly envisage and organize the strategic implementation of long-term planning – i.e., in terms of ensuring future financial viability and sustainability of the organization. As a result, this chapter concludes that the best planning approach would require the assembling of the best organizational context-specific combinations of *incremental planning* and align them with those that match with *visionary planning* (e.g., zero-based planning) – which would lead to *strategic visionary planning.* This then creates a much clearer picture of the organization's strategic value creation imperatives, because *strategic visionary planning* naturally provides a fertile ground for *strategic foresight* to flourish.

Therefore, the litmus test for achieving an organization's vision is to ensure that you achieve it without over compromising your organization's minimum short-term financial viability, and to a limited extent, those of the medium-term. Therefore, for a visionary leader to succeed, besides effectual or non-linear thinking, he or she needs managerial or rational thinking (linear thinking) as well. This would help curb down the excesses of nonlinear thinking. By doing so, it helps to differentiate the ideas that can sustain short term financial requirements of the business from those that are targeted for long term financial viability.

To properly carve out the path toward sustainability leadership, a managerial thinker needs strategic thinking to make him or her a strategic manager, while a visionary thinker needs strategic thinking to make him or her a strategic visionary. Meanwhile, a strategic manager and a strategic visionary would need some schooling in strategic foresight so as to become a sustainability leader. That is, a strategic manager + a strategic visionary = transformational leadership. While transformational leadership + servant leadership qualities = sustainability leadership.

There are also differences between value creation imperatives and strategic value creation imperatives. This chapter concludes that *value creation imperatives* may involve both short-term and long-term considerations of the financial viability of the firm, or it may involve just one of them. In this respect, value creation via managerial thinking - which maximizes profits and reduces costs as much as possible in the short term, has been the dominant force. But at best, it can only ensure low to moderate growth in the short and medium term. At the least, it might lead to declining growth rates and compromise the survival of the firm in the long run. *Strategic value creation imperatives* are long-term value-oriented planning modes. They are realized via strategic thinking, and at a more advanced stage, it embraces strategic foresight. It involves constructing a proper business foresight that ensures short-term profitability and financial viability, with a strategic vision of transitioning these short-term gains via medium-term strategies into the long-term financial viability and sustainability modes. Obviously, it would tend to increase the competitive position of the firm in the long term.

This explains why this book favors *strategic value creation imperatives* because it perfectively aligns with profitability, productivity, and sustainability. Strategic value creation imperatives take the short-term, medium-term, and long-term considerations as constituting alignments in both their individual horizons, and as a synergistic collection of indispensable parameters for a healthy and resilient organization. But over-emphasis on long-term financial viability of the firm without due consideration on short-term profitability and financial health runs a high risk of the firm collapsing quite early – probably even in the short-term. For this reason, this book strongly pushes beyond the boundaries of strategic thinking to strongly embrace strategic foresight. That being said, we can identify five groups of business ideas-oriented priorities:

1. There are those that create value out of little or nothing, which may be sustainable or not sustainable, we call them start-up entrepreneurs.
2. There are those that primarily create more and new values on existing values through new product innovation in a sustainable way – these are the champions.

3. There are others that add distinctive value on existing values; through product life extension and quality improvement for existing products, so as to create impact among leading competitors - these are the runner-ups.
4. There are others that make improvements on existing products through imitative diversification. These imitative products are too often, relatively of lower quality compared to those of the industry champions, and sometimes those of the runner-up. But target underserved markets, or less-privileged niche markets through affordably low prices – these are the imitators.
5. There are those that do not necessarily add distinctive value to existing value, but rely on a continual refurbishing of existing values or income streams, just to stay in business – these are the survivors.

Agreeably, radical innovations bring in revolutions in the industry that usually takes traditionally known business evolutionary patterns off-guard, but is this rare to come by. The pace of global competition is usually dictated by a slight competitive edge of one firm over the others, which we can rightly say, are *evolutionary* in character. But one can equally note that within each *evolutionary* business pattern, it would not be uncommon to find *revolutionary stages*. It is the ability to distinguish these intricacies and act on them by using the appropriate recipes that separate the champions, from those who are runners-up, imitators, and survivors in today's competitive business environment. On this strand of reasoning, there is evidence that those who catch existing waves in the wealth creation enterprise often do so by copying from their predecessors. This applies primarily to survivors, and to imitators to a large extent. Champions, on their part, see and go beyond the historically tinted lenses of their time and the experience of their generation – to create new waves by doing and making things happen. By this approach, champions develop a greater insight that goes far beyond understanding the process and dynamics of wave-catching into mastering the art of creating new waves.

6.1.2 Specific Conclusions

Two Kinds of Leadership Problems That Constrain Value Creation

1. *That most managers in organizations have leaders without strategic vision,* so at best they can only guarantee low to moderate profits in the short term and probably in the medium term. At the least, they can face the risk of very low-profit margins, or the business winding up in the long term due to lack of strategic vision. And that there is a compelling logic in favor of orientating or harnessing the inner and the outer power of managers to become strategic visionaries, by

cultivating in them a built-in strategic foresight (the inner world of values), while upgrading or developing appropriate skills that make them strategic managers (the outer world of values). A combination of these two worlds, make managers become sustainability leaders – a much sought-after quality in today's world.

2. *That there is the existence of many visionary leaders with no appropriate management skills to link their vision to commercial reality.* In other words, there is the absence of a real causality between their business ideas and the business reality. And that there is a compelling logic in favor of orientating or harnessing the inner and the outer power of visionaries to become strategic visionaries, by cultivating in them a built-in strategic foresight (the inner world of values), while matching it proportionately with the building of appropriate skills that makes them strategic managers (the outer world of values). A combination of these two worlds, make visionaries become sustainability leaders – a much sought-after quality in today's world.

The Manager's Role and a Company's Genetic Material

Strangely, the *job of the manager* clearly appears to work somewhat in an *opposite direction* with what which obtains in the OrgDNA formal building blocks, when it comes to successful strategy execution. For example, according to Mintzberg (1990), the manager's job commences from *formal authority*, to *status*, to *interpersonal roles*, and finally to *decision roles.* On the contrary, we saw earlier that to ensure *successful strategy execution,* Neilson *et al.* (2008) identified four fundamental building blocks (OrgDNA) that executives can use to influence those actions. It starts with clarifying *decision rights* and making sure *information flows* where it needs to go, and that, once these two have been properly aligned, then the next logical step is to correct *motivators,* and the types of changes required in the organization's *structure* become obvious. But when an organization fails to execute its strategy, the first thing most managers think of as an effort to improve performance is to *restructure*. In concurrence, Saario (2020) strongly argues that clear roles and responsibilities are the key to successful cooperation. In this regard, when working together, trust and open sharing of information between the partners are required. This means *clarifying decision rights* and designing its appropriate *information flow* is a first and paramount consideration in any sustainably successful strategy execution.

According to Mintzberg (1990), ironically, it is at this level of *structure* (authority and status) where the manager's job starts, whereas under the normal requirements of a company's genetic material, *structure* or *authority and status* should logically present itself after OrgDNA *motivators* have been corrected (*see* Fig. 6.1). Also, note that *motivators is* one of the interpersonal roles in the manager's job.

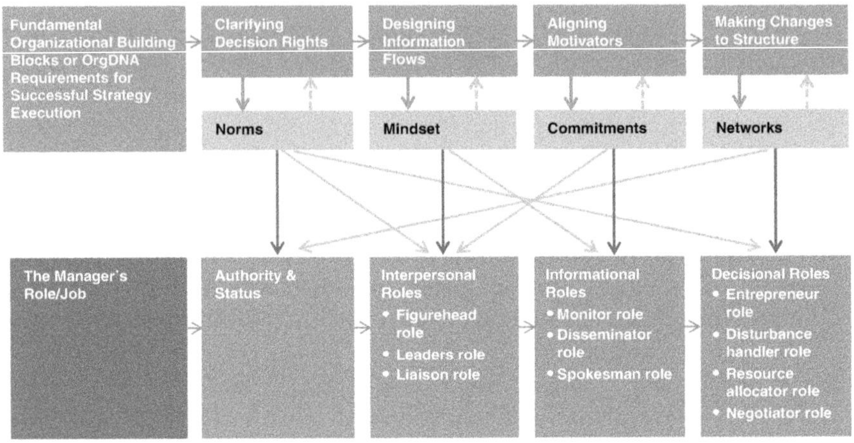

Figure 6.1 Opposite Relationships between the Manager's Role and the OrgDNA Requirements.
Source: Author created.

As shown in Fig. 6.1, the genetic materials of an organization, also known as its Organizational DNA; requires that the proper alignments for successful strategy execution begins from clarifying decision rights, which goes alongside its informal organizational building block requirement (its norms - indicated in the light-grey boxes directly below); and ends up at making the necessary changes to structure, which also goes alongside its informal organizational building block requirement (its networks). On the contrary, with respect to successful strategy execution, the manager's job begins with authority and status (which is the formal OrgDNA equivalent to structure), and then ends up with decisional roles (which is the formal OrgDNA equivalent to decision rights). These misalignments are indicated in the dark-grey horizontal arrows at the extremes. Additionally, the two other dark-grey horizontal arrows at the middle also show other misalignments between the manager's job and the genetic materials of the organization.

As you can see, the **light-grey** arrows linking the manager's role and the OrgDNA are supposed to be the proper alignments for successful strategy execution. Again, the **dark-grey horizontal** arrows linking the OrgDNA formal building blocks with their informal building blocks are known as **the OrgDNA** *synthesized templates*. While the dotted light-grey horizontal arrows linking the informal OrgDNA building blocks with their formal building blocks is called the *reverse transcription* of the OrgDNA synthesized templates. From the foregoing, these natural misalignments between the manager's job and the alignment requirements of the OrgDNA can be corrected by equally taking into consideration the informal OrgDNA building blocks, in addition to its formal organizational building blocks components.

In concurrence, Neilson *et al.* (2008) found that unclear decision rights not only paralyze decision making but also impede information flow. And blocking the information flow results in poor decisions, limited career development, and a reinforcement of structural misalignments.

Again, as we saw in *Chapter 2*, Estupiñán and Neilson (2014) argue that formal OrgDNA elements are attractive to companies because they are *tangible* – as they can be easily defined and measured. But they are only half the story as the *intangible* elements also matter in the life of an organization. Supposedly as companies often realize this after they've made significant changes – reassigned decision rights, reworked the organization chart, established new incentives, or set up knowledge-sharing systems – yet don't see the results they expect. That's because they ignored the informal, intangible elements. These include norms (what people think is the right way to behave), commitments (the promises people feel motivated to keep) mind-sets (deeply held attitudes and beliefs), and networks (connections among employees outside the formal structure). All these add up to influence the ways people think, feel, communicate, and behave. From the foregoing, Estupiñán and Neilson (2014) hold that until you learn to influence these factors, your efforts to build performance will be unbalanced.

6.2 Suggestions

It pays off to establish an executable business model that clearly fits into the OrgDNA, and reflected in the causal links between profitability, productivity, and sustainability. A prerequisite for the successful implementation of organizations' strategy would require that corporate management and employees alike should be schooled on it. This should include clearly identifiable benefits that the organization, management, and employees would reap from it.

There are two key advantages this approach can bring to an organization. First, this is to ensure that the benefits that accrue from any of these alignment components should eventually flow to the others. Second, that early failure signals emanating from any of them should be quickly identified and checked so that it does not creep into the other alignment components and then contaminate them.

In another development, to build a proper brand name faster, it would appear you have to market the highest quality goods at the lowest reasonable price – by constantly creating products that create value in the minds of customers that are surprisingly even greater than they would have imagined or expected. In this direction, you grow your revenue stream and profit margin on turnover and not through unnecessarily higher prices.

With regards to the *mindset of value creation,* this book argues that it should theoretically and or practically metamorphose through entrepreneurial resilience to the *culture of value creation;* if the process is NOT abandoned along the way. In other words, it requires persistence and consistency in the transitional phrases from the mindset of value creation activities, to the culture of value creation. This should be embedded in an unshakable belief that, while you need to constantly learn from others, the burden of executing business projects lies on your shoulders. As a result, the insight to surmount such challenges, as well as the responsibility to do and make things happen - resides in no other place but inside you. In addition, this belief should not only be within your reach but found deep inside you - and which must be jealously tapped, and constantly converted into a culture of creating superior-upon-superior quality of added-value activities in wealth creation.

Conclusion

As far as today's world is concerned, the human mindset and its innate learning abilities as applied to value creation, have not really changed that much, when compared to that obtained in ancient civilizations. But what has really been changing is the way humans have been expressing and sharing ideas and information regarding value creation over time. Consequently, start-up ventures, established organizations, and countries that fail to tap from the vast array of available information, and then appropriately package them into their specific compartments that relate to profitability, productivity, and sustainability challenges – are doomed from the beginning, or if only partially harnessed and not upgraded over time, will be facing impending doom. But for those that are "lucky" to escape it, and not take appropriate steps to align these three elements, later on, are only preparing themselves to take the role of mere business survivors or losers for decades upon decades to come.

Due to the increasing complexities in consumer tastes and preferences, the rapid pace at which closely related and even loosely related disciplines are increasingly cross-interlinked, is shaping a new paradigm in the way science, social, economic, and political issues have to be tackled now and in the future. As a result, it is imperative that in order to stay at the driver's seat in the competitive environment or create your own space in the midst of the shakers and movers in a competitive world, you need not only be a strategically focused and dynamic curious learner, but also, you must be equally excited about it – so as to sustain the momentum of learning, which underpins the discovery of new knowledge, as well as the hidden combinations of existing knowledge.

Works Cited

Estupiñán, Jaime and Gary L. Neilson. "The 10 Principles of Organizational DNA." *Strategy-business.com*, 27 Oct. 2014, pp. 1–3.

Mintzberg, Henry. "The Manager's Job: Folklore and Fact." *Harvard Business Review*, 1990 Mar./Apr., pp. 12–20.

Neilson, Gary L., et al. "The Secrets to Successful Strategy Execution." *Harvard Business Review*, Jun. 2008, pp. 61–70, https://hbr.org/2008/06/the-secrets-to-successful-strategy-execution.

Saario, Ari. "Five Steps to Successful Commercialization of an Innovation – Can the Pitfalls Be Avoided?" *Valmet.com*, https://www.valmet.com/media/articles/experts-voice/five-steps-to-successful-commercialization-of-an-innovation/.

List of Abbreviations

AI	Artificial Intelligence
BMD	Business Model Design
BP	Business Plan
BCG	Boston Consulting Group
BHAGs	Big Hairy Audacious Goals
BiC	Best-in-Class Analysis
CalRecycle	California's Department of Resources Recycling and Recovery
CBM	Condition-Based Maintenance
CDIO	Conceive, Design, Implement, Operate
CE	Circular Economy
CPPSs	Cyber-Physical Production Systems
CSA	Customer Success Association
CSM	Customer Success Management
CS	Customer Success
CST	Customer Success Team
CTB Model	Critical Thinking Business Model
CX	Customer Experience
DIY	Do-It-Yourself Culture
DMAIC	Define, Measure, Analyze, Improve, Control
DNA	Deoxyribonucleic Acid
ERRC Grid	Eliminate, Raise, Reduce, Create
GCI	Global Competitiveness Index
HBRAS	Harvard Business Review Analytics Services
HERO	Healthy and Resilient Organizations
HG	High Growth Ventures
HR	Human Resource
IRS	Internal Revenue Service
4^{TH}IR	Fourth Industrial Revolution (or Industry 4.0)
3^{TH}IR	Third Industrial Revolution (or Industry 3.0)
2^{TH}IR	Second Industrial Revolution (or Industry 2.0)
1^{ST}IR	First Industrial Revolution (or Industry 1.0)
LPA	Least Product Approach
LSA	Lean Startup Approach

MGI	McKinsey Global Institute
mRNA	Messenger Ribonucleic Acid
MVP	Minimum Viable Products
MSE	Materials Science and Engineering
mtDNA	Mitochondrial DNA
OP	Organizational Performance
OrgDNA	Organizational DNA
PA	Product Architecture
PDR&D	Product Design, Research, and Development
PDCA	Plan, Do, Check, and Act
PLG	Product-Led Growth
PM	Planned Maintenance
PPS	Profitability, Productivity, and Sustainability
SaaS	Software as a Service
UX	User Experience
RNA	Ribonucleic Acid

Index

Note: Pag numbers in **bold** represent tables.

For Product Safety Concerns and Information please contact our EU
representative GPSR@taylorandfrancis.com
Taylor & Francis Verlag GmbH, Kaufingerstraße 24, 80331 München, Germany

www.ingramcontent.com/pod-product-compliance
Ingram Content Group UK Ltd.
Pitfield, Milton Keynes, MK11 3LW, UK
UKHW022348190926
475702UK00015B/2174

* 9 7 8 0 3 6 7 6 0 8 9 3 4 *